Exploring Queensland's parks and forests

Your guide to national parks, state forests, forest reserves, conservation parks, recreation areas and resources reserves.

Queensland Government

Environmental Protection Agency
Queensland **Parks and Wildlife Service**

Mt Spec, Paluma Range National Park

Darren Jew

Exploring Queensland's parks and forests

Your guide to national parks, state forests, forest reserves, conservation parks, recreation areas and resources reserves.

Acknowledgements

Parks and forests are set aside for nature conservation, heritage protection and forest production. They are also for people. Special thanks go to the rangers and other staff of the Queensland Parks and Wildlife Service and Environmental Protection Agency for sharing their knowledge of parks and forests so everyone can enjoy these special places. Thank you for caring for parks and forests.

Text: Pamela Harmon-Price   Design: Trish Salisbury, Karen Stobbs
Base maps: Roger Thomson   Editor: Don Marshall

Photographs: Many talented photographers and keen naturalists provided photographs for this book. Where possible, their names appear beside their photos. Special thanks go to Queensland Museum photographers Bruce Cowell, Gary Cranitch and Jeff Wright, Tourism Queensland, past and present Environmental Protection Agency photographers Paul Candlin, Adam Creed, Darren Jew, Damian McGreevy and Steve Parish, Queensland Parks and Wildlife Service staff Robert Ashdown, John Augusteyn, Terry Harper, Col Limpus, Keith McDonald, Tom Mumbray and Michael O'Connor, and external photographers Darran Leal, Lin Martin, Ross Naumann, Tim Peek, Greg Teschner and John Young.

Front cover photo: Isla Gorge National Park (Paul Candlin)

Technical support: Many people helped make this book relevant and accurate, including Dr Andrew Dennis, CSIRO Sustainable Ecosystems and Rainforest Cooperative Research Centre, Lisa Bourke, Marnie Crossman, Cathy Gatley, Keith McDonald, Neil Kershaw, John Moye, Sue Olsson, Doug Schulz, Karen Smith, Nickie Stewart, Bob Thomson and Tamara Vallance.

Copyright

Disclaimer

While this book was prepared with care, the information is a guide only. Visitors are reminded that conditions change constantly and all parks and forests are subject to closure without notice. No liability is accepted by the Queensland Government for any decisions or actions taken on the basis of information in this publication.

National Library of Australia Cataloguing-in-Publication

Harmon-Price, P. (Pamela)
Exploring Queensland's parks and forests: your guide to national parks, state forests, forest reserves, conservation parks, recreation areas and resources reserves.

Includes index.
ISBN 0 7242 9977 7.

1. National Parks and reserves — Queensland.
2. Forest Reserves — Queensland.
I. Queensland. Parks and Wildlife Service. II. Title.

363.6809943

Bk44 September 2003
Printer: Fergies

Contents

Hill Inlet, Whitsunday Island, Whitsunday Islands National Park

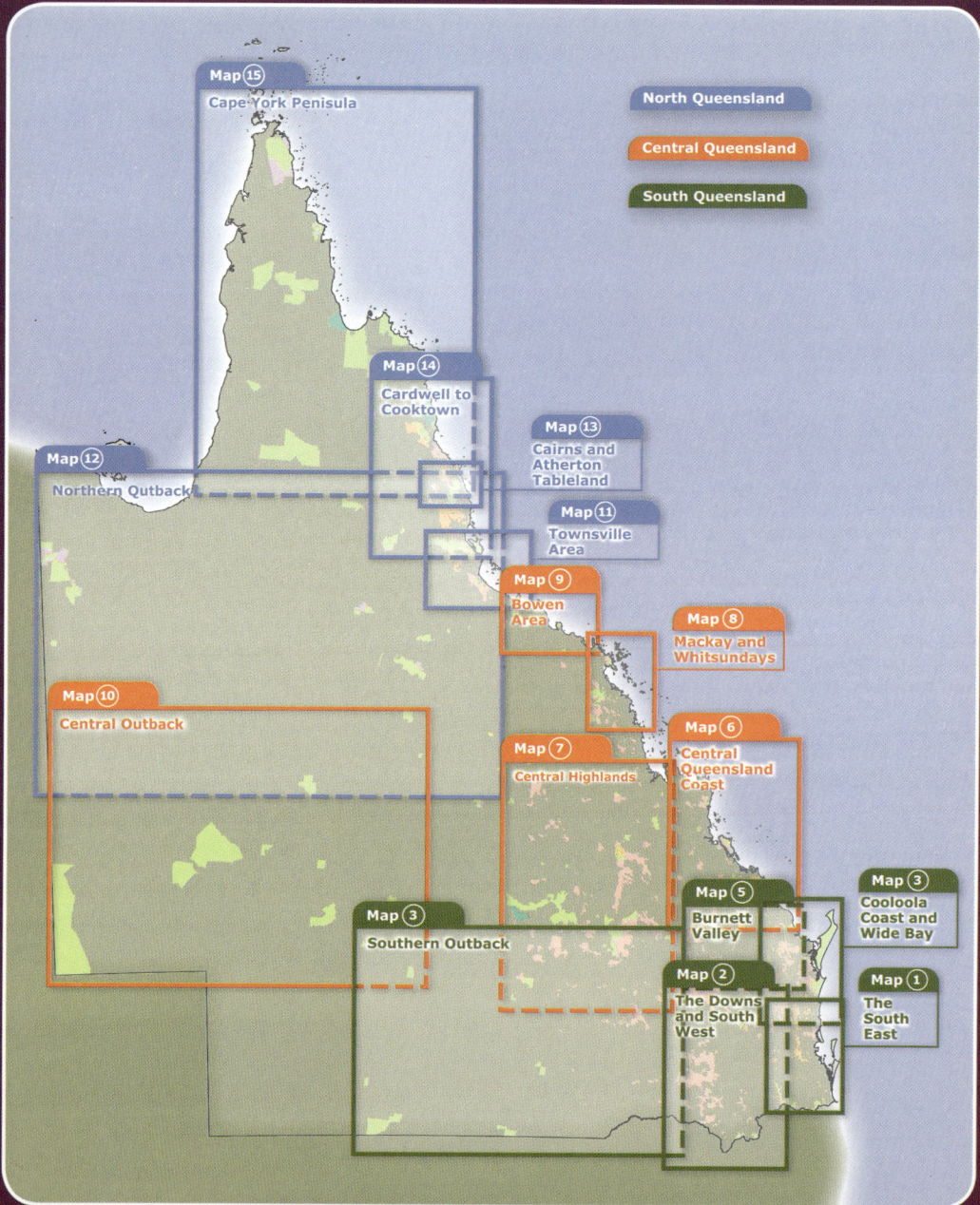

Key Map

North Queensland

Central Queensland

South Queensland

Map 15
Cape York Peninsula

Map 14
Cardwell to Cooktown

Map 13
Cairns and Atherton Tableland

Map 12
Northern Outback

Map 11
Townsville Area

Map 9
Bowen Area

Map 8
Mackay and Whitsundays

Map 10
Central Outback

Map 6
Central Queensland Coast

Map 7
Central Highlands

Map 4
Southern Outback

Map 5
Burnett Valley

Map 3
Cooloola Coast and Wide Bay

Map 2
The Downs and South West

Map 1
The South East

Park and forest map contents

① The South East

Around Brisbane
Brisbane Forest Park
Mt Mee FR
Daisy Hill FR
Venman Bushland NP
Fort Lytton NP
St Helena Island NP
Blue Lake NP
Moreton Island NP
Bunyaville FR
Gold Coast and hinterland
Burleigh Head NP
Mt Cougal (Springbrook NP)
Tamborine NP
Springbrook NP
Natural Bridge (Springbrook NP)
Numinbah FR
Nerang FR
Lamington NP
Near Boonah
Mt Barney NP
Moogerah Peaks NP
Sunshine Coast and hinterland
Bribie Island NP
Glass House Mountains NP
Beerburrum SF/FR
Bellthorpe FR
Kenilworth SF/FR
Imbil SF/FR
Conondale NP
Jimna SF/FR
Kondalilla NP
Mapleton Falls NP
Delicia Road CP
Mapleton FR
Currimundi Lake CP
Parklands FR
Mooloolah River NP
Mt Coolum NP
Tewantin FR
Noosa NP

② The Downs and South West

Near Warwick
Main Range NP
Goomburra FR
Queen Mary Falls (Main Range NP)

Granite Belt
Girraween NP
Sundown NP
Around Toowoomba
Yarraman SF
Ravensbourne NP
Crows Nest NP
Benarkin SF/FR
Bunya Mountains NP
The Palms NP
Western Downs
Lake Broadwater CP
Southwood NP

③ Southern Outback

Around Charleville
Currawinya NP
Lake Bindegolly NP
Tregole NP
Culgoa Floodplain NP
Mariala NP

④ Cooloola Coast and Wide Bay

Great Sandy Region
Cooloola (Great Sandy NP)
Inskip Peninsula RA
Fraser Island (Great Sandy NP)
Woody Island (Great Sandy NP)
Near Gympie
Woondum SF/FR
Amamoor SF/FR
Brooyar SF
Near Maryborough
Tuan SF
Poona NP
Wongi SF/FR
Near Bundaberg
Baldwin Swamp CP
Mon Repos CP
Woodgate, Burrum Coast NP
Kinkuna, Burrum Coast NP

⑤ Burnett Valley

Near Kilkivan
Kilkivan FR
Boat Mountain
Jack Smith Scrub
Near Biggenden
Woowoonga FR
Mt Walsh NP

Good Night Scrub NP
Coalstoun Lakes NP
Upper Burnett
Auburn River NP
Tolderodden CP
Cania Gorge NP
Kalpowar SF

⑥ Central Queensland Coast

Around Miriam Vale
Mouth of Baffle Creek CP
Broadwater CP
Castle Tower NP
Deepwater NP
Eurimbula NP
Joseph Banks CP
Bulburin FR
Capricorn Coast
Capricorn Coast NP
Curtis Island NP
Keppel Bay Islands NP
Byfield NP
Byfield SF
Near Rockhampton
Mt Archer NP
Mt Etna Caves NP
Mt Jim Crow NP
Capricornia Islands
Capricornia Cays NP
Near Biloela
Mt Scoria CP
Kroombit Tops NP/FR

⑦ Central Highlands

Central Highlands
Minerva Hills NP
Blackdown Tableland NP
Near Taroom
Isla Gorge NP
Expedition NP
Lake Murphy CP
Carnarvon NP
Carnarvon Gorge (Carnarvon NP)
Mt Moffatt (Carnarvon NP)
Salvator Rosa (Carnarvon NP)
Ka Ka Mundi (Carnarvon NP)

NP – National Park
CP – Conservation Park
SF – State Forest
FR – Forest Reserve
RR – Resources Reserve
RA – Recreation Area

Park and forest map contents

NP – National Park
CP – Conservation Park
SF – State Forest
FR – Forest Reserve
RR – Resources Reserve

Discover Queensland ... naturally

From the bush to the beach, from the outback to the reef, Queensland has some of the best scenery Australia has to offer.

Enjoy the bush on your doorstep. Visit Queensland's national parks and State forests. Parks and forests protect the best places in the state and facilities are provided to help you enjoy them.

Have a bush barbecue, boil a billy, make a damper, go for a bushwalk, camp in the great outdoors, be amazed by big skies and starry nights, rediscover life's simple pleasures, savour the sights and sounds of the Australian bush, get close to nature or simply relax and enjoy the peace in Queensland's parks and forests.

With more natural variety than any other state or territory, Queensland is a great place to see wildlife. Go birdwatching or spotlighting or enjoy fascinating wildlife spectacles like whale watching or turtle nesting.

This is your guide to the most popular parks and forests in Queensland. Some are the top tourist destinations in the state. You will be lucky to see another visitor in others.

See spectacular gorges and escarpments, tumbling waterfalls, boulder-strewn creeks, crystal-clear lakes, sandy beaches, tall rainforests, wildflower-filled heaths, limestone caves, wide grassy plains and outback billabongs.

Be dazzled by nature's masterpieces — vibrantly-coloured cliffs, spectacular sunsets, and colourful birds, fungi and wildflowers. Be humbled by thousands of years of living indigenous culture reflected in rock art on cliffs, rock shelters and caves.

Stay close to civilisation with home comforts or get as far away as possible and be totally self-reliant.

Discover all this and more in our wonderful parks and forests, the best that nature has to offer. With five World Heritage Areas, hundreds of parks and forests, thousands of plant species and hundreds of reptiles, birds, mammals, insects, corals, fish and frogs, Queensland hosts many natural wonders. So, get out there and explore our parks and forests. But don't forget to take this book!

Paul Candlin

Regent bowerbird

About parks and forests

Mahogany glider
John Young

Protecting the state's natural diversity is the goal of the Queensland Parks and Wildlife Service, Environmental Protection Agency, the State's nature conservation authority. Keeping the balance between protecting these natural assets while helping people enjoy them is a constant challenge.

Protected areas, mostly national parks, conserve about two-thirds of the state's ecosystems in more than seven million hectares (4.5 percent of the state). Forests and related reserves protect a further 3.6 million hectares (2 percent of the state).

National parks are very special places. While their primary purpose is to conserve nature and our cultural heritage, parks and other protected areas are also places where people can get-away-from-it-all and get close to nature. Nature-based, low-impact activities are welcome and facilities are provided to help people enjoy parks without spoiling them for later visitors.

Conservation parks and other protected areas provide a level of heritage protection similar to national parks. Some conservation parks and resources reserves cater for visitor use.

Why are national parks so important? They are totally protected, providing a biological bank for the future. The species we protect today could greatly improve the quality of human life tomorrow.

Parks provide a home for our native plants and animals — the essence of the Australian bush and what makes Australia special. The threat of wildlife extinction is real — places where animals can roam free and undisturbed are an important part of an overall strategy to prevent species loss.

State forests are multiple-use reserves which meet a variety of community needs from timber production to nature conservation, forest recreation, plant harvesting for the nursery and floral trade, cattle grazing, bee-keeping and water catchment protection.

Forest reserves are state forests which are in the process of being converted to another conservation tenure, usually national park. Current approved uses are allowed to continue until the change to a protected area tenure happens.

Global treasures

Like the seven wonders of the world, World Heritage areas protect the best examples of the world's natural and cultural heritage. Five of Australia's 14 properties are located wholly or partly in Queensland:

> Great Barrier Reef
> Wet Tropics
> Fraser Island
> Central Eastern Rainforests Reserves (Australia)
> Riversleigh, Australian Fossil Mammal Sites

In 1981, the Great Barrier Reef became Australia's first world heritage area, meeting all four natural criteria for listing. Stretching more than 2000km along the Queensland coast and covering 35 million hectares, the Great Barrier Reef is the world's largest coral reef and probably the richest. For thousands of years, the Reef has been the sea country of Aboriginal people and Torres Strait Islander people.

Extending from Cooktown to Townsville, the Wet Tropics World Heritage Area protects many parks and forests. A third of Australia's marsupial species, a quarter of the frogs and reptiles and about 60 percent of bat and butterfly species live in the wet tropics. Listed in 1988, the Wet Tropics contains Australia's most extensive wet tropical rainforests and a living rainforest indigenous culture dating back 50,000 years.

At Fraser Island, listed in 1992, the unique processes of change which created the world's largest sand island can still be seen. The island's sands provide an excellent record of the ageing processes of sand dunes and are an outstanding example of geological and biological processes working together. The Butchulla people lived on Fraser Island for more than 5000 years. Their special heritage is preserved in Fraser Island's sands.

The Central Eastern Rainforests Reserves (Australia) World Heritage Area, originally listed in 1986 to cover rainforests in New South Wales, was extended in 1994 to include rainforests on the Queensland side of the border. This property contains the world's largest subtropical rainforest remnants and nearly all of the world's Antarctic beech cool temperate rainforests, and more frog, snake, bird and marsupial species than anywhere else in Australia.

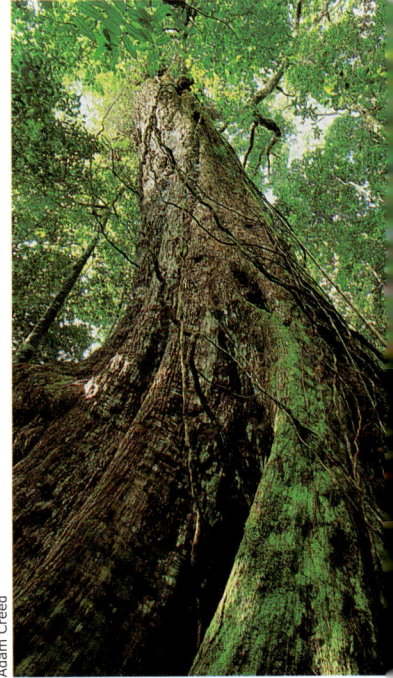

Adam Creed

Mt Whitfield Conservation Park

Global treasures

Listed in 1994 as part of the Australian Fossil Mammal Sites World Heritage Area, Riversleigh in north-west Queensland is a natural museum, helping scientists understand why Australia's native animals, isolated from the rest of the world, are so different. The Riversleigh fossils preserve at least 20 million years of evolutionary history, one of the best records of Australian mammal history.

Lake McKenzie, Fraser Island, Great Sandy National Park

Visiting parks and forests

You can enjoy Queensland's parks and forests all year round (closures are uncommon). The best time to visit Cape York Peninsula and inland parks is April–September, cooler and drier months. Many popular parks and forests are crowded during holidays, especially Christmas, Easter, June and long weekends.

Before you visit

Check the website www.epa.qld.gov.au and find out as much as possible before you visit. Be prepared with the right equipment and gear to have an enjoyable visit. Choose a place with plenty of facilities and go for walks which suit your fitness level.

Regular visitors

Take some responsibility for your own safety in the bush. Remember these are wild places with natural hazards. Be careful and enjoy your visit.

Never assume you know what to expect. Road and weather conditions change. Facilities change too. Check whether camping areas are accessible and open, water supply is available, roads are passable, or fire bans have been introduced.

Read signs and brochures

Signs and brochures are provided to help you enjoy your visit. Read them carefully and pay attention to any warnings.

Check the website before you visit and download any brochures or information to help you explore the park or forest — www.epa.qld.gov.au.

Walks and talks

Rangers, volunteers and commercial guides provide guided walks, slide shows and other activity programs on parks and forests. Fees may apply. Join in and have fun.

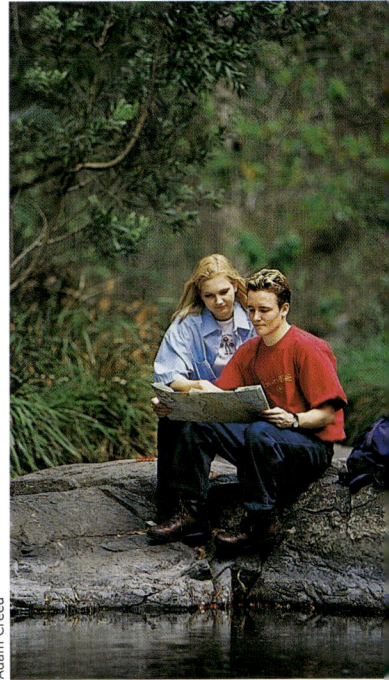

Adam Creed

Cedar Creek, Tamborine National Park

Camping

Paul Candlin

You can camp in most parks and forests in this book provided you obtain a camping permit first. Fees apply.

Book and pay for your campsite through *Smart Service Queensland* on 13 13 04 or book online at www.qld.gov.au/camping. This booking service is being gradually introduced throughout the state. Some parks and forests have on-site, self-serve camping stations where you pay your fees and get your permit. Check with the Integrated Contact Centre or QPWS office about the preferred way to book or confirm your campsite.

Camping checklist

Basic facilities are provided in most park and forest campgrounds. Campers must be as self-sufficient as possible.

Here's a handy checklist of things you should take:
- Sturdy rubbish bags (Few places have bins.)
- Secure food storage containers (which animals can't open!)
- Drinking water (Supplies can be limited or require treatment. Allow seven litres/day/person if no water is available.)
- A fuel stove and fuel supply (Campfires are banned in some places.)
- Waterproof matches
- Your own firewood (where fires are allowed and firewood is not supplied)
- Plenty of non-perishable food (You can be stranded in bad weather. Take extra supplies.)
- Cooking utensils
- Gas lights and a torch for walking at night
- Sleeping bags and mats or swags
- Spare shoes (Thongs are unsuitable.)
- Waterproof tent and poles/frame/tent pegs
- Tomahawk for chopping supplied firewood, mallet for sandy campsites and small shovel for digging holes for human waste (if toilets are not provided)
- Camera, film, binoculars
- Insect repellent, sunscreen, hat
- Raincoat or waterproof jacket
- Two-way radio (remote places)
- Broadcast radio (for weather forecasts) and spare batteries
- Well-stocked first aid kit (Medical help is rarely nearby.)
- Map, park/forest brochure, compass

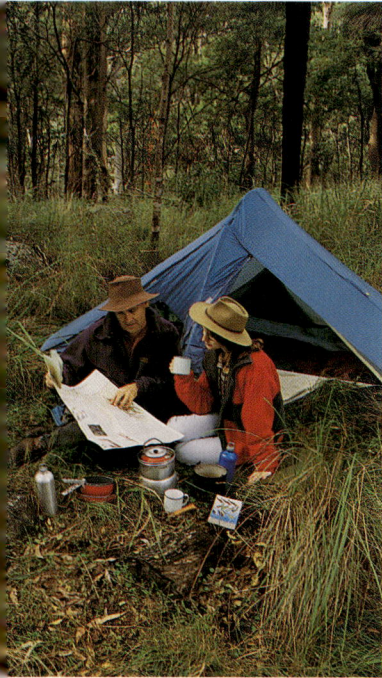

Lamington National Park

Adam Creed

Camping

Caravans and motorhomes

Most park/forest campgrounds have tent sites close to carparks. Some have sites for caravans, camper trailers and motorhomes. No sites are powered, though private campgrounds with powered sites are located close to some parks and forests. Places where you can take caravans and motorhomes are indicated in this book.

Camp fees

Current camping fees for parks and forests are:
$4/person/night or $16/family/night. For parks, a family group is two adults and accompanying children between 15 and 18. For forests, a family group is four or more people over 4 years with no more than two over 15. Children under 5 are free.

Inskip Peninsula Recreation Area

Bushwalking

Paul Candlin

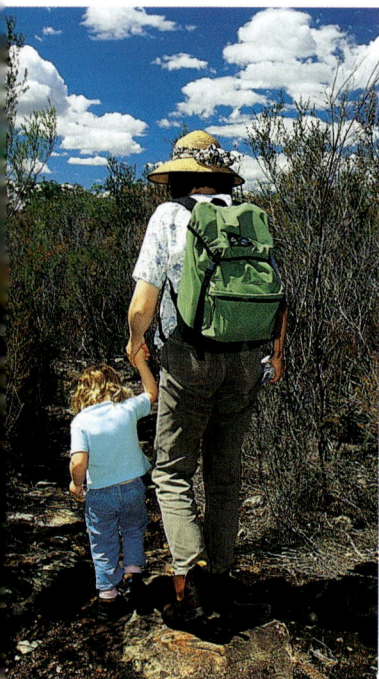

Adam Creed

Mt French, Moogerah Peaks National Park

Walking is increasingly popular in parks and forests. Improve your fitness while you enjoy the sights. Choose from a range of specially graded walking tracks which showcase the major attractions. Match the walk to your fitness and mobility. Experienced bushwalkers can tackle longer walks and unmarked trails.

Take a backpack

Get into the good habit of taking a backpack when bushwalking. You may decide to walk further than planned. Be prepared.

Here's a checklist for your day pack:
- Nutritious, energy-boosting nibbles (muesli bars, chocolate, nuts, dried fruit)
- Drinking water
- Insect repellent
- Sunscreen
- Basic first aid supplies
- Camera
- Binoculars
- Raincoat or waterproof jacket
- Plastic bags for rubbish and to sit on
- Mobile phone (You will be out of range in many places.)

Bushwalker safety form

Some parks and forests require walkers to complete a bushwalker registration form providing details of any planned hikes. Leave a copy with the ranger (if required) and a responsible friend or family member. You must advise your friend or family of your safe return. The Service does not check whether you return safely. The information on the form is used if a rescue operation is necessary.

Search and rescue operations are very costly and risk other lives. Be careful and try to prevent getting lost or injured. Carry a personal positioning beacon if you go off-track. It may save your life. Never rely on mobile phones. They are usually out of range.

Great Walks

An exciting new concept in long-distance walking will become a reality in 2004 when two of the Great Walks of Queensland open. Under this $10million State Government initiative, six walking tracks will be developed by 2006. The walks will give visitors a new way to explore some of the most beautiful places in the state.

Six three-to-four-day adventure walks are being established:

> Fraser Island 85km
> Whitsundays 36km
> Gold Coast hinterland
> Sunshine Coast hinterland
> Mackay Highlands
> Wet Tropics

At Fraser Island, follow the traditional pathways of the Butchulla people from Dilli Village to Lake Garawongera past crystal-clear freshwater lakes, forests, woodlands and heaths.

Take a walk on the wild side through subtropical rainforest in Lamington and Springbrook National Parks in the Gold Coast hinterland.

Quaint craft villages, coffee shops and country B'n'Bs will be a short detour from the Sunshine Coast Hinterland Great Walk along the picturesque Blackall Range.

The Mackay Highlands Great Walk will appeal more to serious walkers. Starting in Eungella National Park, this walk will pass through some of the state's most ruggedly beautiful mountain scenery.

For a refreshing change in the beautiful Whitsundays, discover tropical rainforests and rocky creeks along the Conway Range behind Airlie Beach.

See tumbling waterfalls and picturesque Herbert River Gorge in north Queensland on the Wet Tropics Great Walk.

The first two Great Walks — the Fraser Island and Whitsundays walks — will open in July 2004. Check the EPA website www.epa.qld.gov.au/GreatWalks for regular updates.

Lamington National Park

great!walks *queensland*

Other activities

People can enjoy parks and forests without jeopardising their conservation values and sustainability. You can walk but you cannot always ride. Take photographs but nothing else. When you go, leave nothing but footprints. The most popular activities are camping, bushwalking, picnicking and nature study.

Picnicking

Having a barbecue or picnic is one of the best ways to enjoy the bush. Many parks and forests have picnic facilities. Information about picnic facilities is provided throughout this book. Make sure you enjoy your picnic. Feed yourself, not the animals. Let them find their own food. Secure your food before going for a walk or it may be gone when you get back!

Never assume that water is safe to drink. Unless the water supply is signed as "drinking water", boil it for at least five minutes or treat the water before drinking. If bins are not provided, take your rubbish home with you.

Check whether you need to bring your own firewood or fuel stove if you plan to have a barbecue.

Adam Creed

Mt Cougal, Springbrook National Park

Other activities

Driving

While walking is the preferred way to see parks and forests, many have opportunities for four-wheel-driving and scenic driving.

Driving permits
You need a permit to drive on recreation areas at Moreton and Fraser Islands. Fees apply. You also need a permit to travel on many forest roads. No fees apply.

Permits to traverse forests
In forests, you can drive to camping and picnic areas and along forest drives without a permit. If you plan to travel beyond these "public" areas, you must obtain a permit to traverse before you arrive.

This permit system protects you and the forest. Permits to traverse are free to licensed drivers with registered vehicles. You must first complete an application form. To find out how to obtain your permit, contact the QPWS office listed in the *Further information* section of the forest you wish to visit.

With a permit to traverse, you are allowed to use signposted restricted access roads in forests.

Driving safety in forests
Timber trucks, other traffic and wildlife share the road in state forests and forest reserves. Forest roads are unsealed with sharp bends and steep grades.

Four-wheel-driving

Some access roads and internal roads in many parks and forests in this book are suitable only for four-wheel-drive vehicles.

Make sure you have driving experience before negotiating rough roads and sandy surfaces. Follow the specifications recommended by the manufacturer of your vehicle when reducing tyre pressure to drive in sand. Re-inflate your tyres to drive on normal road surfaces. Make sure your vehicle has a winch in case you get stuck.

You can apply to go four-wheel-driving in many other forests not included in this book. Contact your local QPWS office for more information. Permits are required.

Tips for driving safely in forests

- Obtain a permit if driving on a restricted access road.
- Obey all road signs.
- Keep left, especially at sharp bends and crests.
- Pull to the side to let other traffic pass or take photographs.
- Watch for and give way to any bushwalkers, cyclists or horse riders.
- Never take a conventional vehicle on a road marked "four-wheel-drive only". Roads deteriorate past these points and you may get stuck.

Paul Candlin

Fraser Island

Other activities

Paul Candlin

Adam Creed

Kuranda State Forest

Horse riding

Horse riding is allowed in some forests in this book, but not permitted in national parks. You can also apply to go horse riding in many other forests. Permits are required. Contact your local QPWS office for more information.

Bike riding

In some forests, bike riding is allowed by permit. Horse riders and cyclists often share the road with walkers, so be careful and courteous. For your safety and to protect the forest, you should always stay on existing tracks and roads. Bike riding is not allowed in parks.

Trail bike riding

Trail bike riding is allowed in some forests in this book, but not permitted in most forests or any national parks. Permits are required.

Extreme sports

Hang gliding, caving, abseiling and rockclimbing are allowed in some parks and forests. For your safety, talk to the ranger first. Permits and restrictions may apply.

Accessibility

Mobility, vision and hearing impairment, and literacy can restrict the way people enjoy their park/forest visit. Providing better access to parks and forests is a challenge which the Queensland Parks and Wildlife Service is keen to meet. In this book, information on services which help people access park and forest facilities is presented in the *Accessibility* section for each park and forest. Most existing services are wheelchair access to toilets and tracks. A graphic icon next to the park/forest heading indicates whether special facilities are provided.

Mt Edith, Danbulla Forest Reserve

Public transport

Daisy Hill Forest Reserve

Adam Creed

Few parks and forests are readily accessible by public transport or commercial tour. Most are only accessible by private vehicle.

With some effort, you can catch public transport or a tour bus/boat to the following places in this book:

- Brisbane Forest Park
- Daisy Hill Forest Reserve
- Bunyaville Forest Reserve
- Fort Lytton National Park
- St Helena Island National Park
- Moreton Island National Park
- Burleigh Head National Park
- Tamborine National Park
- Lamington National Park
- Main Range National Park
- Glass House Mountains National Park
- Noosa National Park
- Fraser Island and Cooloola, Great Sandy National Park
- Capricorn Coast National Park
- Capricornia Cays National Park
- Brampton Islands National Park
- Whitsunday Islands National Park
- Molle Islands National Park
- Lindeman Islands National Park
- Conway National Park
- Townsville Town Common Conservation Park
- Magnetic Island National Park
- Edmund Kennedy National Park
- Hinchinbrook Island National Park
- Barron Gorge National Park
- Green Island National Park
- Fitzroy Island National Park
- Cape Tribulation, Daintree National Park
- Chillagoe-Mungana Caves National Park
- Lizard Island National Park

Contact your local QPWS office or local tourism centre about other places you may be able to reach by public transport or commercial tour.

The weather

Paul Candlin

Queensland has a tropical to subtropical climate and is reputed to be beautiful one day... perfect the next. While this slogan is often true, Queensland can also be:

> hot in summer;
> wet in summer;
> wild and windy during storms and cyclones; and
> cold at night in winter, especially in the outback and the south-east corner.

Suggested times to visit (or stay away from) parks and forests are given in this book. Be aware of climate extremes and the potential dangers of unusual weather events such as storms and cyclones. Never plan to visit any park or forest when a cyclone (or prolonged rain) is forecast. Never bushwalk during an electrical storm.

Darren Jew

Storm clouds gather over the Mitchell Grass Downs in western Queensland

Caring for parks and forests

Bruce Cowell

Adam Creed

Moogerah Peaks National Park

Because parks and forests are places which protect the nature of Queensland, rules apply to ensure parks and forests stay special.

Pets

Pets (cats, dogs, birds etc) and domestic animals such as horses are not allowed in national parks. On-the-spot fines apply.

Dogs on leashes are allowed in some forest picnic and camping areas, as indicated in this book. Places where you can currently camp with your dog include:

» Clancy's, Benarkin State Forest
» Gheerulla Creek, Mapleton Forest Reserve
» Amamoor Creek, Amamoor State Forest and Forest Reserve
» Glastonbury Creek, Brooyar State Forest
» Inskip Peninsula Recreation Area
» Wongi State Forest and Forest Reserve
» Tuan State Forest
» Kalpowar State Forest
» Red Rock, Byfield State Forest

Campfires

Wildfires threaten people, livestock, native wildlife, vegetation, crops and buildings. Help prevent wildfires by being very careful with fire in parks and forests.

Ideally, you should take a fuel stove. If you enjoy a campfire and fires are permitted in the place you are visiting, please follow these rules:

» Light fires only in constructed fireplaces or previous fire rings.
» Collect no firewood in the park/forest. Even dead wood and leaf litter provide homes for animals. Leave it on the ground.
» Use supplied firewood sparingly or take your own.
» Build your fire carefully and avoid smoking out your neighbours.
» Put your fire out with water, never sand, whenever you leave your campsite. (Children have been badly burnt by smouldering embers hidden under sand which retains intense heat for hours.)

Caring for parks and forests

Robert Ashdown

Weeds

Weeds can spread rapidly through bushland spoiling the natural beauty and smothering the natural vegetation. You can help minimise the damage. Wash the undercarriage of your four-wheel-drive vehicle carefully after driving on unsealed roads. If you plan to visit more than one park or forest, talk to the local QPWS staff to find out whether you should avoid some areas to prevent the spread of weeds.

Leave no trace

Parks and forests protect Queensland's wonderful natural diversity and scenery. Please help keep these places special by following the rules when visiting:

» **Protect the wildlife.** Remember, plants and animals are protected. Try not to trample plants when walking or erecting your tent.
» **Be careful with fire.** Use fireplaces, where provided, not an open fire. Put the fire out when you leave your campsite.
» **Use a fuel stove.** Preferably use a fuel stove for cooking. Don't collect firewood from the reserve.
» **Leave no rubbish.** Take your rubbish when you leave or use bins (where provided). Don't bury rubbish.
» **Be considerate.** People visit parks and forests to enjoy nature, not noisy radios or generators.
» **Camp, walk and drive softly.** Leave your campsite better than you found it. Stay on track.
» **Use toilets.** If toilets are not provided, bury human wastes well away from tracks and water bodies.
» **Take no pets.** Leave domestic animals at home. Cats and dogs disturb native wildlife and other campers. Horses are not allowed in national parks.
» **Protect creeks and lakes.** Use no soap, toothpaste or detergent in freshwater lakes and creeks — they pollute the water. Apply sunscreen after your swim.
» **Respect indigenous culture.** Rock art and other sites on parks and forests represent thousands of years of living culture of special significance to indigenous people. These sites are easily damaged yet irreplaceable. Look at, enjoy, but do not touch or damage these sites.

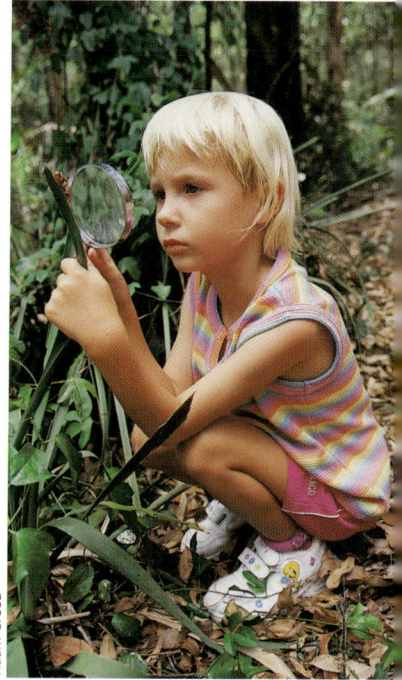

Adam Creed

Daisy Hill Forest Reserve

Look after yourself

Bruce Cowell

Adam Creed

Adam Creed

Girraween National Park

Parks and forests are wild places with hidden dangers for the unwary visitor. Safety advice is provided throughout this book and on-site warning signs are located near severe hazards. Pay close attention to such advice. It is not given lightly.

For your safety, follow this advice to minimise your risks and have an enjoyable visit:

» **Be prepared.** Plan your trip carefully. Make sure your camping equipment, vehicle or boat are in good working condition. Take a first aid kit and wet weather gear.

» **Take care near water.** Swim with extreme caution. Creeks have hidden dangers and swift currents. National park beaches are unpatrolled. People have been seriously injured and killed diving into rockpools, lakes and the sea. Supervise your children around water.

» **Stay on the track.** You may get lost if you head off the road or walking track. Take a map and brochure and follow any signs. Let someone responsible know your plans in case you get lost.

» **Watch your step.** Stay well back from cliff edges and waterfalls. Cliff edges may crumble and rocks near waterfalls may be slippery. Always stay behind safety fences to avoid tragedy.

» **Be wary of wild animals.** Tragedies have occurred. Stay well back from snakes, cassowaries, crocodiles, wild pigs and dingoes. Follow local advice about these animals.

» **Never feed or play with wildlife.** You may get bitten or scratched. Human foods may be harmful to wild animals. Birds, dingoes and kangaroos can become aggressive towards people when fed.

» **Watch out for biting, sucking, scratching things.** Wear protective clothing and insect repellent to protect yourself from stings, scratches and insect bites. Detour around snakes; never provoke them.

» **Be sun-smart.** Wear a hat and sunscreen, even on overcast days, to avoid sunburn. Drink frequently to avoid dehydration.

» **Think before you drink.** Even mountain streams can be contaminated. Boil (for five minutes) or treat creek or lake water before drinking to avoid giardia and diarrhoea. Or take your own supply.

» **Drive carefully.** Follow normal road rules whether you are driving on the beach or on a forest track. Watch for oncoming traffic and pedestrians and share the road. Pull off to take photographs.

Great Barrier Reef islands

Paul Candlin

Many islands listed in this guide are in the Great Barrier Reef Marine Park, a World Heritage Area. Seasonal closures apply to some islands and some activities are restricted or not allowed.

Protect yourself and the islands and reefs when you visit:

❯ Help prevent the spread of weeds and feral animals. Check your clothing and equipment to ensure it is clean before visiting the islands.
❯ Check the zoning plan for restrictions on line fishing and collecting shells. Spearfishing using scuba gear and collecting coral are prohibited.
❯ Take extra supplies of food and water in case you are stranded by sudden weather changes.
❯ Be aware of tidal variations and strong currents. Anchor boats securely.
❯ Anchor in sand or mud to avoid coral damage. Preferably use a lightweight reef pick with plastic tubing over the anchor chain.
❯ Watch for sudden weather changes, particularly storms and cyclones. Be prepared to evacuate if necessary.
❯ Don't throw it, stow it. Dumping plastic and other rubbish at sea is illegal and can harm or even kill aquatic animals and seabirds.
❯ Carry a marine band radio transceiver. (Most sites in this book are out of range for mobile phones.)

Lizard Island Group National Park

Paul Candlin

Introduction 19

How to use this guide

Eastern grey kangaroos

Parks and forests for nature-based recreation are included in this guide. Each national park, conservation park, resources reserve, recreation area, State forest and forest reserve has its own entry.

Parks and forests are listed by location and grouped so you can find places to visit in a particular area. A map at the beginning of each section shows the parks and forests featured on the following pages. The key map shows how the state has been divided. An alphabetical index is provided at the back of the book, if you know the name of the place you want to visit.

For each park/forest entry in the book, graphic icons in the heading (the name of the park or forest) indicate whether a park/forest has facilities for:

Bushwalking

Camping

Picnicking

Disability access   *Special services to help people access the park/forest*

Some parks and forests have no graphic icons beside the heading. You can still enjoy visiting these places, but do not expect any facilities for your activities. Camping is not allowed.

Each park/forest entry has:
> A brief description of the park/forest's special values;
> Suggested ways to explore and enjoy the park/forest;
> Walking track names, distances and approximate walking times and advice about safe bushwalking;
> Information on facilities which make parks and forests more accessible, for example wheelchair access, if available;
> Directions for getting to the park/forest and the closest place for supplies and fuel;
> Address(es) for further information and permits; and
> Symbol signs for recreation facilities and possible visitor activities.

How to use this guide

Most symbols are self-explanatory but you can check their meanings on this page or the inside front cover of this book.

Most track distances are return unless stated one-way. Circuit tracks take you back to where you started.

Once you have decided where to go, if you wish to camp, contact *Smart Service Queensland* on 13 13 04 or book online at www.qld.gov.au/camping. For any other advice or permits to traverse, contact the office given at the end of each entry or check the website www.epa.qld.gov.au.

The following abbreviations are used:

QPWS   Queensland Parks and Wildlife Service
NP   National Park
SF   State Forest
FR   Forest Reserve
CP   Conservation Park
RA   Recreation Area
RR   Resources Reserve

Rangers help you make the most of your visit.

*   Special access to help visitors with disabilities enjoy parks and forests. This symbol usually refers to toilets.
**   Occasionally suitable for motorhomes. Check first.
***   No facilities are provided for rubbish disposal at these places. You must bag and remove your rubbish.
****   Marine stingers are present in coastal waters and estuaries north of Agnes Water between October and May. Never swim unprotected at this time of year.
*****   Estuarine crocodiles living in coastal waters and estuaries north of Maryborough pose a serious threat to humans. Never swim where you see this sign.

Symbol signs

- ⓘ Information centre
- Staff on-site
- Patrolled site
- Boat-patrolled site
- Toilets
- Disability access*
- Picnic tables
- Shelter shed
- Barbecues or fireplaces
- Drinking water
- Showers
- Car camping
- Bush camping
- No camping
- Suitable for caravans**
- Campfires prohibited
- No rubbish disposal***
- Walking track(s)
- Self-guiding trail
- Hiking trail (not graded)
- Lookout
- Public phone
- Forest drive (signposted)
- 4WD access recommended
- Beware stingers****
- Beware crocodiles*****

Carnarvon Gorge, Carnarvon National Park

The South East

Map 1

Legend

National Park	State Forest	Highway
Conservation Park	Timber Reserve	Major connecting road
Forest Reserve	Resource Reserve	Minor access road

0   12.5   25
km

N

Amamoor SF
Pomona
Great Sandy NP
Tewantin FR
Noosa
Cooroy
Noosa NP
Imbil
Imbil SF
Imbil FR
Mapleton FR
Mt Coolum NP
Kenilworth
Delicia Rd CP
Parklands FR
Jimna SF/FR
Mapleton
Nambour
Kenilworth FR
Mapleton Falls NP
Conondale NP
Kondalilla NP
Maleny
Mooloolah River NP
Blackbutt
Bellthorpe FR
Currimundi Lake CP
Caloundra
Benarkin SF
Kilcoy
Beerburrum SF
Glass House Mountains NP
Woodford
Beerburrum FR
Bribie Island NP
Caboolture
Mt Mee FR
Crows Nest NP
Esk
Dayboro
Moreton Island NP
Ravensbourne NP
Redcliffe
Samford
Bunyaville FR
Lowood
Brisbane Forest Park
St Helena Is NP
Fort Lytton NP
Gatton
BRISBANE
Dunwich
Laidley
Ipswich
Logan
Daisy Hill FR
Blue Lake NP
Venman Bushland NP
Beenleigh
Tamborine NP
Pine Ridge CP
Goomburra FR
Nerang FR
Southport
Boonah
Beaudesert
Nerang
Gold Coast
Moogerah Peaks NP
Main Range NP
Burleigh Head NP
Numinbah FR
Palm Beach
Queen Mary Falls
Rathdowney
Springbrook NP
Mt Barney NP
Natural Bridge
Mt Cougal
Killarney
Lamington NP
NEW SOUTH WALES
Murwillumbah

Brisbane Forest Park

Eucalypt forest near
Wivenhoe Outlook

Bruce Cowell, Queensland Museum

What's special?

Right on Brisbane's doorstep, Brisbane Forest Park is a scenic mosaic of natural bushland with many places to bushwalk, bush camp and picnic close to the city. Reputedly the largest tract of bushland near a major capital city in Australia, Brisbane Forest Park also contains Brisbane's closest and most accessible rainforest.

Here, national park, forest reserve and Brisbane City Council lands are jointly managed for nature-based recreation and conservation. A haven for native plants and animals, Brisbane Forest Park is a great place to relax and unwind from the pressures of city life.

Exploring Brisbane Forest Park

Visit the park headquarters before you head up the mountain. Obtain information and brochures and check out the native animals at Walk-about Creek Wildlife Centre. (An admission fee applies.)

Enjoy a picnic with a view at Jolly's Lookout or Maiala, or bush picnic at Boombana in D'Aguilar National Park. You can also picnic at Mt Coot-tha, Bellbird Grove, Camp Mountain, Wivenhoe Outlook, Cedar Flats, Ironbark Gully and Lake Manchester.

Enjoy spectacular views over Brisbane, the Samford Valley, Moreton Bay and the Glass House Mountains from Jolly's Lookout. On a clear day, you can see the scenic rim of mountains from Western Window north of Maiala.

Go for a scenic drive through the park to Lake Wivenhoe, stopping at lookouts and picnic areas along the way. Contact the park about places where horse riding and mountain bike riding are allowed.

Enjoy the "Go Bush" nature-based activity program throughout the year with guided bushwalks, spotlighting, wildlife talks, kids' activities and other activities. Contact the park for "Go Bush" details and bookings and information about school and community programs. Fees apply for these programs.

Bush camping by permit is allowed in some parts of Brisbane Forest Park. Book through the park.

Brisbane Forest Park

Walking

See the rainforest, gold mining relics and open forest along the park's many short walks. Wear a hat and sunscreen and take water. Wear insect repellent in summer to discourage leeches. Talk to the staff about the long-distance walking trail being developed in the park.

Accessibility

The first part of the Pitta circuit is suitable for strollers and wheelchairs. The start of the Maiala circuit is suitable for strollers and, possibly, wheelchairs. The park headquarters is wheelchair-accessible.

Getting there

Brisbane Forest Park headquarters is located at 60 Mt Nebo Road, just 20–30 minutes from central Brisbane via Waterworks Road. Jolly's Lookout and Boombana are a further 15 minutes along Mt Nebo Road while Manorina is 55 minutes from Brisbane on the Mt Nebo Road. Maiala can be reached by Mt Nebo Road or Samford-Mt Glorious Road and is just over one hour's drive from central Brisbane.

Westridge Outlook

Tracks

Egernia circuit, Jolly's Lookout
1·5km, 20–30 mins

Thylogale track
8km return, 2–3 hours

Pitta circuit, Boombana
1·1km, 20–30 minutes

Turrbal circuit, Bellbird Grove
1·7km, 30–45 minutes

Golden Boulder track
1km return, 30 minutes

Atrax circuit, Manorina
1·5km, 30–40 minutes

Morelia track, Manorina
6km return, 2–2·5 hours

Maiala circuit
1·9km, 30–45 minutes

Greene's Falls track
4·3km return,
1 hour–1 hour 30 minutes

Cypress Grove track
2·5km return,
45 minutes–1 hour

Westside track
Maiala 7km return,
1·5–2·5 hours

Further information

Brisbane Forest Park
60 Mt Nebo Road
THE GAP QLD 4061
ph (07) 3300 4855
fax (07) 3300 5347
e-mail: brisbaneforestpark@epa.qld.gov.au

Mt Mee State Forest and Forest Reserve

What's special?

At the northern end of the D'Aguilar Range, Mt Mee State Forest and Forest Reserve contains beautiful open forests, scribbly gum forests, rainforest remnants, hoop pine plantations and picturesque creek scenery.

Exploring Mt Mee

Have a picnic at the Gantry picnic area where you can see the remains of the old sawmill which operated here until 1981. Toilets, picnic tables, barbecues, water and bins are provided.

Go bushwalking. Find out about the forest along the Piccabeen walk. Enjoy magnificent views over Lakes Somerset and Wivenhoe along the Somerset trail. Discover the rainforest along the Mills rainforest walk.

Choose from two small camping areas in the forest. Neurum Creek is 6km from the Gantry picnic area. Tent sites, toilets, fire rings, firewood, bins and water are provided.

You can also camp beside Neurum Creek at Archer camping area, 16km from the Gantry picnic area along Loveday's Road. Obtain a camping permit and permit to traverse the forest beforehand. Toilets, barbecues and firewood are provided. Boil the creek water for five minutes before drinking.

Bruce Cowell, Queensland Museum

Neurum Creek

Bruce Cowell, Queensland Museum

Rocky Hole

Mt Mee State Forest and Forest Reserve

Both camping areas are unsuitable for caravans or camper trailers.

Enjoy the view over the picturesque Neurum Valley and Bulls Falls from the Falls Lookout, 1km past the picnic area. Access to the lookout is by a 500m walking track along a four-wheel-drive road. Vehicle permits are required.

Take care if swimming in waterholes along Neurum Creek.

Walking

Wear sturdy shoes and take drinking water when walking.

Accessibility

Gantry picnic area is wheelchair-accessible. The Piccabeen walk is suitable for wheelchairs with assistance.

Getting there

Mt Mee is about 90 minutes' drive or 60km north-west of Brisbane. From the south, travel through Samford and Dayboro then follow Mount Mee and Sellin Roads to the forest. From the north, turn off the D'Aguilar Highway at D'Aguilar south of Woodford. Access to the camping areas is suitable for conventional vehicles.

Tracks

Falls Lookout
1km return, 20 minutes

Mills rainforest walk
1·4km, 40 minutes

From Gantry Day Use Area:
Piccabeen walk
1km circuit, 20 minutes

Somerset trail
13km circuit, 3–4 hours

From Neurum Creek camping area:
Lophostemon walk
750m, 10 minutes

Further information

Naturally Queensland Information Centre
Ground Floor
160 Ann Street, Brisbane
PO Box 155 BRISBANE ALBERT STREET QLD 4002
ph (07) 3227 8185
fax (07) 3227 8749
e-mail: nqic@epa.qld.gov.au

Vehicle permits:
ph (07) 3227 7800

Campsite bookings: 13 13 04 or www.qld.gov.au/camping

View towards Mt Glorious from Mt Mee

Bruce Cowell, Queensland Museum

Daisy Hill Forest Reserve

See koalas at Daisy Hill

Paul Candlin

What's special?

On Brisbane's southern outskirts, Daisy Hill Forest Reserve protects forest and woodland remnants, most of which have disappeared from the metropolitan area.

Open forests with grey gum, spotted gum, narrow-leaved ironbark and tallowwood and paperbark woodlands grow in the forest.

Together with other reserves, the forest is managed as part of a coordinated conservation area to protect this important koala habitat.

Exploring Daisy Hill

Daisy Hill is one of the few urban forests in south-east Queensland where you can picnic, bushwalk, cycle and horse ride.

Have a picnic in a grassy open forest setting in the lower picnic area. Barbecues, shelter sheds, firewood, picnic tables, toilets, bins and drinking water are provided. Large groups should contact the office first. Dogs on leashes are allowed in the picnic area. You can reserve particular sites for private functions.

The upper picnic area is smaller and popular with horse riders. Barbecues, firewood, picnic tables, toilets, bins and drinking water are provided.

Join in a "Go Bush" activity at Daisy Hill during school holidays.

Adam Creed

Daisy Hill Forest Reserve

Find out about trees along the Tree Discovery trail. Discover why koalas are an Australian icon from the educational display in the Daisy Hill Koala Centre. The centre is open 10am to 4pm every day except Christmas Day, New Year's Day and Good Friday. Admission is free. "Go Bush" nature activities for families are conducted in the school holidays. Fees apply.

Cycling and horse riding are allowed along unsealed tracks starting from the upper picnic area where parking for horse floats and a corral are provided. Cyclists and horse riders can also share the Stringybark and Spotted Gum trails with walkers. Permits are not required.

Camping is not allowed in the forest and the entrance gate to the lower picnic area is closed at night.

Accessibility

The lower picnic area, toilets and the Daisy Hill Koala Centre are wheelchair-accessible. The Paperbark trail is wheelchair-assisted.

Getting there

Daisy Hill is 25km south-east of Brisbane. Turn off the Pacific Highway at the Shailer Road exit or take the Winnetts Road exit and travel to the forest along Winnetts and Daisy Hill Roads. From the south, take the Loganlea exit off the Pacific Highway.

Tracks

From the lower picnic area:
Tree Discovery trail
800m circuit, 45 minutes

Spotted Gum trail
4km one-way, 1·5 hours

Stringybark trail
5·7km one-way, 2 hours

Paperbark trail
450m circuit, 15 minutes

Further information

Daisy Hill Koala Centre
PO Box 5116
DAISY HILL QLD 4127
ph (07) 3299 1032
fax (07) 3299 1217
e-mail: koala.centre@epa.qld.gov.au

Paperbark trail, Daisy Hill Forest Reserve

Venman Bushland National Park

See red-necked wallabies in the picnic area.

Adam Creed

What's special?

Together with other bushland remnants, Venman Bushland National Park is an important koala habitat. The Koala Coast, extending from the Gateway Motorway east to Moreton Bay and south to the Logan River, contains up to 5000 koalas, the largest suburban koala population in Australia.

Brisbane's closest national park contains one of the largest eucalypt forest remnants in the near-metropolitan coastal lowlands. The open forest, with its mixture of eucalypt and angophora trees and well-developed understorey of flowering shrubs, is home to koalas, brushtail and ringtail possums, sugar gliders, greater gliders, swamp and red-necked wallabies, powerful owls and many other birds.

The park protects the headwaters of Tingalpa Creek and its tributaries. For most of the year, the creeks are dry or just a string of waterholes, as the creeks flow underground. Frogs, water-rats and water dragons live in and around the creeks.

The park has been a popular Brisbane recreation site for decades and was donated to the Queensland Parks and Wildlife Service by local Jack Venman (1911–94).

Exploring Venman Bushland

Have a bush picnic or barbecue. Picnic tables, wood barbecues and firewood are provided. Boil the water for five minutes before drinking, and remove your rubbish.

See red-necked wallabies in the picnic area but please do not feed them. (Animals can become a nuisance when fed. Let them find their own food — native herbs and grasses.)

Go birdwatching. The forest is home to many different birds. You might glimpse the rarely seen powerful owl. See the wildflowers in spring.

Camping is not allowed in the park.

Venman Bushland National Park

Walking

The park has many gravel roads, rough footpads and fire trails to explore. Get a map from the information sign in the picnic area carpark. Wear a hat and sunscreen and carry water, especially in summer. Do not drink the creek water. Choose from several tracks from a few hundred metres to a few kilometres. Allow up to two hours for your walk.

Accessibility

The toilets and a picnic table are wheelchair-accessible and disability parking is provided.

Getting there

Venman Bushland National Park is 40km or half an hour's drive south of Brisbane on West Mt Cotton Road via the Southeast Freeway or Mt Cotton Road. Travel south along the Southeast Freeway and take the Cleveland turnoff. Head towards Redland Bay turning left onto California Creek Road. Follow the signs to the park. The gates and toilets are closed at night.

Further information

Venman Bushland NP
c/- Daisy Hill Koala Centre
Daisy Hill Road
PO Box 5116
DAISY HILL QLD 4127
ph (07) 3299 1032
fax (07) 3299 1217
e-mail: koala.centre@epa.qld.gov.au

Open forest in Venman Bushland National Park

Fort Lytton National Park

Adam Creed

Inside the fort

What's special?

Near the mouth of the Brisbane River lie the remains of Fort Lytton, one of several coastal fortifications built along Australia's coast before federation to safeguard shipping lanes and ports from possible enemy raids.

For half a century from 1881, Fort Lytton was Brisbane's frontline of defence and is regarded as the birthplace of Queensland's military history. Regular training camps in military warfare were a highlight of Queensland's political and social calendar.

This classic example of a coastal fortress was surrounded by a water-filled moat, and its heavy armaments were concealed behind grassy ramparts connected by underground passages. After World War II, the fort had outlived its usefulness and fell into disrepair until Ampol took over the site in 1963. The fort became a national park in 1988 and today protects this important link with our military past.

Exploring Fort Lytton

Visit the fort 10am to 4pm on Sundays or public holidays. Entry fees apply. Go on a 90 minute–two hour guided tour on Sundays with an experienced and knowledgeable volunteer guide. Groups can book weekday tours through the ranger.

Buy a brochure or map to help you explore the park. Visit the museum and discover Fort Lytton's special stories. Thanks to the efforts of the Fort Lytton volunteers, you can learn how the disappearing gun worked and see guns similar to the fort's original arsenal.

After your tour of the fort, enjoy a picnic on the banks of the Brisbane River.

Learn more about our past or simply enjoy a cuppa in the canteen run by the volunteer guides. (Small fee applies.) Purchase a souvenir of your visit.

Experience gun firing demonstrations and military re-enactments. Check with the ranger about likely dates.

Fort Lytton National Park

Walking

There are no tracks at the park but walking routes are easy to follow from brochures and rope barriers. Wear a hat and sunscreen. Stay behind the safety barriers. The grass pathways are unsuitable for strollers or wheelchairs.

Getting there

Fort Lytton is 15km from central Brisbane at Lytton on the southern bank of the Brisbane River. Drive east along Lytton Road past the Gateway Arterial through Hemmant. Just past Lindum Road, turn left (still Lytton Road) then drive through the gate to the fort. From Wynnum, drive west to the end of Tingal Road, left into Pritchard Street and right into South Street.

Further information

Fort Lytton NP
South Street, Lytton
PO Box 293 WYNNUM QLD 4178
ph (07) 3393 4647
fax (07) 3893 1780

Hear the guns fire on special open days.

St Helena Island National Park

What's special?

St Helena Island's picturesque setting in inner Moreton Bay is a striking contrast to its turbulent past as a high security prison. Queensland's first historic national park, St Helena Island National Park contains the ruins of the State's first penal settlement which operated here from 1867 until 1932.

St Helena Island provides a fascinating insight into life in the 19th Century. The island was virtually self-supporting and the site of Queensland's first tramway and sugar mill. Today, the vegetation is an interesting mix of the original vine forest, crops such as the grove of olive trees and remnants of beautifully landscaped gardens.

The park also contains evidence of the lifestyle of Aboriginal people who visited the island in search of seasonal delicacies such as flying-foxes and shellfish. A large shell midden on the south-western side of the island has been carbon-dated at 2000 years.

Wetlands around the island are a haven for migratory wading birds. The surrounding waters are protected in Moreton Bay Marine Park.

Old Stores building

Darren Jew

St Helena Island National Park

Exploring St Helena Island

Have a picnic on the foreshore overlooking the beach and the distant suburbs of Brisbane. Access beyond the picnic area and shore is restricted to protect the ruins.

Explore the historic ruins in the company of a guide. Fees apply. Commercial tours operate daily. Ranger-guided tours of the ruins operate on weekends from the picnic area. Contact the ranger to check times and availability.

Capture the picturesque ruins on camera. For your safety and to protect the ruins, stay behind rope barriers.

Look for turtles, dugong and dolphins in the surrounding Moreton Bay waters. Take your binoculars and go birdwatching.

Visit the museum in the restored Chief Warder's Cottage and see displays about the island's past. (Access to the museum is by guided tour only.) Educational tours for school groups can be arranged through the Moreton Bay Environmental Education Centre on (07) 3906 9111, www.moretonbayeec.qld.edu.au.

Camping is not allowed on the island.

Walking

The island has no formal tracks but the historic crushed coral roads and grassy paths are easy to follow. Wear comfortable walking shoes, a hat, sunscreen and insect repellent, especially in summer. Carry drinking water.

Getting there

St Helena Island is 7km north-east of Manly and 45 minutes by boat. Regular ferry services depart from Manly and New Farm. Check the Yellow Pages for details. The Moreton Bay Environmental Education Centre operates its own service to the island for school groups. Book through the centre.

Further information

St Helena Island NP
PO Box 293 WYNNUM QLD 4178
ph (07) 3396 5113,
ph (07) 3393 4647
fax (07) 3396 5715

Moreton Bay Environmental Education Centre
PO Box 373 WYNNUM QLD 4178
ph (07) 3906 9111
fax (07) 3906 9100
e-mail: moreton.bay@moretoneec.qld.edu.au
website: www.moretonbayeec.qld.edu.au

Prisoner's graveyard

Blue Lake National Park

What's special?

On North Stradbroke Island, Blue Lake National Park protects coastal wallum and a freshwater lake of special significance to the local Quandamooka people.

Blue Lake or "Karboora" is a window lake formed within a hollow in the island's water table. Tortoise Lagoon, a small seasonal swamp, is a perched lake, located above the water table. Fringed with paperbarks, eucalypts, reeds and banksias, these lakes provide a quiet haven for native animals and visiting bushwalkers. Blue Lake's crystal clear, blue waters are home to the soft-spined sunfish. Reed-filled Tortoise Lagoon is sometimes dry.

Exploring Blue Lake

Walk through wallum woodlands with stunted eucalypt trees, wallum banksias and a flowering heath understorey to Blue Lake.

Sit quietly by the lake and have a bush picnic. Swimming is not recommended. (Hidden snags and shallow water pose risks for visitors.)

Take your camera and binoculars. Look for birds, sand goannas and swamp wallabies early morning and late afternoon. Enjoy the wildflowers in spring.

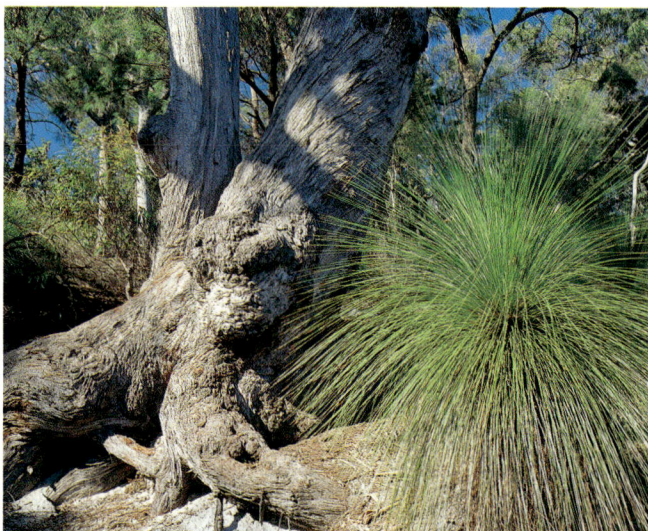

Jeff Wright, Queensland Museum

Wallum banksia flower

Bruce Cowell, Queensland Museum

Open woodland, Blue Lake National Park

Blue Lake National Park

Paul Centurin

Bruce Cowell, Queensland Museum

Blue Lake

Walk to Neembeeba Lookout for a magnificent view over the southern part of North Stradbroke Island, the Pacific Ocean and the Gold Coast.

Visitors must be self-sufficient. There are no facilities. Please remove your rubbish from the park.

Camping is not allowed in the park. Private accommodation is available at Dunwich, Amity and Point Lookout. Local authority campgrounds are at Amity and Point Lookout.

Walking

Explore the wallum on two tracks through the park. Walk in the cooler months. Wear a hat and sunscreen and take drinking water. Wear insect repellent in summer.

Getting there

Water taxis and vehicle ferries from Cleveland provide regular access to North Stradbroke Island. The water taxi takes about 20 minutes and the ferry takes about 90 minutes. From Dunwich, drive 9km along Tazi Road to the park entrance. The walking track to the lake is the best way to see the park.

Tracks

Neembeeba Lookout track
6km return, 1·5–2·5 hours

Karboora track
5km return, 1·5–2 hours

Further information

QPWS
127 Russell Street
PO Box 402
CLEVELAND QLD 4163
ph (07) 3821 9000
fax (07) 3821 9001

Moreton Island National Park

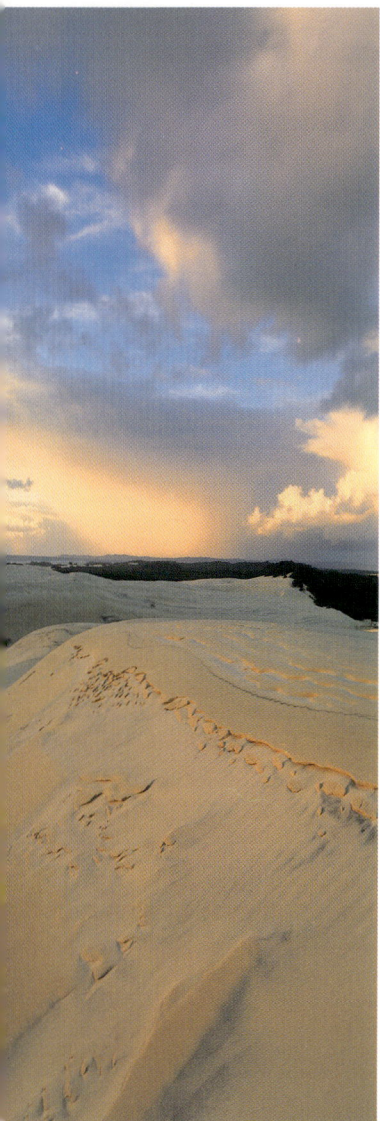

What's special?

Moreton Island is the most natural of the large sand islands protecting Moreton Bay's sheltered waters. Most of the island is national park and a recreation area managed for nature-based recreation.

The park contains freshwater creeks and lakes, coastal heath, rocky headlands, paperbark swamps, an historic lighthouse and the ruins of coastal forts. Mt Tempest, the highest sand dune on the island, is the highest stable coastal sand dune in the southern hemisphere.

Migrating wading birds flock to the island between September and April, and nesting turtles occasionally come ashore in summer. The adjacent bay waters are protected in Moreton Bay Marine Park.

Exploring Moreton Island

Explore the island by four-wheel-drive and walking. Look for migrating humpback whales in late winter and spring. Go birdwatching. Cool off in Blue Lagoon. Enjoy the wildflowers in spring.

See the remains of coastal defences at Toompani Beach and Cowan Cowan. Discover the island's special stories in the information centre at the Cape Moreton lighthouse complex.

Camp at Blue Lagoon, Eagers Creek, Ben-Ewa, the Wrecks or Comboyuro camping areas or specific sites along the beach. (Check with the rangers before setting up camp along the beach.) Facilities are fairly basic and showers are cold. Be prepared for busy holiday times, especially Christmas, New Year and Easter. Get supplies (fuel, groceries and bait) at Bulwer and Kooringal. Vehicle access to the Wrecks campground may be restricted in peak periods.

Fresh water points are provided at the Big Sandhills (western beach), Rous Battery track (eastern beach), North Point and the campgrounds at Blue Lagoon, Eagers Creek, Comboyuro Point, the Wrecks and Ben-Ewa. Boil the water before drinking.

Big Sandhills, Moreton Island

Paul Candlin

Moreton Island National Park

Paul Candlin

Paul Candlin

Paperbark woodland, Moreton Island

Walking

Walking in sand can be tiring. Wear sturdy shoes, a hat and sunscreen. Always carry drinking water.

Getting there

Access to the island is by barge or launch. The barge trip from Whyte Island near Lytton or Scarborough takes two hours. Tangalooma Resort operates a passenger launch from Pinkenba. Pre-booking is essential for all transport. Four-wheel-drive is necessary to get around the island.

Native iris

Robert Ashdown

Tracks

Mt Tempest track
2·5km return, 2 hours

Rous Battery track
18km return, 7 hours

Old Telegraph Road
16km return, 6 hours

Further information

Moreton Island NP
via Tangalooma
MORETON ISLAND QLD 4025
ph (07) 3408 2710
fax (07) 3408 2555
e-mail: moretonisland@
epa.qld.gov.au

Bunyaville Forest Reserve

Picnic area, Bunyaville
Paul Candlin

Tracks

Bunyaville Forest walk
30 minutes

Further information

**Naturally Queensland
Information Centre**
Ground Floor
160 Ann Street, Brisbane
PO Box 155 BRISBANE ALBERT
STREET QLD 4002
ph (07) 3227 8185
fax (07) 3227 8749
e-mail: nqic@epa.qld.gov.au

**Cycling and horse
riding permits:**
ph (07) 3227 7800

What's special?

On Brisbane's north-western outskirts, Bunyaville Forest Reserve is a peaceful retreat and wildlife haven close to the busy metropolitan area.

Spotted gum, grey ironbark, narrow-leaved ironbark, white mahogany, tallowwood, forest red gum, grey gum and brush box grow in the open forests. The forest protects a small community of the broad-leaved spotted gum *Corymbia henryi* found only in the Brisbane region.

Exploring Bunyaville

Have a picnic or barbecue in the forest. Barbecues, firewood, picnic tables, drinking water and toilets are provided. Large groups should contact the QPWS before visiting.

Horse riding and cycling are allowed by permit. For your safety and to minimise damage to the forest, stay on existing tracks.

Find out about the forest and the way it is managed on the Bunyaville Forest walk which starts in the picnic area.

Education Queensland operates an environmental education centre in the forest. The centre provides educational programs for schools. Contact the centre for details and bookings (07) 3353 4356, www.bunyavileec.qld.edu.au.

Camping is not allowed in the forest. The Bunyaville Nursery (07) 3353 1770 is open to the public on weekdays.

Walking

A number of gravel roads are shared by walkers, cyclists and horse riders. Give way to horse riders using the same tracks. Take drinking water.

Accessibility

The picnic facilities are wheelchair-accessible.

Getting there

Bunyaville State Forest is 15km north-west of central Brisbane between the suburbs of Albany Creek and Everton Hills. Access is from the Old Northern Road. The entrance gate is locked at night.

Burleigh Head National Park

What's special?

Right in the heart of the busy Gold Coast, Burleigh Head National Park provides a peaceful haven for wildlife and walkers. Remnants of past volcanic activity, littoral rainforest and reminders of the living culture of the Kombumerri people are protected in this park. The Kombumerri call the headland "Jellurgal".

In spite of its small size, the park is quite diverse, with fringing mangroves along the creek, and windswept tussock grassland, open forest, rainforest and coastal vegetation around the headland.

Exploring Burleigh Head

Sit quietly on Echo Beach at Tallebudgera Creek and enjoy the scenery. Watch for passing dolphins or humpback whales from Tumgun Lookout.

Picnic on the Burleigh foreshore just outside the park. Toilets are located here and near the park's southern entrance.

Visit the Burleigh Head Information Centre on the Gold Coast Highway to find out about the park, Kombumerri culture and nearby hinterland parks.

Walking

See the park's vegetation and scenery along the walking tracks. Do the circuits in a clockwise direction. Wear a hat and sunscreen and stay on the track. A section of the lower coastal track is occasionally closed after rain when there is a risk of rockfall.

Getting there

The park lies between Burleigh Heads and the Tallebudgera Creek estuary and is about 70 minutes from Brisbane. Access is from the Gold Coast Highway near the Tallebudgera Creek bridge or from Goodwin Terrace, Burleigh Heads.

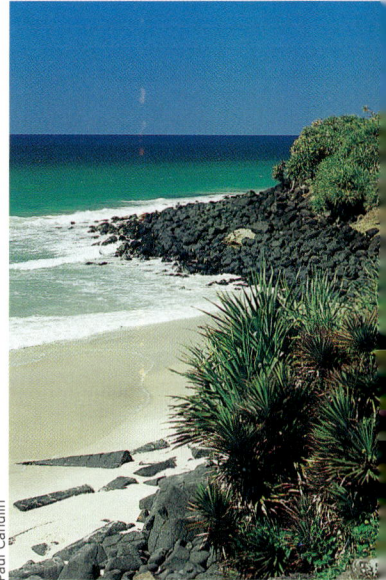

Paul Candlin

Basalt rocks on the foreshore

Tracks

Coastal track
1·2km one-way, 20 minutes

Ocean View circuit
2·8km, 1–1·5 hours

Rainforest walk
*705m one-way,
1–1·5 hours as circuit*

Further information

**Burleigh Head
Information Centre**
1171 Gold Coast Highway
PO Box 203
BURLEIGH HEADS QLD 4220
ph (07) 5535 3032

Mt Cougal Springbrook National Park

Paul Candlin

Rainforest, Mt Cougal

What's special?

Just behind the Gold Coast, Mt Cougal's twin peaks overlook the scenic Currumbin Valley. This small section of Springbrook National Park protects a subtropical rainforest remnant, scenic cascades and the headwaters of Currumbin and Tallebudgera Creeks.

The Mt Cougal Section is an important wildlife habitat and the most easterly known location of the Lamington spiny cray. One of the world's largest skinks, the land mullet, also lives here.

The Yugambeh people lived in this valley for at least 6000 years and still have a close connection with the park. A dreaming story is associated with Cougal's twin peaks.

A bush sawmill operated here from 1942 until 1954 producing timber for housing and to crate bananas grown in the Currumbin Valley. The remains of the partly restored sawmill are located at the end of the walking track.

The Mt Cougal Section of Springbrook National Park is part of the Central Eastern Rainforest Reserves World Heritage Area.

Adam Creed

Bush sawmill

Mt Cougal, Springbrook National Park

Bruce Cowell

Exploring Mt Cougal

Go for a scenic drive through the picturesque Currumbin Valley. Have a bush picnic by the creek or just sit quietly and enjoy the peaceful sounds of the bush away from the noise and bustle of the nearby Gold Coast. Take drinking water.

See the local wildlife. Eastern water dragons, sooty owls, water-rats, brushtail possums, brush-turkeys and logrunners are some of the animals you might see. Please do not feed the animals.

Read about the park's world heritage values at the display shelter at the start of the walking track and signs along the track.

Be careful around the creek. People have been seriously injured jumping and diving into the creek.

Camping is not allowed in the park. A public phone, toilets, barbecues and picnic facilities are provided 6km away at the Currumbin Rockpool.

Walking

See cascades and rockpools along the walk to the bush sawmill. Wear insect repellent to discourage ticks and leeches.

Accessibility

Mt Cougal has wheelchair-accessible toilets and picnic tables. Wheelchairs could possibly negotiate the sealed track with assistance.

Getting there

Mt Cougal is just 35 minutes' drive from Palm Beach on the Gold Coast, 43km from Nerang or 113km from Brisbane. Turn off the Pacific Motorway south of Palm Beach and drive 19km along the Currumbin Creek Road to Mt Cougal.

Ross Naumann

Cascade treefrog at Mt Cougal

Tracks

Cougal Cascades track
1·6km return, 30–45 minutes

Further information

**Mt Cougal Section
Springbrook NP**
PO Box 203
BURLEIGH HEADS QLD 4220
ph (07) 5576 0271
fax (07) 55209613
e-mail: GoldCoast@epa.qld.gov.au

Tamborine National Park

What's special?

In the Gold Coast hinterland, Tamborine National Park contains precious remnants of subtropical rainforest and open forest on and around the slopes of the scenic Tamborine Mountain Plateau.

Much of the subtropical rainforest is dominated by the distinctive piccabeen palm. The unusual cycads *Lepidozamia peroffskyana* growing on the mountain are relics of plants which flourished 150 million years ago.

The park is home to many rainforest animals including the rare Albert's lyrebird and one of the world's largest skinks, the land mullet. The Richmond birdwing butterfly and noisy pitta migrate seasonally to the park from nearby higher altitude rainforests.

Basalt columns, cliffs, rocky outcrops and waterfalls are a lasting legacy of volcanic eruptions 23 million years ago. Tamborine is the most northerly remnant of these flows from a volcano centred on Mt Warning.

Queensland's first national park was established here at Witches Falls on 28 March 1908.

Exploring Tamborine

Escape to the mountains at Tamborine. Enjoy a picnic and a short walk through the forest.

Start your visit at the information centre at Doughty Park, North Tamborine. The Centre is open every day except Christmas Day from 10.30am until 3.30pm.

The best picnic spots are The Knoll and Witches Falls. You can also picnic at MacDonald Park and Cedar Creek, halfway up the mountain. Witches Falls has electric barbecues. Cedar Creek has wood-fired barbecues. Joalah, Palm Grove and Zamia Grove have no picnic facilities.

Tamborine is a great place for a scenic drive. Stop at Palm Grove, Witches Falls or The Knoll for spectacular views over the surrounding countryside. See the ancient cycads at Zamia Grove.

Camping is not allowed in the park but there is plenty of private accommodation on the mountain.

Open forest, Witches Falls

Darren Jew

Tamborine National Park

Walking

With 22km of graded walking track, Tamborine is a great place for bushwalking. Most walks take less than half a day. Wear insect repellent to discourage leeches. Take drinking water, especially on the more exposed tracks. Never drink the creek water.

Accessibility

The toilets at Cedar Creek are wheelchair-accessible.

Getting there

Tamborine is about 80km or one hour's drive south of Brisbane or 36km and 30 minutes north-west of the Gold Coast via the Pacific Highway and Tamborine-Oxenford Road. You can also drive to the park from Brisbane via Tamborine Village or from Nerang via the Nerang-Beaudesert Road.

The volunteer-run information centre is at Doughty Park, North Tamborine. The park office is on Knoll Road at North Tamborine.

Adam Creed

Cedar Creek

Tracks

Curtis Falls track, Joalah
1·5km return, 35–45 minutes

Joalah circuit
4·2km return, 1·5 hours

Cameron Falls circuit
2·6km return, 1 hour

Rainforest circuit, MacDonald Park
1·4km, 30–45 minutes

Palm Grove circuit
3km return, 1 hour

Jenyns Falls circuit
5·4km, 2 hours

Witches Falls circuit
3km, 1 hour

Witches Chase track
6·5km return, 2–3 hours

Cedar Creek circuit
3.5km, 1-2 hours

Further information

Tamborine NP
Knoll Road
NORTH TAMBORINE QLD 4272
ph (07) 5545 1171
fax (07) 5545 4031
e-mail:
mt.tamborine@epa.qld.gov.au

Bruce Cowell, Queensland Museum

Buttressed tree in rainforest at Witches Falls

Springbrook National Park

White-eared honeyeater

Adam Creed

What's special?

Over thousands of years, water and volcanic activity have carved a spectacular landscape of cliffs, gorges and waterfalls around the Springbrook Plateau just behind the Gold Coast. Almost 3000ha of rainforest, open forest and montane heath are protected in Springbrook National Park. Picturesque creeks, tumbling waterfalls and panoramic views make Springbrook one of the state's most popular parks.

More than 100 bird species live in the park and rare and threatened animals like the Richmond birdwing rely on Springbrook's forests for their survival. Ten percent of the plants are only found locally.

Aboriginal names are a reminder that this is a special place for indigenous people. Gwongorella means "dancing waters" while Warrie means "rushing". The plateau was not opened up for grazing selection until 1906 and forestry was a thriving industry in the early 20th Century.

Springbrook is part of a chain of mountains and forest remnants on both sides of the Queensland/New South Wales border known as the "Scenic Rim". These forests are protected in the Central Eastern Rainforest Reserves World Heritage Area.

Exploring the park

Springbrook is a refreshingly cool retreat from the summer heat. The park's picnic areas and walking tracks are very popular.

Take a scenic drive to Springbrook and enjoy spectacular views over the Gold Coast and hinterland. Go for a short walk or simply relax in the bush.

Find a perfect picnic spot at Goomoolahra, Tallanbana or Gwongorella. You might see brush-turkeys, satin bowerbirds, noisy miners and crimson rosellas. Toilets, a shelter shed, picnic tables and barbecues are provided. Gwongorella has electric barbecues. Boil the water for five minutes before drinking or take your own water supply.

Enjoy a bushwalk in the fresh mountain air. Look for logrunners in the rainforest leaf litter or listen for the call of the Albert's lyrebird. The Twin Falls circuit is a great introduction to the park. See rainforest, open forest and montane heath, waterfalls and scenic views on this short walk.

Springbrook National Park

You can camp at Purling Brook Falls. Campsites are limited and bookings are essential. The campground has very basic facilities (no showers or bins) and is unsuitable for caravans. Bush camping is not allowed in the park.

Discover the plateau's fascinating past and the present-day forests at the Springbrook Information Centre. The centre is housed in a 1911 schoolhouse.

Walking

Choose from graded tracks between 700m and 17km. The Purling Brook Falls circuit is the most popular walk. **WARNING: Serious injury or death can result from walking near the cliff edge. Stay on the track. Supervise children closely.**

Accessibility

Goomoolahra picnic area has a wheelchair-accessible picnic area, toilets and sealed 100m walking track. At the information centre, a 100m boardwalk suitable for wheelchairs and strollers leads to a lookout over the Gold Coast.

Getting there

Springbrook is 90 minutes by road from Brisbane or 45 minutes from the Gold Coast via Nerang or Mudgeeraba. Both routes are steep and winding. Food and fuel are available on the Plateau.

From Brisbane, take the Pacific Highway about 70km south to Mudgeeraba, then drive 29km to Springbrook. From Nerang, 65km south of Brisbane, take the Nerang-Murwillumbah Road to Numinbah Valley and drive a further 18km to Springbrook.

Tracks

Purling Brook Falls circuit
4km, 1·5–2 hours

Twin Falls circuit
4–4·5km, 1·5–2 hours

Warrie circuit
17km, 5–6 hours

Bilborough Lookout
3km return, 1–2 hours

Best of All Lookout
700m return, 15–30 minutes

Further information

Springbrook NP
2873 Springbrook Road
SPRINGBROOK QLD 4213
ph (07) 5533 5147
fax (07) 5533 5991

Campsite bookings: 13 13 04 or www.qld.gov.au/camping

Lamington spiny cray

Paul Candlin

View from Canyon Lookout

Paul Candlin

Natural Bridge Springbrook National Park

What's special?

In the Gold Coast hinterland, the Natural Bridge Section of Springbrook National Park protects subtropical rainforest remnants and an intriguing rock arch formation over Cave Creek. This is a popular destination for hinterland visitors.

Cave Creek once flowed over a waterfall in front of the present stone bridge. Over time, water gouged out a cavern in the softer rock behind the waterfall, while a pothole formed in the creek above. Eventually, the water broke through the roof of the cavern. Like a natural bridge (or arch), Cave Creek now plunges through that hole into the cavern below. One of Australia's largest glow-worm colonies lives beside the track and on the roof of this cave.

Natural Bridge is part of the traditional lands of the Kombumerri people. Aboriginal people commonly travelled through the Numinbah Valley when attending gatherings and ceremonies. This section also contains reminders of the early timber-getters who came to the Numinbah Valley searching for prized red cedar trees.

Rainbow lorikeet

Darren Jew

Exploring Natural Bridge

Have a bush picnic in the rainforest. Coin-operated electric barbecues, picnic tables and a shelter shed are provided. Boil tap water for five minutes before drinking.

Look for noisy pittas, rainforest dragons and rainbow lorikeets in the forest. At night, you can spotlight possums in the trees and see glow-worms inside the cave under the rock arch. After dusk in summer is the best time to see the glow-worms. Please do not disturb the glow-worms or shine your torches on them. Commercial tours operate.

Camping is not allowed in this section of the park but you can camp on the nearby Springbrook plateau or stay in private accommodation in the Numinbah Valley.

Find out about the forest at the information shelter at the start of the walking track.

Natural Bridge, Springbrook National Park

Walking

Enjoy a short rainforest walk and see the natural arch over Cave Creek. Stay behind the safety fence above the arch. People have been seriously injured diving in the creek.

Accessibility

The small picnic area has wheelchair-accessible toilets. Several steps make the whole circuit unsuitable for wheelchairs. If you go anti-clockwise, you can get to the lookout over the arch with a stroller and, possibly, a wheelchair.

Getting there

Natural Bridge is 30km from Nerang or 42km from Mudgeeraba via the Springbrook plateau. The drive from Brisbane takes about 90 minutes.

Tracks

Rainforest circuit
1km, 20–40 minutes

Further information

Springbrook NP
Via MUDGEERABA QLD 4215
ph (07) 5533 5147
fax (07) 5533 5991

Bruce Cowell, Queensland Museum

Natural arch

Numinbah Forest Reserve

Nerang River,
Numinbah Forest Reserve

Adam Creed

Further information

**Naturally Queensland
Information Centre**
Ground Floor
160 Ann Street, Brisbane
PO Box 155 BRISBANE ALBERT
STREET QLD 4002
ph (07) 3227 8185
fax (07) 3227 8749
e-mail: nqic@epa.qld.gov.au

**Cycling and horse
riding permits:**
QPWS
PO Box 3454
BURLEIGH TOWN LPO
BURLEIGH HEADS QLD 4220
ph (07) 5520 9600

Group activity permits:
QPWS
158 Hume Street
PO Box 731
TOOWOOMBA QLD 4350
ph (07) 4639 4599
fax (07) 4639 4524

What's special?

In the scenic foothills of the border ranges lies Numinbah Forest Reserve, the gateway to some of the most popular Gold Coast hinterland parks. This large forest protects rugged mountain scenery, dry open eucalypt forests and wet sclerophyll forests fringing the Nerang River and picturesque Waterfall Creek. Tall flooded gums and orange-flowering silky oaks grow in these forests.

Exploring Numinbah

Go for a scenic drive through the Numinbah Valley and stop here for a picnic or barbecue beside the Nerang River. Barbecues, firewood, picnic tables, a shelter shed and toilets are provided. Dogs on a leash are allowed in this forest.

Horse riding and cycling are allowed by permit. Queensland Association of Four Wheel Drive clubs can apply to go scenic four-wheel-driving in the forest. For safety and to minimise damage to the forest, stay on existing tracks.

Camping is not allowed in the forest.

Walking

There are no formal tracks but you can walk along the forest roads with care. Give way to horse riders using the same tracks. Take drinking water.

Accessibility

The picnic area has wheelchair-accessible toilets and picnic tables.

Getting there

Numinbah Forest Reserve is 25km south-west of Nerang or 40km north of Murwillumbah along the Nerang-Murwillumbah Road.

Nerang Forest Reserve

What's special?

In the Gold Coast hinterland, Nerang Forest Reserve forms a green backdrop to the township of Nerang. Dry rainforest and open eucalypt forests of grey gum, blue gum, stringybark and tallowwood grow in the hilly reserve.

Exploring Nerang

Relax and enjoy nature in this largely undeveloped forest. Go birdwatching. Watch glossy black-cockatoos feeding in the casuarina groves.

Horse riding and cycling are allowed by permit available from the QPWS office at Burleigh Heads. Queensland Association of Four Wheel Drive clubs can apply to go scenic four-wheel-driving in the reserve. For safety and to minimise damage to the forest, stay on existing tracks.

Trail bike riding and camping are not allowed in the forest.

Walking

Cyclists and walkers share the Casuarina Grove track through the dry open forest and along the creek. You can also explore the forest along roads and other tracks. Give way to horse riders who use some tracks.

Getting there

Nerang Forest Reserve is on Nerang's north-west outskirts, 12km from Surfers Paradise or 70km south of Brisbane. Conventional vehicle access is possible from Matilda or Coolibah Roads off the Pacific Motorway, Nerang township or the Beaudesert-Nerang Road.

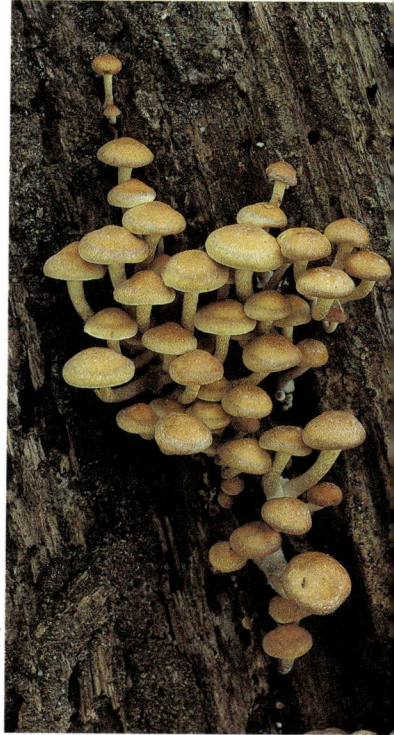

Bruce Cowell, Queensland Museum

Gilled fungi, Nerang Forest Reserve

Tracks

Casuarina Grove track
2.8km return, 1 hour

Further information

Burleigh Head Information Centre
1171 Gold Coast Highway
PO Box 203
BURLEIGH HEADS QLD 4220
ph (07) 5535 3032

Lamington National Park

What's special?

Rugged mountain scenery, tumbling waterfalls, rainforest, wildflower heaths, tall open forests, picturesque creeks, varied wildlife and some of the best bushwalking in Queensland are protected in Lamington National Park.

One of Queensland's best-loved parks, Lamington is the core of the Central Eastern Rainforest Reserves Australia World Heritage Area along the Queensland-New South Wales border ranges. The park's beautiful rainforests include the largest subtropical rainforest remnant in the world and one of the most extensive Antarctic beech cool temperate rainforests in Australia.

Lamington is home to an incredible variety of wildlife including rare and threatened plants and animals such as the Coxen's fig-parrot, eastern bristlebird, Richmond birdwing butterfly, milk-vine and blotched sarcochilus, a beautiful orchid.

For thousands of years, Aboriginal people lived in and visited these mountains. Early European settlers also valued the area, and fought to make it one of the first parks in Queensland. The O'Reilly family established a guesthouse near the park in 1926 and founding members of the National Parks Association of Queensland built Binna Burra Lodge next to the park in the 1930s.

Exploring Lamington

Have a picnic at Binna Burra or Green Mountains. Picnic tables, toilets, electric barbecues and tap water are provided. See colourful crimson rosellas, king parrots, pademelons and brush-turkeys around the picnic areas. Go birdwatching during the day or spotlighting at night.

The best way to see the park is bushwalking. Choose from many short or full-day walks which take you to the park's best attractions. Let someone reliable know your bushwalking plans and advise them of your safe return.

Stay overnight at campgrounds or resorts at Binna Burra or Green Mountains. Bookings are essential, especially for public and school holidays and weekends.

Both the national park campground at Green Mountains and the private campground at Binna Burra have good facilities including toilets, hot showers and water supply. Take a fuel stove for Green Mountains. Open fires are not allowed.

See many waterfalls in Lamington National Park.

Robert Ashdown

Binna Burra

Green Mountains

Lamington National Park

You can bush camp in the park between February and November. Bush camping is only allowed in specific places. Conditions apply. You must book through the Green Mountains office and pay for your campsite at least three weeks in advance.

The southern end of Lamington National Park has no formed tracks. If you wish to bush camp overnight in this remote area, you must complete an application form and pay your camping fees at least three weeks in advance through the Green Mountains office. Take plenty of food and water, a map and compass, well-stocked first aid kit, a torch, warm clothing, rain gear and a warm sleeping bag. Never walk alone.

Visit the information centres at Binna Burra or Green Mountains to learn more about the park. Read the information displays at the start of the walking tracks to determine the best walk for you.

Orange-eyed green treefrog at Running Creek

Tracks

From Binna Burra:
Border track
21·4km one-way, 6–8 hours

Daves Creek circuit
12km return, 3·5–4·5 hours

Rainforest circuit
1·2km return, 20–30 minutes

Tullawallal circuit
5km return, 1·5–2 hours

Coomera circuit
17·5km, 6–7 hours

Upper Ballunjui track
11km return, 2·5–3 hours

Illinbah circuit
16·6km return, 7–8 hours

Gwongoorool track
6km return, 1·5–2 hours

Caves circuit
5km return, 1·5–2 hours

Bellbird Lookout track
2km return, 40 minutes–1 hour

Ships Stern circuit
19km return, 7–8 hours

Lower Bellbird circuit
12km return, 3–4 hours

Mt Hobwee circuit
20·4km return, 6–8 hours

Araucaria track
18km return, 6–7 hours

Mt Merino track
23km return, 8–9 hours

Lamington National Park

Robert Ashdown

Tracks

From Green Mountains:
Rainforest circuit
1·3km return, 20–35 minutes

Border track
21·4km one-way, 6–8 hours

Python Rock track
3·4km return, 1 hour

Morans Falls track
4·6km return, 1·5–2 hours

West Canungra Creek circuit
13·9km, 5–6 hours

Box Forest circuit
10·9km, 3·5–4.5 hours

Elabana Falls
7·4km return, 2–3 hours

Toolona Creek circuit
17·4km, 6–7 hours

Albert River circuit
20·6km, 7–8 hours

Further information

Lamington NP
Binna Burra Section
Beechmont
via NERANG QLD 4211
ph (07) 5533 3584
fax (07) 5533 3767

Binna Burra Campsite
(privately run)
BEECHMONT QLD 4211
(07) 5533 3622

Green Mountains Section
via CANUNGRA QLD 4275
ph (07) 5544 0634
fax (07) 5544 0633
9–11am and 1–3.30pm weekdays

Campsite bookings: 13 13 04 or
www.qld.gov.au/camping

Paul Candlin

Australian king-parrot

The Binna Burra Information Centre is open 8am to 3.30pm weekdays and 9am to 3.30pm weekends, public holidays and some school holidays. The Green Mountains Information Centre is open 9am to 11am on Mondays, Wednesdays and Thursdays, 1pm to 3.30pm weekdays and 9am to 3.30pm most weekends.

Private kiosks and public phones are located at Green Mountains and Binna Burra. Fuel is available at Binna Burra Mountain Resort.

Walking

Take drinking water and wet weather gear when walking in Lamington. Allow 15–20 minutes to walk one kilometre. Wear insect repellent.

Accessibility

The toilets and picnic tables at Binna Burra are wheelchair-accessible. A trail for sight-impaired people is located on private land near Binna Burra Mountain Resort.

Getting there

Binna Burra is near Beechmont, about 110km or 1 hour 40 minutes' drive from Brisbane, or an hour from the Gold Coast via either Canungra or Nerang.

Green Mountains is about 115km or almost two hours from Brisbane and 70km or 90 minutes from the Gold Coast via Canungra.

The mountain roads are narrow and winding and unsuitable for caravans. Tour buses operate to both places.

Mt Barney National Park

What's special?

Mts Barney, Maroon, May and Lindesay rise majestically above the surrounding farmlands in Mt Barney National Park on the Queensland–New South Wales border. These rugged peaks are the remains of the ancient Focal Peak Shield Volcano which erupted 24 million years ago. Mt Barney is the second highest peak in south-east Queensland.

The park has extremely varied vegetation with open forests around the foothills of the peaks, subtropical rainforest above 600m, montane heath shrublands towards the summit of the peaks, cool temperate rainforest on the summit of Mt Ballow, and mallee eucalypt shrublands on Mt Maroon. Many rare and unusual plant species grow in the park including the endangered Maroon wattle *Acacia saxicola*, and the rare mallee eucalypt *Eucalyptus codonocarpa*, Mt Barney bush pea *Pultanaea whiteana* and *Eucalyptus michaeliana*.

Most of Mt Barney National Park is in the Central Eastern Rainforests Reserves Australia World Heritage Area.

Exploring Mt Barney

Experienced, well-equipped bushwalkers can enjoy this remote park's special attractions. Most trails are unmarked.

Have a picnic at Yellow Pinch at the base of Mt Barney. Toilets, barbecues and picnic tables are provided. Read about the park and walking safety at information displays located at Yellow Pinch and the Lower Portals carpark.

Enjoy spectacular views over the border ranges and scenic rim forests from the summit of Mt Barney. The most challenging route up Mt Barney is Logan's Ridge. Peasant's or South Ridge is a better choice for less experienced climbers.

Robert Ashdown

View from South East Ridge of Mt Barney

Paul Candlin

Mt Barney

Mt Barney National Park

Robert Ashdown

Tracks

Lower Portals track
7·4km return, 2·5–3 hours

Upper Portals track
8km return, 2·5–3 hours

Cronan Creek track
13km return, 4·5–6 hours

Mt Barney summit
8–10 hours return

Further information

QPWS
3522 Ipswich–Boonah Road
COULSON QLD 4310
ph (07) 5463 5041
fax (07) 5463 5042
e-mail: Boonah@epa.qld.gov.au

Allow plenty of time for the ascent and descent, which take between 8 and 10 hours, depending on the route and your level of fitness. Walkers need navigational and bushwalking skills and sound physical fitness. Never walk alone or take unfit walkers in your party.

Nearby Mt Maroon is popular for rockclimbing.

Bush camping is allowed at Mt May and Mt Barney. Restrictions apply during peak holiday times. Book your campsite at least three weeks before your visit.

You can also camp nearby at Mt May. Private campgrounds at Flanagan's Reserve near Yellow Pinch, Bigriggen and Mt Barney Lodge, just outside the park, provide toilet and shower facilities for family camping.

Walking

Bushwalks are rough trails with steep pinches unsuitable for young children, the elderly and anyone without sound fitness. Walkers must complete a bushwalker safety form and leave it with a reliable friend or family member. Take warm, waterproof clothing, plenty of food and water (at least two litres a day for each person), a compass, the Mt Lindesay 1:25 000 topographic map, a torch and spare batteries, a cyalume light stick (optional), matches and a first aid kit.

Accessibility

Wheelchair-accessible toilets are provided at the Lower Portals carpark and Yellow Pinch picnic area.

Getting there

Mt Barney is about 90 minutes to two hours' drive or 117km from Brisbane, via the Mt Lindesay Highway and Boonah–Rathdowney Road.

Take the Mt Lindesay Highway south to Rathdowney. Turn into the Boonah–Rathdowney Road 1km past Rathdowney and travel 8km to the Barney View–Upper Logan Road. Turn left and follow the signs 12km to Yellow Pinch. For the Lower Portals, turn right off the Barney View–Upper Logan Road into Sidenspinner Road.

From Boonah, drive 39km south and turn off to Yellow Pinch and the Lower Portals on the Upper Logan Road, just past the Logan River crossing. Access to Graces, off Boonah–Rathdowney Road, is suitable for four-wheel-drive vehicles only.

Moogerah Peaks National Park

What's special?

Craggy volcanic peaks rise above the scenic, cultivated Fassifern Valley around Boonah. Four peaks are protected in Moogerah Peaks National Park.

Open forest, dry rainforest and montane heath remnants are preserved in the Mt Moon, Mt Greville, Mt Edwards and Mt French sections of the park. The park contains most of the remaining rainforest in the once-extensive Fassifern Scrub. Dry rainforest with emergent hoop pines and low montane heath grow towards the summits of the peaks.

Frog Buttress at Mt French is regarded as one of Queensland's best rockclimbing sites with more than 300 climbs for experienced climbers. Mt Moon is home to the brush-tailed rock-wallaby which is threatened with extinction.

Exploring Moogerah Peaks

Have a picnic at Mt French or beside Lake Moogerah near Mt Edwards. Enjoy views over the Fassifern Valley, Cunningham's Gap and Mt Barney from lookouts at Mt French.

With its mixture of open forest and vine forest, Moogerah Peaks is a great place for birdwatching. See pale-headed rosellas and brush-turkeys at Mt French and colourful finches at Mt Edwards.

Enjoy the wildflowers at Mt French. In spring and summer, yellow dogwoods and creamy Leptospermum transform the park while the rich ruby-red pea flowers of *Bossiaea rupicola* brighten the picnic area in July and December.

Go spotlighting at night at Mt French. Please do not feed the brushtail possums and secure your food if camping here.

Tent and vehicle camping are allowed at Mt French. Only 14 sites are provided, so book your campsite, especially in the winter climbing season. You can also camp at private campgrounds around Lake Moogerah.

Adam Creed

Mt French

Moogerah Peaks National Park

Paul Canfin

Tracks

East Cliff Lookout circuit, Mt French
800m circuit, 20–30 minutes

North Cliff Lookout track, Mt French
720m return, 15–30 minutes

Mt Edwards track
6km return, 2·5–3·5 hours

Mt Greville track
6km return, 2–3 hours

Further information

QPWS
3522 Ipswich-Boonah Road
COULSON QLD 4310
ph (07) 5463 5041
fax (07) 5463 5042
e-mail: Boonah@epa.qld.gov.au

Campsite bookings: 13 13 04 or
www.qld.gov.au/camping

Walking

Moogerah Peaks has a walk to suit everyone, from wheelchair-accessible tracks with lookouts over the Fassifern Valley on the top of Mt French to rough trails to the summits of Mts Edwards and Greville with spectacular views over the surrounding countryside. Only fit walkers should attempt the tracks up Mt Edwards and Mt Greville.

Accessibility

The North Cliff track at Mt French is wheelchair-accessible.

Getting there

This park is about 100km or 80 minutes' south-west of Brisbane via the Cunningham Highway and Ipswich-Boonah Roads. Mt French is 10km west of Boonah. Mt Edwards is 17km south-west of Boonah or 9km south of Aratula via the Cunningham Highway. Mt Greville is 25km south-west of Boonah via Mt Alford or about 11km south of Lake Moogerah.

Bruce Cowell, Queensland Museum

Mt Greville

Bribie Island National Park

What's special?

Wildflower heaths, open forests and woodlands, teatree wetlands, freshwater creeks and lagoons, cultural sites, migratory birds, and a variety of other wildlife are protected in Bribie Island National Park.

The park covers the northern third of this low-lying sand island, stretching from sheltered Pumicestone Passage to the ocean beach. The surrounding tidal lands and waters are protected in Moreton Bay Marine Park.

Middens along the coastline are a reminder of the Aboriginal people who once lived on the island. The remains of World War II coastal fortifications are also within the park.

Exploring Bribie Island

Bribie Island is a quiet retreat for self-sufficient nature lovers. Go boating or fishing or paddle a canoe along a creek, freshwater lagoon or Pumicestone Passage.

Go boating along Pumicestone Passage and stop for a bush picnic at Lighthouse Reach or the Lions Park on the northern spit or Mission Point. Picnic tables and fireplaces are provided. Take firewood or a fuel stove and drinking water. Toilets are located at Lions Park, Mission Point and Poverty Creek.

Bush camp at Gallaghers Point, Poverty Creek, Mission Point, Lime Pocket or along a 3km stretch of the ocean beach, 16km north of the access road to the beach. Basic facilities are provided at Mission Point and Poverty Creek. Take your own drinking water and firewood and take your rubbish home for disposal.

Go wildlife watching. Look for swamp wallabies, echidnas, emus and frilled lizards. Stroll along the beach. (Beware of passing traffic on the eastern beach). Look for migratory birds in summer. Go birdwatching at nearby Buckley's Hole Conservation Park on the south-western side of the island. A bird hide overlooks the lagoon.

Enjoy the wildflowers in spring. Visit the Park Office at White Patch for more information.

Bruce Cowell, Queensland Museum

Bungwall ferns in paperbark wetland on Bribie Island

Bribie Island National Park

Paul Canlin

Bruce Cowell

Swamp orchid

Tracks

Bicentennial bush walks
3·8km, 45 minutes–1 hour

Lighthouse Reach to the ocean beach
1·5km one-way, 30 minutes

Further information

Bribie Island NP
White Patch Esplanade
PO Box 324
BRIBIE ISLAND QLD 4507
ph (07) 3408 8451
fax (07) 3408 8495
7.30am–4pm weekdays

Walking

Discover the wonderful natural variety of Bribie Island along the Bicentennial bush walks. Obtain a brochure first from the Community Arts Centre on Sunderland Drive. Wear a hat, insect repellent and sunscreen.

Getting there

Bribie Island is one hour or 65km north of Brisbane, or 70km south of Caloundra, via the Bruce Highway. Roads within the park are suitable for four-wheel-drives only and impassable after heavy rain. Enter the park from the end of White Patch Esplanade or the Eighth Avenue carpark off North Street, Woorim. You must obtain a permit from Caboolture Shire Council or Bongaree Caravan Park to drive along the ocean beach. Mission Point, Lime Pocket, Lighthouse Reach and Lions Park are accessible only by boat. For your safety, access restrictions sometimes apply to this park. Check with the ranger.

Access to Buckley's Hole is via Bongaree along Welsby Parade and Toorbul Street.

Bruce Cowell, Queensland Museum

Pumicestone Passage

Glass House Mountains National Park

What's special?

Craggy volcanic peaks tower over a scenic patchwork of pine plantations, bushland and cultivated fields in the Sunshine Coast lowlands north of Brisbane. Eight of the 16 peaks are protected in Glass House Mountains National Park — Mts Beerwah, Tibrogargan, Ngungun, Coonowrin (Crookneck), Miketeeburnulgrai, Mt Cooee, Elimbah (Saddleback) and Coochin Hills.

Named by Cook during his epic voyage along Australia's east coast, the Glass Houses are rhyolitic volcanic plugs left by volcanic activity millions of years ago. This area has special significance for the Gubbi Gubbi Aboriginal people.

Remnants of the open eucalypt woodland and mountain heath vegetation, which once covered the coastal plains, provide a home for an interesting variety of wildlife including 26 rare and threatened plants.

The Glass House Mountains are surrounded by a scenic patchwork of forests and farmlands.

Adam Creed

Glass House Mountains National Park

Robert Ashdown

Adam Creed

Mt Tibrogargan

Tracks

Trachyte circuit
5·7km, 2–3 hours

Mt Ngungun track
1·4km return, 1–2 hours

Mt Beerwah track
3–4 hours

Mt Tibrogargan track
2–3 hours

Further information

QPWS
Bells Creek Road
BEERWAH QLD 4519
ph (07) 5494 0150
fax (07) 5494 6307

Exploring the Glass House Mountains

Go for a scenic drive stopping to walk, picnic or enjoy the view. Picnic at the base of Mt Beerwah or Mt Tibrogargan in the park or nearby at Mt Beerburrum, Wild Horse Mountain, Glass House Mountains Lookout or Mary Cairncross Park, Maleny overlooking the park.

Go birdwatching. Enjoy the spring wildflower display along the Trachyte circuit.

Camping is not allowed in the park but you can camp at nearby private campgrounds on the Glass House Mountains Road or at Coochin Creek in Beerburrum State Forest and Forest Reserve.

Walking

Most walkers can reach lookouts part way up the peaks. Only very experienced walkers should climb to the summits. Mt Coonowrin is closed for public safety. Wear a hat and sunscreen. Take drinking water on your walk. Rocks are slippery when wet. Tracks may be closed when the bush fire danger is high.

Accessibility

The Tibrogargan toilets are wheelchair-accessible.

Getting there

The Glass Houses are west of the old highway between Beerburrum and Beerwah. Access to Mt Ngungun and Mt Beerwah is from the Glass House Mountains township via Coonowrin and Fullertons Road. Mt Tibrogargan is off Marshs and Barrs Roads between Beerburrum and Glass House Mountains townships. Mt Ngungun is 2km from the Glass House Mountains railway station. Mt Tibrogargan is 3km away. Coochin Creek is 9km east of Beerwah.

Beerburrum State Forest and Forest Reserve

What's special?

Exotic pine plantations, open forest, rainforest and coastal wallum remnants and the scenic Glass House Mountains make Beerburrum State Forest and Forest Reserve in the Sunshine Coast lowlands a picturesque place to visit.

Between 1881 and 1890, the thriving timber town of Campbellville flourished on the banks of Coochin Creek when red cedar and eucalypt trees were harvested from the nearby forests. Paddle steamers and sailing cutters transported the timber down the creek to the port of Brisbane.

Exploring Beerburrum

Go for a scenic drive. Signs indicate points of interest. Stop at the Glasshouse Mountains Lookout for the best, most accessible view in the area.

Have a picnic here in the grassy open forest. Toilets, picnic tables, drinking water and wood barbecues are provided. Firewood is supplied.

Enjoy magnificent views over the coastal lowlands from the Glass House Mountains, Wild Horse Mountain or Beerburrum Mountain Lookouts. Walk through scribbly gum and wet sclerophyll forests around Glass House Mountains Lookout.

Camp or picnic among the pine trees at Coochin Creek camping area, on the east side of the highway, 3km upstream from the Pumicestone Passage. Grassy campsites suitable for caravans and tents, toilets, drinking water and barbecues are provided. Take insect repellent.

Sit quietly by the creek and imagine what this place was like in its timber-getting heyday. Go boating or fishing or explore the waterways by canoe. A boat ramp is provided.

Horse riding, cycling, trail bike riding and four-wheel-driving are allowed by permit. For your safety and to minimise damage to the forest, stay on existing tracks.

Dogs on a leash are allowed in the lookout picnic areas and walking tracks but not in the Coochin Creek picnic and camping area.

Paul Candlin

Coochin Creek

Beerburrum State Forest and Forest Reserve

Robert Ashdown

Tracks

Melaleuca walk
1·3km return, 40 minutes

Mooloolah River circuit
500m, 15 minutes

Glass House Mountains Lookout circuit
400m return, 25 minutes

Beerburrum Mountain Lookout track
1·4km return, 45 minutes

Wild Horse Mountain Lookout track
1·4km return, 45 minutes

Further information

QPWS
Bells Creek Road
BEERWAH QLD 4519
ph (07) 5494 0150
fax (07) 5494 6307

Cycling, horse riding and driving permits:
ph (07) 3227 7800

Walking

Wear sturdy shoes, a hat and sunscreen when walking. All tracks except the Melaleuca walk and Mooloolah River circuit are steep in places.

Accessibility

The Melaleuca walk and Mooloolah River circuit through rainforest and wet sclerophyll forest along the Mooloolah River at Jowarra are wheelchair-accessible. Signs help you explore the forest. The tracks are located next to the rest area near the Rustic Cabin just off the Caloundra Road.

The Coochin Creek camping area toilets are wheelchair-accessible.

Getting there

Beerburrum State Forest is about one hour's drive north of Brisbane via the Bruce Highway and the Glass House Mountains Road. Beerburrum Mountain Lookout is just off the old Beerburrum-Caboolture Road near Beerburrum township. Wild Horse Mountain Lookout is on the east side of the Bruce Highway. Turn off at the Mobil service station and drive along Johnson Road to the walking track to the lookout. Coochin Creek picnic and camping area is on Roys Road 5km east of the highway and north of the Glass House Mountains turnoff.

Paul Candlin

Coochin Creek camping area

Bellthorpe State Forest and Forest Reserve

What's special?

Natural bushland at the southern end of the Conondale Range is protected in this small forest. Bellthorpe State Forest and Forest Reserve is quite rugged with open forest, rainforest, and waterfalls and cascades along picturesque Stony Creek. The rockpool is a popular cool retreat in summer.

Exploring Bellthorpe

Have a bush picnic or barbecue beside a rockpool at the junction of Stony and Branch Creeks. Toilets, picnic tables, drinking water and wood barbecues are provided. Firewood is supplied. Dogs on a leash are allowed in the picnic area.

Be careful exploring around the creek. Never jump or dive into the waterhole.

Walking

There are no formal tracks but you can walk along the forest roads with care.

Accessibility

The toilets are wheelchair-accessible.

Getting there

Bellthorpe is off the D'Aguilar Highway west of Beerwah. Turn off the highway at Stony Creek Road 10km past Woodford. The forest is about 90 minutes' drive north-west of Brisbane.

Robert Ashdown

Reflections, Bellthorpe

Further information

QPWS
61 Bunya Street
MALENY QLD 4552
ph (07) 5494 3983
fax (07) 5494 3986
7.30am–4pm weekdays

Robert Ashdown

Hyacinth orchid

Kenilworth State Forest and Forest Reserve

Sunshine Coast and hinterland

Tall open forest, Kenilworth

Bruce Cowell, Queensland Museum

What's special?

In the rugged Conondale Range lies one of the state's most popular and picturesque forests, Kenilworth State Forest and Forest Reserve. Waterfalls, cascades, boulder-strewn creeks, rainforest, tall open forest, plantation forests of hoop and exotic pines, and spectacular scenery make this forest well worth a visit.

The diverse forests provide a home for a wonderful variety of wildlife including more than 120 species of birds and many mammals. The threatened but seldom-seen yellow-bellied glider lives in the open forest.

At the junction of Peters and Booloumba Creeks, scenic Booloumba Gorge features cascades, falls and rockpools.

Kenilworth is the site of an annual horse-riding endurance event.

Exploring Kenilworth

Stop for advice and brochures at the QPWS office 6km south of Kenilworth. A public phone is located here. Explore the forest from your base at Booloumba Creek or Charlie Moreland camping and picnic areas. A 37km forest drive takes you into the heart of the forest. Allow 90 minutes for the forest drive.

Stop at the halfway point, Peters Creek, for a short break. See riverine rainforest and tall open forests with Sydney blue gums, blackbutt, tallowwood, grey ironbarks, flooded gums and brush box.

Have a picnic in the rainforest overlooking the creek at the Booloumba Creek picnic area. In summer, the orange-flowering blackbeans are a picture.

Choose from three rainforested Booloumba Creek camping areas. Toilets, picnic tables, barbecues, firewood, cold showers (Area 1 only), water, bins and a public phone are provided. Bookings are required for Booloumba 1 and 3. (Both campgrounds have individual tent sites.) Booloumba Creek 4, a self registration camping area, is suitable for large groups and caravans.

Camp or picnic at Charlie Moreland on the banks of Little Yabba Creek. Picnic tables, toilets, wood-fired barbecues, firewood, water and bins are provided.

Darren Jew

The campground is suitable for families, large groups and caravans. Pay your fees on-site. Horse riding and bike riding are allowed. A horse paddock is provided. Permits are required to ride in State forest areas. Check with the ranger.

Backpack camping for horse riders, cyclists and bushwalkers is allowed by permit away from camping areas and roads. (Always check with the ranger.)

Hike to Mt Allan for a view over the forest. Picnic facilities and tank water are provided at the Mt Allan fire tower.

Walking

Forest walks range from short strolls to the challenging Mt Allan hiking trail with views over Booloumba Gorge. Wear sturdy shoes and be careful not to walk on slippery rocks. The Mt Allan trail is easier when tackled from Charlie Moreland.

Accessibility

Fig Tree walk is a sealed, wheelchair-accessible track on the banks of the Mary River near Little Yabba Creek Rest Area on the Maleny-Kenilworth Road. The toilets in the camping areas are wheelchair-accessible but some assistance would be needed to negotiate the camping area. The Booloumba Creek picnic area and toilets are wheelchair-accessible.

Getting there

Kenilworth is about two hours' drive north of Brisbane via the Maleny-Kenilworth Road. Access to the camping areas is suitable for conventional vehicles and caravans. The turnoff to the forest office is about 6km south of Kenilworth or 13km north of Conondale. The office is a further 0·5km and Charlie Moreland is 5km from the turnoff. The turnoff to Booloumba Creek is signposted 12.5km north of Conondale. Access to the Booloumba Creek areas, 6km from the Maleny-Kenilworth Road, may be restricted by flooded creek crossings following heavy rain.

Tracks

Fig Tree walk
1km return, 45 minutes

From Charlie Moreland:
Little Yabba Creek circuit
1·3km circuit, 45 minutes

Piccabeen circuit
3·3km circuit, 1·5–2 hours

Mt Allan hiking trail
8km return, 3–4 hours

From Booloumba Creek:
Mt Allan hiking trail
4km return, 3 hours

Gold Mine walk
5·2km return, 2·5–3 hours

From Booloumba Gorge picnic area:
Booloumba Falls walk
3km return, 1 hour

From Peters Creek:
Peters Creek walk
500m circuit, 20 minutes.

Further information

QPWS
Sunday Creek Road
PO Box 52
KENILWORTH QLD 4574
ph (07) 5446 0925
fax (07) 5446 0966
7.30am–4pm weekdays

Campsite bookings: 13 13 04 or www.qld.gov.au/camping

Bruce Cowell, Queensland Museum

Booloumba Creek

Imbil State Forest and Forest Reserve

What's special?

Surrounding Lake Borumba, Imbil State Forest and Forest Reserve contain Queensland's first hoop pine plantation, established in the early 1900s. Hoop pine *Araucaria cunninghamii* grows naturally from northern New South Wales to Papua New Guinea and is a valuable timber species.

Exploring Imbil

Take the scenic all-weather drive from Borumba Dam to Imbil through the forest. The 14km forest drive takes about an hour and includes eight stops, a lookout and a short walk. Drive carefully. Permits are required to travel along other forest roads.

Have a picnic and listen to the sweet sounds of bellbirds calling in the Bellbird Feature Protection Area, home to a colony of bellbirds. Picnic tables and barbecues are provided and dogs are allowed on a leash.

Go birdwatching. More than 120 species of birds live in this area and nearby Amamoor State Forest and Forest Reserve.

Visit nearby Borumba Dam. You can boat, canoe, fish and camp here. Camping is not allowed in the forest. Showers, barbecues, picnic tables, toilets and water are provided in the Borumba Dam camping area.

Walking

See red cedar trees and other rainforest species along a short walk through gallery rainforest.

Accessibility

The toilets at the Borumba Dam camping area are wheelchair-accessible.

Getting there

Imbil State Forest and Forest Reserve are near Imbil, 32km south-west of Gympie or 36km west of Cooroy. Borumba Dam is 12km west of Imbil. Access is suitable for conventional vehicles towing caravans. Bellbird Feature Protection Area is on the Imbil-Kenilworth Road.

Paul Candlin

View from lookout

Further information

QPWS
Sunday Creek Road
PO Box 52
KENILWORTH QLD 4574
ph (07) 5446 0925
fax (07) 5446 0966
7.30am–4pm weekdays

Conondale National Park

What's special?

West of the Mary River valley, Conondale National Park protects important remnants of grassy open eucalypt forest, tall wet sclerophyll forest and subtropical rainforest. These forests were once more extensive in the Sunshine Coast hinterland.

The park is the central undisturbed core of an extensive area of forest reserves in the Conondale Range and an important refuge for many rare and threatened animals. The catchments of Bundaroo and Peters Creeks which flow into Booloumba Creek are protected in the park.

Exploring Conondale

This park is undeveloped and suitable only for experienced bushwalkers.

Drive through the park on the 37km Kenilworth Forest Drive or hike along Goods Road, a fire management trail within the park.

Picnic or camp at nearby Booloumba Creek or Charlie Moreland in Kenilworth State Forest and Forest Reserve.

Walking

Hike along a fire trail or bushwalk through the nearby forest reserve to Mt Allan (4km return), the gold mine (5·2km return), Peters Creek Falls (0·5km return), or the Breadknife and Booloumba Creek Falls (3km return).

Getting there

Conondale National Park is about 100km or 90 minutes northwest of Brisbane in the Sunshine Coast hinterland. Access is through Kenilworth State Forest and Forest Reserve.

Bruce Cowell, Queensland Museum

Peters Creek

Further information

QPWS
Sunday Creek Road
PO Box 52
KENILWORTH QLD 4574
ph (07) 5446 0925
fax (07) 5446 0966
7.30am–4pm weekdays

Bruce Cowell, Queensland Museum

Lichens on a piccabeen palm, Conondale National Park

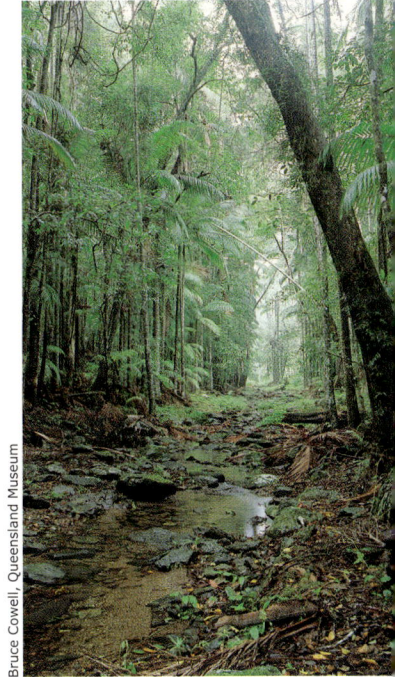

Jimna State Forest and Forest Reserve

Tall open forest, Jimna

Bruce Cowell, Queensland Museum

What's special?

On the scenic Jimna and Conondale Ranges, Jimna State Forest and Forest Reserve form a watershed between the Brisbane and Mary River systems.

Towering hoop pine plantation forests, rainforest and open forest remnants, panoramic mountain views and crystal-clear mountain streams make Jimna a popular destination. More than 140 species of birds and other animals live in this diverse forest. Both hoop and bunya pines grow in the rainforest.

In the late 1800s, Jimna thrived when prospectors flocked here searching for gold. Today, the Sunday Creek Environmental Education Centre is on the site of the old gold diggings, a former steam-driven sawmill and the old forest camp. Jimna Fire Tower, the highest in Queensland, took three years to build.

Exploring Jimna

Relax and enjoy the outdoors in this tranquil bush setting. Go for a scenic drive through the forest, stopping for a picnic at Peach Trees, Marumba viewing area or the base of the fire tower. Tables, fireplaces, tap water and toilets are provided at Peach Trees and the fire tower. Marumba has picnic tables and fireplaces. You must obtain a permit to traverse if you plan to explore along the forest roads.

Enjoy the 360-degree view over the surrounding mountain ranges from the Jimna fire tower platform or views over the forest from Marumba or Yednia Lookouts.

Look for platypus in the creek along the Yabba Creek walk at dawn or dusk. Go birdwatching along the Eugenia circuit early morning or late afternoon. Look for bell-miners, finches, fantails and wrens. Paddle a canoe in the waterhole on Yabba Creek just above Tungi Road bridge in nearby Jimna township.

Stay overnight at Peach Trees on the grassy banks of Yabba Creek. Bookings are recommended for school holidays and long weekends. Campers must register and pay camping fees at the self-registration hut. Coin-operated hot showers, toilets, firewood, water and a public phone are provided. Take drinking water. Hikers wishing to bush camp must get a permit beforehand.

Jimna State Forest and Forest Reserve

Darren Jew

Dogs on leashes are allowed in the forest, but not in the camping area.

Find out more about the forest at the forestry office in Jimna. Contact the nearby Sunday Creek Environmental Education Centre about special programs available for schools, (07) 5497 3139, www.sundaycreec.qld.edu.au.

Walking

Short walks and hiking trails start at Peach Trees.

Accessibility

The toilets at Peach Trees and the fire tower are wheelchair-accessible.

Getting there

The Jimna forests are about two hours' drive north of Brisbane and 40km north-west of Kilcoy along the Kilcoy-Murgon Road.

Conventional vehicle access is possible but the road is unsuitable for caravans.

Peach Trees is about 4km off the Kilcoy-Murgon Road, just north of the Jimna township exit. The fire tower is 500m further along the road from the Peach Trees turnoff.

Tracks

From the far end of the camping area:
Yabba Creek walk
700m, 20 minutes

Araucaria walk
4·5km circuit, 1·5–2 hours

From the entrance to the camping area:
Eugenia walk circuit
2·5km, 45 minutes–1 hour

Further information

QPWS
Sunday Creek Road
PO Box 52
KENILWORTH QLD 4574
ph (07) 5446 0925
fax (07) 5446 0966
7.30am–4pm weekdays

Hoop pine forest on the road to Peach Trees

Bruce Cowell, Queensland Museum

Kondalilla National Park

Kondalilla Falls

Adam Creed

What's special?

In the Sunshine Coast hinterland, Kondalilla National Park is a cool retreat with tall open eucalypt forest, subtropical rainforest and a spectacular waterfall, Kondalilla Falls. The falls drop 90m over Skene Creek into a rainforest valley.

Surrounded by farms and quaint villages, this park is an important refuge for many animals and plants including the rare Australian marsupial frog *Assa darlingtoni* and the bopple nut *Macadamia ternifolia* which is vulnerable to extinction. More than 107 species of birds have been seen in the park, and 70 species of reptiles and 32 species of frogs have been recorded from the Blackall Range and nearby Conondale Range.

Part of the traditional lands of the Gubbi Gubbi people, Kondalilla National Park has special meaning for the Aboriginal people who travelled here when the bunya nuts were in season. Kondalilla Falls got its name from the Aboriginal word meaning "rushing waters".

Exploring Kondalilla

Escape the summer heat in this small pocket of remnant bushland in the heart of the scenic Blackall Range.

Have a bush picnic or barbecue. See brush-turkeys, lace monitors and kookaburras in the picnic area. Don't be tempted to feed them. Let them find their own food.

Take your binoculars and go birdwatching early morning or late afternoon.

Camping is not allowed in the park but there are plenty of places to stay nearby.

There is no drinking water in the park so take your own supply and carry water on your walks. The creek water is unsuitable for drinking.

Kondalilla National Park

Paul Candlin

Walking

The falls and rockpool are very popular. Walk early morning, mid-afternoon or mid-week to avoid the crowds. Wear a hat and sunscreen. Take drinking water. For your safety, never dive or jump into the rockpool. The tracks may be closed during wet weather due to flooding.

Getting there

Travel 54km north of Brisbane along the Bruce Highway then follow the scenic Glass House Mountains Road 22km north to the Landsborough turnoff. Drive a further 20km to Montville and travel 4km north of the town. The park is signposted on the left. From the north, travel to Nambour, then head 15km west to Mapleton. Continue 10km towards Montville to the park turnoff.

Tracks

Picnic Creek circuit
2·4km return, 45 minutes–1 hour

Kondalilla Falls circuit
4·6km return, 1·5–2 hours

Further information

QPWS
61 Bunya Street
MALENY QLD 4552
ph (07) 5494 3983
fax (07) 5494 3986
7.30am–4pm weekdays

Kookaburras

Paul Candlin

73

Mapleton Falls National Park

View of Mapleton Falls
from the lookout

Paul Candlin

Further information

QPWS
61 Bunya Street
MALENY QLD 4552
ph (07) 5494 3983
fax (07) 5494 3986
7.30am–4pm weekdays

What's special?

On the scenic Blackall Range, Mapleton Falls National Park protects a small remnant of the forests which once covered this part of the Sunshine Coast hinterland.

Hexagonal columns in Pencil Creek near the picnic area remain from volcanic activity 25 million years ago. Pencil Creek plunges 120m into the valley below.

Together with nearby Kondalilla National Park, this park provides an important refuge for native wildlife.

Exploring Mapleton Falls

See the spectacular view from the lookout over Mapleton Falls. Read about the park at the information shelter.

Have a picnic before or after your walk. Wood barbecues, firewood and toilets are provided. Take your own drinking water — the creek water is unsuitable for drinking.

Listen for the wompoo fruit-dove's booming call. Look for birds early morning and late afternoon.

Enjoy the view over the scenic Obi Obi valley from Peregrine Lookout along the walking track.

Visit nearby Kondalilla National Park and Delicia Road Conservation Park or take the forest drive through Mapleton Forest Reserve.

Camping is not allowed in the park but there is plenty of accommodation on the range.

Walking

Walk through the rainforest and open eucalypt forest. Take drinking water. Check for leeches after your walk.

Accessibility

The lookout to see the falls is accessible by strollers and wheelchairs.

Getting there

Drive to Nambour via the Bruce Highway, then take the Mapleton and Montville turnoff 17km west to Mapleton. Turn west into Obi Obi Road. Continue about 3km to the signposted turnoff to Mapleton Falls.

Delicia Road Conservation Park

What's special?

This small park protects a small rainforest remnant on the scenic Blackall Range and is home to the great barred frog, *Mixophyes fasciolatus*. Delicia Road Conservation Park is known locally as Linda Garrett Park.

Exploring Delicia Road

Go for a short walk through the rainforest or go birdwatching early morning or late afternoon.

Camping is not allowed. Stay nearby in private accommodation on the Blackall Range.

Walking

Walk through wet eucalypt forest and a palm grove along tracks and a boardwalk and return along a fire management trail. Wear insect repellent and check for leeches after your walk in summer.

Getting there

Drive to Nambour via the Bruce Highway, then take the Mapleton and Montville turnoff 17km west to Mapleton. Turn west into Obi Obi Road. Turn right into Delicia Road at the Linda Garrett Park sign and continue to the park.

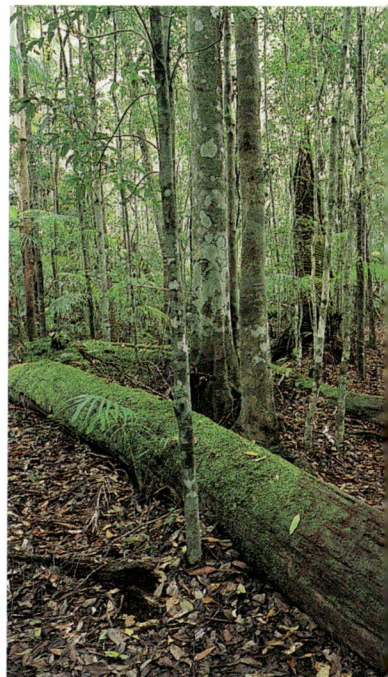

Paul Candlin

Rainforest walk at Delecia Road Conservation Park

Tracks

Delicia Road circuit
2·2km, 40 minutes–1 hour

Further information

QPWS
61 Bunya Street
MALENY QLD 4552
ph (07) 5494 3983
fax (07) 5494 3986
7.30am–4pm weekdays

Great barred frog
Steve Parish

Mapleton Forest Reserve

View from Pt Glorious

Paul Candlin

Tracks

Pilularis forest walk
800m return, 20 minutes

Piccabeen palm groves walk
400m return, 10 minutes

Further information

QPWS
61 Bunya Street
MALENY QLD 4552
ph (07) 5494 3983
fax (07) 5494 3986
7.30am–4pm weekdays

Permits and campsite bookings:
QPWS
Sunday Creek Road
PO Box 52
KENILWORTH QLD 4574
ph (07) 5446 0925
fax (07) 5446 0966
7.30am–4pm weekdays

What's special?

At the northern end of the rugged Blackall Range, Mapleton Forest Reserve protects rainforest remnants with bunya pines, piccabeen palm groves, tall open blackbutt forests and picturesque mountain scenery.

Exploring Mapleton

See the forest along the Mapleton Forest Drive starting just north of Mapleton. Have a picnic on the site of the old forest station in the headwaters of Cedar Creek. Picnic tables, toilets, barbecues, firewood and drinking water are provided.

Stop at Poole's Dam and walk to the top of a waterfall for views over the forested valley below. Beware of slippery rocks. See the bunya pines along the walk through the piccabeen palm groves. The forest drive ends with spectacular views of the coast and hinterland from Point Glorious.

Camp at Gheerulla Creek camping area. Picnic tables, toilets, barbecues, firewood and drinking water are provided. Pay your camping fees on-site. Dogs on leashes are allowed overnight.

Trail bike riding is allowed by permit in the specified Trail Bike Area only. The forest has a short beginners circuit and a more challenging 34km route with views over the Mary Valley from the Oaky Creek Lookout.

Walking

Enjoy the forest on two short walks. See the tall wet sclerophyll forest along the Pilularis forest walk.

Getting there

Mapleton lies between Nambour and Kenilworth, about two hours' drive north of Brisbane. To reach the Gheerulla camping area and trail bike area, turn off the Eumundi-Kenilworth Road at Sam Kelly Road, 6km east of Kenilworth. The camping area is 2km off the main road.

Currimundi Lake Conservation Park

What's special?

In the middle of the busy resort of Caloundra lies Currimundi Lake (Kathleen McArthur) Conservation Park, a small remnant of wallum heath once common on the Sunshine Coast.

Exploring Currimundi Lake

Discover the special beauty of this unspoilt stretch of coastline. Go for a quiet stroll beside the lake.

Look for birds in the heath. See brown honeyeaters, fairy wrens, native finches, noisy friarbirds. Enjoy the wildflowers late winter and spring.

Picnic next door in the local authority picnic area where picnic tables and barbecues are provided. Camping is not allowed in the park.

Walking

A short track leads from Coongarra Esplanade through the park to the beach. Wear a hat and sunscreen.

Wheelchairs can access the first 130m of the walking track.

Getting there

The park is on Currimundi Lake's northern shore, just north of Caloundra. Head north along the Nicklin Way. Turn right into Gayandi Street then right into Madara Drive which becomes Coongarra Esplanade and leads to the park.

Tracks

Heath circuit
1·5km, 40 minutes

Further information

QPWS
Bells Creek Road
BEERWAH QLD 4519
ph (07) 5494 0150
fax (07) 5494 6307
7am–3.30pm

Currimundi Lake

Paul Candlin

Parklands Forest Reserve

Open forest, Parklands

Paul Candlin

Tracks

Track One
5km circuit, 1·5 hours

Track Two
5.5km circuit 1·5–2 hours

Track Three
5km circuit 1·5 hours

Further information

QPWS
School St
POMONA QLD 4568
ph (07) 5485 1027
fax (07) 5485 2940

What's special?

Just near Nambour, Parklands Forest Reserve protects a tall open eucalypt forest remnant in the Sunshine Coast lowlands.

Exploring Parklands

Escape the bustle of the Sunshine Coast and motorised traffic when you visit Parklands Forest Reserve. The forest has no facilities but you can bushwalk, cycle or ride your horse along 15km of roads and tracks. Permits apply for horse riding and cycling.

The tracks are colour coded for easy identification. The give way code applies. Bikes give way to horses and people, and walkers give way to horses.

Walking

Riders, cyclists and walkers share the same trails. Wear a hat and sunscreen and take drinking water when hiking in the forest.

Getting there

Parklands is about 90 minutes' drive north of Brisbane. Take the Parklands exit off the Bruce Highway just north of Nambour. The forest is on the eastern side of the highway.

Paul Candlin

Parklands is just to the left of the Bruce Highway.

Mooloolah River National Park

What's special?

Most of the coastal lowlands in southern Queensland have been cleared for development. Mooloolah River National Park protects valuable remnants of wallum heath, open eucalypt woodlands and tea-tree swamps and woodlands near the Mooloolah River.

Exploring Mooloolah River

This is a quiet retreat for nature lovers. No facilities are provided.

Paddle your canoe along the Mooloolah River or ride past the park along the bike trail to the Sunshine Coast University.

Explore the park along fire management trails. Take your camera and binoculars. Enjoy the wildflower display in late winter and spring.

Walking

No tracks are provided but you can walk along the many fire trails through the park. Wear a hat and sunscreen and take drinking water.

Getting there

The park straddles the Sunshine Motorway near Mooloolaba and is accessible from Claymore Road, Sippy Downs past Sunshine Coast University. The Mooloolah River forms the south-eastern boundary of the park. No vehicle access is allowed.

Bruce Cowell, Queensland Museum

Mooloolah River

Bruce Cowell, Queensland Museum

Riparian rainforest, Mooloolah River National Park

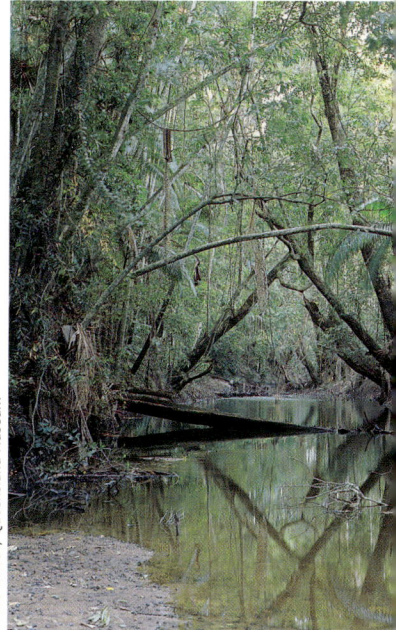

Further information

QPWS
61 Bunya Street
MALENY QLD 4552
ph (07) 5494 3983
fax (07) 5494 3986
7.30am–4pm weekdays

Mt Coolum National Park

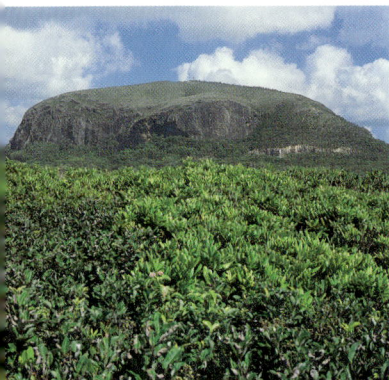

Mt Coolum

Paul Candlin

What's special?

Dome-shaped Mt Coolum rises 208m above sugar cane fields and coastal resorts to dominate the skyline in the Sunshine Coast lowlands. Mt Coolum National Park contains most of the mountain with its craggy cliffs. After rain, waterfalls cascade over the sides.

Open eucalypt forest skirts Mt Coolum's lower slopes while grasslands and montane heath grow towards the summit. This is one of only two coastal places where montane heath grows. The park extends south and west of Mt Coolum protecting coastal wallum, paperbark wetlands and rainforest remnants which have largely disappeared from this part of the Sunshine Coast lowlands.

The park contains rare and threatened plant species, *Allocasuarina thalassoscopica* and *Bertya sharpeana*. About 40 percent of known fern families grow in the park. Peregrine falcons nest along the cliff faces.

Mt Coolum is significant to the Gubbi Gubbi people and features in stories about the way the landscape was formed.

Exploring Mt Coolum

Have a picnic. Wood barbecues are provided. The rest of the park is undeveloped and suitable only for keen bushwalkers. Take your binoculars and go birdwatching.

Enjoy spectacular 360-degree views from the top. See wildflowers in winter and spring.

Camping is not allowed in the park but private camping areas are located at nearby Mudjimba and Coolum.

Walking

A rough 800m trail on the eastern side of the mountain leads from a carpark to the summit. Only fit walkers should attempt the climb. Wear a hat, sunscreen and sturdy shoes. Take drinking water. Allow two hours for the return hike.

Getting there

Mt Coolum is about 90 minutes' drive north of Brisbane via the Bruce Highway and the Sunshine Motorway. The park straddles the Sunshine Motorway and extends to the David Low Way near the township of Coolum. Turn off the David Low Way 5km north of Coolum or 2km south of Marcoola.

Further information

Noosa NP
Park Road
NOOSA HEADS QLD 4567
ph (07) 5447 3243
fax (07) 5447 2698

Tewantin Forest Reserve

What's special?

Rainforest, open eucalypt forest and wallum remnants between Noosa and Cooroy are protected in this hilly near-coastal forest, Tewantin Forest Reserve.
Mt Tinbeerwah (265m) is a volcanic plug remaining from volcanic activity millions of years ago.

The forest is home to the endangered *Triunia robusta*, a straggly, multi-stemmed small tree with white flowers and red fruit.

Exploring Tewantin

Have a picnic among coastal she-oaks and bloodwood trees at Wooroi day use area, just a few kilometres west of Tewantin. Picnic tables, barbecues and drinking water are provided. Please do not feed the butcherbirds and cheeky noisy miners. See tall flooded gums hundreds of years old and cabbage tree palms along the walking track. Dogs on leashes are allowed here.

Towards Cooroy, stop and walk to Mt Tinbeerwah Lookout for a 360-degree view over the Noosa River system with its string of lakes, the coast and hinterland forests.

Camping is not allowed in the forest.

Walking

Enjoy a 30-minute walk through the cabbage palm forest along Wooroi Creek.

Accessibility

A sealed 130m track at Mt Tinbeerwah provides wheelchair access to a lookout over the coast.

Getting there

Tewantin Forest Reserve is just west of Noosa and Tewantin along the Cooroy-Noosa Road. To reach Tinbeerwah Lookout, turn off the road and follow the signs to the carpark.

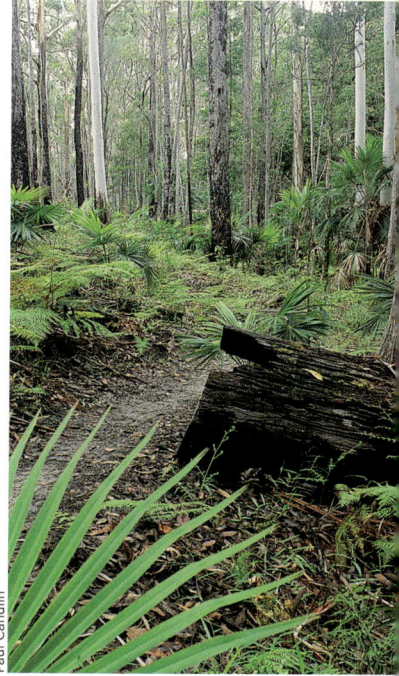

Paul Candlin

Palm Grove track

Tracks

Palm Grove track
30 minutes

Mt Tinbeerwah Lookout track
260m return, 10 minutes

Further information

QPWS
School St
POMONA QLD 4568
ph (07) 5485 1027
fax (07) 5485 2940

Noosa National Park

What's special?

South-east Queensland's only stretch of undisturbed, rocky coastline and the largest wallum heath remnant close to Brisbane make Noosa National Park one of the state's most picturesque parks.

Open woodlands with a heath understorey and low wallum heath cover most of the park. Hoop and kauri pines tower above small rainforest pockets growing on sand in sheltered sites away from the sea breezes.

The park includes the popular scenic headland near Noosa Heads, parts of Lake Weyba, a large shallow, saltwater lake in the Noosa River system, and coastal lowlands extending south towards Coolum.

Exploring Noosa

Have a picnic overlooking beautiful Laguna Bay with its sweeping views from Noosa to Cooloola. Electric barbecues, toilets, drinking water and picnic tables are provided. Parking is limited, especially at weekends and holiday times.

Go for a walk. See coastal rock formations, such as the Boiling Pot and Hells Gates, pandanus-lined Teatree Bay, rocky Granite Bay, historic Winch Cove and the sweeping beach of Alexandria Bay. The beaches, though inviting, are not patrolled. Alexandria Bay often has rips. Please be very careful. Toilets are provided at Teatree Bay and an emergency phone is located at the northern end of Alexandria Bay.

Escape the crowds and the summer heat on the Tanglewood track and rainforest circuit in the Noosa Headland Section. Walk through the heath at Peregian.

Explore the Weyba sections of the park on the fire trails only. During World War II, this area was a training ground and unexploded ordnance may be present. Contact the ranger before visiting this part of the park. Maps are not available.

Camping is not allowed in the park but there is plenty of private accommodation nearby. A camping and caravan park is at Munna Point, Noosaville.

Learn about the park or buy light refreshments and field guides at the information centre near the park entrance at Noosa Heads. The centre is open 9am to 3pm seven days a week.

Ross Naumann

Climbing pandanus, Noosa National Park

Noosa National Park

Paul Candlin

Walking

The best way to enjoy Noosa's special attractions is bushwalking. Wear a hat and sunscreen and take drinking water. You can also explore along fire trails. Be very careful around cliff edges. Never walk alone in the park.

Accessibility

The Coastal track to Teatree Bay is suitable for wheelchair-assisted access and strollers. Safety signs at track entrances are in German, Japanese and English.

Getting there

Noosa National Park is about two hours' drive north of Brisbane via the Bruce Highway and the Sunshine Motorway or one hour south of Gympie via Cooroy and Tewantin.

The Noosa Headland Section is a 10-minute walk from Hastings Street, Noosa, along the coastal boardwalk or a short drive along Park Road. Access is also from Parkedge Road and McAnally Drive, Sunshine Beach. Parking is restricted at McAnally Drive.

The Peregian Section is next to the David Low Way, 3km north of Coolum. Contact the ranger before visiting the Weyba sections of the park.

Tracks

Coastal track
5·4km return, 1·5–2·5 hours

Alexandria Bay track from McAnally Drive
2km return, 30–45 minutes

Alexandria Bay track from Parkedge Road
*4·6km return,
1 hour 15 minutes–2 hours*

Noosa Hill track
3·4km circuit, 1–1·5 hours

Palm Grove circuit
1km, 15–30 minutes

Tanglewood track
8·4km return, 2–3 hours

Peregian track
1km return, 15–25 minutes

Further information

Noosa NP
Park Road
NOOSA HEADS QLD 4567
ph (07) 5447 3243
fax (07) 5447 2698

Teatree Bay

Paul Candlin

Map 2

The Downs and South West

Legend

- National Park
- Conservation Park
- Forest Reserve
- State Forest
- Timber Reserve
- Resource Reserve
- Highway
- Major connecting road
- Minor access road

0   20   40
km

N

Murgon

Kingaroy

Nanango

Miles

Chinchilla

The Palms NP

Bunya Mountains NP

Yarraman

Yarraman SF

Blackbutt

Benarkin SF

Cooyar

Dalby

Crows Nest NP

Lake Broadwater CP

Crows Nest

Esk

Oakey

Ravensbourne NP

Toowoomba

Gatton

Moonie

Southwood NP

Millmerran

Goomburra FR

Main Range NP

Queen Mary Falls

Warwick

Killarney

Inglewood

Goondiwindi

Stanthorpe

Sundown NP

Ballandean

Texas

Girraween NP

Wallangarra

WALES

NEW

SOUTH

Tenterfield

Main Range National Park

What's special?

In the Central Eastern Rainforests Reserves Australia World Heritage Area, Main Range National Park forms the western part of a semi-circle of mountains in south-east Queensland known as the scenic rim. The park extends from Mt Mistake south to Wilson's Peak on the New South Wales border and includes Mt Superbus, southern Queensland's highest peak.

The park's open forests, rainforests and montane heath provide habitat for many animals, including the eastern bristlebird, Coxen's fig parrot and black-breasted button-quail, which are threatened with extinction.

Spicer's Gap is believed to be a traditional pathway for Aboriginal people travelling between the inland and the coast. In 1828, Allan Cunningham discovered the route through the mountains now called Cunningham's Gap. Stockman Henry Alphen discovered Spicer's Gap in 1847. The Spicer's Gap Road, used to carry supplies to and from the Darling Downs, is the best remaining example of sophisticated 19th century engineering in Queensland.

Exploring Main Range

Picnic facilities and walking tracks at Cunningham's Gap, Spicer's Gap and Queen Mary Falls help visitors enjoy the park. The rest of the park is trackless and rugged wilderness suitable only for experienced, well-equipped bushwalkers.

Have a bush picnic beside West Gap Creek near Cunningham's Gap, at the Pioneer Picnic Area at Spicer's Gap, or at Queen Mary Falls. Picnic tables, wood barbecues and toilets are provided. West Gap Creek also has a shelter shed and tank water. Boil the water before drinking.

Re-discover the past on the Spicer's Gap Road — the route taken by early pioneers still shows evidence of early road construction. A small cemetery marks the resting place for a number of early travellers.

Enjoy spectacular views from Governor's Chair, Sylvester's or Fassifern lookouts or the summits of Mts Cordeaux and Mitchell.

Go birdwatching along the Box Forest track. Hear bellbirds calling. See satin bowerbirds, Australian ground thrush and king parrots. See spear lilies and flowering orchids in spring.

Bruce Cowell, Queensland Museum

Looking towards Mt Mitchell from Mt Cordeaux with spear lilies in foreground

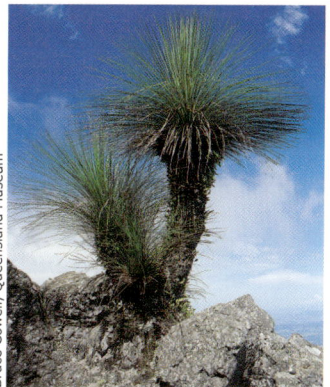

Bruce Cowell, Queensland Museum

Grasstrees on Mt Cordeaux

Main Range National Park

Bruce Cowell

Tracks

Box Forest track
8·4km return, 2 hours

Rainforest circuit
1·4km, 25 minutes

Gap Creek Falls trail
9·4km return, 6 hours

Palm Grove circuit
4·4km return, 2 hours

Mt Cordeaux track
6·8km return, 2·5–3 hours

**Morgan's Walk and
Bare Rock track**
12·4km return, 4·5 hours

Mt Mitchell track
10·2km return, 3 hours

Sylvester's Lookout track
940m return, 20 minutes

Mt Matheson trail
8·1km return, 3 hours

**Governor's Chair
lookout track**
300m return, 10 minutes

Heritage trail
3·2km return, 1 hour

Further information

Main Range NP
Cunningham's Gap
MS 394 WARWICK QLD 4370
ph (07) 4666 1133
fax (07) 4666 1297
e-mail:
main.range@epa.qld.gov.au

Campsite bookings: 13 13 04 or
www.qld.gov.au/camping

**Coral
fungus**

Paul Candlin

Mt Wilson on the Scenic Rim

Bruce Cowell, Queensland Museum

Camp at Spicer's Gap. Bookings are essential for all public holiday long weekends. Toilets, picnic tables, tank water and wood barbecues are provided. Bush camping is allowed in the more remote areas of the park by permit from the ranger at Cunningham's Gap.

Walking

Enjoy short or half-day walks in the park or go hiking. Check for ticks in spring and summer. **WARNING: Anyone hiking in undeveloped parts of the park must be physically fit and have sound navigational skills.** Leave your trip details with someone reliable and advise your safe return. Take a positioning beacon, topographic map, compass, mobile phone, first aid kit and plenty of food, water and warm clothing.

Accessibility

The toilets at Spicer's Gap are wheelchair-accessible.

Getting there

Main Range is 116km south-west of Brisbane or 50km east of Warwick on the Cunningham Highway. Cunningham's Gap is on the highway. Spicer's Gap camping area is on the Spicer's Gap Road, which is unsuitable for camper trailers and caravans. Turn off the Cunningham Highway 5km west of Aratula and follow the signs. The western approach leaves the highway 1·5km past the park headquarters and ends 1·6km before Governor's Chair carpark. (There is no through route.) This western approach is suitable for four-wheel-drive vehicles only and closed in wet weather.

Goomburra Forest Reserve

What's special?

Nestled in the scenic western foothills of the Great Dividing Range, Goomburra Forest Reserve protects open eucalypt forests and lush rainforests in the Central Eastern Rainforest Reserves Australia World Heritage Area.

The dry open forest contains New England blackbutt and manna gums. The distinctive manna gum, with its long ribbons of shedding bark, is at its northern limit here. The forest is an important refuge for wildlife.

Exploring Goomburra

Get away from it all in this beautiful forest. Enjoy the local wildlife. See platypus, koalas and echidnas. Go spotlighting at night. Look for feathertail gliders and mountain brushtail possums.

Picnic or camp on the grassy banks of Dalrymple Creek. Two camping areas are provided — Poplar Flat and Manna Gum. Both have toilets, drinking water and barbecues. Limited firewood is supplied. Bookings are essential for all public holiday long weekends.

A small picnic area next to the Poplar Flat camping area has picnic tables, fireplaces and firewood.

Walk to the upper reaches of Dalrymple Creek along the Cascades or North Branch trails or walk to the base of Araucaria Falls along the Araucaria trail. Enjoy panoramic views eastwards over mountains and valleys from the Mt Castle and Sylvesters Lookouts.

Dogs on leashes are allowed in the picnic area, walking trails and Mt Castle Lookout track but not in the camping area.

Walking

Wear sturdy shoes and take drinking water when walking. Most walks have moderate to steep grades and require reasonable fitness.

Accessibility

Wheelchair-accessible toilets are provided in both camping areas. Wheelchair-assisted access is possible along the Dalrymple circuit.

Robert Ashdown

Boil the billy at Goomburra

Goomburra Forest Reserve

Tracks

Dalrymple circuit
1·2km, 30 minutes

Mt Castle Lookout track
1·2km return 1 hour

Sylvesters Lookout
940m return, 30 minutes

Cascades trail
6km circuit, 3 hours

Ridge trail
5km circuit, 2·5 hours

North Branch trail
7km, 3·5 hours

Araucaria trail
3km, 1·5 hours

Further information

Main Range NP
Cunningham's Gap
MS 394 WARWICK QLD 4370
ph (07) 4666 1133
fax (07) 4666 1297
e-mail:
main.range@epa.qld.gov.au

Campsite bookings: 13 13 04 or
www.qld.gov.au/camping

Getting there

Goomburra Forest Reserve is 175km south-west of Brisbane. Turn off the Cunningham Highway just west of Cunningham's Gap and follow Goomburra and Inverramsay Roads 35km to the forest. From the New England Highway south of Toowoomba, take the Inverramsay Road 40km to the forest. The last 6km is unsealed and may be impassable following heavy rain. The road to the lookouts may be closed after rain.

Bracket or pore fungus at Sylvester's Lookout

Queen Mary Falls Main Range National Park

What's special?

In the western foothills of the Great Dividing Range lies Queen Mary Falls, a small scenic section of Main Range National Park.

Millions of years ago, the now extinct Main Range volcano erupted, covering the surrounding lands with basalt lava flows. Over time, Spring Creek eroded through the basalt to the softer sedimentary rocks below, creating the spectacular waterfall known as Queen Mary Falls.

Queen Mary Falls is in the headwaters of the Murray-Darling, Australia's longest river system. Spring Creek flows through the park before joining the Condamine River.

Most of the section is open eucalypt forest but a small pocket of subtropical rainforest grows in the gorge below the waterfall. The brush-tailed rock-wallaby, considered vulnerable to extinction, lives in the section's rocky cliffs. About 100 bird species live in or visit the park section, including the rare Albert's lyrebird, king parrot, crimson rosella, golden whistler and satin bowerbird.

Exploring Queen Mary Falls

Go for a scenic drive over Cunningham's Gap or Teviot Gap to Queen Mary Falls. Enjoy a picnic in the open forest. Picnic tables, toilets, a shelter shed, wood barbecues, firewood and water are provided. Boil the water for five minutes before drinking.

Take your binoculars and camera and go birdwatching early morning or late afternoon. Walk to the lookout or down to the bottom of the falls. Look for eastern water dragons sunbaking on the rocks or spiny cray around the rockpools.

You can camp across the road at the privately operated Queen Mary Falls Tourist Park where a kiosk and public phone are located. Cabins and powered sites are available, phone (07) 4664 7151.

Walking

The easiest way to walk the circuit is to start at the bottom end of the picnic area and walk in a clockwise direction.

Adam Creed

Queen Mary Falls

Queen Mary Falls, Main Range National Park

Tracks

Queen Mary Falls circuit
2km, 40 minutes–1 hour

Further information

QPWS
Hermitage Research Station
via WARWICK QLD 4370
ph (07) 4661 3710
fax (07) 4661 7001

Accessibility

The toilets are wheelchair-accessible. Most of the circuit track is sealed but only the first few hundred metres of each track are wheelchair-accessible. You would need assistance to get to the track through the picnic area.

Getting there

Queen Mary Falls is about 42km east of Warwick and 11km east of Killarney on the Killarney-Boonah Road near the New South Wales border. This section is about 2·5 hours south-west of Brisbane via Boonah or Beaudesert and the Teviot Gap Road or via Cunningham's Gap and Freestone or via Warwick.

Darren Jew

Satin bowerbird

Girraween National Park

What's special?

Huge granite boulders tower above open forests in this spectacular park nestled on the Queensland/New South Wales border. Few parks can match the spectacular wildflower display seen in this park every spring.

Bracing winter temperatures, outstanding wildlife and picturesque granite and creek scenery make Girraween a special place. The park's wildlife includes plants and animals rarely seen elsewhere in the state, such as the common wombat, spotted-tailed quoll, turquoise parrot and Wallangarra white gum.

Girraween was known as "the meeting place" to the Aboriginal people who lived in and passed through this area. Former vineyards and fruit farms are now part of the park.

Exploring Girraween

Enjoy a bush picnic by Bald Rock Creek. Barbecues, toilets and picnic tables are provided. Go for a scenic drive through the park to Storm King Dam and Stanthorpe or to the quiet picnic area behind Mt Norman. Toilets and picnic tables are provided here.

Stay in secluded bush campsites at Bald Rock Creek campground or shady campsites at Castle Rock campground. Both have tent, campervan, motorhome and large group sites, hot showers, washing tubs, picnic tables and barbecues. Take your own firewood or purchase it outside the park. Book early, especially for Christmas, Easter, long weekends and school holidays. Visitors must bag and remove all rubbish.

Go backpack camping and visit Bald Rock National Park just next door. Book through the park office at least 10 days in advance. Restrictions apply to group size and campsite locations.

Take your camera and binoculars and go wildlife watching. See kangaroos, brushtail possums and many colourful birds. Go birdwatching early morning or late afternoon or try spotlighting at night. Enjoy the colourful wildflower displays in spring.

Adam Creed

Enjoy the wildfowers of Girraween.

Girraween National Park

Tracks

The Pyramid track
3km return, 1·5–2 hours

The Junction track
5km return, 2·5 hours

Granite Arch track
1·5km circuit, 30 minutes

Castle Rock track
3km return, 1·5–2 hours

Mt Norman track
*10·4km return, 6 hours from
Pyramids Road or 4km return,
2 hours from Mt Norman
picnic area*

**The Sphinx and
Turtle Rock track**
7·4km return, 4 hours

**From Pyramids Road, 4km
east of the information centre
Dr Roberts' Waterhole track**
1·2km return, 35 minutes

Underground Creek track
*2·8km return, 45 minutes–
1·5 hours*

Further information

Girraween NP
via BALLANDEAN QLD 4382
ph (07) 4684 5157
fax (07) 4684 5123

Campsite bookings: 13 13 04 or
www.qld.gov.au/camping

The Pyramids

Climb The Pyramid or Castle Rock for 360 degree views
over the park and surrounding farmlands. Be very careful
swimming in the cold water at Girraween. Hidden
underwater boulders and slippery rocks can be dangerous.

Find out more about the park in the information centre or
join a ranger-led slide show, spotlight tour or guided walk
in holiday times.

Walking

Girraween is a great park for bushwalking with 17km of
graded walking tracks and many fire trails taking you to
the park's best features. Wear a hat and sunscreen.
Choose your walk carefully. Signs at the start of every
track explain that some walks require considerable
stamina. **WARNING: granite rocks are slippery when
wet. Wear sturdy shoes with good grip.**

Getting there

Girraween is 260km or three hours' drive south-west of
Brisbane via the New England Highway. Turn off the
highway 18km north of Wallangarra or 40km south of
Stanthorpe and drive 8km to the information centre. The
drive to the Mt Norman picnic area through Wallangarra
takes about half an hour. Ask the ranger for directions.

Sundown National Park

What's special?

On the Queensland/New South Wales border, Sundown National Park is a rugged wilderness park with spectacular steep-sided gorges, sharp ridges and peaks rising to more than 1000 metres.

The vegetation is mainly box-ironbark-cypress woodland with tea trees, river red gums and river oaks along the river, stringybark-yellow box forest in some high eastern areas and pockets of dry vine scrub in sheltered gorges.

More than 150 species of birds have been recorded in the park, some seasonal visitors. Grey kangaroos are common. Red-necked wallabies and swamp wallabies and wallaroos also live in the park. The once common brush-tailed rock-wallaby now survives only in the northern end of the park.

Sundown has a history of early selection, subdivision in the late 1800s, extensive clearing for grazing and fine wool production, and tin, copper and arsenic mining from the 1870s. Pastoral relics and old surface diggings remain.

Exploring Sundown

Sundown is a great place to get away from it all. Visitors must be fairly self-sufficient as few facilities are provided.

Camp at The Broadwater, a large waterhole on the Severn River. Individual grassy campsites, pit toilets, fireplaces, firewood, water and donkey boiler showers are provided. Remove all your rubbish except recyclable glass and cans. Secure your supplies and rubbish from goannas and currawongs. The closest supplies are at Glenlyon Dam.

Go birdwatching early morning or late afternoon. See ducks, herons, cormorants and tiny azure kingfishers along the river. Watch eastern grey kangaroos browsing on the grassy flats around The Broadwater late afternoon and early morning.

Read about the park's vegetation and bushwalking at the information shelter in The Broadwater camping area.

Four-wheel-drive campsites are located along the river at Burrows' Waterhole and Reedy Waterhole. Burrows' Waterhole has pit toilets. Reedy Waterhole has no facilities. You can also camp closer to the park entrance at Red Rock Gorge. A pit toilet and lookout are located here. You must bag and remove your rubbish from the park.

Robert Ashdown

Blue Gorge

Sundown National Park

Red-necked wallaby

Tracks

**The Permanent
Waterhole track**
2km return, 45 minutes

Red Rock Gorge Lookout
500m return, 15 minutes

Further information

Sundown NP
Via Glenlyon Dam Road
MS 312
Via STANTHORPE QLD 4380
ph (02) 6737 5235
fax (02) 6737 5325

Camping and walking are best between May and September when you can expect cold nights, frosty mornings and warm, clear days. Summer can be hot and humid.

Walking

Few tracks are provided but you can explore along side gorges at Ooline and McAllister's Creeks near The Broadwater and Blue Gorge downstream from Rats' Castle. Check with park staff at The Broadwater and take a copy of the 1:50,000 park map when walking. Wear a hat and sunscreen and carry water.

Getting there

Sundown is 3–4 hours' drive south-west of Brisbane. The Broadwater camping area at the southern end of the park can be reached by conventional vehicle from Stanthorpe along 76km of bitumen road and 4km of good gravel road. You can also travel from Tenterfield 52km west on the Bruxner Highway to Mingoola and a further 12km to the park entrance.

From Ballandean, a 16km road leads to the park's eastern boundary and a rough four-wheel-drive track leads 20km to campsites along the river. The drive takes about two hours.

Yarraman State Forest

What's special?

Subtropical rainforest with hoop and bunya pines towering above the forest, open eucalypt forest and native hoop pine plantations grow in Yarraman State Forest.

Horse teams used to haul the native hoop and bunya pine logs out of the forest to a tramway, which carried the logs to the sawmill at Yarraman.

Exploring Yarraman

See the forest along a 45-minute (one-way) forest drive from the highway to Meandu Coal Mine Lookout. Experimental exotic parana pine can also be seen along the drive.

Stop and have a picnic or barbecue under the hoop pines at Rogers Park. Shelter sheds, toilets, picnic tables, drinking water, barbecues and firewood are provided.

Continue along the forest drive to Stables camp, the site of the former barracks for forestry workers. Stop at two lookouts for a view over Tarong Power Station and the nearby Meandu Coal Mine. Follow the signs to the end of the forest drive.

Camping is not allowed in the forest.

Walking

Two short self-guided forest walks are located at Rogers Park. One takes 10 minutes, the other is about an hour. See how rainforest is invading the open forest along the 10 minute Tree identification circuit, further along the forest drive.

Getting there

Yarraman State Forest is on the D'Aguilar Highway 2km north of the township of Yarraman. Turn off the highway between Nanango and Yarraman at the signposted Yarraman Forest Drive. The forest is 165km or about two hours' drive north-west of Brisbane.

Adam Creed

Rogers Park

Further information

QPWS
158 Hume Street
TOOWOOMBA
PO Box 731
TOOWOOMBA QLD 4350
ph (07) 4639 4599
fax (07) 4639 4524

Ravensbourne National Park

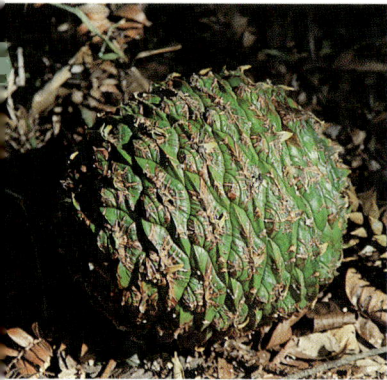

Steve Parish

Bunya cone

What's special?

Small remnants of the rainforest and wet eucalypt forest that once covered this part of the Great Dividing Range are preserved in Ravensbourne National Park. Evidence suggests the rainforest is slowly overtaking the open forest.

More than 80 species of birds visit or live in this park including the black-breasted button-quail, which is threatened with extinction, fruit doves and six species of owls.

Ravensbourne is along one of the pathways taken by Aboriginal people when visiting the Bunya Mountains for the bunya nut festival, providing a reliable source of food for travelling Aboriginal people.

Exploring Ravensbourne

Have a bush picnic. Two picnic areas are provided. Both have picnic tables, wood barbecues, firewood, water and toilets. The Cedar Block picnic area also has a shelter shed. Boil or treat the water before drinking.

Enjoy a panoramic view over the range towards Brisbane, the Scenic Rim and the Lockyer Valley from the Gus Beutel Lookout.

Michael O'Connor

Rainforest at Ravensbourne

Ravensbourne National Park

Go birdwatching. You might see satin bowerbirds, pigeons or red-backed fairy-wrens. On the edge of the Cedar Block circuit track, you may notice circular hollows on the rainforest floor made by the black-breasted button-quail *Turnix melanogaster* as it spins around while feeding on the rainforest floor. Spectacular red-tailed and glossy black-cockatoos feed on casuarina seeds in the open forest in winter. Listen for the call of the green catbird and paradise riflebird.

Camping is not allowed but you can stay at nearby Crows Nest National Park or Cressbrook Dam.

Walking

This is a great park for short, less crowded bushwalks. Most tracks start in the Blackbean picnic area. A self-guiding walk starts in Cedar Block picnic area. Wear a hat, sunscreen and insect repellent.

Getting there

Ravensbourne is located between Esk and Toowoomba just off the Esk-Hampton Road. From Toowoomba, travel 32km along the New England Highway to Hampton then 17km along the Esk Road to the park. From Esk, drive 33km along the Esk-Hampton Road to the park.

Tracks

Cedar Block walk
500m circuit, 15 minutes

Rainforest circuit
1·7km, 30–45 minutes

Palm circuit
3·5km, 1 hour–1 hour 30 minutes

Caves track
3·1km return, 1 hour

Buaraba Creek track
6·8km return, 2 hours

Further information

Ravensbourne NP
PO Box 68
CROWS NEST QLD 4355
ph (07) 4698 1296
3.30–4pm weekdays

Red-backed wren

Darran Leal

Crows Nest National Park

What's special?

Spectacular creek scenery, granite outcrops, a scenic waterfall and eucalypt forest remnants in the headwaters of Crows Nest Creek are protected in Crows Nest National Park on the Great Dividing Range west of Brisbane.

Few places have such a wonderful variety of eucalypt trees from gums to stringybarks, bloodwoods and ironbarks, delighting the amateur naturalist. The park is a haven for wildlife including platypus, swamp wallabies, echidnas, bandicoots, lace monitors, birds, and the brush-tailed rock-wallaby *Petrogale penicillata*, which is vulnerable to extinction in Queensland.

Exploring Crows Nest

Go wildlife watching. Look for platypus in the creek near the picnic area and brush-tailed rock-wallabies on the rocky cliffs along the creek. Be patient and quiet and you may be rewarded. For your safety and to protect the wallaby habitat, stay on the track.

Go birdwatching during the day. See pale-headed rosellas, magpies, yellow robins, thornbills, golden whistlers, eastern spinebills, grey fantails or blue-faced honeyeaters. Try spotlighting for sugar gliders, brushtail possums, ringtail possums and greater gliders along the walking track. Enjoy the wildflowers in spring.

Have a bush picnic or explore around the creek. Be careful — rocks and stepping-stones can be slippery, especially after rain. Follow the steep-sided gorge in the upper reaches of Crows Nest Creek to a lookout overlooking Crows Nest Falls. Continue to Koonin Lookout for a spectacular view over a deeper gorge known locally as the Valley of Diamonds.

Bush camp in the eucalypt forest. Tent and caravan sites, toilets, showers (operating on a self-serve donkey boiler system), barbecues, firewood, water and bins are provided. Bookings are recommended for school holidays and long weekends. Boil or treat the water before drinking.

Brush-tailed rock-wallaby at Crows Nest

Robert Ashdown

Crows Nest National Park

Valley of Diamonds

Walking

Wear a hat and sunscreen and carry water on your walk. Stay away from the waterfall and stay on the track. Never dive or jump into the pool below the falls.

Getting there

Crows Nest National Park is just outside the town of Crows Nest near Toowoomba. Take the New England Highway north from Toowoomba and drive 50km to Crows Nest. Turn off the highway and drive 6km east to the park.

Tracks

Kauyoo Loop track
1·3km return, 30–45 minutes

Crows Nest Falls Lookout
2km return, 40–50 minutes

Koonin track
3·4km return, 1·5–2 hours

Further information

Crows Nest NP
PO Box 68
CROWS NEST QLD 4355
ph (07) 4698 1296
3.30–4pm weekdays

Benarkin State Forest and Forest Reserve

What's special?

In the Blackbutt Range, hoop pines tower over subtropical rainforest in Benarkin State Forest and Forest Reserve. The forest contains hoop pine plantations established in the 1920s and open eucalypt forests with blackbutt, tallowwood, white mahogany, grey gum, blue gum and ironbarks.

The National Bicentennial Trail passes through the forest.

Exploring Benarkin

Have a picnic then go for a scenic drive through the forest. The 13km forest drive starts east of Blackbutt on the D'Aguilar Highway and finishes at the camping areas. A small shelter shed, toilets, barbecues, firewood and picnic tables are provided in the Benarkin picnic area.

Camp or picnic beside Emu Creek, a tributary of the Brisbane River. Clancys camping area is beside the Bicentennial National Trail. The nearby creek is quite shallow making this an ideal family campsite. Emu Creek camping and picnic area, a further 2km along the forest drive, is set among tall trees near a large waterhole, a haven for wildlife.

Toilets, barbecues, firewood, picnic tables and tap water are provided at both camping areas. Emu Creek also has cold showers. (The water supply is seasonal so showers may not be available late winter and spring.)

Follow the Bicentennial Trail through the forest. Tether your horses away from the camping area and water them downstream.

Trail bike riding, horse riding, cycling and four-wheel-driving are allowed along the logging roads by permit only. Dogs on leashes are allowed overnight at Clancys only and in the Emu Creek and Benarkin day use areas

Walking

Look for wildlife along the track beside Emu Creek connecting the two camping areas. See goannas, water dragons, freshwater turtles, red-backed wrens and star finches.

Hoop pine forest at Benarkin

Bruce Cowell, Queensland Museum

Tracks

Silky Oaks walk
3·4km return, 1 hour 15 minutes

Benarkin State Forest and Forest Reserve

Robert Ashdown

Accessibility

The toilets at Emu Creek are wheelchair-accessible.

Getting there

Benarkin is about two hours' drive north-west of Brisbane off the D'Aguilar Highway.

Turn off at the Benarkin Day Use area, a popular stopover on the highway for travellers. The camping areas are 18–20km from Blackbutt along the forest drive. Conventional access is possible with care along 16km of gravel with steep, narrow, winding sections.

Further information

QPWS
158 Hume Street
PO Box 731
TOOWOOMBA QLD 4350
ph (07) 4639 4599
fax (07) 4639 4524

Open forest at Benarkin

Bruce Cowell, Queensland Museum

Bunya Mountains National Park

What's special?

High above the cultivated plains of the Darling Downs and the South Burnett Valley, Bunya Mountains National Park protects the most extensive remaining bunya pine rainforests in south-east Queensland.

The park is the most westerly rainforest park in southern Queensland and conserves valuable remnants of tall, cool subtropical rainforests with bunya pines, figs, red cedars and giant stinging trees, dry vine thickets with bottle trees emerging above the canopy, open eucalypt forests and rare high altitude grasslands. About a quarter of these grasslands have disappeared in the past 50 years. Some of the state's tallest grasstrees grow in the park's open forests and grasslands.

The park is home to about 120 species of birds and many species of mammals, frogs and reptiles.

About every three years in summer until the late 1800s, Aboriginal people visited the mountain when the bunya nut was in season to take part in what was known in Waka Waka language as the "bonye bonye" festival.

Darren Jew

Crow's ash seedpod

Sunset at Burton's Well

Bunya Mountains National Park

Darren Jew

Today, the park has great spiritual significance for the Aboriginal people who still visit the park.

Bunya Mountains became Queensland's second national park in 1908.

Exploring Bunya Mountains

Start your visit at the information centre at Dandabah, next to the camping area.

Have a picnic at Dandabah, Westcott, Cherry Plain or Burton's Well. Dandabah has toilets, picnic tables, electric barbecues and tap water. See the local wildlife, but please do not feed them. Keep wildlife wild.

Camp at Dandabah or bush camp at Burton's Well or Westcott. Dandabah has hot showers, toilets, a shelter shed, coin-operated electric barbecues and tap water. Open fires are not allowed. Take a gas stove. Westcott has toilets, picnic tables, wood barbecues, firewood and tap water. Cherry Plain has picnic tables but no barbecues. Burton's Well has toilets, a shelter shed, picnic tables, wood barbecues, firewood, water supply and donkey boiler showers. Boil or treat the water before drinking.

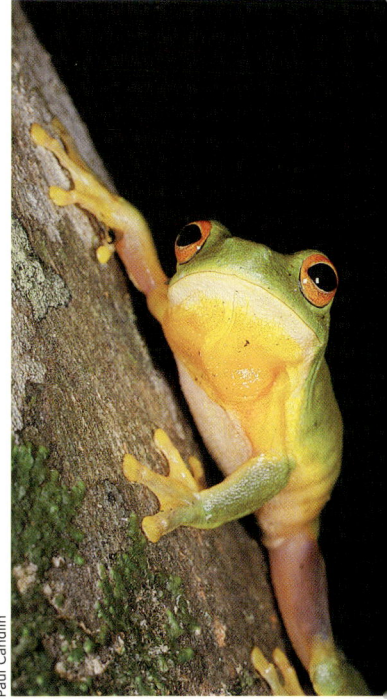

Paul Candlin

Orange-eyed green treefrog

Paul Candlin

Bunya Mountains National Park

Grassy bald at Bunya Mountains

Darren Jew

Tracks

Scenic circuit track
4km, 1·5 hours

Bunya Bunya track
500m, 15–20 minutes

Barker Creek circuit
10km, 3–4 hours

Cherry Plain track
6km one-way or 8·4km return,
3–4 hours

Mt Kiangarow track
2·3km return, 1–1·5 hours

Westcott Plain track
4·8km one-way or 6·6km return,
2–3 hours

Koondaii circuit track
2·5km, 1–1·5 hours

Westcliff track
3·2km one-way or 4·7km return,
2–3 hours

Further information

Bunya Mountains NP
MS501
via DALBY QLD 4405
(07) 4668 3127
fax (07) 4668 3116
2–4pm daily

Campsite bookings: 13 13 04 or
www.qld.gov.au/camping

The Burton's Well and Westcott camping areas are suitable for tents only, not motorhomes, campervans or camper trailers. Vehicles must stay on nearby sealed carparks. The Dandabah camping area has vehicle access.

Enjoy watching wildlife. You will probably see red-necked and black-striped wallabies, red-necked pademelons, satin bowerbirds, noisy pittas, crimson rosellas, king parrots, honeyeaters, wrens, thornbills, scrub-turkeys, orange-eyed tree frogs and lots of butterflies. Go spotlighting at night to see mountain brushtail and ringtail possums, owls, frogmouths and luminous fungi.

Watch the nightly emergence around dusk of the chocolate wattle bats from the old schoolhouse at Dandabah. Go on a Ranger-guided walk during the school holidays to discover the special stories of the Bunyas.

For a special experience, visit in winter when nights are cold and mornings are frosty.

Apart from camping, there are plenty of places to stay on the mountain, but the park does not take bookings for private accommodation.

Walking

Wear a hat and sunscreen and take drinking water. Walking can be hot in summer. Stay on the track and cover up to avoid being scratched or stung by nettles, stinging tree leaves, prickly vines and thorny shrubs.

Accessibility

The Dandabah, Westcott and Burton's Well camping areas have wheelchair-accessible toilets.

Getting there

Bunya Mountains is 63km north-east of Dalby or 58km south-west of Kingaroy. The drive from Brisbane takes about 3 hours via Yarraman and Maidenwell or 3·5-4 hours via Toowoomba and Jondaryan. The Maidenwell route has about 6km of gravel. No access routes are suitable for caravans or trailers.

The Palms National Park

What's special?

In the Brisbane River headwaters, The Palms National Park protects a small remnant of mixed palm vine forest and subtropical rainforest.

Exploring The Palms

The Palms is a great place for a stopover on your way to Bunya Mountains. Have a bush picnic with the local wildlife. Boil or treat the water before drinking.

Walk through the forest. Look for grey-headed flying-foxes camping over the creek in summer and visiting black-breasted button-quails winter and spring.

Walking

See piccabeen palms, a large strangler fig, bunya and hoop pines, and buttressed trees along the track and boardwalks through the rainforest.

Getting there

The park is 7km north-east of Cooyar. Turn off the New England Highway 1km north of Cooyar then drive 6km to the park.

Adam Creed

Bracket fungi on a tree trunk in The Palms National Park

Tracks

The Palms circuit
800m, 15–20 minutes

Further information

QPWS
158 Hume Street
TOOWOOMBA
PO Box 731
TOOWOOMBA QLD 4350
ph (07) 4639 4599
fax (07) 4639 4524

Adam Creed

Palm forest in The Palms National Park

Lake Broadwater Conservation Park

Pelican

Paul Candlin

What's special?

Lake Broadwater, the only natural lake on the Darling Downs, is an important refuge for waterbirds and other wildlife. Surrounded by cypress pine, eucalypt and brigalow open woodland, this shallow lake fills after heavy rains and is occasionally dry.

The park preserves valuable remnants of the vegetation types which once covered the western Downs before settlement.

Aboriginal people camped here and remains of ceremonial sites indicate this was a special place for the local community. Teamsters and early settlers travelling west from Jondaryan used the lake as an overnight watering stopover.

Exploring Lake Broadwater

Have a picnic under the shady river red gums and blue gums on the lake's shores. Sheltered tables, barbecues and toilets are provided.

Stay overnight at Lake Broadwater or Wilga Bush camping areas. Lake Broadwater has grassy campsites overlooking the lake, toilets, hot showers and picnic facilities, and is suitable for caravans and motorhomes. Wilga Bush camping area has shady, secluded campsites on the northern side of the lake, toilets, fireplaces and a shelter shed. Pay your camping fees at the self-registration station in the picnic area or get your camping permit beforehand.

Boating is by permit, available from the on-site caretaker. No boats are allowed in The Neck, a bird nesting area. Go birdwatching from a hide near the neck of the lake.

Learn about the park's vegetation along the walking track which skirts the lake. See the remains of an old dingo fence built in the 1860s for St Ruth Station.

Guided activities can be arranged through the Lake Broadwater Natural History Association.

Walking

A 2km track along the lake's shore joins the two camping areas. A 1km side track leads to the lake overflow. See the vegetation along a 5km track starting near the main camping area.

Lake Broadwater Conservation Park

Paul Candlin

Open woodland at Lake Broadwater

Darren Jew

Accessibility

The Lake Broadwater toilet and shower block is wheelchair-accessible.

Getting there

From Dalby, drive 20km west along the Moonie Highway then turn left into Broadwater Road. Drive a further 9km to the picnic and camping area.

Further information

Wambo Shire Council
26 Wood Street
PO Box 549
DALBY QLD 4405
ph (07) 4662 2922

The Caretaker
**Lake Broadwater
Conservation Park**
Lake Broadwater Road
DALBY QLD 4405
ph (07) 4663 3562 after hours

Galahs at Lake Broadwater

Darren Jew

Southwood National Park

What's special?

Brigalow-belah forest remnants are conserved in this park on the western Darling Downs. Few intact examples of this vegetation type remain on the Downs. Cypress pine, poplar box, wilga bush, false sandalwood, western teatree and other plant species common throughout the semi-arid lands also grow in the park.

Southwood's scrubby forests are a refuge for wildlife. More than 92 species of birds have been seen in the park. The wonga pigeon is close to the inland limit of its range here. Large depressions known as gilgais are scattered through the park. These form by constant wetting and drying of the heavy clay soils.

This is the traditional land of the Bigambul people. Explorers Allan Cunningham and Thomas Mitchell passed this way but the surrounding area was slow to attract settlers. Formerly known as "Wild Horse Paradise", Southwood became a national park in 1970.

Exploring Southwood

Break your journey between Toowoomba and Quilpie at Southwood. Have a bush picnic in the peaceful natural surroundings. Take drinking water. Remove your rubbish. Be careful with open fires.

Take your binoculars and go birdwatching. Glossy black-cockatoos feed on the seed-filled cones of the belah trees. Go spotlighting at night to see sugar or feathertail gliders. Camping is not allowed.

Walking

The park has no walking tracks but you can explore the forest along the roads with care.

Getting there

Southwood is about four hours' drive west of Brisbane or 130km south-west of Dalby on the Moonie Highway. Four-wheel-drive is recommended on Fabians Road which dissects the park. Roads become boggy when wet.

Brigalow forest

Darren Jew

Further information

QPWS
158 Hume Street
PO Box 731
TOOWOOMBA QLD 4350
ph (07) 4639 4599
fax (07) 4639 4524

Southern Outback

Map 3

Legend

▢ National Park	▢ State Forest	— Highway
▢ Conservation Park	▢ Timber Reserve	— Major connecting road
▢ Forest Reserve	▢ Resource Reserve	— Minor access road

0   30   60   90
km

N

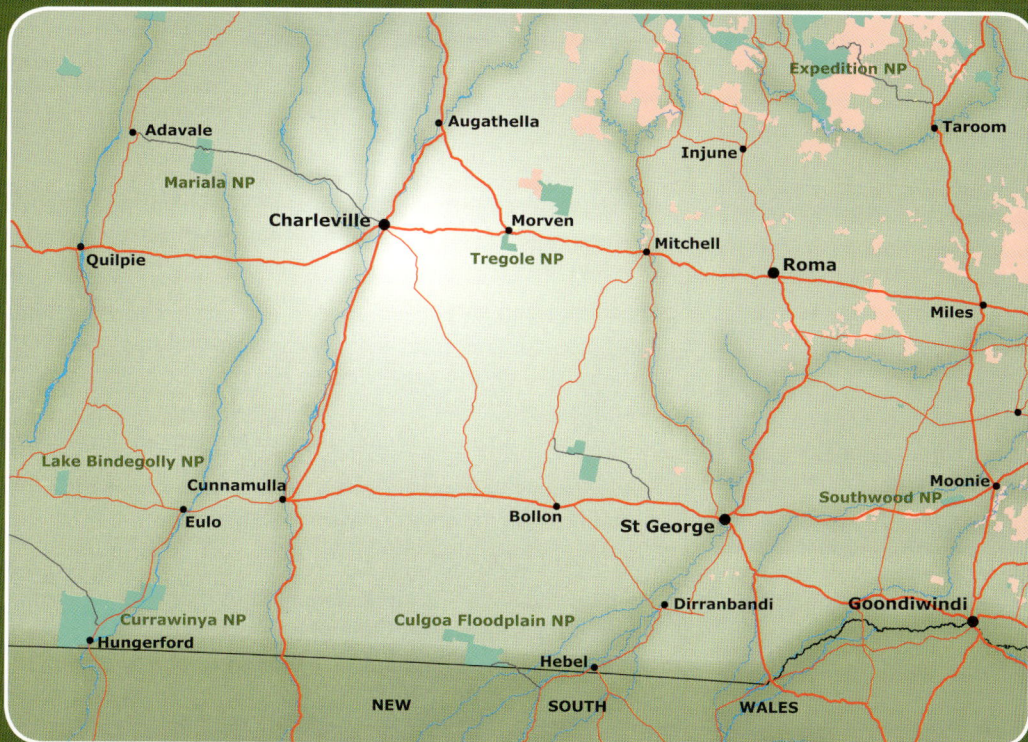

Adavale

Mariala NP

Augathella

Taroom

Expedition NP

Injune

Charleville

Morven

Mitchell

Roma

Quilpie

Tregole NP

Miles

Lake Bindegolly NP

Cunnamulla

Moonie

Eulo

Bollon

St George

Southwood NP

Currawinya NP

Culgoa Floodplain NP

Dirranbandi

Goondiwindi

Hungerford

Hebel

NEW   SOUTH   WALES

Western grey kangaroos at Culgoa Floodplain National Park

Paul Candlin

Currawinya National Park

Adam Creed

Currawinya Woolshed

Adam Creed

What's special?

Currawinya's large lakes, rivers and muddy waterholes contrast strikingly with stark red sandy plains, claypans and rocky ranges in semi-arid south-western Queensland. Saline, clear, Lake Wyara, freshwater Lake Numulla, seasonal waterholes along the Paroo River and other lakes form a major wetland of international significance, providing refuge for thousands of birds.

More than 200 bird species live in the park. Following good rain, thousands of black swans, coots, ducks and grebes flock to Lake Wyara. Lake Numulla is a refuge for pink-eared, hardhead, black and wood ducks and the rare freckled duck, and is a safe breeding ground for many other birds.

Evidence of thousands of years of Aboriginal occupation, and more recent relics of pastoral activities dating from the 1860s, are scattered across the park.

Mulga woodlands are most common but many other shrub and tree species grow in the park, including turpentine, hopbush, poplar box, gidgee, black bluebush and belah.

Community donations have paid for a 25 square kilometre predator-proof fence to protect a captive-bred bilby colony in the park. This population is part of a national strategy to protect the endangered greater bilby, which has disappeared from much of its home range in inland Australia.

Exploring Currawinya

The best way to explore Currawinya is by driving. The 85km return trip from the Currawinya ranger base to the lakes takes two to three hours. Drive carefully.

Bush camp at Ourimperee Waterhole behind the Woolshed or at sites along the Paroo River near Caiwarro. Toilets and tank water are provided at Ourimperee Waterhole and a pit toilet is located at Caiwarro ruins. Take extra drinking water and a fuel stove. Remove your rubbish. Organised groups can stay in the former shearer's quarters at the old Currawinya Woolshed. Showers, toilets, cabins, a public phone and kitchen facilities are provided. Fees apply and bookings are recommended during Queensland and New South Wales school holidays. Visitors must be self-sufficient in food, fuel and water. Meals are available at Hungerford where fuel and some groceries can be obtained at the Royal Mail Hotel.

Currawinya National Park

Paul Candlin

Go birdwatching around the lakes and waterholes. Watch for brolgas dancing. Look for imigrating waterbirds from the northern hemisphere. See mallee ringnecks, mulga parrots and blue bonnets in the low woodlands.

Picnic under the black box trees on the shores of Lake Numulla. Go canoeing or swimming. Motorised boats and jet skis are not allowed on the lakes. Fishing is allowed at specific sites. Check with the ranger and bring your own bait.

Photograph the old woolshed or the ruins of Caiwarro Homestead. Climb The Granites, 15km from the information centre, for a panoramic view over the park. See wildflowers in spring. Information signs at the park office turnoff help you explore the park.

Summer days are extremely hot and winter nights are frosty. April to September is the best time to visit.

Walking

There are no tracks but you can walk along the sandy shores of Lake Numulla. Overnight hiking is allowed. Take drinking water and a fuel stove.

Getting there

Currawinya lies on the Queensland/New South Wales border, next to the township of Hungerford, 217km north-west of Bourke. The park is 170km south-west of Cunnamulla. Travel towards Thargomindah, turning off to Hungerford 4km west of Eulo and continue 60km to the park and a further 40km to the park office. The park office is 4·5km north of the Ten Mile Bore or 20km north of Hungerford. Conventional access is possible but four-wheel-drive is necessary to reach the lakes. The sandy roads become boggy when wet.

Further information

Currawinya National Park
PMB 25
Via CUNNAMULLA QLD 4490
ph (07) 4655 4001
fax (07) 4655 4085
e-mail: currawinya@epa.qld.gov.au
UHF channel 6 (duplex) or
UHF channel 2 (simplex)

QPWS
Park Street
PO Box 149
CHARLEVILLE QLD 4470
(07) 4654 1255
fax (07) 4654 1418

Caiwarro Waterhole

Adam Creed

Lake Bindegolly National Park

What's special?

A string of salt and freshwater wetlands at Lake Bindegolly National Park form an important wildlife refuge in the arid zone. The park is home to more than 195 species of birds, 80 other kinds of animals and 300 species of plants. Saline Lakes Bindegolly and Toomaroo and freshwater Lake Hutchinson attract more than 60 species of waterbirds including pelicans, swans and the rare freckled duck. The lakes are dry about once a decade.

This diverse 14,000ha park has samphire flats, claypans, sand dunes, hard and soft red mulga country, gidgee woodlands, and Eremophila shrublands. The park was established in 1991 to protect the *Acacia ammophila* tree which grows along the sand dunes fringing the eastern side of the lakes. This is one of only two known populations of this gnarled tree which is threatened with extinction.

Mulga-studded gibber plains rise to a ridge on the western side of the lake known locally as Mt Bindegolly.

Sunset at Lake Bindegolly

Adam Creed

Lake Bindegolly National Park

Robert Ashdown

Exploring the park

Drive to the park entrance and read about the park's wildlife and history at the display in the picnic shelter. Have a picnic or walk to the lake.

Take your binoculars and go birdwatching. A bird viewing site is 4·5km from the carpark. See thousands of waterbirds on the lake and wedge-tailed eagles, blue bonnets, pink cockatoos and mulga parrots in the shrublands.

To protect the fragile lake edges and samphire flats, vehicles are not allowed on the park. See wildflowers in spring.

Fuel, food and accommodation are available at nearby Thargomindah. Camping is allowed on a reserve just outside the park on the southern side of the Bulloo Developmental Road. No facilities are provided and firewood collection is not allowed.

Visit in the cooler months.

Walking

Explore around Lake Bindegolly on a 9·2km circuit track which skirts the lake edge then returns along scrub-covered sandhills. The track may be flooded after rain. Follow the markers and stay on the sandy track to protect the park's fragile vegetation. Wear a hat and sunscreen and take water.

Getting there

Lake Bindegolly is half an hour or 40km east of Thargomindah on the Bulloo Developmental Road.

Tracks

Lake Bindegolly circuit
9·2km, 2–3 hours

Further information

QPWS
Sams Street
PO Box 101
THARGOMINDAH QLD 4492
ph (07) 4655 3173
fax (07) 4655 3208

The lakes attract pelicans
and other waterbirds.

Paul Candlin

Tregole National Park

What's special?

In semi-arid, south-western Queensland, Tregole National Park straddles the boundary between two of the state's natural regions, the brigalow belt and the mulga lands.

The park protects a small, almost pure stand of ooline *Cadellia pentastylis*, an attractive dry rainforest tree dating back to the Ice Ages. Ooline has been extensively cleared and is now uncommon and considered vulnerable to extinction. Tregole's ooline forest survives in the less than ideal semi-arid conditions.

Mulga grows on the ridges while poplar box woodlands cover the alluvial plains, brigalow woodlands grow on areas with heavy clay soils and Mitchell grasslands are found on the park's undulating plains.

Exploring Tregole

Relax and enjoy the bush. Read the signs in the information shelter to discover more about the park.

Have a bush picnic. A gas barbecue is provided. Open fires are not permitted. See sand goannas or caper white butterflies flitting around the wild orange bushes. Please do not feed the animals. Take some drinking water and remove your rubbish when you leave.

Take your binoculars and camera and go birdwatching. Camping is not allowed in the park. Accommodation is available in nearby Morven.

Walking

See the park's major vegetation types on a 2·1km circuit track. Walk through the ooline forest, along a ridge and back to the picnic area. Look for the black orchid growing on the ooline tree trunks. Plants numbered along the track are identified in the park brochure. Wear a hat and sunscreen and allow up to an hour for the walk.

Getting there

Tregole is located between Roma and Charleville, just 10km south of Morven on the Morven-Bollon Road. The road between Morven and the park is sealed and narrow.

**Eremophila flower,
Tregole National Park**

Jeff Wright, Queensland Museum

Further information

Tregole NP
Park Street
PO Box 149
CHARLEVILLE QLD 4470
ph (07) 4654 1255
fax (07) 4654 1418

Culgoa Floodplain National Park

What's special?

An important floodplain in the Murray-Darling Basin, Aboriginal cultural sites and diverse woodland vegetation are preserved in Culgoa Floodplain National Park.

Coolibahs, black box and grasses flourish on the floodplains, brigalow and gidgee are found on the flat plains, and mulga and western bloodwood grow on red earth and stony ridges. The park is a birdwatcher's haven with more than 150 species including 10 honeyeaters, Australia's six species of woodswallow and beautiful parrots.

Stone tool scatters and cooking sites remind visitors that Aboriginal people have had a long association with this place. Relics of the pastoral and grazing industries are found throughout the park, which was formerly Byra Station.

Exploring Culgoa Floodplain

Bush camping is allowed at several sites. Visitors must be self-sufficient. Take a fuel stove, first aid kit, vehicle spare parts and extra supplies of drinking water, food, and fuel. Take your rubbish from the park when you leave.

Go birdwatching early morning at creeks and waterholes. The park is also good for wildlife watching. See kangaroos, sand goannas, shingleback lizards and bearded dragons.

Take your camera and try to capture the subtle shades of green reflected in the many different plants which grow in the park.

Walking

The park has no tracks. Ask the ranger for a detailed park map before exploring.

Getting there

Culgoa Floodplain is on the Queensland–New South Wales border 130km south-west of Dirranbandi. From St George, travel 160km south to Hebel on a sealed road then 45km south to Goodooga along an unsealed road which becomes impassable after rain. From Goodooga, turn right into Brenda Road then take the left fork after the cattle grid and follow the "Byra 7km" sign. Four-wheel-drive is recommended.

Paul Candlin

Red kangaroo at Culgoa Floodplain

Further information

Culgoa Floodplain NP
PO Box 51
GOODOOGA NSW 2831
ph (07) 4625 0942
fax (07) 4625 0956

QPWS
Park Street
PO Box 149
CHARLEVILLE QLD 4470
ph (07) 4654 1255
fax (07) 4654 1418

Campsite bookings: 13 13 04 or www.qld.gov.au/camping

Mariala National Park

What's special?

Deep red earth contrasts with the silver-grey foliage and yellow flowers of mulga trees in this remote park. Mulga trees and shrubs grow alongside mountain yapunyah, Dawson gum, poplar box and wattles in the open woodlands.

Mariala National Park was the first park established to protect Queensland's Mulga Lands. This former grazing property was used to breed horses for Cobb and Co. stagecoaches in the early 1900s.

A colony of threatened yellow-footed rock-wallabies has been established in the park. Other local wildlife include the threatened pink cockatoo and the rare square-tailed kite. More than 140 bird species live in the park.

Exploring Mariala

Bush camp in the park. Visitors must be totally self-sufficient as there is no ranger on the park, the local water supply is unreliable and unsuitable for drinking, and there are no facilities. Take a first aid kit and a fuel stove. Take extra food, water, fuel and spare parts for your vehicle. Remove your rubbish from the park.

Go birdwatching early morning. See or hear butcherbirds, spiny-cheeked honeyeaters, brightly-coloured Australian ringnecks or Hall's babblers. Look for emus, echidnas and wallaroos in the mulga shrublands.

Enjoy a view over the park from the main road through the park.

Visit in the cooler months. Summer days can be very hot and winter nights can be cold.

Walking

Take a compass when exploring. There are no formal walking trails.

Getting there

Mariala is 128km north-west of Charleville on the main road to Adavale. All roads are unsealed and may become impassable when wet. Four-wheel-drive is recommended. Leave gates as you find them.

Mulga woodland at Mariala

Jeff Wright, Queensland Museum

Further information

QPWS
Park Street
PO Box 149
CHARLEVILLE QLD 4470
ph (07) 4654 1255
fax (07) 4654 1418

Cooloola Coast and Wide Bay

Legend

National Park	State Forest	—— Highway
Conservation Park	Timber Reserve	—— Major connecting road
Forest Reserve	Resource Reserve	—— Minor access road

0   12.5   25
km

N

Map 4

Burnett Heads

Mon Repos CP

Baldwin Swamp CP

Bundaberg

Gin Gin

Kinkuna

Burrum Coast NP

Woodgate

Woodgate

Fraser Island

Childers

Hervey Bay

Good Night
Scrub NP

Woowoonga FR

Woody Island

Wongi SF

Great Sandy NP

Biggenden

Wongi FR

Coalstoun
Lakes NP

Maryborough

Mt Walsh NP

Poona NP

Tiaro

Tuan SF

Inskip Point

Inskip Peninsula RA

Rainbow Beach

Tin Can Bay

Great Sandy NP

Kilkivan FR

Cooloola

Kilkivan

Jack Smith Scrub CP

Boat Mountain CP

Brooyar SF

Goomeri

Gympie

Murgon

Woondum FR

Boreen Point

Amamoor SF

Noosa

Tewantin FR

Cooroy

Imbil

Noosa NP

Imbil SF

Imbil FR

Mapleton FR

Jimna SF/FR

Kenilworth

Mapleton

Mt Coolum NP

Nanango

Kenilworth FR

Jimna

Nambour

Kondalilla NP

Conondale NP

Maleny

Cooloola Section Great Sandy National Park

What's special?

Sand, wind and water have sculpted a varied landscape at Cooloola, the largest coastal vegetation remnant on southern Queensland's mainland. High sand dunes, coloured sand cliffs, sweeping beaches, sandblows, freshwater lakes, tall forests, paperbark swamps and wildflower heath plains make this a spectacular part of Great Sandy National Park.

Cooloola protects the headwaters of the Noosa River, the cleanest river in south-east Queensland and the only coastal river in Queensland with most of its catchment protected in a national park.

Cooloola is a refuge for plants and animals whose habitats have dwindled with coastal development. Some of the animals living here, such as the Cooloola acid frog and ground parrot, are rare or threatened with extinction, and the park has one of the few remaining emu populations in coastal Queensland.

For thousands of years, Cooloola has been a special place for Aboriginal people. Through timber-getting, agriculture and sand mining, Cooloola has undergone many changes in the past 150 years. Today, Cooloola protects valuable coastal remnants and is one of the most popular tourist destinations in the state.

Exploring Cooloola

Exchange the bustle of the busy coastal resorts for Cooloola's peace and tranquillity. Canoe the calm Noosa River waters, walk through flowering heaths and forests or discover the early timber-getting industry.

Explore the beach around low tide. See coloured sands, jagged sand cliffs, migrating humpback whales and the Double Island Point lighthouse. Go fishing at Teewah Beach, the Noosa River and Kin Kin Creek. Restrictions apply.

See flowering banksias, heath shrubs, ground orchids and Christmas bells in spring and summer. Go birdwatching by day or spotlighting at night.

Stop for a picnic on the shores of Lake Cootharaba at Mill Point, or picnic at Fig Tree Point, Harrys or campsites along the upper reaches of the Noosa River.

Coloured sands at Cooloola

Paul Candlin

Cooloola Section, Great Sandy National Park

You can also picnic at Freshwater, Seary's Creek or in the rainforest at Bymien. Toilets, barbecues and picnic tables are provided at Bymien, Freshwater, Fig Tree Point and Harrys. Seary's Creek has toilets and tables but no barbecues. Take insect repellent.

Camp overnight at Harrys, Fig Tree Point, Freshwater, campsites along the Noosa River or along Teewah Beach. Picnic tables, toilets, barbecues, firewood and water are provided at Fig Tree Point and Harrys. Take your rubbish home with you or put it in the bins at Teewah Beach. Boil the water for five minutes before drinking. The Freshwater camping area has tent and caravan sites, water, toilets, showers, a public telephone and bins. Book your campsite in the holidays. Take insect repellent.

The Cooloola Wilderness Trail has bush camping areas without facilities at Neebs and Wandi waterholes. Take fresh water and a fuel stove for the Trail, the Noosa River campsites, beach campsites and Poverty Point camping area. Open fires are not allowed. Remove all rubbish.

Boat landing sites are provided along the Noosa River. A private campground is located at Elanda Point.

Go for a scenic drive along the Cooloola Way, between Rainbow Beach Road and Kin Kin–Wolvi Road. Discover more about the park by visiting information centres at Kinaba and Rainbow Beach or reading signs at Bymien, Seary's Creek, Harrys, Freshwater and Elanda Point.

Accessibility

Wheelchair-accessible toilets are at Harrys, Figtree Point and Freshwater camping areas and Freshwater picnic area.

View from Double Island Point

Paul Candlin

Pig-face flower

Greg Teschner

Tracks

From Elanda:
Elanda circuit via Mill Point
5·1km, 1·5–2 hours

Kinaba track
12·2km return, 3–4 hours

Mangrove self-guiding walk
500m circuit, 20 minutes

**Elanda Point to
Fig Tree Point track**
21km return, 5–7 hours

**Melaleuca circuit at
Fig Tree Point**
500m circuit, 10–15 minutes

Fig Tree Point to Harrys track
13·2km return, 4–5 hours

Boronia track
5km return, 1·5–2 hours

**From Harrys camping and
day-use area:**
Harrys to Campsites 1–3 track
12·6km return, 3–4 hours

Cooloola Sand Patch track
12km return, 3–4 hours

Fig Tree Point to Harrys track
13·2km return, 4–5 hours

Boronia track
5km return, 1·5–2 hours

From Bymien:
Dandathu circuit
230m, 10 minutes

Poona Lake
4·2km return, 1–2 hours

Telegraph track
14·4km return, 4–5 hours

Freshwater Lake track
14·6km return, 4–5 hours

Cooloola Section, Great Sandy National Park

Darran Leal

Tracks

From Freshwater:
Freshwater campground to Freshwater Lake
2·6km return, 1 hour

Freshwater Lake circuit
2·7km, 45 minutes–1 hour

Other walks:
Teewah Beach to Double Island Point Lighthouse
2·2km return, 30–50 minutes

Seary's Creek boardwalk
200m return, 10 minutes

Carlo Sandblow
1·2km return, 30 minutes

Teewah Landing track and Mt Seewah
8km return, 3·5 hours

Cooloola Wilderness Trail
46km one-way, 2–4 days

Further information

Cooloola Section,
Great Sandy NP
Rainbow Beach Road
PO Box 30
RAINBOW BEACH QLD 4581
ph (07) 5486 3160
fax (07) 5486 3335

Freshwater
(07) 5449 7959

Cooloola Section,
Great Sandy NP
Elanda Point
MS 1537 TEWANTIN QLD 4565
ph (07) 5485 3245
ph (07) 5449 7364
fax (07) 5485 3377

QPWS
Great Sandy Information
Centre
240 Moorindl Street
PO Box 818 TEWANTIN QLD 4565
ph (07) 5449 7792
fax (07) 5449 7357
7am–4pm daily

Getting there

Cooloola lies between the coastal resorts of Noosa Heads and Rainbow Beach and is two to three hours' drive north of Brisbane. Conventional access is limited. The best way to see this part of the park is by boat, walking or four-wheel-drive.

For southern Cooloola, walk from Elanda Point or boat along the Noosa River from Boreen Point (which has a boat ramp) or Elanda Point. You can reach Harrys camping and day-use area by conventional vehicle from Cooloola Way via Kin Kin or Rainbow Beach but the road is rough and four-wheel-drive is recommended.

For northern Cooloola, beach access is possible from Rainbow Beach or Tewantin. Take the vehicle ferry across the Noosa River at Moorindl Street, Tewantin and four-wheel-drive along the beach to Freshwater. Drive 3km to Bymien picnic area from the Rainbow Beach Road, 4km south of Rainbow Beach. The 16km sand road from Bymien to Freshwater camping and day-use area is four-wheel-drive only.

The upper Noosa River campsites are accessible by canoe or electric-powered boat only. To reach Poverty Point, turn off 13km south of Rainbow Beach township then drive 6km to the camping area.

Commercial tours operate from Brisbane, Noosa and Rainbow Beach.

Reflections along the Noosa River

Darren Jew

Inskip Peninsula Recreation Area

What's special?

Off the southern tip of Fraser Island at the entrance to Tin Can Bay lies Inskip Peninsula Recreation Area. The Peninsula is bounded by the Pacific Ocean on its eastern side and the still waters of Tin Can Bay and Great Sandy Strait to the west. Coastal vegetation with she-oaks and cypress pines covers this sand spit.

Most of the Peninsula has been set aside as a recreation area managed for nature-based recreation.

Exploring Inskip Peninsula

Relax and enjoy this quiet coastal retreat. Toilets, picnic tables, barbecues, water and bins are provided.

Look for turtles, dolphins and dugong in the adjacent waters. Beware of strong rips and estuary currents if swimming.

Four camping areas are provided. All are named after local shipwrecks. S.S. Dorrigo campground has campsites overlooking the ocean and caravan sites. M.V. Natone and M.V. Beagle campgrounds are accessible by four-wheel-drive only. M.V. Sarawak campground is suitable for larger groups. Only toilets are provided. Put your rubbish in the bins near the road exits from each campground or "The Oaks" beach access track. Camping is by permit only and you must get your permit before you arrive. Take drinking water and a fuel stove. Fresh water is available at the service facility in Rainbow Beach. Firewood may be purchased at Rainbow Beach.

Dogs on leashes are permitted.

Walking

A 900m circuit leads from the carpark to Pelican Bay.

Getting there

Inskip Peninsula is just 9km north of Rainbow Beach along a sealed all-weather road. From Gympie, take the Tin Can Bay-Rainbow Beach Road. You can also travel from Tewantin by four-wheel-drive at low tide along Cooloola's beaches to Rainbow Beach. Four-wheel-drive access is possible along the beach from Rainbow Beach.

Paul Candlin

Aerial view of Inskip Peninsula

Further information

QPWS
Rainbow Beach Road
PO Box 30
RAINBOW BEACH QLD 4581
ph (07) 5486 3160
fax (07) 5486 3335

Campsite bookings: 13 13 04 or www.qld.gov.au/camping

Fraser Island Great Sandy National Park

Adam Creed

What's special?

The world's largest sand island, Fraser Island, was more than a million years in the making. Fraser Island is a World Heritage Area. This complex ecosystem of sand dunes, lakes, soils and forests survives solely on sand, an outstanding global example of continuing biological and geological processes. Most of the island is protected in Great Sandy National Park and managed as a recreation area.

Jagged coloured sand cliffs, stunning sandblows, freshwater lakes, tall forests, wildflower heaths, magnificent rainforests and crystal-clear creeks make Fraser Island a memorable place to visit. More than 40 freshwater lakes — half the world's perched lakes — nestle among the island's sand dunes. The island has the most extensive wallum heath remnants in Queensland. Fraser Island and nearby Cooloola are the only places in the world where tall rainforest grows in sand.

The island's rich forests, heaths and woodlands are a haven for wildlife including migrating birds and rare and threatened animals such as acid frogs, the ground parrot, Illidge's ant-blue butterfly, the beach stone-curlew and the false water-rat. Fraser Island has possibly the purest dingo population in Australia. More than 600 plant species and around 300 vertebrate animal species live on the island.

Dingo on the beach at Fraser Island

Paul Candlin

Looking south to Indian Head from Middle Rocks

Paul Candlin

Fraser Island, Great Sandy National Park

Adam Creed

People have left their mark on this place. The Butchulla people lived here for at least 5000 years. Scattered among the island's ever-shifting sands are many reminders of their special connection with this place. More recently, the island has hosted timber-getting, sand mining and tourism industries. But the island's character is largely unspoilt.

Exploring Fraser Island

Take the time to explore Fraser Island. See coloured sand cliffs and natural sand sculptures along the coast or try your luck at beach fishing. Leave the busy beach behind and enjoy the beauty of Fraser Island's forests, heaths, lakes and creeks.

Sit by a lake or go for a quiet paddle. Go wildlife watching. See wildflowers in spring. Look for honeyeaters and fairy-wrens among flowering heaths, and flycatchers and robins in the forests. See turtles, dugong, dolphins and migrating humpback whales offshore.

Be very careful around dingoes. Stay with your children, walk in groups and never feed or coax them. All wild animals, including goannas, butcherbirds or kookaburras, can be aggressive, even if they are familiar with people. Keep wildlife wild.

Choose from many bushwalks or scenic drives around the island. Signposted tourist drives, suitable only for four-wheel-drive vehicles, start from Central Station and Happy Valley.

Have a picnic or barbecue at historic and picturesque Central Station, Waddy Point, Ocean Lake, Lake Boomanjin, Lake Birrabeen, or Lake Garawongera.

Camp at national park campgrounds on the eastern beach at Waddy Point and Dundubara, on the western beach at Wathumba, or inland at Central Station, Lake Boomanjin and Lake Allom. Basic facilities are provided including coin-operated hot showers, picnic tables, barbecues, firewood, toilets and tap water. No firewood suppied at Central Station. Generators are not allowed. Take insect repellent. Lock all food and rubbish in your vehicle or campground lockers and secure eskies with tight straps to discourage dingoes. Fines apply for not complying. Bookings are essential for Waddy Point and Dundubara during holidays. Dundubara is suitable for caravans.

Tracks

Walks around Waddy Point:
Waddy Point campground to headland walk
3·2km return, 1–1·5 hours

Binngih Sandblow track
750m return, 20–30 minutes

Champagne Pools from Waddy Point
7km return, 2–2·5 hours

Cypress circuit, Ocean Lake
1km return, 20–30 minutes

Middle Rocks Imagine walk to Champagne Pools
1·6km return, 45 minutes–1 hour

Walks around Dundubara:
Wungul Sandblow walk
2km return, 30–45 minutes

Wungul Sandblow circuit
5·5km circuit, 1·5–2 hours

Bowarrady trail via Lake Bowarrady
22km return, 6–8 hours

Lake Allom circuit
1·4km circuit, 30–40 minutes

Lake Coomboo track
4·4km return, 1·5 hours

Forest walk via Hidden Lake
12·4km return, 3·5 hours

Walks around Kingfisher Bay Resort (KBRV), Lake McKenzie and Central Station:
Dundonga Creek mouth walk
3·3km one-way, 1·2 hours

McKenzie's Jetty and Z-Unit Commando Site walk
5km circuit, 1–2 hours

KBRV to Lake McKenzie via Dundonga Creek
11km one-way, 3·5 hours

Lake McKenzie to KBRV via McKenzie's Jetty
9km one-way, 3 hours

Fraser Island, Great Sandy National Park

Paul Candlin

Tracks

Lake McKenzie via Lake Wabby to Ocean Beach
14km one-way, 4·5–5·5 hours

Lake McKenzie to Central Station via Basin Lake track
6·3km one-way, 2–2·5 hours

Central Station to Lake McKenzie-Lake Wabby track via Pile Valley
8km one-way, 3 hours

Walks from Central Station:
Wanggoolba Creek boardwalk
500m one-way, 15–30 minutes

Pile Valley circuit
4·6km return, 1·5–2 hours

Basin Lake track
4km return, 1·5 hours

Central Station to Lake Boomanjin track via Lake Benaroon
14·6km one-way, 4·5–5·5 hours

Lake Boomanjin northern beach walk
2km return, 30–45 minutes

Lake Boomanjin to Dilli Village
6·3km one-way, 2·5 hours

Forest Lakes Trail
75–77km, 4–6 days

Walks from the Ocean Beach:
Ocean Beach to Lake Wabby track
5km return, 1·5–2 hours

Rainbow Gorge–Kirra Sandblow circuit
2·1km circuit, 1 hour

Eli Creek Boardwalk
800m return, 15–30 minutes

You can also camp at signed places along the beach. No facilities are provided and campers must remove all rubbish. Collect your camping tag and information pack before you reach the island. Private campgrounds and other accommodation are also available.

Food, gas refills, ice and fuel are available at Happy Valley, Eurong, Cathedral Beach, Orchid Beach and Kingfisher Bay. Public telephones are located around the island. There is no medical assistance on the island. Take a well-stocked first aid kit.

Find out about the island's special attractions at information signs and centres around the island or join a ranger-led slide show, spotlight tour or guided walk in holiday times.

Walking

When walking, wear a hat and sunscreen. Read your *Be dingo-aware* brochure for advice on what to do if you feel threatened by a dingo. A 100km Great Walk is being established on Fraser Island allowing visitors to hike from Dilli Village to Lake Garawongera. This is part of the Great Walks of Queensland nature-based tourism initiative.

Accessibility

Wheelchair-accessible toilets are at Wanggoolba Creek barge landing, Eli Creek, Lake Garawongera, Lake Birrabeen and Lake Allom.

Getting there

You can reach Fraser Island by air or water from Rainbow Beach or Hervey Bay. Commercial barges operate from Inskip Point near Rainbow Beach to Hook Point on the southern end of Fraser Island, from River Heads near Hervey Bay to Wanggoolba Creek or Kingfisher Bay, and from Urangan Boat Harbour, Hervey Bay to Moon Point. Bookings are required for all barges except Hook Point to Inskip Point where barges operate 6am–5.30pm most days.

A passenger ferry service operates from Urangan Boat Harbour to Kingfisher Bay. Private boats can moor at Kingfisher Bay Resort, Wathumba and Garry's Anchorage.

Passenger flights run daily from Hervey Bay. Contact QPWS Maryborough about the public airstrip at Toby's Gap.

Fraser Island, Great Sandy National Park

The only way to get around this sand island is by four-wheel-drive. Hire companies operate from mainland towns (Rainbow Beach, Hervey Bay) and Eurong Beach, Kingfisher Bay and Happy Valley resorts. A driving safety video is available from the Maryborough office. Obtain a vehicle permit before taking your vehicle to Fraser Island. For safety, travel along the beach 2–3 hours either side of high tide and follow sand-driving guidelines.

Commercial tours of the island operate from Rainbow Beach, the Sunshine Coast, Hervey Bay and Brisbane.

Lake Birrabeen

Further information

Naturally Queensland Information Centre
Ground floor
160 Ann Street, Brisbane
PO Box 155
BRISBANE ALBERT STREET
QLD 4002
ph (07) 3227 8186
fax (07) 3227 8749
e-mail: nqic@epa.qld.gov.au

QPWS
Corner Lennox and Alice Streets
PO Box 101
MARYBOROUGH QLD 4650
ph (07) 4121 1800
fax (07) 4121 1650

QPWS
Rainbow Beach Road
PO Box 30
RAINBOW BEACH QLD 4581
ph (07) 5486 3160
fax (07) 5486 3335

QPWS
Great Sandy Information Centre
240 Moorindl Street
PO Box 818
TEWANTIN QLD 4565
ph (07) 5449 7792
fax (07) 5449 7357
7am–4pm daily

Eurong Information Centre
ph (07) 4127 9128
fax (07) 4127 9150

Central Station Ranger Base
ph (07) 4127 9191
fax (07) 4127 9102

Dundubara Information Centre
ph (07) 4127 9138
fax (07) 4127 9254

Waddy Point Ranger Base
ph (07) 4127 9190
fax (07) 4127 9253

Campsite bookings: 13 13 04 or www.qld.gov.au/camping

Woody Island Great Sandy National Park

Tracks

Middle Bluff lighthouse to North Bluff lighthouse
4km one-way, 3–4 hours return

One Tree to North Bluff
1km, 30 minutes

Gas shed to Middle Bluff
500m, 15 minutes

Further information

Great Sandy (Fraser Island) NP QPWS
Corner Lennox and Alice Streets
PO Box 101
MARYBOROUGH QLD 4650
ph (07) 4121 1800
fax (07) 4121 1650

Campsite bookings: 13 13 04 or www.qld.gov.au/camping

What's special?

In the Great Sandy Strait between Fraser Island and Hervey Bay lie Woody and Little Woody Islands, which together form an undeveloped section of Great Sandy National Park.

Rocky Woody Island's open forests and fringing mangroves are home to a variety of birds. The twin Woody Island lighthouses and associated buildings, built in 1866, remains of telegraph lines and a grave site are heritage-listed for their contribution to the maritime and settlement history of the Maryborough-Hervey Bay area.

Exploring Woody Island

This is a quiet retreat for self-sufficient visitors. No facilities are provided and open fires are not allowed.

Bush camp at Jeffries Beach on the south-eastern side of the island. Take fresh water and a fuel stove.

Relive the fascinating history of Queensland's early lightkeepers as you explore around the lighthouses. For your safety, please do not enter or climb on the lighthouse complex structures.

Walking

There are no formal tracks on the island and trails are not signposted. A rock-lined track which once linked the two lighthouses can still be seen in places.

Getting there

Woody Island is in the Great Sandy Strait, about 5km or 20 minutes east of Urangan, Hervey Bay. Access is by private boat only.

Terry Harper

Sunset over Woody Island

Woondum State Forest and Forest Reserve

What's special?

Subtropical rainforest, tall wet sclerophyll forest and spectacular rocky creeks make Mothar Mountain in Woondum State Forest and Forest Reserve a popular spot for locals and visitors. Here, Woondum and Boulder Creeks join together in a series of picturesque rockpools.

Exploring Woondum

Have a picnic by the creek. Relax and unwind to the sound of water gently cascading over ancient granite outcrops. Picnic tables, barbecues, firewood, water and toilets are provided at the rockpools. Please do not feed the lace monitors. Let them find their own food and keep wildlife wild.

Explore around the creek or go for a short walk through the cool, moist forest. Be careful swimming in the rock pools, never jump or dive into the water and supervise children closely.

Camping is not allowed in the forest. You can camp in campgrounds at Amamoor or Brooyar State Forests near Gympie.

Visit the Woodworks Museum on the Bruce Highway at Gympie for an insight into this area's fascinating timber industry past. The museum is open weekdays and a small entrance fee applies.

Walking

Explore the forest along an easy 530m (one-way) track. Allow half an hour for the walk.

Getting there

Mothar Mountain is just 15 minutes south-east of Gympie. Take the Old Noosa Road then turn left into Hills Road.

Paul Candlin

Mother Mountain

Further information

QPWS
27 O'Connell Street
PO Box 383
GYMPIE QLD 4570
ph (07) 5480 6207
fax (07) 5482 8105

Woodworks Forestry and Timber Museum
Fraser Road
MS 483
GYMPIE QLD 4570
ph (07) 5483 7691
fax (07) 5482 1773

Amamoor State Forest and Forest Reserve

Near Gympie

What's special?

In the scenic foothills west of Gympie, Amamoor State Forest and Forest Reserve protect precious remnants of the beautiful forests which once covered this area. More than 120 species of birds live in this forest and nearby Imbil State Forest.

Riverine rainforest grows along Amamoor Creek. White cedar, red cedar, hoop pine and bunya pine can be seen in the rainforest remnants. The forest also contains hoop and bunya pine plantations.

The Country Music Muster, the largest outdoor music festival in Australia, is held in this forest every August.

Exploring Amamoor

Have a picnic beside the creek at Amama under the shade of a hoop or bunya pine. Picnic tables, wood barbecues and toilets are provided. The open grassy area is suitable for large groups and ball games.

Look for platypus in Amamoor Creek at dawn or dusk. Explore the nearby rainforest. If you have time, take the road opposite Amama to Cooke's Knob fire tower for a spectacular view over the forests and coastal plains. Obtain a permit to traverse first.

Camp at Cedar Grove where grassy sites on the banks of Amamoor Creek are popular all-year-round. Take your own firewood or use supplied firewood sparingly. Pay your fees on-site. Cold showers, toilets, barbecues, water and a public phone are provided here.

See white and red cedar trees in the subtropical rainforest and open forest and hoop pine plantations along the hiking trail.

You can also camp at Amamoor Creek camping area. Dogs on leashes are allowed overnight. The campground is not available for general use during the Muster in late August. Facilities include cold showers, toilets, barbecues and water.

Both camping areas are suitable for motorhomes and caravans.

Look for platypus in Amamoor Creek

Paul Candlin

Amamoor State Forest and Forest Reserve

Walking

Wonga walk starts across the road from Amama and the Cascade circuit continues from the end of this walk.

Accessibility

Platypus Walk starting at the far end of Amama day use area is wheelchair-accessible. This walk follows Amamoor Creek to a small viewing platform where you can watch for platypus.

Getting there

Amamoor is about two hours' drive north of Brisbane. Turn off the Bruce Highway 20km south of Gympie and follow the signs to Amamoor township. The forest is 10km west of Amamoor along the Amamoor Creek Road. Access is suitable for conventional vehicles towing caravans. Collect a brochure at the information shelter at Amamoor before visiting the forest.

Rainforest walk at Cedar Grove

Paul Candlin

Tracks

From Amama:
Platypus Walk
300m one-way, 15 minutes

Wonga walk
1·5km return, 40 minutes

Cascade circuit
2·2km return, 1 hour

From Cedar Grove:
Rainforest walk
1km return, 30 minutes

Hiking trail
4·6km return, 4 hours

Further information

QPWS
27 O'Connell Street
PO Box 383 GYMPIE QLD 4570
ph (07) 5480 6207
fax (07) 5482 8105

QPWS
Sunday Creek Road
PO Box 52
KENILWORTH QLD 4574
ph (07) 5446 0925
fax (07) 5446 0966
7.30am–4pm weekdays

Brooyar State Forest

What's special?

In the scenic Mary Valley north-west of Gympie lies Brooyar State Forest. The campground lies in the hills between Widgee and Glastonbury Creeks. This quiet retreat contains rainforest, open eucalypt forest and hoop pine plantations. Patches of riverine rainforest fringe Glastonbury Creek. Queensland's best hoop pine plantations are in this forest.

Exploring Brooyar

Go for a scenic drive through the forest, stopping to enjoy the view from the lookouts. Turn off the Bruce Highway 20km north-west of Gympie to the Wide Bay Highway. The return trip to Gympie via Bells Bridge is 53km.

Walk through open eucalypt forest with a grasstree understorey to Eagle Nest Lookout for a view over the forest to Black Snake Ranges. Enjoy the view from Point Pure Lookout. Abseiling is allowed at both lookouts for individuals and authorised groups with qualified leaders. For safety, spectators should stay well back.

Camp on the banks of Glastonbury Creek. A grove of white cedars across the creek are a mass a gold flowers in autumn while, in summer, the rich red and yellow flowers of the black bean trees contrast with the orange spikes of the silky oak trees. Toilets, fire rings, firewood and drinking water are provided. Pay your camping fees on-site. The camping area is suitable for caravans and motorhomes. Bookings are unnecessary. Dogs on leashes are allowed.

Have a picnic or barbecue at Glastonbury Creek where there is plenty of room for outdoor games. Picnic tables and wood barbecues are provided. Relax and cool off in the trickling creek. For your safety, never jump or dive into this shallow creek.

If you enjoy your visit to Brooyar, you may like to visit the Woodworks Museum on the Bruce Highway at Gympie to discover the timber-getting history of the Gympie area. Displays include a 619-year-old kauri pine stump. The museum is open weekdays and a small entrance fee applies.

Paul Candlin

Cliffs at Point Pure

Brooyar State Forest

Walking

Walk through the rainforest along an old logging road at Glastonbury Creek. Short walks lead to both lookouts along the Brooyar Forest Drive. See open forest, sandstone outcrops and rock shelters.

Getting there

Brooyar is just 20 minutes north-west of Gympie or two and a half hours' drive north of Brisbane. Head 10km north of Gympie along the Bruce Highway then turn left onto the Wide Bay Highway and drive 7·8km to the turnoff to the campground. Caravan access to the campground is via Peterson Road (partly unsealed) off the Wide Bay Highway.

Further information

QPWS
27 O'Connell Street
PO Box 383
GYMPIE QLD 4570
ph (07) 5480 6207
fax (07) 5482 8105

Woodworks Forestry and Timber Museum
Fraser Road
MS 483
GYMPIE QLD 4570
ph (07) 5483 7691
fax (07) 5482 1773

Paul Candlin

View from Point Pure Lookout

Tuan State Forest

Log dump camping area, Kauri Creek

Paul Candlin

What's special?

Stretching from Tin Can Bay to Boonooroo in the coastal lowlands along the Great Sandy Strait, Tuan State Forest contains some of the most extensive exotic pine plantations in Queensland. The forest also has small coastal wallum remnants along creeks and estuaries.

Tuan is a low-key holiday destination for people who love boating and fishing in the adjacent creeks and Great Sandy Strait.

Exploring Tuan

Enjoy the wildflower display late winter and spring. Go birdwatching in the nearby Great Sandy Conservation Park along Tinnanbar Road.

Go canoeing along the creeks. Wear insect repellent if canoeing or camping.

Choose from several camping areas in the forest. All have water frontage. Hedleys on the banks of Kauri Creek is the most popular and has fewer sandflies and mosquitoes. Access to Hedleys is through private property. A $5 fee is payable to the owners (07) 4129 8177.

The Log Dump on Kauri Creek has toilets, water, a boat ramp and fireplaces. Take your own drinking water supply. Boil the tap water before drinking. Fire rings are provided at Hedleys.

Dogs are allowed on leashes. Pay your camping fees at the self-registration stations onsite.

Walking

The park has no walking tracks but you can explore along numerous sand roads with care.

Accessibility

The toilets at the Log Dump are wheelchair-accessible.

Tuan State Forest

Adam Creed

Paul Candlin

Poona Creek

Getting there

Tuan lies between the Tin Can Bay military training area and the township of Boonooroo. The forest is about 20 minutes' drive east of Maryborough. Head towards Boonooroo then take the Cooloola Coast Road. Drive 19km along the Cooloola Coast Road to the Tinnanbar turnoff. The Log Dump turnoff is 7km along this gravel road and the Hedleys turnoff is a further 4·7km. The Log Dump and Hedleys camping areas are 1km and 3km off the Tinnanbar Road. A wildflower reserve is along the Tinnanbar Road. All sites are dirt road access and may be inaccessible in wet weather. A permit to traverse is required to drive on tracks apart from access roads to designated camping areas.

Further information

QPWS
Corner Lennox and Alice Streets
PO Box 101
MARYBOROUGH QLD 4650
ph (07) 4121 1800
fax (07) 4121 1650

Poona National Park

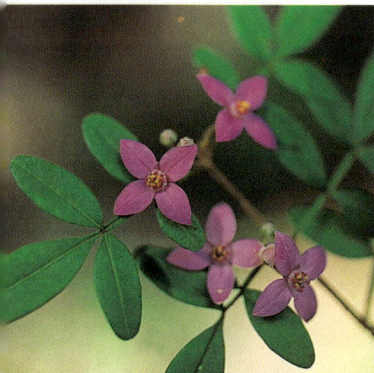

What's special?

Low-lying coastal plains and two small islands in the Great Sandy Strait are protected in this park between the Mary River estuary and Great Sandy Strait. Poona National Park conserves valuable remnants of the wallum heath communities which flourished in the Maryborough-Hervey Bay area before settlement and land clearing.

Paperbark forests and woodlands, mangroves, and banskia and blue gum woodlands also grow in the park. Rare and threatened plants include *Boronia keysii* and *Macrozamia pauli-guilielmi*. The park contains one of the most southerly stands of the broad-leafed paperbark *Melaleuca viridiflora*. Poona National Park is an important wildlife refuge. The endangered ground parrot lives in the park's wallum heath.

The park also protects part of the Kalah Creek catchment. Poona National Park is the traditional country of the Butchulla people who also lived on nearby Fraser Island.

Exploring Poona

This is a great place for low-key nature-based activities such as photography and birdwatching. No facilities are provided and camping is not allowed.

See spectacular wildflower displays in spring and summer. You can fish from the Kalah Creek area only. Camping is not allowed.

Walking

The park has no designated walking tracks but you can explore the bush with care.

Getting there

Poona is just 6km south-east of Maryborough on the northern side of the Maryborough-Cooloola and Boonooroo Road. Access is possible by four-wheel-drive vehicle, boat or walking. The roads inside the park are not signposted and become boggy when wet.

Key's boronia

Darren Jew

Further information

QPWS
Corner Lennox and Alice Streets
PO Box 101
MARYBOROUGH QLD 4650
ph (07) 4121 1800
fax (07) 4121 1650

Wongi State Forest and Forest Reserve

What's special?

A string of beautiful waterholes fringed by paperbarks and rushes and surrounded by eucalypt forest and exotic pine plantations make Wongi State Forest and Forest Reserve special places to visit. Lenthalls Dam, the water supply for Hervey Bay shire, is in the heart of the forest.

Wongi is reputedly an Aboriginal word meaning snake. Tannins leached from the paperbarks stain the water in the waterholes a golden-brown colour. Reflections can often be seen in the still waters.

Hoop pine rainforest, open eucalypt forest, open woodland with a heath understorey, and exotic pine plantations grow in Wongi. The National Bicentennial Trail passes through the forest.

Exploring Wongi

Camp or picnic under the shady eucalypt trees. Cool off in a waterhole in summer. For your safety, never jump or dive into the waterholes. Supervise children closely as the water is deep.

Two picnic areas are provided beside the waterholes. The first picnic area is near the forest entrance and the second is 700m from the entrance next to the camping area. Both have picnic tables and wood barbecues.

Wongi camping area has sites to suit families, groups, caravans, tents and motorhomes. Picnic tables, toilets, cold showers, wood barbecues, firewood and tank water are provided. Take a fuel stove. Boil the water for five minutes before drinking. Dogs are allowed on leashes. Pay your camping fees onsite.

Getting there

Wongi is 25km north-west of Maryborough. Head 12·5km towards Childers on the Bruce Highway then turn left at the signpost and drive 10km into the picnic and camping areas along a gravel road.

Paul Candlin

Wongi waterhole

Further information

QPWS
Corner Lennox and Alice Streets
PO Box 101
MARYBOROUGH QLD 4650
ph (07) 4121 1800
fax (07) 4121 1650

Baldwin Swamp Conservation Park

What's special?

Part of a string of wetland remnants in the Bundaberg area, Baldwin Swamp Conservation Park is a tiny slice of Kakadu right in the heart of the city. Waterways here provide valuable feeding and breeding grounds for a variety of waterbirds and other wildlife. About 75 bird species have been seen in the park, including magpie geese, jacanas, swamp hens, herons and hardheads.

Paperbark trees, sedges, swamp grass and reeds grow in swampland in the western part of the park. Dry vine scrub fringes the watercourses and open eucalypt forest grows on higher ground. The rainforest is a remnant of the Woongarra Scrub which once extended between the Burnett and Elliott Rivers.

The Bunda people camped on the creek banks long before European settlement. The swamp was named after one of Bundaberg's pioneers and the springs provided the settlement's first water supply. Bundaberg City Council and the community have restored the swamplands and are re-establishing the original vegetation.

Jacana

Darran Leal

Exploring Baldwin Swamp

Have a picnic then explore the park. Go birdwatching. Look for waterbirds along the 400m Sunset track beside Bundaberg Creek. A large shelter shed, picnic tables, barbecues and toilets are provided in the adjacent city park.

See brushtail and common ringtail possums, short-nosed bandicoots, insectivorous bats and echidnas mainly at night. Enjoy birdwatching during the day. More than 75 species live in the park.

Camping is not allowed but you can stay overnight in Bundaberg.

Walking

Short boardwalks and walking tracks skirt the wetlands. Take your binoculars and wear insect repellent.

Tracks

Harry Frauca walkway
200m, 10 minutes

Figtree circuit
150m, 5 minutes

Sunset track
400m, 15 minutes

Baldwin Swamp Conservation Park

Darren Jew

Accessibility

The 200m Harry Frauca walkway through teatree forest and riverine scrub is wheelchair-accessible.

Getting there

Baldwin Swamp is 4km from the Bundaberg Post Office along Bargara Road, Scotland and Steindl Streets and Que Hee Street causeway. You can also reach the park via the Bundaberg Port Road (Walker Street) and the causeway.

Further information

QPWS
PO Box 1735
BUNDABERG QLD 4670
(07) 4131 1600
fax (07) 4131 1620

Paul Candlin

Wetland in Baldwin Swamp Conservation Park

Woodgate Burrum Coast National Park

What's special?

Coastal lowland remnants and long, sandy beaches are protected in this section of Burrum Coast National Park between the mouth of the Gregory River and Woodgate.

Remnants of the many vegetation types found in the coastal lowlands can be seen in this section of the park, from mangrove-lined riverbanks to pockets of livistona palm forests, eucalypt and angophora forests and woodlands, wallum heath and paperbark swamps. The park contains plants found only in this local area, such as the rare or threatened *Eucalyptus hallii*, *Melaleuca cheelii* and *Macrozamia lomandroides*.

Exploring Woodgate

Relax and enjoy this coastal retreat away from the crowds. Picnic at Walkers Point or Hoppy Lark's Creek. Toilets are provided just outside the park at Walker's Point. Please do not feed the kangaroos. They can become aggressive when fed.

Canoe across the river. Try your luck at fishing. Go birdwatching. You might see spoonbills, ibis, pelicans, ducks or jabiru from the birdhide over a wetland off Walkers Point Road. See stunning wildflowers in spring along the Banksia track or road to Hoppy Lark's Creek.

Camp behind the beach at Burrum Point. This camping area is suitable for tents, campervans and small caravans. Individual campsites, toilets, town water, cold showers and a pulley system for solar showers are provided. Take a fuel stove. Pay your camping fees onsite. Book six months in advance for the school holidays as campsites are limited. Remove your rubbish to the transfer station outside the park.

Walking

Wear a hat, sunscreen and insect repellent.
Take drinking water.

Jabiru at Woodgate

Darren Jew

Tracks

From 6th Avenue and Acacia Street:
The boardwalk
800m return, 20 minutes

Banksia walk
5·4km circuit, 1·5–2 hours

From campground:
Melaleuca track
12·3km return, 3–4 hours

From Walkers Point picnic area:
Birdhide walk
3km return, 1 hour

Woodgate, Burrum Coast National Park

Paul Cladin

Accessibility

Hoppy Lark's Creek has wheelchair-accessible tracks to a viewing platform with a picnic table and a fishing platform on the banks of the Gregory River. Walkers Point picnic area is also wheelchair-accessible. The boardwalk through a paperbark swamp at the start of the Banksia track, and the picnic area and track at Walker's Point are also wheelchair-accessible. The birdhide walk which follows the Gregory River estuary from Walker's Point is wheelchair-assisted.

Getting there

From Childers, travel 2km east on the Bruce Highway. Turn off to Goodwood then travel 45km to Woodgate township. From Bundaberg, follow Barolin Street (which becomes Goodwood Road) and travel 60km to Woodgate township. Roads within the park are gravel or sand. The camping area is accessible only by four-wheel-drive.

Further information

**Woodgate Section,
Burrum Coast NP**
PO Box 167
WOODGATE QLD 4660
ph (07) 4126 8810

QPWS
46 Quay Street
PO Box 1735
BUNDABERG QLD 4670
ph (07) 4131 1600
fax (07) 4131 1620

Gregory River wetlands

Darren Jew

Mon Repos Conservation Park

What's special?

For more than 35 years, scientists have studied turtle biology at Mon Repos, one of the two largest loggerhead turtle nesting sites in the South Pacific. Mon Repos Conservation Park near Bundaberg is the rookery for the largest number of nesting marine turtles on mainland eastern Australia.

Between November and March, visitors to Mon Repos can witness one of Nature's most fascinating spectacles, the annual onshore pilgrimage of sea turtles, which come ashore to lay their eggs, and the subsequent hatching of young sea turtles and their return to the sea.

The park's other attractions include Woongarra scrub remnants, mangroves, the site of Bert Hinkler's first glider flights, a tidal lagoon, rockpools, and an historic basalt stone wall built by Kanaka labourers brought to Queensland in the late 19th Century to harvest sugar cane.

The offshore waters and the beach are protected in adjacent Woongarra Marine Park.

Mon Repos foreshore

Paul Candlin

Mon Repos Conservation Park

Exploring Mon Repos

Enjoy this quiet retreat during the off-peak season of winter and spring when access to the park is unrestricted. Walk along the beach or go birdwatching. Explore the rockpools or go snorkelling on the fringing reef.

During the turtle season, November to March, thousands of visitors flock to the turtle information centre to watch turtles on guided night tours. The centre opens at 7pm and access to the centre and beach is by ticket only. Fees apply. Audiovisual shows are presented in the amphitheatre, weather permitting.

The best time to see turtles is after dark from mid-November to February. Hatchlings usually leave their nests at night from mid-January until late March. If you visit in January, you might see both nesting turtles and hatchlings.

Visitors should come prepared with warm clothes, rain gear, insect repellent and walking shoes. Small torches are permitted. While time limits apply to beach access, you may have to wait at least two hours before going to the beach. Allow up to six hours for your visit.

Spend time in the visitor centre discovering the special stories of Mon Repos, the sea turtles and nearby Woongarra Marine Park.

Camping is not allowed in the park but a private caravan park adjoins the park. You can also stay nearby at Bargara or Bundaberg.

Walking

A track starting from the information centre lets you explore the park. Wear a hat and sunscreen. Take drinking water.

Accessibility

The Mon Repos Information Centre, toilets, picnic table, boardwalks and the first 600m of the coastal circuit are wheelchair-accessible but there is no special access to the beach.

Getting there

Mon Repos is about four and a half hour's drive north of Brisbane and just 14km or 15 minutes east of Bundaberg.

Turtle watching at Mon Repos

Tracks

Coastal circuit
4km return, 1–1.5 hours

Further information

Mon Repos CP
PO Box 1735
BUNDABERG QLD 4670
ph (07) 4159 1652
fax (07) 4159 1630

QPWS
PO Box 1735
BUNDABERG QLD 4670
ph (07) 4131 1600
fax (07) 4131 1620

Loggerhead hatchling

Kinkuna Burrum Coast National Park

Wedding bush

Bruce Cowell, Queensland Museum

Further information

**Woodgate Section,
Burrum Coast NP**
PO Box 167
WOODGATE QLD 4660
(07) 4126 8810

QPWS
46 Quay Street
PO Box 1735
BUNDABERG QLD 4670
(07) 4131 1600
fax (07) 4131 1620

What's special?

This remarkably unspoilt stretch of coastline features a long, sandy beach backed by low sand dunes, tea-coloured waterways and a variety of coastal vegetation communities from wallum heath to sedgelands, tall open forests, low stunted woodlands and paperbark swamps. The Kinkuna Section of Burrum Coast National Park also protects the catchment of Theodolite Creek.

Exploring Kinkuna

Enjoy the peace and quiet in this undeveloped section of the park. Visitors must be self-sufficient. Take fresh water, a first aid kit and a fuel stove for cooking or take your own firewood.

Walk along the beach or go birdwatching in the heath. See beautiful wildflowers in late winter and spring. Let the ranger know if you intend hiking in this undeveloped part of the park.

Camp behind the sand dunes in the shade of casuarina trees. Use the access ramps to get to the beach. Pay your camping fees at the self-registration station.

Walking

No formal tracks are provided but you can walk along fire trails. Wear a hat and sunscreen. Take drinking water. Register overnight hikes with the ranger at Woodgate.

Getting there

Kinkuna is accessible only by four-wheel-drive. Sand driving experience is essential. Turn off the Bundaberg-Childers Road 17km south of Bundaberg. Follow Coonarr Road for 8km then turn into Palm Beach Road which leads to the park. Palm Beach is 16km north of Woodgate or 30km south of Bundaberg.

Burnett Valley

Map 5

Legend

- National Park
- Conservation Park
- Forest Reserve
- State Forest
- Timber Reserve
- Resource Reserve
- Highway
- Major connecting road
- Minor access road

0   12.5   25
km

N

Cania Gorge NP
Kalpowar SF
Monto
Mon Repos CP
Baldwin Swamp CP
Bundaberg
Gin Gin
Burrum Coast NP
Woodgate
Childers
Tolderodden CP
Eidsvold
Good Night Scrub NP
Woowoonga FR
Wongi SF
Biggenden
Mundubbera
Coalstoun Lakes NP
Maryborough
Gayndah
Mt Walsh NP
Auburn River NP
Kilkivan FR
Kilkivan
Proston
Jack Smith Scrub CP
Boat Mt CP

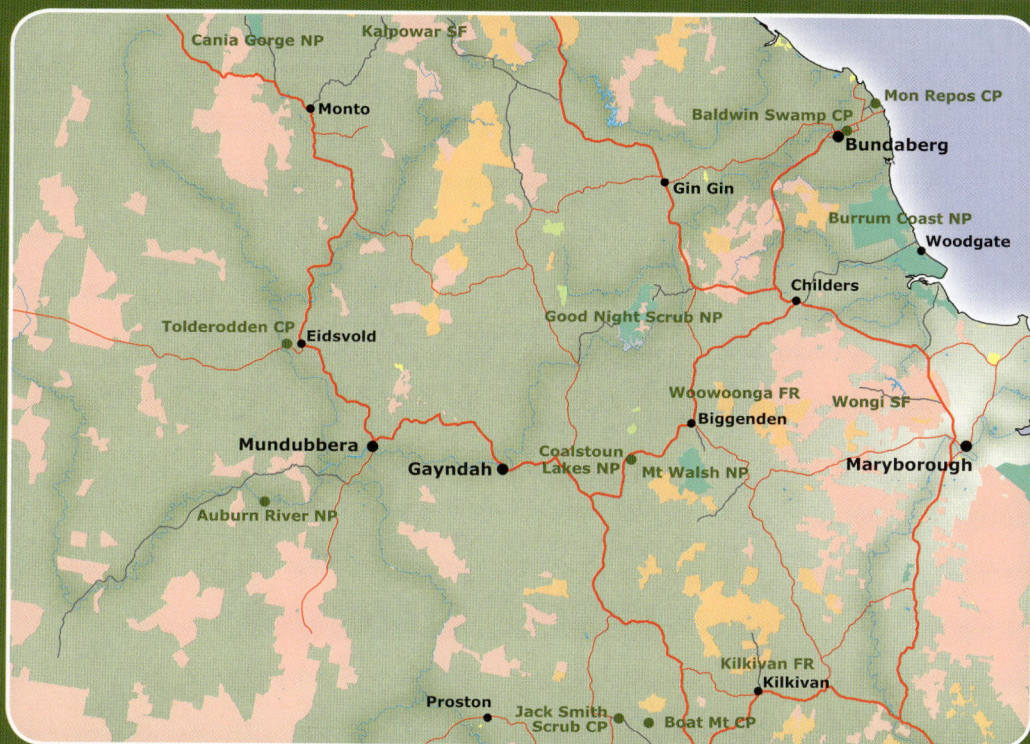

Fern Tree Pool, Cania Gorge National Park

Robert Ashdown

Kilkivan Forest Reserve

What's special?

Just north of Kilkivan on the Mudlo Range, Kilkivan Forest Reserve protects one of the area's few remaining stands of native hoop pine rainforest. Rainforest once covered many of the coastal ranges in the Lower Burnett Valley. Little remains today.

Rainforest covers most of the park. Large hoop pines and occasional bunya pines tower over the rainforest canopy. Many plants are close to the limit of their normal range here and the rare large-leaf chainfruit grows in the park. Open eucalypt woodlands with ironbarks and forest red gums grow on more exposed slopes and foothills.

Mudlo is believed to mean "men's magic stone" but little is known about the Aboriginal people who lived here. Mudlo was a once a timber-getting area and later attracted copper and gold miners to the Kilkivan area.

Exploring Kilkivan

Go for a short scenic drive from Kilkivan to Mudlo Gap. Stop for a picnic or bushwalk beside Scrubby Creek. Only picnic tables are provided.

Walk through the rainforest or uphill to a lookout over Kilkivan and the surrounding countryside. See strangling figs, staghorns and buttressed trees along the track.

Continue your scenic drive to Mudlo Gap for a great view over the surrounding grazing land and forests. Picnic tables, a shelter shed, toilets and a barbecue are provided at the Gap.

Enjoy the local wildlife. See whiptail wallabies, brush-turkeys and wonga pigeons.

Camping is not allowed in the park but you can stay nearby at Kilkivan.

Blue triangle

Adam Creed

Kilkivan Forest Reserve

Walking

Explore the hoop pine rainforest along two walking tracks. The Mudlo Gap track is quite steep with many steps, but the view at the top is your reward for the strenuous climb. Try to arrange to be dropped off at the Gap and walk downhill.

Accessibility

The Scrubby Creek picnic table is wheelchair-accessible.

Getting there

Kilkivan is 8·5km north of Kilkivan. Head north from Kilkivan along James and Bridge Streets towards the Showgrounds. Continue along the Mudlo Road to Scrubby Creek and another 400m to Mudlo Gap.

Tracks

Scrubby Creek circuit
1km, 30 minutes

Mudlo Gap track
4km return, 1·5–2 hours

Further information

QPWS
80 Gore Street
PO Box 260 MURGON QLD 4605
ph (07) 4169 5992
fax (07) 4168 3645

Scrubby Creek, Kilkivan Forest Reserve

Boat Mountain Conservation Park

Start of the walking track

Adam Creed

Tracks

Braithwaites Lookout
370m return, 20 minutes

Silburns Vine Scrub walk
2·2km return, 45 minutes

Boat Mountain circuit
1·8km, 40 minutes

Daniels Lookout
2·2km, 45 minutes

What's special?

This distinctive flat-topped ridge shaped like an upturned boat is covered in dry rainforest and open eucalypt woodland. At 589m, Boat Mountain is a local landmark in the Murgon area and the headwaters of four creeks.

Most of the vegetation was originally hoop pine rainforest but now is a mixture of softwood scrub and vine thicket following logging. More than 130 plant species grow here including rare plants. Common trees include the small-leaved tuckeroo, white tamarind, leopard ash and native holly.

The park also contains grassy open eucalypt woodland with stringybarks and grey gums.

Exploring Boat Mountain

Relax and enjoy nature in this small park. Have a picnic with a view on the edge of the park. Only picnic tables are provided. Walk to two lookouts for views over the surrounding countryside.

Go birdwatching. The park has at least 46 species of birds including rufous whistlers, black-faced cuckoo-shrikes, double-barred finches, red-backed wrens, honeyeaters, fantails, doves and pigeons. You might also see black-striped wallabies and echidnas by day or pygmy-possums and sugar gliders at night.

See the dish-shaped depressions on the track made by the black-breasted button-quail as it spins around feeding. Bandicoot diggings can be seen along the track.

Camping is not allowed in the park.

Walking

See the vine forest and great views along the walking track. Wear protective clothing to avoid being scratched by prickly shrubs. The full circuit includes Braithwaites Lookout and the vine scrub walk.

Boat Mountain Conservation Park

Getting there

Boat Mountain is north-east of Murgon. Head north out of Murgon along Gore Street which becomes Boat Mountain Road. Travel for 9km along Boat Mountain Road then turn right into Levers Road. After 0·6km, turn left into Daniels Road. Continue 1·4km then turn right into Hebbel Drive and drive another 1·4km to the park.

From Goomeri, head 2km towards Nanango then take the Murgon Road 4km to the Manyung Road turnoff. Drive 4·5km then veer right into Reifs Road. Continue for 3·5km then turn right into Daniels Road. Continue 2·8km to the park.

Further information

QPWS
80 Gore Street
PO Box 260
MURGON QLD 4605
ph (07) 4169 5992
fax (07) 4168 3645

Open forest at Boat Mountain Conservation Park

Jack Smith Scrub Conservation Park

Rainforest at Jack Smith Scrub

Adam Creed

Tracks

Owenia nature walk circuit
900m, 20 minutes

Further information

QPWS
80 Gore Street
PO Box 260
MURGON QLD 4605
ph (07) 4169 5992
fax (07) 4168 3645

What's special?

Jack Smith donated this small patch of softwood scrub in hilly country north-west of Murgon. Jack Smith Conservation Park preserves a valuable remnant of the once vast dry rainforests that have since been largely cleared for agriculture. The tall crow apple *Owenia venosa* emerges above the rainforest canopy. Other common trees in the dense vine thicket are python tree, leopard ash and thorny yellow wood.

Exploring Jack Smith Scrub

Have a picnic at the edge of the park overlooking the South Burnett Valley. On a clear day, you can see the Bunya Mountains to the south-west.

Go birdwatching. More than 40 species of birds have been seen in the park including the black-breasted button-quail which leaves circular depressions on the track as it spins around feeding on the forest floor. See brush-turkey mounds beside the walking track.

If you visit in spring, you will see the creamy flowers of the wonga vine which twists around the tree trunks.

Camping is not allowed in the park.

Walking

Explore the park along a short circuit track. Wear protective clothing to avoid being scratched by prickly shrubs.

Getting there

The park is just north-west of Murgon on Smiths Road. Head 5km west of Murgon along the Gayndah Road. Turn right at Tablelands Road and left at Smith Road. Jack Smith Scrub is 3km along this road on the right. Alternatively, head north out of Murgon along Gore Street which becomes Boat Mountain Road. Travel for 9km along Boat Mountain Road then turn left into Levers Road. Continue for 2km through the Tablelands Road intersection into Smiths Road and on to the park.

Woowoonga Forest Reserve

What's special?

Hilly country clothed in dry rainforest with towering hoop pines and open eucalypt forest is protected in Woowoonga Forest Reserve along the Woowoonga Range.

Exploring Woowoonga

Have a picnic or barbecue beside a rocky creek in the forest. A sheltered picnic table, tank water and a wood barbecue are provided.

Hike through the vine thicket and open forest to Mt Woowoonga for spectacular views over the Biggenden and Maryborough area.

Go birdwatching. See flocks of red-tailed black-cockatoos in summer.

Bush camping is not allowed. Accommodation is available in nearby Biggenden.

Walking

A rough trail leads through the vine forest to the summit of Mt Woowoonga. This trail is suitable for experienced bushwalkers only. Take a compass and follow the red markers. Start your walk near the picnic area. Wear a hat and sunscreen. Take water and stay on the trail. The walk to Mt Woowoonga takes about three hours return.

Getting there

Woowoonga is about 90 minutes' drive from Maryborough and 14km north of Biggenden. Turn off the Childers Road into Giles Road 6·5km north of Biggenden. Drive 2·5km then turn left into Woowoonga Hall Road. Continue for 2km then turn right into Mt Woowoonga Road and continue 3km to the picnic area.

Red-tailed black-cockatoos

Robert Ashdown

Further information

QPWS
Corner Lennox and Alice Streets
PO Box 101
MARYBOROUGH QLD 4650
ph (07) 4121 1800
fax (07) 4121 1650

View towards Mt Woowonga

Paul Candlin

Mt Walsh National Park

What's special?

Rising to 703m above sea level in the Coastal Range, Mt Walsh National Park is a rugged park with spectacular exposed granite outcrops and cliffs. The Bluff area of Mt Walsh, at the park's northern end, is a prominent landmark in the Biggenden area.

The park's diverse vegetation includes vine forest in sheltered pockets, scrubland and heath on rock pavements and open eucalypt forest and woodland. Shrubs are common in the forest and woodland understorey, heath and shrubland.

Common rainforest trees include tuckeroo, python tree, canary beech and the native witch hazel with its white perfumed flowers. The park is a wildlife refuge and home to rare and threatened species including the heart-leaved bosistoa *Bosistoa selwynii*, powerful owl *Ninox strenua* and the grey goshawk *Accipiter novaehollandiae*.

View from The Bluff

Robert Ashdown

Exploring Mt Walsh

Have a picnic or barbecue below The Bluff. A shelter shed, toilets, showers, barbecue and tank water are provided in the local authority picnic ground next to the park.

Most of this rugged park is suitable only for experienced, well-equipped bushwalkers with sound bush skills. **WARNING: Granite rocks are slippery when wet. Wear shoes with good grip or avoid walking during or after rain.**

Bush camping is allowed in the park. No facilities are provided so visitors must be totally self-sufficient. Take a fuel stove. Open fires are not permitted. Camping may be closed in periods of high fire danger. Take plenty of drinking water.

You can also stay in Biggenden.

Talk to the ranger before rockclimbing or abseiling in remote parts of the park.

Mt Walsh National Park

Walking

A 300m trail leads from the picnic area through open forest to a rocky creek gully fringed with dry rainforest. Continue 200m to the treeline for views over the surrounding countryside. Only experienced walkers should attempt the 2·5 hour hike to the summit of Mt Walsh.

Walkers should take a topographic map and compass when exploring the park. Never walk alone. Take a first aid kit and plenty of drinking water. Mobile phone reception is available. Wear sturdy shoes and tell someone responsible your bushwalking plans in case you get lost or injured.

Getting there

Mt Walsh is 84km west of Maryborough or 50km south of Childers. Turn off the Maryborough-Biggenden Road 2km east of Biggenden or 79km west of Maryborough. Travel a further 5·3km along the signposted National Park Road to the picnic area.

Further information

QPWS
cnr Alice and Lennox Streets
PO Box 101
MARYBOROUGH QLD 4650
ph (07) 4121 1800
fax (07) 4121 1650

Mt Walsh

Good Night Scrub National Park

Bottle tree scrub in Good Night Scrub

Ross Naumann

What's special?

In hilly country in the Burnett Valley, Good Night Scrub National Park protects an intact remnant of once extensive hoop pine rainforest. Most of this 6670ha park is dry rainforest with tall hoop pines emerging above the forest. Distinctive bottle trees and crows ash are also common. The rest of the park is dry open forest of spotted gum, forest red gum and narrow-leaved red ironbark.

According to local folklore, the scrub was so thick, people could not walk or ride through it. If cattle escaped into the scrub, you could "kiss your cattle goodnight".

Kalliwa Hut, a timber-getter's hut at the park's southern end, is a reminder of the park's former forest logging days. This slab hut was moved here in the 1920s and later had its shingle roof replaced.

Good night Scrub is the last known sighting of the presumed extinct paradise parrot. Part of the park will be flooded by the proposed Paradise Dam on the Burnett River.

Exploring Goodnight Scrub

Enjoy nature in this peaceful retreat. Have a bush picnic in a picturesque bushland setting at Kalliwa Hut. Picnic tables are provided.

Go birdwatching. More than 166 species have been seen in the park, including powerful owls, regent bowerbirds, forest kingfishers and king parrots. See swans, spoonbills and other waterbirds along the river. Go wildlife watching. See black-striped, swamp and red-necked wallabies. More than 60 species of butterflies have been seen in the park.

Enjoy the 360-degree view from the old fire tower at One Tree Hill Lookout. On a clear day, you can see from Bundaberg to Mt Walsh.

Walking

No tracks are provided but you can walk along a firebreak trail. Carry water. Wear a hat and sunscreen.

Good Night Scrub National Park

Darren Jew

Tim Peek

Kalliwa Hut

Further information

QPWS
46 Quay Street
PO Box 1735
BUNDABERG QLD 4670
ph (07) 4131 1600
fax (07) 4131 1620

Getting there

Good Night Scrub is in the Burnett Valley between Gin Gin and Gayndah. Turn right off the Bruce Highway at a signposted junction 10km south of Gin Gin and head south. Or turn west off the highway at Booyal, 27km west of Childers. After 200m on the Biggenden Road, turn right and drive 4km to the Burnett River causeway then another 9km to the junction with the park road. The park is a further 10km from this junction along a gravel road. Access within the park is on gravel road that is suitable for conventional vehicles only in dry weather and can be impassable to four-wheel-drive vehicles in the wet. The steep access road to One Tree Hill Lookout is four-wheel-drive only in dry conditions.

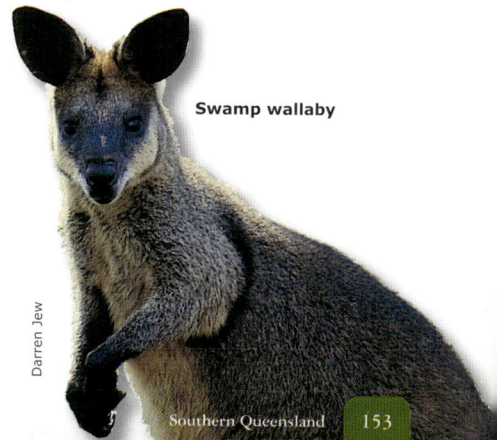

Swamp wallaby

Darren Jew

Coalstoun Lakes National Park

Bottle trees at Coalstoun Lakes

Robert Ashdown

What's special?

Rising 200m above a broad cultivated valley, Mt Le Brun contains two large craters which occasionally fill with shallow lakes. The crater lakes are protected in Coalstoun Lakes National Park. Formed more than 600,000 years ago, the mountain is one of the youngest volcanic formations in Australia.

Melaleucas and blue gums fringe the lakes which are sometimes completely dry and covered in sedgelands. The vine scrub covering the crater sides is one of the few dry rainforest remnants in this area. Bottle trees, crows ash, leopard ash and other trees tower over the dense vine scrub. The heart-leaved bosistoa *Bosistoa selwynii* found in this forest is vulnerable to extinction.

The lakes were named after Coalstoun in Scotland by Wade Brun, manager of nearby Ban Ban Station.

Exploring Coalstoun Lakes

With no facilities, this is a park for birdwatching and nature study. Leave your car at the base of the mountain and walk up the steep outer side of the northern crater for a great view over the vine forest and crater. Continue down into the crater.

See the intact patch of brigalow scrub next door to the park as you head up the northern crater. Camping is not allowed in the park.

Walking

Wear a hat, sunscreen and protective clothing to avoid being scratched by prickly shrubs in the vine thicket.

Getting there

Turn off the Isis Highway 20km south of Biggenden or 4km north of Coalstoun Lakes into Crater Lakes Road. Follow the gravel track to the base of the northern crater.

Tracks

Northern Crater trail
1km return, 30 minutes

Further information

QPWS
Corner Lennox and Alice Streets
PO Box 101
MARYBOROUGH QLD 4650
ph (07) 4121 1800
fax (07) 4121 1650

Auburn River National Park

What's special?

The scenic Auburn River tumbles over massive, water-sculpted, salmon-coloured granite boulders as it flows through a steep-sided gorge in Auburn River National Park.

Weeping bottlebrushes, flowering leptospermum shrubs and stunted figs line the creek banks. Bottle trees grow in the dry rainforest on the northern bank of the river near the camping area. Silver-leaved ironbark and forest red gum grow in the grassy open forests. These western hardwood forests are now uncommon in this area.

This small park contains relics of past gold mining days.

Exploring Auburn River

Camp or picnic in a picturesque bush setting on the northern bank of the river. Only picnic tables are provided. Take drinking water, a fuel stove for cooking or your own firewood. Remove your rubbish.

Go birdwatching in the forests along the clifftops or around the waterholes. If you are lucky, you might see peregrine falcons which nest in the cliffs opposite the camping area. See brush-tailed rock-wallabies around the cliffs and red-necked wallabies in scrubby gullies near the camping area. Enjoy the wildflowers in spring.

Explore around the river. Take water. Do not drink the river water. Visit in the cooler months as this park can be very hot in summer.

Walking

From the picnic and camping area, a short 150m trail leads to a lookout high above the Auburn River. A rough 550m track winds down the side of the gorge to the river. This is a strenuous walk and should only be attempted by fit walkers.

Getting there

Auburn River is 40km or one hour's drive south-west of Mundubbera. Travel 12·5km south along the Mundubbera-Durong Road then take the Hawkwood Road west for about 20km to the park turnoff. Drive a further 7km to the park along an unsealed road. Conventional access is possible. Four-wheel-drive is recommended in wet weather. Stay on the road. The soils are treacherous when wet.

Tim Peek

Scenic Auburn River

Further information

QPWS
Shed 5 Willsons Avenue
PO Box 127
MUNDUBBERA QLD 4626
ph (07) 4165 5120
fax (07) 4165 4800

QPWS
46 Quay Street
PO Box 1735
BUNDABERG QLD 4670
ph (07) 4131 1600
fax (07) 4131 1620

Tolderodden Conservation Park

What's special?

This small park beside the Burnett River was once a camping and water reserve. Today, visitors can enjoy a brief stopover here.

Open eucalypt forest with Moreton Bay ash and blue gum trees and a grassy understorey grows in the park. Tall blue gums line the steep banks of the Burnett River and basalt outcrops dot the park.

The park is managed by Eidsvold Shire Council. Historic Eidsvold Station is nearby.

Exploring Tolderodden

Camp or picnic under the Moreton Bay ash trees on the banks of the Burnett River. Shady, grassy campsites, pit toilets, picnic tables, a shelter shed, wood barbecues, tank water and bins are provided. Take firewood. The camping and picnic area is solar-lit at night.

Walking

A 700m track leads from the camping area up a ridge for a view over the park.

Getting there

The park is on the Cracow Road just 4·5km west of Eidsvold.

Further information

QPWS
PO Box 226
MONTO QLD 4630
ph (07) 4167 8162
fax (07) 4167 8141

QPWS
46 Quay Street
PO Box 1735
BUNDABERG QLD 4670
ph (07) 4131 1600
fax (07) 4131 1620

Darran Leal

Double-barred finch

Kalpowar State Forest

What's special?

In the foothills of the Burnett Range, Kalpowar State Forest protects a mosaic of forests. Patches of dense rainforest with towering hoop pines remain between open eucalpyt forests and hoop pine plantations. More than 150 plant species occur in the hoop pine rainforest which was first logged in 1918.

Fireclay Road got its name from local clay used to make bricks before the plantations were established here. The first hoop pine plantation of about 12 hectares was developed in 1934 and the last available area was planted in 1991.

Paul Candlin

Hoop pine plantation, Kalpowar State Forest

Exploring Kalpowar

Go on the scenic Kalpowar Forest Drive. Starting at the intersection of Fireclay Road and the Gladstone-Monto Road, the 20km drive takes about 90 minutes. This unsealed road is accessible only in dry weather. Signs along the way provide an insight into the forest and the way it is managed.

Enjoy the view over the Kolan River catchment from Bill's Window Lookout on the forest drive. See the remaining huts that once sheltered the Forestry workers while working on the plantation forests. Strangler figs and crows ash trees grow in the rainforest remnants.

Picnic or camp in a tranquil bush setting beside Crane Creek near the end of the forest drive. The open grassy campsites are suitable for families and large groups. Pay your fees at the self-registration station. Dogs are allowed overnight. Remove your rubbish. Boil the tank water for five minutes before drinking.

Getting there

Kalpowar is 37km north-east of Monto on the Monto-Gladstone Road and accessible by conventional vehicle. The Kalpowar can also be reached from the Bruce Highway and is 80km south-west of Gin Gin or 36km north-west of Gin Gin. The camping area is 3km from Kalpowar township along a gravel road.

Further information

QPWS
PO Box 226
MONTO QLD 4630
ph (07) 4167 8162
fax (07) 4167 8141

QPWS
46 Quay Street
PO Box 1735
BUNDABERG QLD 4670
ph (07) 4131 1600
fax (07) 4131 1620

Cania Gorge National Park

Giant's Chair Lookout

Robert Ashdown

What's special?

Cania Gorge is a near-coastal outlier of Queensland's extensive sandstone belt. Here, you can see towering sandstone cliffs, caves and gorges without travelling all the way to "the outback".

Dry open eucalypt forest grows along Three Moon Creek and on ridges above the 70m sandstone cliffs while dry rainforest with mosses, orchids, figs and vines grows in the moist, sheltered gorges, providing a varied habitat for wildlife.

Cania Gorge preserves a valuable remnant of the Brigalow Belt natural region. More than 150 plants grow here in brigalow forest, eucalypt woodland, cypress pine woodland, dry rainforest and grassland. More than 90 species of birds have been recorded in the park. Brush-tailed rock-wallabies and common bent-wing bats are also seen.

Aboriginal people have lived in Cania Gorge for at least 19,000 years. Freehand art on the sandstone walls is a reminder of their special way of life.

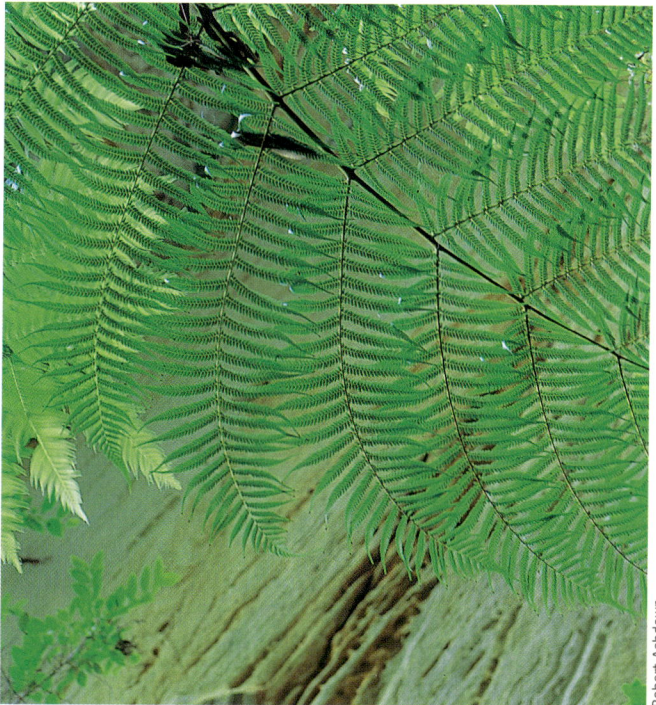

The Overhang

Robert Ashdown

Cania Gorge National Park

Exploring Cania Gorge

Have a picnic at Three Moon Creek below the ochre-coloured cliffs or at the West Track carpark near the entrance. Toilets, picnic shelters, water and electric barbecues are provided at Three Moon Creek.

Find out about the park's wildlife, vegetation and history at the display shelter in the main picnic area. Go bushwalking along one of the many tracks. Climb up a sandstone escarpment to Giant's Chair Lookout for a view over the park.

Go wildlife watching. You might see lace monitors, dollarbirds, king parrots, wompoo pigeons, regent bowerbirds or whiptail wallabies. Look for platypus in waterholes below the dam wall. See red kurrajong flowers in spring.

Camping is not allowed in the park but there are two private campgrounds nearby. Cania Gorge Tourist Retreat is at the park entrance (07) 4167 8110. Cania Gorge Tourist Park is in the gorge 7km north of the picnic area (07) 4167 8188.

Find out about the park's gold mining past at the Shamrock mine. Canoe or picnic at nearby Lake Cania, 11km north of the picnic area.

Walking

See the park's lush rainforests and spectacular cliffs and overhangs on the walking tracks. Some walks are fairly strenuous. Take water and wear a hat and sunscreen.

Getting there

Turn off the Burnett Highway 12km north of Monto or 77km south of Biloela then drive 8km past Moonford to the main picnic area.

Southern spotted gecko

Tracks

From the picnic area:
Picnic area circuit
300m, 15 mins

Dripping Rock
2·2km return, 1 hour

The Overhang
3·2km return, 1·5 hours

Dragon Cave
1·8km return, 1 hour

Bloodwood Cave
2·6km return, 1 hour

Two Storey Cave circuit
1·3km, 1 hour

From West Track carpark:
Fern Tree Pool and Giant's Chair circuit
5·6km, 2–3 hours

Big Foot walk
1km return, 45 mins

Picnic area track
900m one-way, 20 mins

From the carpark 1km south of Lake Cania:
Shamrock mine
1·2km return, 30 mins

Further information

Cania Gorge NP
PO Box 226
MONTO QLD 4630
ph (07) 4167 8162
fax (07) 4167 8141

QPWS
46 Quay Street
PO Box 1735
BUNDABERG QLD 4670
ph (07) 4131 1600
fax (07) 4131 1620

Map 6

Central Queensland Coast

Legend

National Park
Conservation Park
Forest Reserve

State Forest
Timber Reserve
Resource Reserve

Highway
Major connecting road
Minor access road

0   15   30
km

N

Byfield NP
Byfield SF

Keppel Bay Islands NP

Mt Etna Caves NP   Yeppoon   Capricorn Coast NP
Mt Jim Crow NP

North West Island
Capricornia Cays NP

Rockhampton   Mt Archer NP

Curtis Island NP

Mount
Morgan

Masthead Island

Gladstone

Lady Musgrave Island

Calliope

Castle Tower NP

Joseph Banks CP

Eurimbula NP

Biloela   Kroombit Tops FR   Miriam Vale   Deepwater NP

Kroombit Tops NP

Thangool   Broadwater CP
Mt Scoria CP

Mouth of Baffle Creek CP

Bulburin FR

Cania Gorge NP

Mon Repos CP

Baldwin Swamp CP
Monto   Bundaberg

Gin Gin

Burrum Coast NP

Mouth of Baffle Creek Conservation Park

What's special?

Baffle Creek is one of Queensland's few remaining undisturbed coastal rivers. The creek's estuary is protected on both sides by conservation parks. Mouth of Baffle Creek Conservation Park 2 is on the northern shore.

This small coastal remnant features sandy beaches backed by low, open, she-oak woodlands and paperbark woodlands further inland. On the other side of the estuary, Mouth of Baffle Creek Conservation Park 1 is mainly mangrove woodland.

Exploring Mouth of Baffle Creek

This is a peaceful retreat for self-sufficient visitors. Go birdwatching or fishing. If you swim, remember this beach is unpatrolled and beware of marine stingers between October and May.

Camp under the coastal she-oaks behind the dunes overlooking the estuary and sandy beach. Take drinking water and a fuel stove. No facilities are provided. Generators are not allowed. Pay your fees at the self-registration station near the beach access point at Rules Beach.

Getting there

Mouth of Baffle Creek is about one hour north of Bundaberg near Rules Beach. Head towards Miriam Vale and Agnes Water. From Bundaberg, take the Rosedale-1770 Road about 58km to Berajondo. Turn right 500m before Berajondo into Hills Road. Continue to Rules Beach via Wartburg. Drive 1km south along the beach to the camping area. Access is four-wheel-drive only around low tide. Sand driving experience is necessary as getting off the beach can be difficult.

Paul Candlin

Baffle Creek estuary

Further information

General enquiries and bookings:
QPWS
PO Box 1735
BUNDABERG QLD 4670
ph (07) 4131 1600
fax (07) 4131 1620

Local information only:
QPWS
Captain Cook Drive
PO Box 177
AGNES WATER QLD 4677
ph (07) 4974 9350
fax (07) 4974 9400

Broadwater Conservation Park

What's special?

Broadwater is on the coast between Baffle Creek and Deepwater Creek. This small diverse coastal remnant contains casuarina woodland on the foredunes, mangrove-lined creeks and mixed eucalypt open forest and paperbark woodland further inland.

Exploring Broadwater

This is a quiet haven for totally self-sufficient visitors. Go birdwatching or fishing. If you swim, remember this beach is unpatrolled and beware of marine stingers between October and May.

Camp at Mitchell Creek camping area. Take water and a fuel stove. No facilities are provided and generators are not allowed. Pay your fees at the self-registration station near the beach access point at Rules Beach.

Getting there

Broadwater is on the coast 7km north of Rules Beach. Access is by boat or four-wheel-drive along Rules Beach at low tide. Sand driving experience is necessary as getting off the beach can be difficult.

Adam Creed

Look for soldier crabs on the beach.

Further information

General enquiries and bookings:
QPWS
PO Box 1735
BUNDABERG QLD 4670
ph (07) 4131 1600
fax (07) 4131 1620

Local information only:
QPWS
Captain Cook Drive
PO Box 177
AGNES WATER QLD 4677
ph (07) 4974 9350
fax (07) 4974 9400

Castle Tower National Park

What's special?

Towering granite cliffs flank two large granite outcrops, Mts Castle Tower and Stanley in rugged Castle Tower National Park.

Open eucalypt woodland with a shrubby heath understorey covers most of the mountain. The heath contains plants found locally, such as the Byfield spider grevillea *Grevillea venusta*, which is threatened with extinction. Dry rainforest scrub grows along gullies and creeks. The park is the southern limit of white gum *Eucalyptus platyphylla*.

Exploring Castle Tower

Visitors to this undeveloped wilderness park must be totally self-sufficient. Bush camping is allowed. Take drinking water and a fuel stove. Remove your rubbish from the park.

Enjoy the wildflowers late winter and spring.

You can also camp or picnic nearby at Lake Awoonga. Canoe across the lake to the park. Visit in the cooler months as summers can be hot.

Walking

There are no walking tracks so only experienced walkers should hike in the park. Always carry drinking water while bushwalking. Energetic visitors can climb to the summit of Mt Castle Tower for views over the Boyne Valley and Gladstone.

Getting there

Castle Tower is 40km south of Gladstone or 20km north of Bororen. Turn off the Bruce Highway at Christensen Road 30km south of Gladstone or 28km north of Miriam Vale and follow the signposted gravel road to the park boundary. The Mt Stanley Section is accessible via Bororen. Access is also possible by walking or boating across Lake Awoonga.

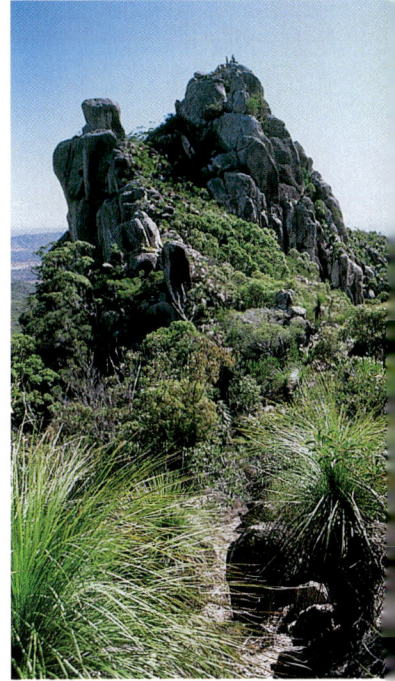

The Spire, Mt Castle Tower

Further information

QPWS
Floor 3, Centrepoint Building
136 Goondoon Street
PO Box 5065
GLADSTONE QLD 4680
ph (07) 4971 6500
fax (07) 4972 1993

Deepwater National Park

What's special?

This park protects sandy beaches, the catchment of near-pristine Deepwater Creek, one of the few remaining undisturbed freshwater streams in Queensland, and vegetation remnants in the coastal lowlands between Bundaberg and Agnes Water.

Paperbark forests, wallum heath and swamplands cover the western part of the park while tall forests of swamp mahogany, paperbark and cabbage palms fringe the creek. Patches of dry rainforest with weeping cabbage palms, Burdekin plums, vines and other rainforest plants flourish behind the high sand dunes. Beautiful open forests of wattles, Moreton Bay ash, banksias and other trees and shrubs grow further inland. Subtropical rainforest grows near the southern boundary of the park.

Deepwater Creek is stained tea-coloured by tannins leached from the surrounding heath communities. Parts of the creek flow only after rain.

Paul Candlin

Brahminy kite

Ross Naumann

Deepwater Creek

Deepwater National Park

Paul Candlin

Exploring Deepwater

Enjoy the peace and quiet of this unspoilt coastal retreat. Picnic behind the dunes at Wreck Rock. Toilets, tank water and picnic tables are provided.

Walk or fish along the vehicle-free beach. Explore the rockpools at Wreck Rock. If you swim, remember this beach is unpatrolled and beware of marine stingers between October and May.

Go birdwatching. Look for brahminy kites, glossy black-cockatoos, honeyeaters and emus. Canoe along the everglade-like waters of Deepwater Creek just outside the park's southern boundary, 5·5km south of Wreck Rock.

Bush camp at Wreck Rock or Middle Rock. Only Wreck Rock has facilities, including shady individual campsites, group campsites, a cold outdoor shower, untreated tap water, picnic tables and toilets. Take a fuel stove for cooking and drinking water for both camping areas. Remove your rubbish. Pay your fees at the self-registration stations. Book for Wreck Rock during the holidays. Sites are limited.

Walking

Walk along the beach from Wreck Rock. Watch for traffic if walking along any roads. Carry drinking water and wear a hat and sunscreen.

Getting there

Deepwater is on the coast between Agnes Water and Bundaberg. Access from the north is four-wheel-drive only. Turn off the Bruce Highway at Miriam Vale and drive to Agnes Water. Head south for 4km then turn right down a sandy track and drive 2km to the park boundary. Continue to Flat Rock, Middle Rock and Wreck Rock camping area.

From Bundaberg, take the Rosedale-1770 Road about 58km almost to Berajondo. Turn right 500m before Berajondo into Hills Road then drive 19·2km to a T-junction. Turn right into Coast Road. Continue for 5·6km then turn left into Fernfield Road. Travel 7·5km then turn left into Deepwater Road. After 10·5km, cross the ford, swing right then turn left into Wreck Rock Road and continue 5·5km to the Wreck Rock turnoff. Conventional access is possible to Wreck Rock from the south in dry weather. The road through the park is unsuitable for conventional vehicles or caravans north of Wreck Rock.

Darren Jew
See emus in the park.

Further information

General enquiries and bookings:
QPWS
PO Box 1735
BUNDABERG QLD 4670
ph (07) 4131 1600
fax (07) 4131 1620

Local information only:
QPWS
Captain Cook Drive
PO Box 177
AGNES WATER QLD 4677
ph (07) 4974 9350
fax (07) 4974 9400

Eurimbula National Park

What's special?

This beautiful stretch of coastline north of Agnes Water was the site of Cook's first landing in Queensland during his discovery voyage in 1770. Botanist Joseph Banks collected plant specimens from the area. Bustard Head was named after a bustard or plains turkey was shot in the vicinity.

Eurimbula's vegetation is special with species from the tropical north as well as southern species. The park has a variety of vegetation types from mangrove-fringed estuaries to freshwater paperbark swamps, lowland eucalypt woodlands with weeping cabbage palms, and tall rainforest with towering hoop pines.

The western part of this large park is rugged and inaccessible.

Exploring Eurimbula

Walk along the wide, sandy beach. Explore Eurimbula Creek by boat or canoe at high tide. Go fishing. If you swim at Bustard Beach, remember the beach is unpatrolled and beware of marine stingers between October and May.

See wildflowers in spring. Go birdwatching. See cormorants and white-breasted sea-eagles along the shore and look for red-tailed black-cockatoos and brolgas in the woodlands.

Enjoy the view over swamps, heathlands and the parallel sand dunes from Ganoonga Noonga Lookout. On a clear day you can see from Round Hill Head to Rodd's Peninsula.

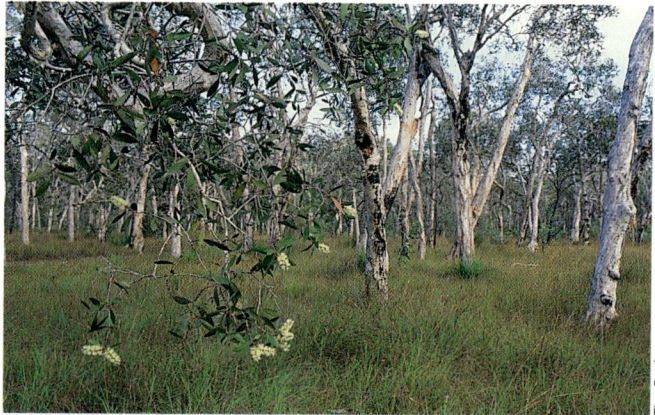

Darren Jew

Melaleuca flower

Tim Peek

Paperbark woodland, Eurimbula

Eurimbula National Park

Paul Cradlin

Camp at Bustard Beach or Middle Creek. Bustard Beach has individual shady campsites, toilets and limited tank water. Middle Creek has no facilities. Pay your fees at the self-registration station. During holidays, book your Bustard Beach campsite in advance through the Bundaberg office. Take water and a fuel stove for cooking. Remove your rubbish. Take plenty of insect repellent.

Bush camping is allowed at Rodd's Peninsula and Bustard Head. Access is by boat or walking only.

Walking

A 360m track leads from a carpark (3km from the park entrance along the Bustard Beach track) uphill to Ganoonga Noonga Lookout. From the lookout, you can see along the coast from Rodd's Peninsula south to Agnes Water.

Getting there

Eurimbula is about one hour north-east of Miriam Vale. Turn off the Bruce Highway at Miriam Vale and drive 46km towards Agnes Water. Turn left at the park sign into Eurimbula Road and travel 4km to the park entrance. A 10km bush track leads to Bustard Beach camping area at the mouth of Eurimbula Creek. Access is possible by conventional vehicles with high clearance in dry weather but four-wheel-drive is recommended after rain. Access is unsuitable for caravans. Middle Creek is 15km from the park boundary along a rough, four-wheel-drive track, accessible only in dry weather. The closest places for supplies are Town of 1770, 4km by boat, or Agnes Water 24km by road from Bustard Beach.

Steve Parish

Australian bustard

Further information

General enquiries and bookings:
QPWS
PO Box 1735
BUNDABERG QLD 4670
ph (07) 4131 1600
fax (07) 4131 1620

Local information only:
QPWS
Captain Cook Drive
PO Box 177
AGNES WATER QLD 4677
ph (07) 4974 9350
fax (07) 4974 9400

Joseph Banks Conservation Park

View from Round Hill Head

Tim Peek

What's special?

This historic coastal peninsula near Agnes Water is a little-known jewel on the central Queensland coast. The rocky headland is bounded by ocean on the east and still waters to the west. The estuary side of Round Hill Head was the site of Lieutenant James Cook's first landing in Queensland on 24 May 1770.

Wind-swept tussock grasslands, small patches of dry vine forest and low woodlands with she-oaks, pandanus, acacias, banksias and eucalypts grow in the park. The surrounding waters are protected in the Great Barrier Reef Marine Park.

Exploring Joseph Banks

Enjoy the natural beauty of this picturesque coastal park. Be careful exploring around the beaches. Tragedies have occurred in the unpatrolled waters and walking around the crumbling and uneven cliff edges can be dangerous.

Stop briefly at the rock cairn monument to Cook's first Queensland landfall then continue 1km up the road to the tracks and lookouts at Round Hill Head. Enjoy the magnificent view north across Eurimbula National Park to Bustard Head and Rodd's Peninsula.

Watch for turtles and dolphins in the clear aquamarine waters below the lookout. See the occasional migrating humpback whale offshore or white-breasted sea-eagles soaring overhead.

Picnic facilities and toilets are provided just outside the park on the foreshore at the Town of 1770. Camping is not allowed in the park but you can stay nearby at the Town of 1770 and Agnes Water.

Walking

Walk 250m through tussock grassland, vine thicket and coastal woodland to a lookout at the tip of the headland. Detour to another lookout over a small sandy cove on your return. The gravel tracks are suitable for strollers but too steep for wheelchairs. Wear a hat and sunscreen.

Joseph Banks Conservation Park

Bottlenose dolphin

Getting there

Joseph Banks is at the Town of 1770, just north of Agnes Water. Turn off the Bruce Highway at Miriam Vale. The park office is at the edge of the park 5km north of Agnes Water and 1·5km south of the monument.

Further information

General enquiries and bookings:
QPWS
PO Box 1735
BUNDABERG QLD 4670
ph (07) 4131 1600
fax (07) 4131 1620

Local information only:
QPWS
Captain Cook Drive
PO Box 177
AGNES WATER QLD 4677
ph (07) 4974 9350
fax (07) 4974 9400

Bulburin Forest Reserve

What's special?

Rugged, high country in the Many Peaks Range is protected in Bulburin Forest Reserve. Mt Boreen Boreen is the highest point.

About half of the forest is covered in beautiful subtropical rainforest, dense stands of dry rainforest with emerging hoop pines, and gallery rainforest. Together, they form the largest rainforest remnant in central Queensland.

The rest of the forest contains open eucalypt forest and woodland and tall open forest with a rainforest understorey. Dry open forests with New England blackbutt, spotted gum and white mahogany grow on the more exposed western ridges and foothills. Mature hoop pine plantations in the State forest are being harvested for timber.

A variety of wildlife lives in the forest including wompoo pigeons, red-necked and red-legged pademelons and orange-eyed green treefrogs. Rare and threatened species like the long-nosed potoroo have also been reported.

The forest protects the catchments for the Boyne and Kolan Rivers and Baffle and Granite Creeks.

Wompoo pigeon

Darren Jew

Exploring Bulburin

Experience one of the best subtropical rainforest remnants in Queensland in this undeveloped forest.

Go birdwatching. See red-crowned pigeons, noisy pittas, regent bowerbirds, satin bowerbirds and paradise riflebirds in the rainforest.

Bush camp along the ridge among planted bunya pines on the site of the former Forestry barracks. No facilities are provided apart from a picnic platform, so campers must be totally self-sufficient. Take drinking water and a fuel stove. Obtain your camping permit beforehand.

Go for a scenic drive through the forest. A four-wheel-drive loop road passes through the rainforest. You must obtain a permit to traverse before driving through the forest.

Bulburin Forest Reserve

Adam Creek

Walking

No tracks are provided. Wear insect repellent when walking in the rainforest.

Getting there

Bulburin is 50km north-east of Monto. Conventional access is possible from Builyan on the Monto-Gladstone Road. Turn at the Dalga Road and continue along the Bulburin Forest Road to the campground, 16km from Builyan. A through route leads 33km to the Bruce Highway. Turn off the highway at Granite Creek Forest Road near the Granite Creek rest area, 64km north of Gin Gin or 38km south of Miriam Vale. This access road is four-wheel-drive only.

Further information

QPWS
Floor 3, Centrepoint Building
136 Goondoon Street
PO Box 5065
GLADSTONE QLD 4860
ph (07) 4971 6500
fax (07) 4972 1993

Paul Candlin

Orange-eyed green treefrog

Capricorn Coast National Park

View towards Bluff Point

Paul Candlin

Tracks

Double Head
730m return, 30 minutes

Bluff Point
2·3km circuit, 45 minutes–1 hour

Further information

QPWS
61 Yeppoon Road
PARKHURST
PO Box 3130
ROCKHAMPTON SHOPPING FAIR
QLD 4701
ph (07) 4936 0511
fax (07) 4936 2171

QPWS
1683 Byfield Rd
BYFIELD QLD 4703
ph (07) 4935 1243
fax (07) 4935 1205

QPWS
John Howes Drive
Rosslyn Bay
PO Box 770
YEPPOON QLD 4703
ph (07) 4933 6595
fax (07) 4933 6619

What's special?

Rocky outcrops along the Capricorn Coast were formed by volcanic eruptions about 130 million years ago.

Five reserves south of Yeppoon are protected in this small park — Double Head, Rosslyn Head, Bluff Point and Pinnacle Point, south of Yeppoon, and Vallis Park to the north. Vallis Park has no public access.

The park protects a variety of vegetation types from windswept low heath with scattered pandanus and she-oaks to eucalypt/wattle open forest, dry rainforest, tussock grassland and mangroves.

Exploring Capricorn Coast

Go for a scenic drive south of Yeppoon, stopping at Double Head or Bluff Point for a bushwalk or picnic.

Next to Rosslyn Bay Harbour, explore Double Head along a sealed 365m walking track which zig-zags up through tangled dry vine thicket and tussock grassland to two lookouts. See the striking fan-shaped cliff formation with hexagonal basalt columns at Fan Rock Lookout, a reminder of the park's volcanic past. Continue to the Rosslyn Bay Lookout for views over this scenic coastline.

Go birdwatching at Rosslyn Head or Bluff Point. You might see brush-turkeys, rufous shrike-thrushes, white-bellied sea-eagles or honeyeaters.

Have a picnic or barbecue on the shore at Bluff Point. Gas barbecues, picnic tables, tap water and toilets are provided. Walk to the lookouts for views over the Keppel Bay islands and Capricorn coastline. Look for dolphins or turtles in the waters below.

Camping is not allowed in the park but you can stay nearby at Yeppoon or Byfield.

Accessibility

Wheelchair-assisted toilets and a wheelchair-accessible picnic table are provided at Bluff Point.

Getting there

Capricorn Coast is south of Yeppoon. See all the park's sections in a short half-hour drive from Yeppoon to Emu Park.

Curtis Island National Park and Conservation Park

What's special?

Off the central Queensland coast between Rockhampton and Gladstone lies Curtis Island. The north-eastern end of this large island is Curtis Island National Park.

A variety of vegetation types grows in the park from heath, grassland, stunted paperbark woodland and open eucalypt forest to extensive patches of dry rainforest.

An historic lighthouse is located at Cape Capricorn.

Exploring Curtis Island

Camp at Yellow Patch. This natural sandblow with bright yellow sand provides a sheltered anchorage for boats. Visitors must be self-sufficient. Obtain your camping permit beforehand. Take drinking water and a fuel stove. Remove your rubbish.

Go fishing or birdwatching.

Walking

There are no tracks but you can spend two to three days hiking along the east coast of the island. Tell someone your plans in case of emergency.

Getting there

The park is accessible only by boat from Gladstone or The Narrows.

Further information

QPWS
Floor 3, Centrepoint Building
136 Goondoon Street
PO Box 5065
GLADSTONE QLD 4680
ph (07) 4971 6500
fax (07) 4972 1993

QPWS
John Howes Drive
Rosslyn Bay
PO Box 770
YEPPOON QLD 4703
ph (07) 4933 6595
fax (07) 4933 6619

QPWS
61 Yeppoon Road
Parkhurst
PO Box 3130
ROCKHAMPTON SHOPPING FAIR
QLD 4701
ph (07) 4936 0511
fax (07) 4936 2171

See brolgas in the wetlands.

Darren Jew

Keppel Bay Islands National Park

Pied oyster-catcher

Paul Candlin

What's special?

The broad sweep of Keppel Bay from Curtis Island to Corio Bay in the central Queensland coast is dotted with a scenic group of 18 islands. Most are protected in Keppel Bay Islands National Park. Steep hills, plunging cliffs, secluded beaches, crystal-clear waters and diverse plant communities are some of the park's attractions.

North Keppel Island has a wonderful variety of plants and vegetation communities including mangroves, palm forests, rainforest, paperbark woodlands, open forests and woodlands with a grasstree understorey, heath, grasslands and dune vegetation. This is the only island in Queensland with such dense stands of weeping cabbage tree palms. Lemon-scented gums also only occur on this continental island. Humpy Island is mainly covered in windswept grasslands and stunted heath.

The surrounding waters are protected in the Great Barrier Reef Marine Park.

Aboriginal people lived on North Keppel Island about 4500 years ago. Remains of the seafoods they gathered and ate are scattered around the shoreline and some of the most significant archaeological sites in the Great Barrier Reef are located on North Keppel Island. Cook named the islands after Rear Admiral Keppel in 1770.

Exploring Keppel Bay Islands

You can bush camp on North Keppel, Humpy, Middle, Miall, Conical, Divided and Pelican Islands. Campers must be self-sufficient. Take drinking water, food, a fuel stove and two-way radio or mobile phone for emergency. If camping on North Keppel, take insect repellent. Remove all rubbish from the park.

The camping areas at Considine Beach, North Keppel Island and the northern beach of Humpy Island have toilets, tap water and cold bush showers. Please do not feed the brushtail possums on North Keppel and store food securely. Middle, Miall and Conical Islands have picnic tables. Divided and Pelican Islands have no facilities.

Keppel Bay Islands National Park

Ross Naumann

Discover the different plant communities along a self-guiding trail between Considine Beach and Mazie Bay on North Keppel Island. Walk to the Keppel Bay Lookout for a view over Mazie Bay and other Keppel islands.

Go birdwatching. See white-bellied sea-eagles, brahminy kites or collared sparrowhawks overhead, terns and pied oystercatchers along the shore and honeyeaters, rainbow bee-eaters and pheasant coucals in the heaths and woodlands. Listen for the mournful cry of the bush stone-curlews.

Go snorkelling or reef walking over the fringing reefs at Mazie Bay (North Keppel), Olive Point headland (Middle Island), Humpy Island or Miall Island. Be careful not to damage the coral. Beware of marine stingers which may be present in the sea from October to May. Restrictions apply to fishing, spear fishing and collecting in the marine park waters.

Education Queensland operates an environmental education centre on North Keppel Island. The centre provides residential educational programs for schools. Contact the centre for details and bookings (07) 4939 2510, www.nkieec.qld.edu.au

Walking

Wear a hat, sunscreen and insect repellent when walking. Take drinking water.

Getting there

Keppel Bay Islands are 15km offshore from Yeppoon. Access is by private boat or charter boat from the Keppel Bay Marina.

Tracks

Considine Beach to Mazie Bay
4·2km return, 1·5 hours

Considine Beach to Keppel Bay Lookout
3·2km return, 1 hour

Further information

QPWS
61 Yeppoon Road
Parkhurst
PO Box 3130
ROCKHAMPTON SHOPPING FAIR
QLD 4701
ph (07) 4936 0511
fax (07) 4936 2212

Campsite bookings: 13 13 04 or www.qld.gov.au/camping

View of North Keppel Island from Conical Island

Tom Mumbray

Byfield National Park and Five Rocks Conservation Park

Swamp banksia
Adam Creed

What's special?

A picturesque sweep of coastline and long, sandy beaches backed by high sand dunes are protected in this central Queensland park. To the north, rugged granite peaks, Mt Atherton and The Peaks, rise above the sandy landscape.

Coastal heath, open woodlands and forests, paperbark swamps, mangroves and rainforest-fringed creeks add to this park's wonderful natural variety.

Tidal wetlands are protected in the southern end of the park around Sandy Point. Endangered little terns nest in this part of the park and vulnerable beach stone-curlews have also been seen.

Exploring Byfield

Relax and enjoy one of Queensland's most unspoilt stretches of coastline.

Go fishing or explore along Farnborough, Nine Mile or Three Rivers Beaches. Beware of marine stingers between October and May. Sandy Point to the south is a popular boating and fishing spot. Camping is not allowed.

Enjoy magnificent coastal views from headlands near Stockyard Point and Five Rocks.

Camp or picnic at Five Rocks, high above the beach, near Stockyard Point township. Cold bush showers, toilets and campsites are provided. Boil or treat the creek water before drinking. Take a fuel stove. Pay your camping fees onsite.

You can also camp on the inside of Water Park Point Headland and along the southern end of Nine Mile Beach. No facilities are provided. Take water and a fuel stove for cooking. Campers must remove all rubbish to the Byfield Ranger Station or take it home. Byfield township is the nearest place for fuel and supplies.

Walking

A 500m track follows Findlay's Creek down to a vehicle-free beach between Stockyard Point and Five Rocks. Allow two hours to walk to Five Rocks Headland and back. Walk around low tide. Access is not possible at high tide.

Byfield National Park and Five Rocks Conservation Park

Accessibility

The toilets at Five Rocks are wheelchair-accessible.

Getting there

Drive 30 minutes north from Yeppoon along the Yeppoon-Byfield Road then turn off and drive 2km to Waterpark Creek campground in Byfield State Forest. Continue 8km along a gravel road to the park entrance. Access from here is four-wheel-drive only and sand driving experience is necessary. Be careful driving in the soft sand and drive for minimal impact. Vehicle access off the Nine Mile Beach may be difficult.

The Sandy Point Section on Corio Bay is accessible by conventional vehicle. Turn right at the roundabout 5km north of Yeppoon and drive for 10km, past the resort. Turn right onto a gravel road at the T-junction and follow this road 10km to Sandy Point.

Further information

QPWS
61 Yeppoon Road, Parkhurst
PO Box 3130
ROCKHAMPTON SHOPPING FAIR
QLD 4701
ph (07) 4936 0511
fax (07) 4936 2171

QPWS
1683 Byfield Road
BYFIELD QLD 4703
ph (07) 4935 1243
fax (07) 4935 1205

Paul Candlin

Bush stone-curlew

Byfield State Forest

What's special?

South of the Shoalwater Bay Military Training Area, Byfield State Forest protects scenic coastal remnants and picturesque creeks next to Byfield National Park.

About one-third of the forest is covered in tall exotic pine plantations which are managed for timber production. Patches of rainforest grow in the ranges and along Waterpark Creek.

This multiple-use forest sustains a variety of commercial uses, including grazing, bee-keeping and timber production, as well as recreation. The distinctive Byfield fern prized by florists is harvested from the forest.

Exploring Byfield

Escape the summer heat and marine stingers in Byfield's crystal-clear and tea-coloured creeks. Wear insect repellent, especially after rain.

Choose from three camping areas with individual campsites, caravan sites and toilets. Bins are not provided so you must bag and remove your rubbish. Make sure you book and get your camping permit before you arrive at Waterpark Creek or Upper Stony camping areas. You can get your camping permit onsite at Red Rock only. Supplies are available at nearby Byfield township. Seek ranger advice about bush camping. Permits to traverse the forest or collect firewood are available from DPI Forestry at Byfield (07) 4935 1115.

Have a picnic or camp by Waterpark Creek. Picnic tables, barbecues and toilets are provided. Two van sites are available. Be careful: bullrouts, freshwater stonefish, live in the creek and can cause a nasty sting. Wear shoes, even when wading. If stung, immerse the affected area in hot (not scalding) water for 20 minutes before seeking medical advice.

You can also camp or picnic at Red Rock. Picnic tables, wood barbecues, water and toilets are provided. Grassy sites in the pine plantation are suitable for vans and motorhomes. Dogs are permitted overnight. Swim with care at Red Rock, a clear, running creek. Do not jump or dive into any waterholes.

Byfield ferns at Waterpark Creek

Ross Naumann

Byfield State Forest

Paul Candlin

Upper Stony camping area is suitable for large groups. Picnic facilities are provided on the other side of the creek. The waterhole is popular in summer. Never dive or jump into the water here and beware of bullrouts.

For your safety, do not go on roads marked "no access". Off-road access is not allowed.

Walking

At Waterpark Creek, walk 300m through the rainforest to the creek. At Red Rock, follow a short track down to the creek. Upper Stony has beautiful rainforest walks around the creek. All have steep sections and steps. Explore along the forestry roads with care.

Accessibility

Wheelchair-accessible toilets and picnic tables are provided at the Waterpark Creek, Red Rock and Upper Stony picnic and camping areas.

Getting there

Byfield is half an hour's drive north of Yeppoon or one hour from Rockhampton via the Yeppoon-Byfield Road. Turn off the sealed main road and drive a further 11km to Upper Stony, 1km to Red Rock and 2km to Waterpark Creek. Access is suitable for conventional vehicles and caravans.

Tracks

From Upper Stony picnic area:

Venusta circuit
900m, 30–45 minutes

Stony Creek circuit
4·3km, 1–2 hours

Freemans Crossing
4km return, 1–2 hours

Further information

QPWS
61 Yeppoon Road
PARKHURST
PO Box 3130
ROCKHAMPTON SHOPPING FAIR
QLD 4701
ph (07) 4936 0511
fax (07) 4936 2171

QPWS
1683 Byfield Road
BYFIELD QLD 4703
ph (07) 4935 1243
fax (07) 4935 1205

Driving permits: DPI Forestry (07) 4935 1115

Campsite bookings: 13 13 04 or www.qld.gov.au/camping

Waterpark Creek, Byfield State Forest

Ross Naumann

Mt Archer National Park

John Augusteyn

Unadorned rock-wallaby

What's special?

On Rockhampton's northern doorstep, Mt Archer National Park protects bushland remnants in the Berserker Ranges, a scenic backdrop to the city. Mt Archer (604m) is the highest peak.

Open forest clothes the mountain while lush subtropical rainforest grows in sheltered pockets, making this park a haven for wildlife.

This is the traditional land of the Darambul people who hunted game and gathered rainforest fruits along the creeks. Mt Archer was named after the early pioneers of the Rockhampton area.

Exploring Mt Archer

Escape the summer heat. Go for a scenic drive up the mountain. Have a picnic in Frazer Park, a local authority-run park on the summit. Picnic tables, shelter sheds, barbecues, firewood, toilets, water and bins are provided.

Enjoy views over the Berserker Range, Rockhampton and the coast from lookouts around the summit. Stay and watch the sunset over the city.

This is a great place for nature lovers. Beautiful rainforest trees, stately eucalypts, ferns, palms, cycads, grasstrees, paperbarks, she-oaks and flowering callistemons are some of the plants you will see if you take the time to explore the park.

See the different forests on the 11km walking track winding from the top of the mountain to the bottom. Arrange to be dropped off and collected. Walking back uphill is quite strenuous.

Relax beside the creek. Look for trout gudgeon and freshwater crays in the waterholes which fill after rain. At sunset, brush-tailed rock-wallabies come to drink. Go birdwatching. Forest fruits attract topknot, brown, wompoo and white-headed pigeons. Glossy black-cockatoos feast on casuarina seeds in summer.

Camping is not allowed in the park.

Mt Archer National Park

Paul Candlin

Walking

Some of the walks at Mt Archer involve a return uphill climb. Take drinking water. Wear a hat and sunscreen.

Accessibility

Frazer Park, on the summit of Mt Archer, has a 500m wheelchair track to two lookouts and wheelchair-accessible toilets and picnic tables.

Getting there

Mt Archer is on Rockhampton's northern outskirts. The summit is reached from Frenchville Road and Pilbeam Drive. The bottom entrance is off Old Norman Road and German Street.

View from Mt Archer summit

Tracks

Grasstree Lookout
1·4km, 30–45 minutes

Zamia walk
14km one-way, 4–5 hours

From the summit:
Sleipner Lookout
2·4km return,
45 minutes–1 hour

Rainforest edge
6km return, 2–2·5 hours

From the bottom:
Casuarina circuit
2km return, 45 minutes–1 hour

Swamp mahogany flats
5km return, 2–2·5 hours

Rainforest crossing
10km return, 3–3·5 hours

Further information

QPWS
61 Yeppoon Road
PARKHURST
PO Box 3130
ROCKHAMPTON SHOPPING FAIR
QLD 4701
ph (07) 4936 0511
fax (07) 4936 2171

Mt Etna Caves National Park

What's special?

Limestone outcrops and dense, decorated caves are protected in Mt Etna Caves National Park. Mt Etna is the roosting site for more than 80 percent of Australia's breeding population of little bent-wing bats. This is also one of the few places in Australia supporting a colony of the endangered ghost bat.

Seabed deposition, volcanic activity and erosion created this rugged karst landscape over millions of years. Grassland, open silver-leaved ironbark forest and semi-evergreen vine thicket grow in the park.

Mt Etna was named after the volcano in Sicily by the Archer Brothers who settled in the Rockhampton area in the 1850s. From 1914 to 1939, the caves were mined for guano, a natural fertiliser, and, from 1925, for limestone. During World War II, commandos trained here. The park was established from 1975 to protect the caves, and a subsequent campaign to save other caves protected Mt Etna.

Exploring Mt Etna Caves

Mt Etna is one of the few places in Queensland where you can go caving. Access to some caves is restricted or prohibited to protect the bats, which are very easily disturbed. Johanssen's Cave is closed between 1 June and 31 January. Caves are a very special environment and easily damaged. Visitors are asked to protect the caves by not touching the limestone while caving.

When caving, go in groups of at least three people and make sure there are at least three torches or light sources within your group. Temperatures inside the caves are fairly constant and cool, so caving is a great way to escape the summer heat.

Have a picnic at Cammoo where toilets, electric barbecues and picnic tables are provided.

Guided night tours of Bat Cleft on Mt Etna operate every summer (December to February) when you can see the spectacular nightly emergence of thousands of little bent-wing bats searching for food. Fees apply.

Ghost bat

Steve Parish

Mt Etna Caves National Park

Robert Ashdown

Paul Candlin

Mt Etna

Ross Naumann

Entrance to Johanssen's Cave

Explore Limestone Ridge. Wear sturdy shoes to protect you from the sharp rocks if walking off-track. The Bat Cleft track is a safer option and provides ready access to the vine thicket and the limestone karst.

Go wildlife watching. Look for brush-tailed rock-wallabies, brushtail possums, bandicoots and echidnas. Go birdwatching. More than 75 bird species have been seen in the park.

Guided cave tours are available at Capricorn Caves outside the park (07) 4934 2883, www.capricorncaves.com.au

Walking

The 1·2km track uphill to Bat Cleft is quite strenuous with many steps. Only relatively fit people should attempt this walk or join the Bat Cleft tour. Walk in the cooler months or early morning to avoid the heat. This track is closed to visitors during the breeding season, 1 November to the end of February, when the tours operate. A 400m track leads to Johanssen's Cave.

Accessibility

The Cammoo picnic area has wheelchair-accessible toilets and a picnic table.

Getting there

Mt Etna Caves is just north of Rockhampton and about three hours south of Mackay. Turn off the Bruce Highway 24km north of Rockhampton or 11km south of Yaamba to The Caves township. The park entrance is a further 2km along the Barmoya and Cammoo Caves Roads.

Further information

QPWS
61 Yeppoon Road
PARKHURST
PO Box 3130
ROCKHAMPTON SHOPPING FAIR
QLD 4701
ph (07) 4936 0511
fax (07) 4936 2171

Mt Jim Crow National Park

Towards the summit of Mt Jim Crow

Paul Candlin

What's special?

Volcanic activity created Mt Jim Crow, a trachyte plug protected in Mt Jim Crow National Park. The base and lower slopes of this impressive dome are covered in semi-evergreen vine thickets and hoop pines tower over the dry rainforest.

Mt Jim Crow is important to the local Aboriginal people. A dreaming legend tells the story of how this mountain was created by the rainbow serpent.

Exploring Mt Jim Crow

Stop on your way between Yeppoon and Rockhampton and tackle the rough trail up this mountain. A walking track leads to a quarry at the base of the mountain and a rough scramble takes experienced climbers to the summit.

Walking

Only experienced walkers should attempt this climb and only in dry weather.

Getting there

Mt Jim Crow is 29km east of Rockhampton, about halfway along the Rockhampton to Yeppoon Road.

Mt Jim Crow from Yeppoon Road

Paul Candlin

Further information

QPWS
61 Yeppoon Road
PARKHURST
PO Box 3130
ROCKHAMPTON SHOPPING FAIR
QLD 4701
ph (07) 4936 0511
fax (07) 4936 2171

Capricornia Cays National Park

What's special?

At the southern end of the Great Barrier Reef, Capricornia Cays National Park protects nine vegetated coral islands or cays. These islands were formed from the ancient remains of animals and plants which once lived in the surrounding reefs. At 100ha, North West is the second largest cay in the Great Barrier Reef.

Pandanus palms and beach she-oaks grow in the open woodland while pisonia trees dominate the dense central forest. North West has one of the most extensive pisonia forests in the world. Masthead has the most diverse vegetation and is the most natural island.

The coral reefs have built up over nearly two million years. A marine park was declared over Heron and nearby Wistari Reefs in 1974. The islands are important rookeries for nesting seabirds and endangered green and loggerhead turtles in summer. Roseate and black-naped terns nest on the islands and migratory birds visit in summer.

Heron Island was named during the 1843 "Fly" survey expedition. Guano mining devastated most of the islands during the late 19th century and a turtle soup industry operated on North West from 1910 until 1928. A resort was established on Heron in 1932 and the Research Station began in 1951. The islands became a park in 1938.

Today, Capricornia Cays National Park is part of the Great Barrier Reef World Heritage Area and the surrounding waters are protected in marine park. These clear waters are rich in marine life and popular for snorkelling and diving.

Sea star

Exploring Capricornia Cays

Bush camp in defined camping areas on Lady Musgrave, North West and Masthead Islands. Toilets are provided on Lady Musgrave and North West Islands. Take fresh water and a fuel stove for cooking. Open fires and generators are prohibited. All rubbish must be removed to the mainland. Take extra food and water in case you are stranded by bad weather. For safety, take a broadcast radio, spare batteries and medical supplies.

Seasonal closures apply to protect turtles and seabirds.

Capricornia Cays National Park

Paul Candlin

Darren Jew

Lady Musgrave Island

Tracks

Lady Musgrave Island track
500m one-way,
30 minutes return

North West Island track
800m one-way,
40 minutes return

Further information

QPWS
Floor 3, Centrepoint Building
136 Goondoon Street
PO Box 5065
GLADSTONE QLD 4810
ph (07) 4971 6500
fax (07) 4972 1993

Campsite bookings: 13 13 04 or
www.qld.gov.au/camping

North West and Lady Musgrave Islands are closed to camping from the day after the Australia Day long weekend until Good Friday. Masthead Island is closed to all visitors from October 14 until Good Friday. Tryon Island is temporarily closed to camping.

Go birdwatching. You might see reef egrets, black noddies, buff-banded rails, bar-shouldered doves, silver gulls, rose-crowned fruit pigeons and silvereyes.

Watch the fascinating dawn exodus of the noisy wedge-tailed shearwaters in summer. Stay out of signposted seabird nesting areas. Watch turtles nest and hatch in summer but use no torches to avoid disturbing the turtles.

Go reef walking, diving or snorkelling. Wear diving boots to protect the coral. Beware of strong currents and changing tides. (Dive compressors may be used only between 9am and 6pm on North West and Lady Musgrave Islands.) Observe fishing and collecting restrictions.

Learn about the island's history and wildlife at the information display on Lady Musgrave Island.

Walking

Trails are provided on North West and Lady Musgrave Islands and walkers can return along the beaches. Take drinking water. Wear a hat and sunscreen. Wear shoes when walking on the coral rubble beaches. Wear sturdy shoes if reef walking and walk only on sand to protect the coral.

Accessibility

The toilet on Lady Musgrave Island is wheelchair-accessible.

Getting there

The Capricornia Cays are 60–100km offshore north-east of Gladstone. Lady Musgrave and North West Islands are accessible by private boat or charter boat.

Mt Scoria Conservation Park

What's special?

Rising 150m above the cultivated plains, Mt Scoria is a striking local landmark protected in Mt Scoria National Park. Formed by volcanic activity 20–26 million years ago, this volcanic plug features many-sided basalt columns.

This small park in Queensland's brigalow belt contains open woodlands with poplar gums, Moreton Bay ash, forest red gums and silver-leaved ironbarks and small patches of brigalow. An open semi-evergreen vine thicket growing on rocky slopes towards the summit and around the base of the mountain is a relict of much wetter times. This vegetation is now uncommon in central eastern Queensland.

Mt Scoria is part of the traditional lands of the Gangulu people.

Exploring Mt Scoria

Have a bush picnic. Picnic shelters, tables, toilets, tank water, wood barbecues and bins are provided. Go birdwatching or simply enjoy the local wildlife.

Please do not strike the basalt columns as this can cause substantial damage. Camping is not allowed in the park.

Walking

No tracks are provided. Beware of the loose scree slopes if you climb to the top of the mountain.

Getting there

Mt Scoria is 6km south of Thangool near Biloela in central Queensland. Access is from the Burnett Highway.

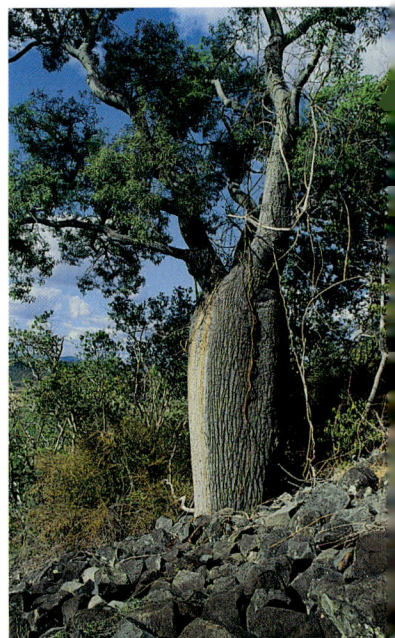

Bottle tree scrub on Mt Scoria

Further information

QPWS
61 Yeppoon Road
PARKHURST
PO Box 3130
ROCKHAMPTON SHOPPING FAIR
QLD 4701
ph (07) 4936 0511
fax (07) 4936 2171

QPWS
Floor 3, Centrepoint Building
136 Goondoon Street
PO Box 5065
GLADSTONE QLD 4860
ph (07) 4971 6500
fax (07) 4972 1933

Kroombit Tops National Park and Forest Reserve

What's special?

Rugged mountain scenery, sandstone cliffs and gorges, creeks, waterfalls and a variety of vegetation types are protected in two adjacent reserves on the 800–900m high Kroombit Tops Plateau. This large protected area is the headwaters for many creeks and a refuge for wildlife including tropical and subtropical rainforest species and animals close to the limit of their usual range. The Kroombit tinkerfrog *Taudactylus pleione*, which is vulnerable to extinction, lives in the rainforest.

Most of the plateau is covered in dry woodland with a heath understorey. Open forests of white mahogany are common. Subtropical rainforest with piccabeen palms grows in sheltered pockets on the wetter eastern side of the plateau. Kroombit Tops is the northern limit of cool temperate white beech rainforest. Dry rainforest with towering hoop pines and tall wet sclerophyll forests with Sydney blue gums grow in the central part of the plateau. Dry bottle tree scrubs grow on the drier western side of he plateau.

Kroombit Tops is the site of a large erosion caldera up to 40m across, formed by past volcanic activity.

Exploring Kroombit Tops

Kroombit Tops is a low-key destination for self-sufficient visitors. Few facilities are provided and most of the park is rugged wilderness. Mobile phone reception points are signposted throughout the forest.

Bush camp at The Wall along the circuit drive or at Griffiths Creek along the forest drive. Campfires are allowed but no facilities are provided. Take drinking water. Creek flow is seasonal. Get your camping permit before you arrive.

Enjoy the view from a lookout on the eastern escarpment. On a clear day, you have stunning views over the Boyne Valley.

Go for a 90-minute scenic drive on a loop road through the park. Most of this circuit is four-wheel-drive only. Allow two hours for the drive. Find out about the tragic plane crash during World War II on the western side of the plateau.

View from a lookout along the forest drive

John Augusteyn

Kroombit Tops National Park and Forest Reserve

Signs help you understand what happened. You must obtain a permit to traverse before driving through the forest.

See the subtropical rainforest and cool temperate rainforest just past the lookout.

Go birdwatching. Glossy black-cockatoos feed in the casuarinas. Enjoy the wildflowers in spring.

A four-wheel-drive road from Cania Gorge is another scenic drive for day-trippers. Horse riding is allowed by permit along the National Bicentennial Trail.

Nights can be cool, especially in winter.

Walking

A 700m return track along the four-wheel-drive scenic drive leads to the site of a 1945 bomber plane crash. Rough tracks lead to other features but should only be attempted with Ranger advice. Be prepared for leeches if you walk through the rainforest.

Getting there

Kroombit Tops is 2·5 hours' drive south-west of Rockhampton via the Bruce Highway, Calliope and the unsealed Tableland Road. Calliope, one hour away, is the closest centre for fuel and supplies. A four-wheel-drive road provides access from Ubobo where fuel and food are also available.

John Augusteyn

Eastern tube-nosed bat

"Beautiful Betsy" crash site

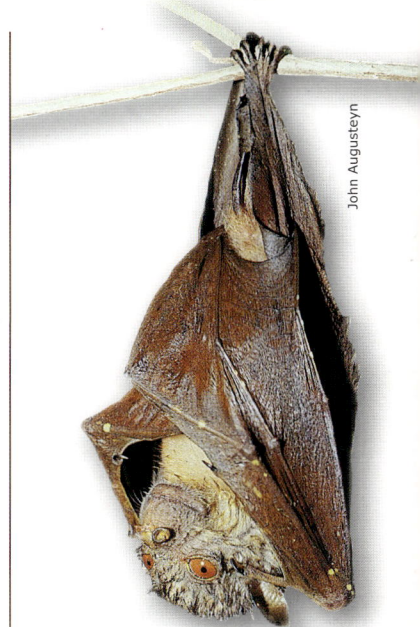

Further information

QPWS
61 Yeppoon Road
PARKHURST
PO Box 3130
ROCKHAMPTON SHOPPING FAIR
QLD 4701
ph (07) 4936 0511
fax (07) 4936 2171

QPWS
Floor 3, Centrepoint Building
136 Goondoon Street
PO Box 5065
GLADSTONE QLD 4860
ph (07) 4971 6500
fax (07) 4972 1993

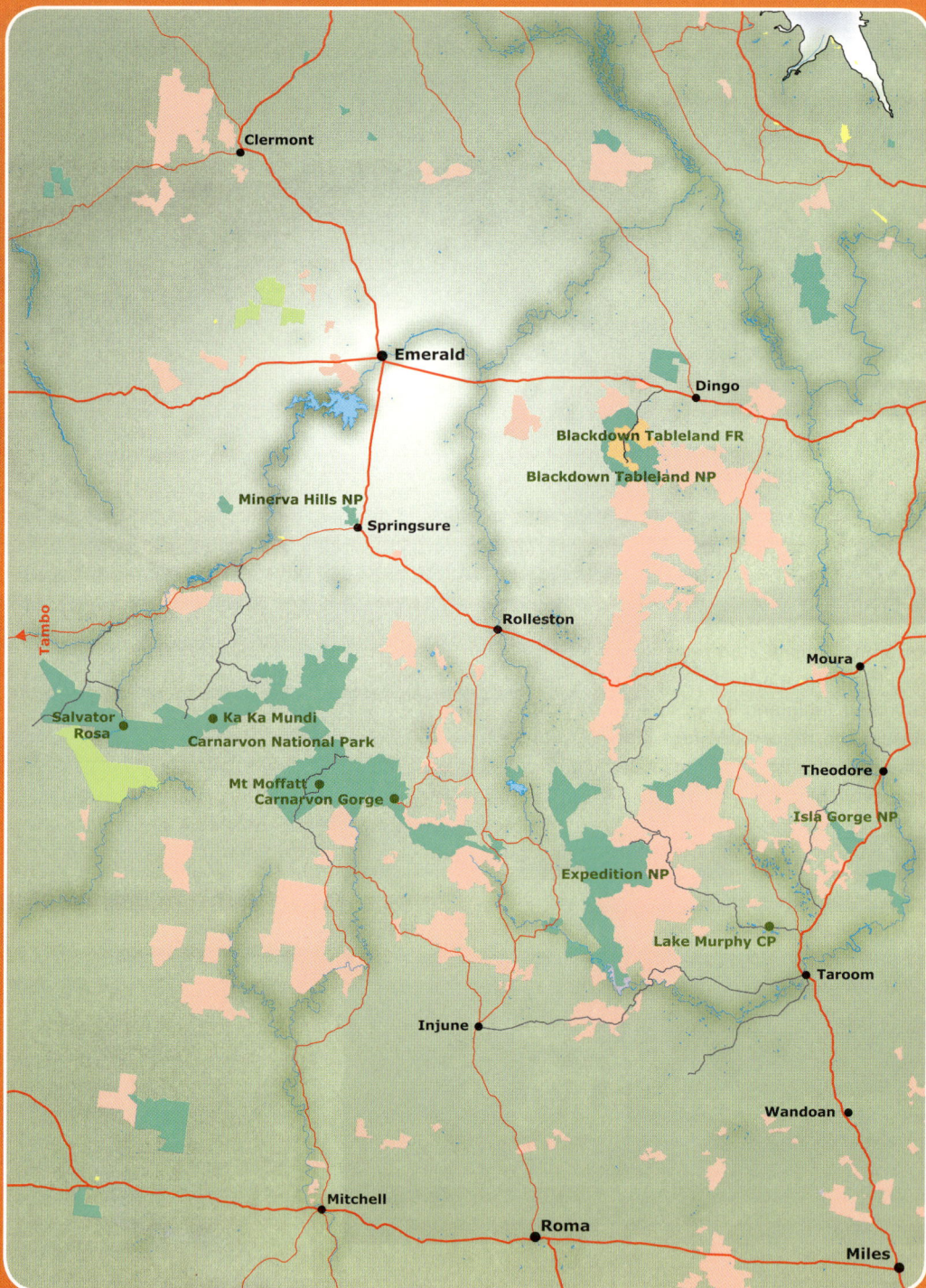

Central Highlands

Map 7

Legend

National Park	State Forest	Highway
Conservation Park	Timber Reserve	Major connecting road
Forest Reserve	Resource Reserve	Minor access road

0   30   60
km

N

Clermont

Emerald

Dingo

Blackdown Tableland FR

Blackdown Tableland NP

Minerva Hills NP

Springsure

Tambo

Rolleston

Moura

Salvator Rosa

Ka Ka Mundi

Carnarvon National Park

Theodore

Mt Moffatt

Carnarvon Gorge

Isla Gorge NP

Expedition NP

Lake Murphy CP

Taroom

Injune

Wandoan

Mitchell

Roma

Miles

Minerva Hills National Park

What's special?

Spectacular jagged peaks provide a scenic backdrop to Springsure in this park in central Queensland. Formed by volcanic activity millions of years ago, Mt Boorambool and cliff-fringed Mt Zamia today dominate the landscape.

In the grassy open woodlands, mountain coolibah, silver-leaved ironbark and gum-topped bloodwood tower over macrozamias and grasstrees. Dry rainforest with figs, stinging trees, pittosporums and vines flourishes in sheltered gorges and at the base of the sheer cliffs. Spinifex grasslands dotted with wattles grow on the summit. The park also supports spotted gum forests and low-lying heath.

Minerva Hills is home to many unusual wildlife including the eastern pebble-mound mouse and fawn-footed melomys.

Stone scatters and rock art are evidence of Aboriginal occupation of this area. Early wagon teams camped near here en route to Rockhampton.

Exploring Minerva Hills

Have a bush picnic with a view at Fred's Gorge. Bring wood for the barbecues. You can also picnic at Springsure Lookout and other sites. Take a fuel stove.

Go wildlife watching during the day. Take your camera and binoculars. See grazing kangaroos and wallabies. If you are lucky, you may spot a koala. Go spotlighting at night to see sugar gliders and greater gliders.

Enjoy panoramic views over the surrounding countryside from lookouts in the park.

Walking

A 2·2km walking track leads to a lookout. Let someone reliable know your plans if you intend walking off-track.

Getting there

Travel 4km west of Springsure on the Tambo road then turn left into Dendle's Drive. Follow this short scenic drive to the park. This unsealed road provides conventional access in dry weather but is unsuitable for caravans.

Paul Candlin

Sugar glider

Further information

QPWS
25 Porphyry Street
PO Box 157
SPRINGSURE QLD 4722
ph (07) 4984 1716
fax (07) 4984 1173

QPWS
99 Hospital Road
PO Box 906
EMERALD QLD 4720
ph (07) 4982 4555
fax (07) 4982 2568

Blackdown Tableland National Park

What's special?

Rising abruptly above the surrounding dry plains, Blackdown Tableland protects spectacular sandstone scenery with gorges and waterfalls at the north-eastern edge of the central Queensland sandstone belt.

Woodlands, tall open forests and heath cover the tableland, providing a home for a variety of plants and animals, several found nowhere else, such as the Blackdown stringybark, a macrozamia, red bottlebrush, the Blackdown "monster" (a type of underground cricket), and a Christmas beetle.

Ferns grow around creeks and gorges. The sheer-drop waterfall at Stony Creek Gorge is dry most of the year.

This is the traditional home of the Ghungalu people who have visited this place for thousands of years and left behind rock art, vivid reminders of their special culture.

The park also contains interesting relics of the park's grazing past. Forest reserve surrounds the park.

Paul Candlin

Rainbow Falls Gorge

Exploring Blackdown Tableland

Stop and enjoy the view over the surrounding grazing lands from Horseshoe Lookout. Read the displays to help you plan your visit.

Discover Aboriginal culture and see the stencil art along the Mimosa Creek cultural trail. Fit walkers can walk through open forest to a spectacular gorge at the bottom of Rainbow Falls. Cool off in the rockpool. Be prepared for a steep climb back.

Have a picnic at Horseshoe Lookout or South Mimosa Creek after your walk. Take drinking water. Remove your rubbish.

Go for a scenic four-wheel-drive around the Loop Road (19km, 1–1·5 hours) in dry weather. See dry open woodland with magnificent sandstone outcrops sheltering king orchids and basket ferns. Stop at Charlevue Lookout for great views over the brigalow belt.

Look for wildlife around the creeks or go spotlighting at night. Wildflower season is one of the best times to visit.

Blackdown Tableland National Park

Enjoy panoramic views from the tableland.

Paul Candlin

Camp in the forest at South Mimosa Creek. Campsites for tents and off-road camper trailers are provided. Be prepared - winter nights can be cold and summer days, quite hot. Take drinking water and a fuel stove. Please do not feed the birds. Let them find their own food. Bookings are taken three months in advance for school and public holidays.

An emergency phone is located at the ranger base opposite Horseshoe Lookout.

Walking

Walking tracks take you to heritage sites, creeks and lookouts. Wear a hat and sunscreen and carry water. Talk to the ranger about possible overnight hikes. Register and pay camping fees before undertaking overnight hikes.

Accessibility

The lookout, picnic tables and toilets at Horsehoe Lookout are wheelchair-accessible.

Getting there

Blackdown Tableland is about 2·5 hours' drive west of Rockhampton via the Capricorn Highway. The park turnoff is 11km west of Dingo, 110km east of Emerald or 35km east of Blackwater. The 8km climb up the Tableland is steep, winding and slippery and unsuitable for towing caravans. The camping area is a further 8km. Conventional access to most of the park is possible with care but four-wheel-drive is necessary around the loop road to Charlevue Lookout. Access may be restricted during wet weather or high fire danger.

Tracks

Two Mile Falls
4km return, 1–1·5 hours

Mimosa culture track
2·8km return, 1 hour

Officers Pocket
2·4km return, 45 mins

Rainbow Falls
4km return, 1–2 hours

Rock Holes
4km return, 1 hour 30 minutes

Stony Creek Gorge
10km return, 3–4 hours

Further information

Blackdown Tableland NP
Via DINGO QLD 4702
ph (07) 4986 1964
fax (07) 4986 1325
UHF channel 6
7.30am–4pm

QPWS
61 Yeppoon Road, Parkhurst
PO Box 3130
ROCKHAMPTON SHOPPING FAIR
QLD 4701
ph (07) 4936 0511
fax (07) 4936 2212

QPWS
99 Hospital Road
PO Box 906
EMERALD QLD 4720
ph (07) 4982 4555
fax (07) 4982 2568

Isla Gorge National Park

Whiptail wallaby

Paul Candlin

What's special?

At the southern end of the Dawson Range, Isla Gorge National Park protects spectacular sandstone scenery in the central highlands. Here, among a complex maze of gorges, sandstone outcrops and striking rock formations change colour throughout the day. Scenic Isla Gorge is fairly broad and contains Gorge Creek, a tributary of the Dawson River.

Open eucalypt forests, brigalow and softwood scrubs and patches of dry rainforest with distinctive bottle trees grow in the park. The park is home to many rare and threatened plants including *Eucalyptus beaniana*, an ironbark found west of the lookout and *Eucalyptus curtisii*, a mallee. The plateau has brilliant wildflower displays in spring.

Rock engravings and stencils are a reminder that Aboriginal people have a close connection with this place. The remains of an old hand-paved road, constructed in 1864 to transport wool from the Roma district to the coastal port of Rockhampton, can still be seen in the western end of the park.

Exploring Isla Gorge

Isla Gorge is a great place for an inland stopover. The picnic and camping area overlooks the gorge and is just 1·3km off the highway. **Be careful: cliff edges may crumble.** Stay well back.

Watch the sunset over the orange-coloured cliffs of Isla Gorge. Camp overnight. The small camping area is suitable for caravans and motorhomes. Take drinking water and firewood. Pay your camping fees at the self-registration station.

Go birdwatching. See wedge-tailed eagles and peregrine falcons soaring above the gorge or honeyeaters splurging on wattle, eucalypt, boronia and grevillea flowers from mid-winter to summer. See whiptail wallabies and grey kangaroos in the valley. (The Herbert's rock-wallabies which live in the park are rarely seen.)

Go for a scenic drive and walk to see the remains of the historic road near Flagstaff Hill. Have a picnic near the carpark.

Isla Gorge National Park

View from the lookout near the picnic and camping area

Walking

Follow a rough 1km trail from the picnic area to a lookout over Isla Gorge. Only very experienced and well-equipped walkers should descend into the gorge. Get advice from the ranger beforehand. Take a map (Ghinghinda 1:100,000 or the Forestry 1:50,000 Isla Gorge map) and let someone responsible know your plans. Follow the gorge to Dave Gordon's spring where lush vine thickets grow. Take water. Creek flow is seasonal.

Take the 2km circuit track past the remaining 137m of stone-paved road just 150m from the carpark near Flagstaff Hill.

Getting there

Turn off the Leichhardt Highway, 55km north of Taroom or 35km south of Theodore, and drive 1·3km to the picnic and camping area. To reach Flagstaff Hill, turn left off the highway at the "Flagstaff via Waterton" signpost, 31km north of Taroom. Follow this road for 49km (ignoring the "Flagstaff" sign pointing to the left halfway along) then turn left and drive 1·6km to the carpark and picnic area at Flagstaff Hill. From the north, turn off the Leichhardt Highway 8km south of Theodore. Travel 14km along the Glenmoral Roundstone and DPI Brigalow Research Station Road. Turn left into Glenbar Road, continue 3·6km then turn right into Flagstaff Road. Drive 9km then turn right into the park. Roads can become impassable after rain.

Tracks

Isla Gorge Lookout
2km return, 30–45 minutes

Flagstaff Hill circuit
2km, 30–45 minutes

Further information

QPWS
41 Miller Street
PO Box 175
TAROOM QLD 4420
ph (07) 4627 3358
fax (07) 4627 3448

Expedition National Park

Mt Cannondale

Macrozamia moorei **seed cone**

What's special?

On the Expedition Range in central Queensland lies remote and rugged Expedition National Park, the closest outback park to Brisbane. Scenic Robinson Gorge winds 14km between sheer sandstone cliffs from a broad shallow basin in the north to a narrow gorge towards its southern end.

Dry eucalypt forest covers most of the park. The mature spotted gum forest is the only intact forest of this type. Mt Cannondale in the Amphitheatre contains one of the largest intact softwood scrub remnants in the central highlands. Patches of dry rainforest scrub grow in narrow side gorges and wildflowers flourish along the cliff tops. Sandy Robinson Gorge is lined with cabbage palms (a relic from the dinosaur era), bottlebrushes and wattles. The park is home to several rare plant species including *Eucalyptus rubiginosa* and *Leucopogon grandiflorus*.

For thousands of years, Aboriginal people lived in this area, leaving behind stencil art and other sacred sites. Leichhardt visited in 1844 during his journey to Port Essington near Darwin.

Exploring Expedition

Camp among the wattles beside a permanent waterhole on Starkvale Creek at the southern end of the park. Spotted Gum camping area in the north has no facilities. Take a fuel stove and water (seven litres/person/day) for both campsites. Pay for your campsite at the self-registration stations at each campsite.

Go birdwatching. Listen for the grey shrike-thrush all-year-round or look for golden whistlers and grey and rufous fantails in winter. In summer, honeyeaters, rainbow lorikeets, friarbirds and king parrots feed on flowers and fruits.

See beautiful wildflowers in winter and spring, the best times to visit.

Enjoy the view of Arcadia Valley to the Carnarvon Range from a lookout off the Carnarvon Developmental Road in the remote Lonesome Section of the park.

Expedition National Park

Walking

From Starkvale, a track leads to a lookout over Robinson Gorge. Turn off the same track to reach the only access into the gorge along a steep, rough 20-minute trail. There are no trails in the gorge. Only experienced walkers should hike along the gorge to the Cattle Dip.

The Shepherd's Peak trail leads 2·5km from Starkvale camping area to a flat-topped mesa, Shepherd's Peak, with views over the surrounding peaks and creeks. Continue 4·5km to a lookout over the "Cattle Dip", a spectacular permanent waterhole in the gorge. Allow five hours to do the whole trail. You can also drive 1·5km from Starkvale to the Cattle Dip carpark then walk to the lookout.

Getting there

Expedition is 128km or two hours' north-west of Taroom along a road with about 100km of gravel. Travel 18km north of Taroom on the Leichhardt Highway, then turn left at the Bauhinia Downs Road. Turn left 2km further on towards Glenhaughton and Reedy Creek. Continue 86km to the turnoff to the park. Starkvale Creek is a further 23km and accessible only by four-wheel-drive. Alternatively, turn off the Dawson Highway 1km east of Bauhinia Downs and follow the Mapala-Fairfield Road for 93km. Turn right at Oil Bore Road. Continue 7km before turning left and driving a further 16km along a four-wheel-drive signposted track. Roads are impassable in wet weather. The nearest supplies are at Taroom (128 km) or Bauhinia Downs (116km).

For your safety, advise a friend or relative about your planned visit and your safe return.

Spotted gum forest by moonlight at Expedition National Park

Tracks

Robinson Gorge Lookout track
4km return, 1–1·5 hours

Shepherd's Peak trail
8km return, 3–5 hours

Cattle Dip track
800m return, 30 minutes

Further information

QPWS
41 Miller Street
PO Box 175
TAROOM QLD 4420
ph (07) 4627 3358
fax (07) 4627 3448

The Amphitheatre

Lake Murphy Conservation Park

Steve Parish

Greater glider

Tracks

Lake Murphy circuit
4km, 1–1·5 hours

Further information

QPWS
41 Miller Street
PO Box 175
TAROOM QLD 4420
ph (07) 4627 3358
fax (07) 4627 3448

What's special

Nestled beneath the low Murphy's Range in the central highlands, Lake Murphy remains largely unchanged from the days when the first Europeans passed this way.

Ludwig Leichhardt and his exploration party camped under the forest red gums on the shore of this lake on 19 November 1844, during their epic journey from the Darling Downs to Port Essington in the Northern Territory. This expedition paved the way for pastoral expansion in the Dawson district during the 1840s and 1850s. Lake Murphy was named after the young man in Leichhardt's party who first saw the lake. Lake Murphy is the party's only remaining campsite on public land in the Taroom area.

Lake Murphy provides a seasonal refuge for waterbirds. This perched lake fills only when nearby Robinson Creek overflows, and has been dry five times in the past two centuries.

Exploring Lake Murphy

Today, visitors can camp or picnic near the lake. Shady, grassy campsites are provided. Take your own drinking water supply and remove your rubbish from the park.

Look for koalas in the forest red gums or red-necked wallabies grazing the grassy plains. See waders when the lake is full and woodland birds in the forest. Go spotlighting at night. You might see brushtail possums or greater gliders in the trees along the walking track.

Read about Leichhardt's expedition in the picnic area. Watch the sunset over the lake. Even when the lake is dry, this is a peaceful and beautiful spot.

Walking

Walk 300m from the picnic and camping area to the lake shores. A 4km circuit track skirts the lake's southern shore before following Robinson Creek through the forest red gums and then returning through the woodland to the picnic area.

Getting there

Lake Murphy is 31km north-west of Taroom. Drive 18km north of Taroom along the Leichhardt Highway then turn west into Bauhinia Downs Road. Travel 2km to the Glenhaughton and Reedy Creek Road turnoff. Turn left and drive 11km to Lake Murphy. Conventional access is possible in dry weather.

Carnarvon Gorge Carnarvon National Park

What's special?

Carnarvon Gorge is an oasis in the semi-arid heart of Queensland. Here, in the Carnarvon Gorge Section of Carnarvon National Park, towering white sandstone cliffs form a spectacular steep-sided gorge with narrow, vibrantly coloured and lush side gorges. Boulder-strewn Carnarvon Creek winds through the gorge.

Remnant rainforest flourishes in the sheltered side gorges while endemic *Livistona nitida* cabbage tree palms, ancient cycads, ferns, flowering shrubs and gums trees line the meandering main gorge. Grassy open forest grows on the cliff-tops. The park's creeks attract a wide variety of animals including more than 173 species of birds.

Aboriginal rock art on the sandstone overhangs is a fragile reminder of the Aboriginal people who used the gorge for thousands of years. Rock engravings, ochre stencils and freehand paintings at Cathedral Cave, Baloon Cave and the Art Gallery include some of the finest rock art in Australia.

This rugged 16,000ha section is the most popular tourist destination in Queensland's central highlands.

Exploring Carnarvon Gorge

Take a few days to explore Carnarvon Gorge and discover its secrets. Camp or stay nearby at Takarakka Bush Resort, Carnarvon Gorge Wilderness Lodge or Warremba Farmstay.

You can camp in the Carnarvon Gorge visitor area only during the Easter, June/July and September/October Queensland school holidays. Bookings are essential. Take a fuel stove. Open fires are not permitted. Remove all rubbish from the park. Basic supplies are available from Takarakka Bush Resort, 4km away.

A small hike-in camping area is located at Big Bend, 9·6km from the information centre. Only a toilet is provided, so campers must be self-sufficient. No fires are permitted. Take a fuel stove and treat the water before drinking. Remote bush camping must be booked through the park.

Go wildlife watching. Watch for platypus in the creek early morning or late afternoon. Look for grazing whiptail wallabies and busy fairy-wrens. See brushtail possums, yellow-bellied gliders and greater gliders at night.

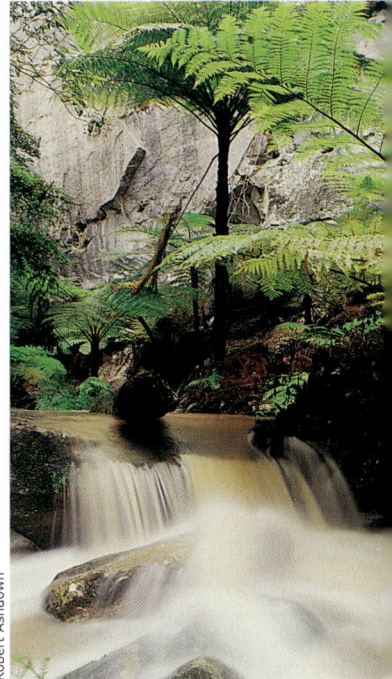

Robert Ashdown

Mickey Creek Gorge

Carnarvon Gorge, Carnarvon National Park

Robert Ashdown

See creeks, waterfalls and lush rainforest on bushwalks through the park. Climb Boolimba Bluff or Battleship Spur for breathtaking views over the park.

Learn about Aboriginal culture and rock art at the Art Gallery, Cathedral Cave and Baloon Cave.

Walking

Carnarvon Gorge has 21km of walking tracks to help you explore the park. Wear a hat and sunscreen and take drinking water. Most tracks start in the gorge visitor area. All track distances are one-way except the Nature Trail. Only fit experienced walkers should attempt the Battleship Spur hike and other remote walks.

Accessibility

The visitor area has wheelchair-accessible toilets and picnic tables and disability car parking.

Aerial view of Carnarvon Gorge

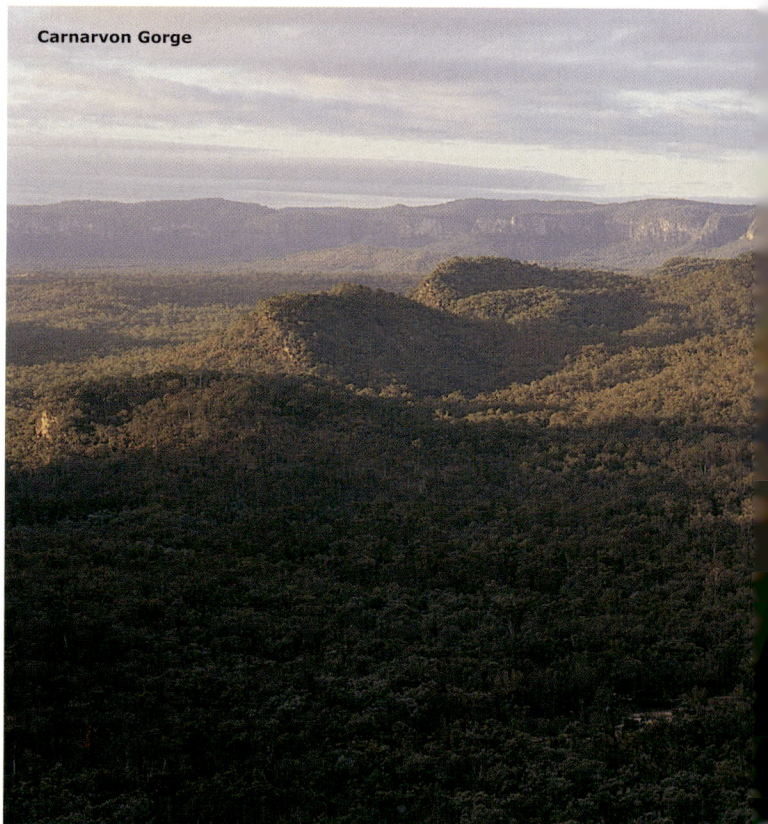

Adam Creed

Tracks

From the carpark:

Baloon Cave self-guided walk
500m, 30 minutes return

Mickey Creek Gorge
1·5km, 1 hour return

Rock Pool
2km, 1–1·5 hours return
(1km from the Lodge)

Nature Trail 1km circuit starting at creek crossing no. 1,
30 minutes

Boolimba Bluff
3·2km, 2–3 hours return

Moss Garden
3·4km, 2–3 hours return

Amphitheatre
4·1km, 3–4 hours return

Lower Aljon Falls and Ward's Canyon
4·7km, 3–4 hours return

The Art Gallery
5·4km, 3–4 hours return

Cathedral Cave
9km, 5–6 hours return

Battleship Spur
14km, 8–10 hours return

Carnarvon Gorge

Carnarvon Gorge, Carnarvon National Park

Adam Creed

Getting there

Carnarvon Gorge is between Roma and Emerald. From Roma, drive north 90km to Injune then a further 160km along the Carnarvon Highway. From Emerald, drive south 65km to Springsure then east 70km to Rolleston, and a further 61km to the Carnarvon turnoff. The 44km road to the park has 21km of unsealed gravel surface. It is suitable for conventional vehicles and caravans in dry weather but can become impassable following rain. Always check road conditions with the park, RACQ or local commercial operators before travelling.

The Wilderness Lodge is 3km from the visitor area. Takarakka is 4km away and Warremba Farmstay is 57km from the park on the Carnarvon Highway 13km south of the Carnarvon turnoff.

Further information

QPWS
36 Quintin Street
PO Box 981
ROMA QLD 4455
ph (07) 4622 4266
fax (07) 4622 4151
8.30am–5pm

Campsite bookings: 13 13 04 or www.qld.gov.au/camping

Carnarvon Gorge Section Carnarvon NP
Via ROLLESTON QLD 4702
ph (07) 4984 4505
fax (07) 4984 4519
8am–5pm seven days

Takarakka Bush Resort
ph (07) 4984 4535
fax (07) 4984 4556
www.takarakka.com.au

Carnarvon Gorge Wilderness Lodge
ph (07) 4984 4503
fax (07) 4984 4500
www.carnarvon-gorge.com

Warremba Farmstay
ph/fax (07) 4626 7175
www.warrembafarmstay.com.au

Paul Candlin

Eastern grey kangaroo in the visitor area

Robert Ashdown

Mt Moffatt Carnarvon National Park

What's special?

Sculpted sandstone outcrops, spectacular gorges and high country in Queensland's central highlands are protected in this remote section of Carnarvon National Park. Known as the "Roof of Queensland", Consuelo Tableland is the watershed for some of Australia's major river systems.

Mt Moffatt is the spiritual home of the Nuri and Bidjara people who have left behind a rich culture and rock art spanning the past 19,500 years. Kenniff Cave is Australia's finest Pleistocene archaeological site. Explorers Thomas Mitchell and Edmund Kennedy passed through the park in 1846–47. The notorious Kenniff Brothers are part of the park's colourful pastoral past.

The park's rich mosaic of open grassy woodlands and forests are home to more than 54 species of mammals, 160 species of birds, 63 reptiles and 17 frogs.

Forest red gums and poplar boxes grow around the creeks and small patches of softwood scrub (dry rainforest) thrive in sheltered gullies. Dense patches of white cypress grow in wide, sandy valleys and spectacular natural grasslands flourish on Marlong Plain, home to the vulnerable native thistle. Macrozamias grow in the grassy understorey of the tall open mahogany forest on the Consuelo Tableland.

Exploring Mt Moffatt

Go for a scenic drive through the park. See fascinating rock sculptures such as Marlong Arch, Cathedral Rock, The Duchess, Lot's Wife and The Chimneys. Drive to the head of Carnarvon Creek for magnificent views over the central highlands. See the intriguing mahogany forest. A round trip within the park can be well over 100km, so take plenty of fuel for exploration and allow at least a full day.

See stencil art at The Tombs and rock engravings and stencil art at Kookaburra Cave. (Kenniff Cave is closed for public safety.) Relive the story of the infamous Kenniff brothers. Enjoy a picnic with a view at the Top Shelter Shed.

Go birdwatching. See raptors gliding overhead, colourful honeyeaters, lorikeets and parrots, or squatter pigeons searching for seeds on the ground. Spotlight for sugar, feathertail, yellow-bellied and greater gliders or reptiles at night.

Hardenbergia flowers, Mahogany Forest

Robert Ashdown

Mt Moffatt, Carnarvon National Park

Stay overnight in four low-key camping areas. Get your camping permit at the information hut near the ranger station. Book in the school holidays as campsites are limited. Conventional access is possible to Dargonelly Rock Hole and West Branch in dry weather. Toilets and tank water are provided. Take drinking water as the supply is limited. A small camping area at the Rotary Shelter Shed has a picnic shelter, drinking water, a toilet, barbecue and exceptional views to Mt Moffatt, Consuelo Tableland and Carnarvon Gorge. The Top Moffatt camping area has a toilet only. Both camping areas are accessible only by four-wheel-drive.

Spring and autumn are the best times to visit as winter mornings can be frosty and summer days quite hot. Be self-sufficient. Take plenty of food, fuel and water, vehicle spare parts and a fuel stove. The nearest supplies are at Injune.

Walking

Mt Moffatt is a drive-oriented park with short walks to special attractions. Walk 840m to Kookaburra Cave or The Duchess. The Chimneys and Marlong Arch are 120m from the road. The walk to The Tombs is 800m via The Chimneys track. Only experienced walkers should attempt cross-country hikes. Seek ranger advice first.

Getting there

Mt Moffatt is 220km from Mitchell or 160km from Injune. From Injune, travel via Womblebank or Westgrove Station. Womblebank can become impassable after rain. Conventional access is possible in dry weather but four-wheel-drive (4WD) high clearance vehicles are recommended. The nearest fuel is at Mitchell or Injune.

Further information

Mt Moffatt Section Carnarvon NP
via MITCHELL QLD 4465
ph (07) 4626 3581
fax (07) 4626 3651
UHF Channel 8 in emergency

QPWS
36 Quintin Street
PO Box 981
ROMA QLD 4455
ph (07) 4622 4266
fax (07) 4622 4151

Campsite bookings: 13 13 04 or www.qld.gov.au/camping

Marlong Plain

Robert Ashdown

Salvator Rosa Carnarvon National Park

The Eye of the Needle, Salvator Rosa

Jeff Wright, Queensland Museum

What's special?

Spring-fed Nogoa River and Louisa Creek wind through a picturesque broad valley beneath craggy sandstone outcrops in the Salvator Rosa Section of Carnarvon National Park. At the western edge of central Queensland's sandstone belt, Salvator Rosa contains deeply eroded and spectacular rock formations, such as Spyglass Peak and the Sentinel, which dominate the skyline.

Eucalypt woodland and open forest cover most of the park. The wildflower displays are spectacular in spring. At least 10 of the park's recorded 300 plant species are rare or threatened.

Explorer Thomas Mitchell named this valley during his 1846 Gulf of Carpentaria expedition and established a base camp here later that year.

Exploring Salvator Rosa

This remote park has few facilities, so visitors must be totally self-sufficient.

Bush camp in the Nogoa River camping area. Take plenty of food, fuel and vehicle spare parts. Take a fuel stove for cooking. Boil the creek water before drinking. Remove your rubbish.

Follow the self-guiding trail through the park to see the park's main attractions, including crystal-clear Belinda Springs and the historic site of Major Mitchell's camp.

Go birdwatching around the watercourses and springs. See sacred kingfishers, herons, plum-headed finches and honeyeaters. Listen to the pheasant coucal calling from the swamp.

Watch the sunrise over the park's buffs and spires. Scramble up the sandstone range near the campsite for a view over the park.

Between April and September is the best time to visit this section as summers can be very hot.

Salvator Rosa, Carnarvon National Park

Robert Ashdown

Walking

See the vivid orange-barked yellow-jacket trees as you walk 500m to the base of Spyglass Peak. Be careful, the sandstone crumbles easily.

Getting there

Salvator Rosa lies between Springsure and Tambo. From Springsure, head 114km west along Tambo Road to the park turnoff. From Tambo, head 42km north on the Alpha Road then turn east towards Springsure and drive 102km to the Salvator Rosa turnoff. At the turnoff, drive south for 50km via "Cungelella" to the park boundary and a further 4km to the campsite. Conventional access to the camping area is possible but four-wheel-drive is essential inside the park. The access roads become impassable after rain. The nearest fuel is at Springsure or Tambo.

Further information

QPWS
PO Box 157
SPRINGSURE QLD 4722
ph (07) 4984 1716
fax (07) 4984 1173

**Salvator Rosa Section
Carnarvon NP**
Lake Salvator MS 420
SPRINGSURE QLD 4722
ph/fax (07) 4984 1715

Jeff Wright, Queensland Museum

Sandstone outcrops tower over the valley.

Ka Ka Mundi Carnarvon National Park

Australian king-parrot
John Augusteyn

What's special?

Across the undulating plains, Ka Ka Mundi's sandstone cliffs dominate the clear blue skyline. This remote section of Carnarvon National Park contains more than 30km of escarpments and plateaus in the central highlands.

This section protects bonewood, softwood and brigalow scrubs on clay soils in central Queensland's brigalow belt. Poplar box and silver-leaved ironbark forests and grassy downs grow on the richer black soils. Lush oases with rainforest scrub flourish around springs at the base of the cliffs and the creeks, attracting king parrots, wompoo fruit-doves and fig birds.

Aboriginal people have close ties with this place and there are many stories associated with Ka Ka Mundi. They believed harmful spirits lived in the caves around the Bunbuncundoo Springs but the springs had healing powers. Old cattle yards near the springs are a reminder of the early pastoral history. Ka Ka Mundi was grazed for more than a century before it became national park in 1974.

Exploring Ka Ka Mundi

Go wildlife watching. See red-necked and swamp wallabies and wallaroos.

Bush camp around Bunbuncundoo Springs. Get your camping permit from the self-registration station. Visitors must be totally self-sufficient. Take water, plenty of food and fuel, and a gas stove for cooking.

Visit in the cooler months. Winter mornings can be frosty and summer days are very hot.

Walking

There are no tracks in this section. Take a compass and the Sunmap 1:100,000 Cungelella map (no. 8348) if bushwalking.

Getting there

Ka Ka Mundi is 130km or two hours' drive south-west of Springsure. Head west on the Springsure-Tambo Road for 50km then turn south into Buckland Road. Follow signed tracks to the park. Conventional access is possible in dry weather. The roads become impassable when wet. The nearest supplies are at Springsure or Tambo.

Further information

QPWS
25 Porphry Street
PO Box 157
SPRINGSURE QLD 4722
ph (07) 4984 1716
fax (07) 4984 1173

QPWS
Government Offices
Hospital Road
PO Box 906
EMERALD QLD 4720
ph (07) 4982 4555
fax (07) 4982 2568

Mackay and Whitsundays

Map 8

Legend

National Park	State Forest	Highway
Conservation Park	Timber Reserve	Major connecting road
Forest Reserve	Resource Reserve	Minor access road

0   10   20
km

N

Gloucester Islands NP

Hook Island

Whitsunday Islands NP

Dryander NP

Airlie Beach

Molle Islands NP

Whitsunday Island

Conway SF

Proserpine

Conway NP

Lindeman Islands NP

Repulse Islands NP

Smith Islands NP

Goldsmith Island

Cathu SF

Brampton Islands NP

Carlisle Island

Newry Islands NP

Scawfell Island

Cape Hillsborough NP

Eungella NP

South Cumberland Islands NP

Eungella

Finch Hatton

Pinnacle

Mackay

Mia Mia SF

Crediton SF

Sarina

Cape Palmerston NP

Cape Palmerston National Park

What's special?

Windswept rocky headlands, mangroves, swamps, rainforest and sand dunes are part of Cape Palmerston National Park's rugged beauty. Open eucalypt woodland with ironbark and poplar gum grows on the ridges while paperbarks grow in the gullies. The distinctive 344m Mt Funnel towers over the park.

Midden heaps are a reminder of the special connection Aboriginal people have with this place. Named by Cook in 1770, Cape Palmerston is one of the few remaining areas of natural coastline in the Mackay area.

The false water-rat lives in the park's mangroves while beach stone-curlews frequent the beaches. Both are considered vulnerable to extinction. Pied imperial-pigeons which visit late winter and spring are close to the southern limit of their range.

The adjacent waters and the Cape Creek system are part of the Great Barrier Reef Marine Park.

Osprey

Adam Creed

Exploring Cape Palmerston

Relax and enjoy nature in this undeveloped, remote park. Take insect repellent, especially in summer.

Go birdwatching. See ospreys and sea eagles soaring overhead or white-breasted woodswallows in the flowering grasstrees. Look for birds around the swamp on the road into the camping areas.

Try your luck at fishing but beware of estuarine crocodiles. Swimming is dangerous when box jellyfish are present in the sea from October to May.

Bush camp at Windmill Bay or Cape Creek. Campers must be self-sufficient. Only picnic tables are provided. Take water, food and a fuel stove. Remove all rubbish from the park.

Walking

Scramble up Cape Palmerston for a magnificent view of the Northumberland Isles and Mt Funnel.

Cape Palmerston National Park

Getting there

Cape Palmerston is 115km south-east of Mackay. Access is by four-wheel-drive vehicles only. Turn off the Bruce Highway at Ilbilbie and drive east towards Greenhill. The park is a further 6·5km. Allow 45 minutes to reach the Cape Creek camping area from the park boundary. Take care driving in soft sand along the beach and beware of the extreme tidal range.

Further information

QPWS
River and Wood Streets
PO Box 623
MACKAY QLD 4740
ph (07) 4944 7800
fax (07) 4944 7811

Darran Leal

White-breasted woodswallow

Eungella National Park

What's special?

High above the surrounding plains, Eungella's mist-shrouded and forest-clad mountains provide a home for a fascinating variety of unusual plants and animals, including the Eungella gastric brooding frog, Mackay tulip oak, Eungella spiny cray and Eungella honeyeater. This isolated mountain refuge lies close to the boundary between subtropical and tropical rainforests and supports species from both vegetation types.

Much of the park is wilderness dissected by gorges. Open eucalypt woodland grows on Dick's Tableland in the rugged north-western part of the park. Rainforest trees, flowering bottlebrushes and tall river she-oaks line the meandering Broken River. Rainforest also grows around Finch Hatton Gorge.

Eungella is one of Queensland's most ecologically diverse parks with 860 plant species, including plants close to their distribution limit such as the Eungella satinash, regent bowerbird and Sydney blue gum. This diversity is matched by a wonderful variety of wildlife.

Exploring Eungella

Go for a scenic drive to Eungella or stay for a longer visit. Stop at Sky Window for a picnic or take a short walk for spectacular views over the Pioneer Valley.

Enjoy a bush picnic at Broken River in tall open forest of swamp mahogany and forest red gums. Picnic tables, a gas barbecue and water are provided. (Boil the water before drinking.) Have morning or afternoon tea at the kiosk next to the information centre. Please do not feed the birds or other animals. Help keep wildlife wild.

Look for platypus, eels and turtles in Broken River. A viewing platform is provided for platypus watching. August is the best month for platypus activity. Water quality makes the river unsuitable for swimming.

Eungella is great for bushwalking. Explore the rainforest along the discovery trail or take a longer walk. Learn about Biri culture on the Sky Window circuit. See beautiful waterfalls along the tracks.

Paul Candlin

Rainforest at Broken River

Eungella National Park

Stay nearby or camp at Fern Flat near the creek and picnic area. A few tent sites, toilets, hot showers, fireplaces and untreated water are provided. Pay your fees at the self-registration station. Take your own firewood or a fuel stove for cooking. Experienced walkers can bush camp by permit. Boil the creek water for five minutes before drinking. Private campsites and cabins are available on the mountain.

Go spotlighting at night. See greater gliders, tawny frogmouths, sugar gliders and brushtail possums. Go birdwatching during the day. See rainbow lorikeets, red-browed finches and blue-faced honeyeaters.

Picnic or walk at Finch Hatton Gorge. Gas barbecues are provided. Please do not feed the goannas.

Join in special ranger-led activity programs in the holidays. Find out more about the park in the information centre which is open weekdays and every day in the holidays.

Walking

Eungella has more than 20km of walking tracks. Wear insect repellent and sturdy shoes when walking. Arrange to be dropped off for the Crediton Creek and Clarke Range tracks to save the return walk. For your safety, do not walk back along the busy Eungella Dam Road. Do not attempt to go beyond the pool on the Araluen Cascades track. Beware of slippery rocks.

Accessibility

The Sky Window circuit, toilets and picnic tables are wheelchair-accessible.

Getting there

Turn off the Bruce Highway 91km south of Proserpine and drive 9km to Marian. Continue 62km to the park. From Mackay, drive 80km west along the Pioneer Valley Road to Eungella township. Continue 6km south to Broken River. The road up the mountain is not recommended for caravans. Finch Hatton Gorge is at the base of the range. Turn off the Eungella Road 1km east of Finch Hatton (60km west of Mackay) and continue 11km to the picnic area. This narrow road is gravel for 6km and closed when creek crossings flood.

Tracks

From Broken River:
Rainforest Discovery Walk
1km circuit, 30 minutes

Granite Bend circuit
2·1km, 1 hour

Crediton Creek trail
8·5km one-way, 4–5 hours

Wishing Pool circuit at end of Crediton Creek trail
1·5km return, 1 hour

Clarke Range track
6·5km one-way, 3–4 hours

Palm Walk circuit
1·5km, 45 minutes

Sky Window circuit
100m, 15 minutes

Cedar Grove track (Sky Window to Eungella Chalet)
3km one-way, 2 hours

From Eungella Chalet:
Pine Grove circuit
1·5km, 1 hour

From Finch Hatton Gorge:
Araluen Cascades track
1·5km one-way, 1–2 hours return

Further information

Eungella NP
c/- Post Office
DALRYMPLE HEIGHTS QLD 4757
ph (07) 4958 4552

QPWS
River and Wood Streets
PO Box 623
MACKAY QLD 4740
ph (07) 4944 7800
fax (07) 4944 7811

Liem's frog

Crediton State Forest

Cockatiels

Adam Creed

What's special?

Picturesque creek scenery, lush rainforest remnants and grassy open eucalypt forest make Crediton State Forest worth a visit. Tall, stately rose gums more than a century old remain along The Loop Road. This is the northern limit of these beautiful trees.

The forest contains relics of gold mining exploration during the 1880s.

Exploring Crediton

Go for a scenic drive through the Cockies Creek area. Continue to Mia Mia State Forest.

Bush camp on peaceful grassy flats at The Diggings beside a permanent waterhole on the Broken River, or beside the seasonally dry Cockies, Raspberry or Timbilla Creeks. Obtain your permit to traverse and camping permit from the Mackay office beforehand. These campsites are best in winter when the creeks are still flowing. Summers can be hot.

Campers must be totally self-sufficient as no facilities are provided. Take drinking water. Creek flow is seasonal. Boil the creek water for five minutes before drinking. Collect firewood from the ground only. Chainsaw use is not permitted. Preferably take a fuel stove. Carefully extinguish any fires when you leave your campsite.

Visit nearby Eungella National Park.

Further information

QPWS
River and Wood Streets
PO Box 623
MACKAY QLD 4740
(07) 4944 7800
fax (07) 4944 7811

Getting there

Crediton is west of Eungella township. High-clearance conventional vehicles can reach The Diggings, along a rough gravel road 2·5km from Eungella. The Cockies Creek drive is four-wheel-drive only. Roads may be closed in wet weather or high fire-danger periods. Mia Mia State Forest is 38km from Cockies Creek.

Mia Mia State Forest

What's special?

Nestled in the foothills of the Clarke Range, Mia Mia State Forest is mostly open eucalypt forest.

Fireclay Road got its name from local clay which was used to make bricks before the plantations were established here. The first hoop pine plantation of about 12 hectares was established in 1934 and the last available area was planted in 1991.

Exploring Mia Mia

Go for a scenic drive through the forest to Pinnacle. Obtain your permit to traverse before your visit.

Bush camp at Captains Crossing beside Teemburra Creek. Visitors must be self-sufficient. Take drinking water.

Getting there

Mia Mia is west of Mackay. Turn off at Pinnacle and drive 20km south-west to the forest. The rough, gravel access road is four-wheel-drive only. Get your permit to traverse before entering the forest. Roads may be closed in wet weather or high fire danger periods. You can also drive to the park through Crediton State Forest.

Paul Candlin

Rainforest rainbow skink

Further information

QPWS
River and Wood Streets
PO Box 623
MACKAY QLD 4740
ph (07) 4944 7800
fax (07) 4944 7811

Cape Hillsborough National Park

Paperbarks, Cape Hillsborough

Adam Creed

What's special?

Rock-strewn, sandy beaches, hoop pine-dotted hillsides plunging towards the sea, subtropical rainforest and mangrove-fringed wetlands make Cape Hillsborough one of the most scenic parks along the central Queensland coast.

Open eucalypt forest with a grassy understorey covers the hills and headlands while sheltered valleys and creeks support lush rainforest. Patches of low heath grow on exposed slopes. West of the picnic area, mangrove forests provide an important breeding and feeding ground for marine wildlife. The surrounding waters are part of the Great Barrier Reef Marine Park.

Rhyolite boulders scattered over the headlands and foreshore are a reminder of volcanic activity millions of years ago.

The Juipera people lived in this area for thousands of years and have left behind reminders of their special connection to the Cape. Cook named the Cape in June 1770 after the Earl of Hillsborough.

Exploring Cape Hillsborough

Have a picnic on the foreshore overlooking the sea. Gas barbecues, shelter sheds, picnic tables, bins, toilets, cold showers and water are provided. See kangaroos hopping along the beach late afternoon. Please do not feed the wildlife.

Explore the tidal rockpools. Fishing is allowed but swimming is not recommended. Estuarine crocodiles live in these waters and box jellyfish are present in the sea from October to May.

Bush camp at Smalleys Beach. Toilets, town water and sites suitable for caravans are provided but the campground is quite small. Pay your fees at the self-registration station. Take a fuel stove for cooking. You can also stay near the picnic area at a private resort and caravan park or at nearby Seaforth.

Go bushwalking. Learn about mangroves on the boardwalk or discover how Aboriginal people use plants along the Juipera Plant Trail. Look for wildlife early morning or late afternoon. Wear insect repellent, especially in summer.

Cape Hillsborough National Park

Walking

Enjoy the view over the coast from the Beachcomber Cove and Andrews Point tracks. Walk to Wedge Island on a falling tide and return 500m along the beach from Andrews Point at low tide. Wear insect repellent and a hat and sunscreen. Carry drinking water.

Accessibility

The mangrove boardwalk is wheelchair-accessible for the first 300m.

Getting there

Cape Hillsborough is off the Bruce Highway north of Mackay. Take the Seaforth Road 20km north of Mackay and continue 20km to the Cape Hillsborough turnoff then a further 10km to the park. (The gravel road to Smalleys Beach is signposted about 6km east of the Seaforth turnoff.) From the north, turn off the highway 79km south of Proserpine and drive 15km towards Seaforth. Turn right then left and drive another 10km to the park. The partly unsealed Mt Ossa Road is unsuitable for caravans.

Tracks

Juipera Plant trail
1·5km circuit, 45 minutes

Beachcomber Cove track
1·6km one-way, 1·5 hours return

Andrews Point track
2·6km one-way, 2 hours return

Mangrove walk
2·4km return, 1 hour

Further information

QPWS
River and Wood Streets
PO Box 623
MACKAY QLD 4740
ph (07) 4944 7800
fax (07) 4944 7811

Inlet, Cape Hillsborough National Park

Cathu State Forest

Bracket fungi, Cathu

Adam Creed

What's special?

Along the rugged Clarke Range behind the Whitsunday coast is Cathu State Forest. Forests and woodlands range from distinctive poplar gum *Eucalyptus alba* woodlands and exotic Caribbean pine plantations on the creek flats to dense rainforest, hoop pine plantations and tall wet eucalpyt forest along the range. The rainforests were selectively logged during the 1960s and 70s.

Exploring Cathu

This is a quiet retreat for people who like to relax and enjoy the bush. Go wildlife watching. See Ulysses butterflies, whiptail and agile wallabies and northern quolls. Take your binoculars and go birdwatching. More than 100 species of birds have been seen in the forest.

Picnic or camp beside Pandanus Creek at Jaxut, 200m past the old forest station site. Grassy, shady campsites, toilets, picnic tables, tap water, bins and fireplaces are provided. Pay your camping fees at the self-registration station. Take firewood and drinking water. Creek flow is seasonal.

Go for a scenic drive beyond the camping area. Enjoy spectacular views over the beautiful Whitsunday coast from the Clarke Range Lookout, 7km from the camping area. From Windy Point, you can see Eungella National Park to the south. Mountain bike riding is allowed in the forest.

Walking

At Jaxut, a 1km walk follows Pandanus Creek. See the rainforest along Muirs Road and the old Kangaroo Creek Road. Both are closed to traffic.

Getting there

Cathu is west of the Bruce Highway, 72km or one hour north of Mackay or 51km south of Proserpine. Jaxut is 12km off the highway. The access road is rough and unsuitable for caravans but conventional access is possible. High fire danger and wet weather can close the roads. To travel beyond the camping area, you need a permit to traverse. Four-wheel-drive is necessary to complete the Loop Road. This road is closed during wet weather.

Tracks

Muirs Road track
4km return, 1 hour 30 minutes

Kangaroo Creek track
4km return, 1 hour 30 minutes

Further information

QPWS
River and Wood Streets
PO Box 623
MACKAY QLD 4740
ph (07) 4944 7800
fax (07) 4944 7811

South Cumberland Islands National Park

What's special?

Off the central Queensland coast lies the Cumberland group protected in South Cumberland Islands National Park.

Scawfell Island is the largest island in the group. Granite cliffs line this hilly continental island's rocky, indented coastline. Open eucalypt woodland covers most of the island and hoop pine-dotted rainforest grows on steep, sheltered slopes. Scawfell is an important turtle rookery.

Cockermouth is a hilly island covered mainly in open grassland. The western side has sandy beaches and a sheltered anchorage. A remnant ancient Pleistocene reef is exposed at low tide in the shallow lagoon on the island's western side.

The islands and surrounding waters are part of the Great Barrier Reef World Heritage Area and are protected. This is part of the sea country of the Ngaro people.

Exploring South Cumberlands

Bush camp on Scawfell Island. A shelter shed and toilets are provided. Take fresh water, a fuel stove for cooking and insect repellent. Open fires and generators are prohibited. Remove all rubbish to the mainland. Bookings are essential in holidays.

Refuge Bay on the northern side of Scawfell Island is a popular anchorage. Fishing is allowed only here.

Beware of marine stingers and cyclones during the warmer months.

Getting there

Scawfell Island is 60km north-east of Mackay. Access is by private boat or water taxi.

Adam Creed

Scawfell Island

Further information

QPWS
Cnr River and Wood Streets
PO Box 623
MACKAY QLD 4740
ph (07) 4944 7800
fax (07) 4944 7811

Campsite bookings: 13 13 04 or
www.qld.gov.au/camping

Newry Islands National Park

Blue tiger on a grasstree flower
spike on outer Newry Island

Adam Creed

What's special?

Nestled close to the coast north-west of Mackay is a group of hilly continental islands. Newry, Rabbit, Outer Newry, Acacia, Mausoleum and Rocky Islands are protected as part of Newry Islands National Park. The islands are wild and windswept with rocky, exposed headlands and sandstone cliffs. Rabbit, the largest island, has sandy beaches.

Grassy open forest with gnarled ironbarks, bloodwoods and blue gums covers most of Newry Island. Small patches of dry rainforest grow in sheltered pockets on the southern slopes. Hoop pines tower over the canopy of Mackay tulip oaks and mountain ash. Orange-footed scrubfowl build nesting mounds in the rainforest. This is the most southerly limit of the pied imperial-pigeon, a migratory bird which feeds on rainforest fruits.

The islands and surrounding waters are part of the Great Barrier Reef World Heritage Area and are protected. Seagrass beds around the islands provide a habitat for the threatened dugong. In summer, green turtles nest on Rabbit Island.

Exploring Newry Islands

Protected from south-easterly winds, the Newry Islands are a popular boating destination.

Have a picnic on the western side of Newry Island overlooking Rabbit Island.

Go wildlife watching. See koalas, bandicoots and echidnas. Spotlight for possums at night. Go birdwatching. See brahminy kites, ospreys and white-bellied sea-eagles soaring above the coast and noisy pittas and rose-crowned pigeons in the rainforest.

Bush camp on Rabbit and Outer Newry Islands. Book ahead for holidays periods. Picnic tables, shelter sheds and toilets are provided. Rabbit Island has a gas barbecue. Take fresh water, a fuel stove for cooking and insect repellent. Open fires and generators are prohibited. Remove all rubbish to the mainland.

Beware of marine stingers and cyclones in the warmer months and estuarine crocodiles.

Newry Islands National Park

Adam Creed

Walking

See the rainforest and open forest along the walking track on the southern end of Newry Island. Enjoy views over the islands and mainland from lookouts along the way.

Getting there

The islands are 5km north-west of Seaforth, 46km by road north-west of Mackay. Access is by private boat from the boat ramp at Victor Creek, 4km west of Seaforth.

Tracks

Circuit track
2km, 1 hour

Further information

QPWS
Cnr River and Wood Streets
PO Box 623
MACKAY QLD 4740
ph (07) 4944 7800
fax (07) 4944 7811

Campsite bookings: 13 13 04 or www.qld.gov.au/camping

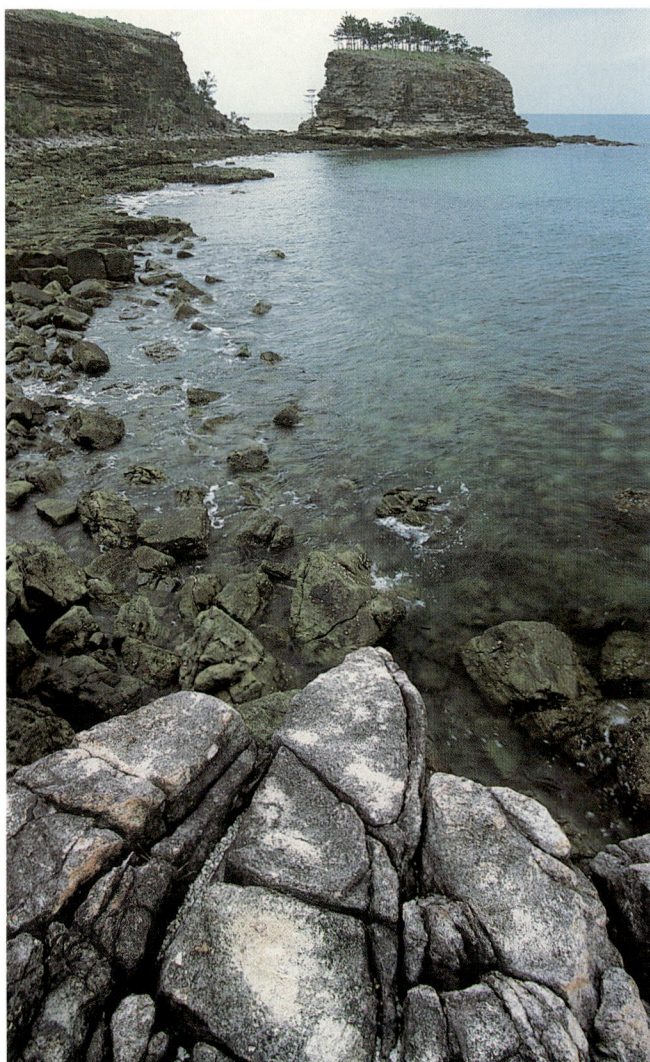

Adam Creed

Outer Newry Island

Brampton Islands National Park

White-bellied sea-eagle

Paul Candlin

What's special?

Rocky headlands dotted with hoop pines, open grasslands, woodlands, sheltered bays, and coral rubble and long sandy beaches make these islands some of the most scenic off the Queensland coast. This park consists of Brampton and Carlisle Islands.

Brampton Island rises from sea level to 214m at Peak Lookout. The island has a variety of vegetation types; open eucalypt forest on ridges and sheltered slopes, dense vine forest in gullies and valleys, dry rainforest with towering hoop pines on headlands, grasstrees scattered through native grasslands, coastal scrub and mangroves.

Carlisle is densely clothed in eucalypt forest with rainforest in sheltered gullies.

Turtles feed in the surrounding marine park waters and the islands are important turtle rookeries. This is the sea country of the Ngaro people who also visited the Whitsunday islands further north. Cook named the group after the Duke of Cumberland.

The islands and surrounding waters are part of the Great Barrier Reef World Heritage Area and are protected.

Exploring Brampton Islands

Go birdwatching. See orange-footed scrubfowl in the forests and majestic white-bellied sea-eagles and ospreys soaring above the cliffs. Watch nesting flatback and green turtles in summer.

At low tide, you can cross from Brampton to Carlisle Island. Bush camp on Carlisle Island. Book ahead for holiday periods. Picnic tables, a shelter shed, toilets, and a gas barbecue are provided. Take fresh water, a fuel stove for cooking and insect repellent. Open fires and generators are prohibited. Remove all rubbish to the mainland.

Take the 7km circuit around Brampton Island, passing through many vegetation types. Stop for a picnic at a secluded bay. Walk 2km to the lookouts at the peak for views over nearby islands and the mainland. Get a brochure to find out more about the island's plants.

Beware of marine stingers and cyclones during the warmer months.

Brampton Islands National Park

Paul Candlin

Adam Creed

Brampton Island in foreground; Carlisle Island in background

Walking

The circuit track starts at the park entrance steps opposite the runway. Wear a hat and sunscreen. Take drinking water.

Getting there

Brampton and Carlisle Islands are 32km north of Mackay. Access is by private boat or commercial operators. Contact QPWS (Mackay) for details.

Steve Parish

Flatback hatchlings

Tracks

Brampton Island circuit
7km, 2·5 hours

Further information

QPWS
Cnr River and Wood Streets
PO Box 623
MACKAY QLD 4740
ph (07) 4944 7800
fax (07) 4944 7811

Campsite bookings: 13 13 04 or www.qld.gov.au/camping

Smith Islands National Park

What's special?

Goldsmith is the largest island in this group of continental islands off Mackay, protected in Smith Islands National Park. Goldsmith has a rocky coastline and is covered in low open forest and woodland with brush box trees and a wattle and grasstree understorey. Long, sandy beaches on the island's northern and western sides are fringed with pandanus trees and coastal she-oaks.

The islands and surrounding waters are part of the Great Barrier Reef World Heritage Area and are protected.

Exploring Smith Islands

Bush camp on Goldsmith Island. Bookings are essential in holidays. Toilets and picnic tables are provided. Take fresh water, a fuel stove for cooking and insect repellent. Open fires and generators are prohibited. Remove all rubbish to the mainland.

Two bays on the north-western side of Goldsmith Island provide a sheltered anchorage for small craft. Go snorkelling over the fringing reef.

Beware of marine stingers and cyclones during the warmer months.

Getting there

Goldsmith Island is 30km north-east of Seaforth. Access is by private boat or water taxi.

Goldsmith Island

Further information

QPWS
Cnr River and Wood Streets
PO Box 623
MACKAY QLD 4740
ph (07) 4944 7800
fax (07) 4944 7811

Campsite bookings: 13 13 04 or www.qld.gov.au/camping

Whitsunday Islands National Park

What's special?

Hilly islands dotting the aquamarine waters of the scenic Whitsunday Passage are protected in Whitsunday Islands National Park. The Whitsunday group of continental islands formed when changing sea levels drowned a mountain range. Whitehaven Beach on Whitsunday Island is world-renowned for its pure, white, silica sands and crystal-clear waters.

The Whitsunday reefs have outstanding coral cover and variety. From May to September the Whitsundays are an important calving ground for migrating humpback whales. The islands and surrounding waters are part of the Great Barrier Reef World Heritage Area and are protected.

The Ngaro people, one of the earliest recorded Aboriginal groups in Australia, were seen by Cook while exploring the Whitsunday Passage. The "Island People" lived throughout the island chain known as the Whitsundays and the nearby mainland for hundreds of years. Rock art and middens at Nara Inlet (Hook Island) provide a record of their special way of life.

Adam Creed

Hook Island

Exploring Whitsunday Islands

A variety of campsites are available on Whitsunday, Hook, Cid and Henning Islands. Some have spectacular views over nearby islands. Facilities vary but are limited to toilets and picnic tables. Campers must be self-sufficient. Take fresh water, a fuel stove for cooking and insect repellent. Open fires and generators are prohibited. Remove all rubbish to the mainland.

While water is usually clearer at the northern sides of the outer islands, snorkelling over the reef flat at high tide can still be rewarding.

Beware of marine stingers and cyclones during the warmer months. Restrictions apply to activities such as spearfishing, fishing, collecting and anchoring. Check first.

Whitsunday Islands National Park

Further information

QPWS
Whitsunday Information Centre
Cnr Shute Harbour and
Mandalay Roads
PO Box 332
AIRLIE BEACH QLD 4802
ph (07) 4946 7022
fax (07) 4946 7023
e-mail:
whitsundays@epa.qld.gov.au

Campsite bookings: 13 13 04 or
www.qld.gov.au/camping

Walking

Walk through woodland from Tongue Bay (Whitsunday Island) to a lookout for a fantastic view over Hill Inlet and Whitehaven Beach. A 1km track connects Dugong and Sawmill Beaches (Whitsunday Island). A short walk leads to a rock art site at Nara Inlet (Hook Island). Talk to the local rangers before walking off-track.

Getting there

The Whitsunday Island group is readily accessible from Airlie Beach or Shute Harbour by private boat or commercial tours. Commercial boats will drop off and collect campers. Arrange your passage before booking your campsite.

Nara Inlet

Repulse Islands National Park

What's special?

Just off Cape Conway, Repulse Islands National Park protects a small group of islands overlooking the Lindeman Group and the rugged Conway Range.

The islands and surrounding waters are part of the Great Barrier Reef World Heritage Area and are protected.

Exploring Repulse Islands

The small camping area in a sheltered bay at West Beach (South Repulse Island) has a good anchorage. Campers must be self-sufficient. Take fresh water, a fuel stove for cooking and insect repellent. Open fires and generators are prohibited. Remove all rubbish to the mainland.

From 1 October to 31 March seasonal bird restrictions apply. You must observe a 6-knot speed limit within 200m of high water mark and no beach access is permitted within the seabird nesting area at the southern end of West Beach.

Beware of marine stingers and cyclones during the warmer months.

Walking

There are no walking tracks in this park. Talk to the local rangers before walking off-track.

Getting there

Access is by private boat only.

Adam Creed

South Repulse Island

Further information

QPWS
Whitsunday Information Centre
Cnr Shute Harbour and Mandalay Roads
PO Box 332
AIRLIE BEACH QLD 4802
ph (07) 4946 7022
fax (07) 4946 7023
e-mail:
whitsundays@epa.qld.gov.au

Campsite bookings: 13 13 04 or www.qld.gov.au/camping

Molle Islands National Park

What's special?

Windswept hillsides, rocky headlands with majestic hoop pines, sandy beaches, secluded coves, natural grasslands, open forest and rainforest make the inshore Molle Islands a wildlife refuge and a scenic retreat for nature lovers.

Open eucalypt forests clothe the hillsides, rainforest grows in sheltered gullies and grasslands cover the more exposed slopes. A seasonal colony of black flying-foxes lives on South Molle Island.

The Ngaro people lived on and visited these islands for thousands of years. They used fire to flush out game and maintain the natural grasslands. A stone quarry for making tools and weapons remains on South Molle Island.

The Molle Islands were first named in 1815 when Jeffreys was charting the Great Barrier Reef islands. Initially used for grazing, South Molle Island later became a national park and a resort was established in 1937.

The islands and surrounding waters are part of the Great Barrier Reef World Heritage Area and are protected.

Exploring Molle Islands

You can spend a few idyllic hours or a week exploring this beautiful park. Go birdwatching or look for tiny jewel and orb weaver spiders along the walking tracks.

If time is limited, walk from the resort through rainforest and grassland to Paddle Bay. Walk to Spion Kop, Mt Jeffreys or Lamond Hill for a spectacular view over the Whitsundays. Take water and wear a hat and sunscreen.

Stay at the resort or bush camp at Sandy or Paddle Bays on South Molle. You can also camp on North Molle, Long, Tancred, Planton and Denman Islands. Cockatoo Beach (North Molle), Sandy Bay (Long Island) and the South Molle campgrounds have picnic tables and toilets. Campers must be self-sufficient. Open fires and generators are prohibited. Take water, a fuel stove and insect repellent. Remove all your rubbish from the islands.

Paddle Bay campers can only access the walking tracks at low tide. The small Tancred, Planton and Denman Island camping areas have a dry rainforest setting.

Molle Islands National Park

While water is usually clearer at the northern ends of the outer islands, snorkelling over the reef flat at high tide can still be rewarding.

Go snorkelling at Sandy Bay, sailing or visit another nearby park in the beautiful Whitsundays.

Beware of marine stingers and cyclones during the warmer months.

Walking

The park provides many opportunities for bushwalking with 9km tracks on Long Island and 15km on South Molle Island. Talk to the local rangers before walking off-track.

Getting there

The Molle group is just east of Shute Harbour. Access is by private boat or commercial boat. Arrange your passage before booking your campsite.

Molle Group with Shute Harbour in foreground

Tracks

South Molle Island
Spion Kop
2·2km one-way, 40 minutes

Oyster Bay
1·9km one-way, 30 minutes

Mt Jeffreys
2·8km one-way, 1 hour

Sandy Bay
4·1km one-way, 1·5 hours

From western end of the resort:
Paddle Bay
500m one-way, 15 minutes

Lamond Hill
1·4km one-way, 30 minutes

Further information

QPWS
Whitsunday Information Centre
Cnr Shute Harbour and Mandalay Roads
PO Box 332
AIRLIE BEACH QLD 4802
ph (07) 4946 7022
fax (07) 4946 7023
e-mail:
whitsundays@epa.qld.gov.au

Campsite bookings: 13 13 04 or www.qld.gov.au/camping

Lindeman Islands National Park

Paul Candlin

Forest kingfisher

What's special?

Beyond the Whitsunday Passage lies the Lindeman group of islands. Like other islands in the Whitsundays, this group formed when a mountain range was drowned by rising sea levels.

Lindeman was formed from the remains of molten rubble spewed from large volcanoes. Smaller islands have a resistant volcanic core while larger islands in the group are made up of granite.

Lindeman Island has a variety of vegetation types including rainforest in sheltered pockets, open forest in drier areas, grasslands and wetlands. The Aboriginal people who visited these islands knew Lindeman as "Yara-Kimba", the place of snapper and bream. Frequent burning maintained the grasslands on Lindeman Island.

The islands and surrounding waters are part of the Great Barrier Reef World Heritage Area and are protected.

Exploring Lindeman Islands

Camp at Boat Port (Lindeman Island) Neck Bay (Shaw Island) or Naked Lady Beach (Thomas Island).

Boat Port is a quiet campsite in a beach scrub setting with a toilet and a picnic table. Neck Bay (Shaw Island) and Naked Lady Beach (Thomas Island) have no facilities but a beautiful sandy beach. Campers must be self-sufficient. Open fires and generators are prohibited. Take water, a fuel stove and insect repellent. Remove all your rubbish from the islands.

Enjoy the sunset over Lindeman Island from the Neck Bay camping area. Walk to Mt Oldfield on Lindeman Island for a magnificent view over the islands.

While water is usually clearer on the northern sides of the outer islands, snorkelling over the reef flat at high tide can still be rewarding.

Go birdwatching around the wetlands on Lindeman Island. See forest kingfishers, swamphens and bush stone-curlews.

Lindeman Islands National Park

Seasonal bird restrictions apply from 1 October to 31 March. Beach access is not permitted within the seabird nesting area on Shaw Island (the beach east of Burning Point) and visitors must observe a 6-knot speed limit within 200m of high water mark.

Beware of marine stingers and cyclones during the warmer months.

Walking

More than 16km of bushwalks are available on Lindeman and Seaforth Islands. Talk to the local rangers before walking off-track.

Getting there

Access is by commercial or private boats or aircraft.

Shaw Island

Adam Creed

Tracks

Lindeman Island
Mt Oldfield walk
9km return, 3–4 hours

Coconut Beach-Boat Port walk
1km one-way, 30 minutes

Coconut Beach-Boat Port Loop walk
8·5km circuit, 2·5–3 hours

Boat Port to resort
3·3km one-way, 1 hour

Resort to Gap Beach and Butterfly Valley
6km return, 2 hours

Resort to Plantation Beach
8km return, 2·5–3 hours

Further information

QPWS
Whitsunday Information Centre
Cnr Shute Harbour and Mandalay Roads
PO Box 332
AIRLIE BEACH QLD 4802
ph (07) 4946 7022
fax (07) 4946 7023
e-mail: whitsundays@epa.qld.gov.au

Campsite bookings: 13 13 04 or www.qld.gov.au/camping

Gloucester Island National Park

Gloucester Island

Adam Creed

What's special?

Just off the mainland between Airlie Beach and Bowen lies Gloucester Islands National Park, a scenic group of inshore continental islands. Gloucester Island, the largest, is home to a colony of endangered Proserpine rock-wallabies. Sandy and coral rubble beaches, rainforest and seclusion are some of this park's main attractions.

The islands and surrounding waters are part of the Great Barrier Reef World Heritage Area and are protected.

Exploring Gloucester Island

More remote than other parks in the Whitsundays, these islands offer a quiet retreat.

Camp at Bona or East Side Bays (Gloucester Island) or at Armit or Saddleback Islands. Bona Bay (Gloucester Island), the largest campground, has a good anchorage, toilets, picnic tables, and a shelter shed. East Side Bay (Gloucester) is set between two rocky headlands. Armit Island has a toilet and picnic tables. Saddleback is close to the mainland.

Campers must be self-sufficient. Take fresh water, a fuel stove for cooking and insect repellent. Open fires and generators are prohibited. Remove all rubbish to the mainland.

From 1 October to 31 March seasonal bird restrictions apply. You must observe a 6-knot speed limit within 200m of high water mark and no beach access is permitted within seabird nesting areas on south beach (Armit Island), west beach (Double Cone Island), south beach (Grassy Island), Little Armit Island, and Old Rock. These restrictions apply all year round at Eshelby and Little Eshelby Islands.

Beware of marine stingers and cyclones during the warmer months.

Walking

There are no walking tracks in this park. Talk to the local rangers before walking off-track.

Getting there

Take a private boat from Dingo Beach, Hydeaway Bay, Bowen or Airlie Beach to reach these islands.

Further information

QPWS
Whitsunday Information Centre
Cnr Shute Harbour and Mandalay Roads
PO Box 332
AIRLIE BEACH QLD 4802
ph (07) 4946 7022
fax (07) 4946 7023
e-mail:
whitsundays@epa.qld.gov.au

Campsite bookings: 13 13 04 or www.qld.gov.au/camping

Conway State Forest

What's special?

On the rugged Conway Range behind Airlie Beach lies Conway State Forest. This beautiful forest contains lowland tropical rainforest remnants and picturesque rocky creeks. The forest has been selectively logged over the past 70 years for sought-after rainforest timber. Trial plantations of hoop pines were established in the forest. Logging ended in 1993.

Volcanic activity millions of years ago created this rugged landscape and the offshore islands. The volcano was centred over Pentecost Island.

The forest is home to many animals including the buff-breasted paradise-kingfisher which migrates here to breed each summer.

Exploring Conway

The forest is largely undeveloped, so visitors must be self-sufficient.

Go birdwatching or bushwalking. See exquisite Ulysses butterflies and hear the call of the wompoo fruit-dove. See the remains of old snigging tracks used to remove felled trees during the logging days.

Camping is not allowed in the forest but there are plenty of places to stay nearby at Cannonvale and Airlie Beach.

A Great Walk is being developed in the forest with bush campsites, lookouts and trails. The walk should be ready mid-2004.

Walking

Enjoy the Kingfisher Rainforest circuit which winds down to a creek. Take a brochure from the stand at the start of the track to help you explore the forest. (Please return it afterwards.) See large rainforest trees, Alexandra palms, cauliflorous figs and strangler figs.

Getting there

Head west from Airlie Beach for 10km or 13km east from Proserpine along the Shute Harbour Road. Turn off to the Brandy Creek Road and drive 6km along a mostly gravel road to the carpark before a locked gate. Park here near the Kingfisher Rainforest circuit. Access is suitable for conventional vehicles.

Adam Creed

View of Conway Range

Tracks

Kingfisher Rainforest circuit
2km, 45 minutes

Further information

QPWS
Whitsunday Information Centre
Cnr Shute Harbour and Mandalay Roads
PO Box 332
AIRLIE BEACH QLD 4802
ph (07) 4946 7022
fax (07) 4946 7023
9am–5pm weekdays

Conway National Park

View of Conway National Park

Adam Creed

What's special?

Forested hills along the Conway Range fringe the scenic Whitsunday Passage in Conway National Park. Conway is very similar to the offshore islands because the sea level rose thousands of years ago, drowning the coastal ranges and creating the islands.

Dry vine thicket, mangroves, open forests with a grasstree understorey, paperbark and pandanus woodlands, and patches of lowland rainforest with twisted vines grow in the park. The park is home to two of Australia's mound-building birds, the Australian brush-turkey and the orange-footed scrubfowl.

For thousands of years, the Ngaro and Gia people roamed these forests, harvesting the riches of the forests and the adjoining sea country. Today, the adjacent waters are protected in marine parks.

Exploring Conway

Get away from it all in this peaceful park with its beautiful forests, panoramic lookouts and secluded beaches. Beware of marine stingers October to May. Wear insect repellent.

Stop for a picnic and short walk at the picnic area on the Shute Harbour Road. Toilets, a shelter shed and electric barbecues are provided.

Bush camp beside a secluded, pebbly beach overlooking Daydream (West Molle) Island. This is a walk-in camping area only. Sites are limited. Tank water, a shelter shed, a pit toilet and bush campsites are provided. Take a fuel stove and drinking water. The supply is limited and seasonal. Boil the water for five minutes before drinking.

Walk uphill to the Mt Rooper Lookout for a spectacular view over Hamilton, Dent, Long and Henning Islands. Walk 700m up a ridge from Coral Beach for a view over the Molle Islands. Find out why this area is so important to the local Ngaro people on the Coral Beach track.

Go birdwatching. See emerald doves, sulphur-crested cockatoos and brush-turkeys.

Conway National Park

Walking

Tracks take you through the main vegetation types to lookouts with magnificent views over the Whitsundays. Wear insect repellent, a hat and sunscreen. Take drinking water and avoid walking in summer and the middle of the day.

Accessibility

The toilets in the picnic area have wheelchair-assisted access.

Getting there

Conway straddles the Airlie Beach-Shute Harbour Road just a few kilometres south of Airlie Beach.

Tracks

Swamp Bay track
4·2km return, 1 hour

Mt Rooper circuit
5·4km, 90 minutes–2 hours

Mt Rooper circuit and Swamp Bay
7·5km return, 2–3 hours

Coral Beach track
2km return, 40 minutes

Picnic area circuit
1km, 30 minutes

Further information

QPWS
Whitsunday Information Centre
Cnr Shute Harbour and Mandalay Roads
PO Box 332
AIRLIE BEACH QLD 4802
(07) 4946 7022
fax (07) 4946 7023
9am–5pm weekdays

Campsite bookings: 13 13 04 or www.qld.gov.au/camping

Sulphur-crested cockatoo

Dryander National Park

Drylander National Park

Adam Creed

Further information

QPWS
Whitsunday Information
Centre
Cnr Mandalay and Shute Harbour
Roads
PO Box 332
AIRLIE BEACH QLD 4802
ph (07) 4946 7022
fax (07) 4946 7023
9am–5pm weekdays

Campsite bookings: 13 13 04 or
www.qld.gov.au/camping

What's special?

Overlooking the scenic Whitsunday Islands, Dryander
National Park is a large coastal park north of Proserpine.
Fringing reefs just offshore are protected in marine parks.

Exploring Dryander

Relax and enjoy nature in this peaceful coastal retreat.

Bush camp at Grimstone Point. Toilets and picnic tables are
provided but visitors should be totally self-sufficient. Take a
fuel stove, drinking water and insect repellent.

Check the zoning plan for permitted activities in the
adjacent marine park waters. Beware of marine stingers
October to May.

Getting there

Access is by boat from Airlie Beach or Dingo Beach.

John Augusteyn

Rufous owl

Cape Upstart National Park

What's special?

Flanked by sandy beaches, Cape Upstart is an imposing granite headland covered in a range of vegetation types from vine thicket to heath.

This is an important place for the Juru people.

The surrounding waters are part of the Great Barrier Reef Marine Park.

Exploring Cape Upstart

This is a low-key park for self-sufficient visitors. Camp at Coconut Beach or bush camp in a secluded campsite on the northern side of the Elliot River. No facilities are provided. Take drinking water and a fuel stove.

Check the marine park zoning plan for advice on activities permitted in the adjacent marine park waters. Beware of marine stingers October to May. Beware of estuarine crocodiles at Coconut Bay.

Getting there

Cape Upstart is on the coast between Ayr and Bowen. There is no vehicle access to the park. Access is by boat only. Launch your boat at ramps south of Gumlu at Molongle Bay or the Elliot River near Guthalungra.

Further information

QPWS
Whitsunday Information Centre
Cnr Shute Harbour and
Mandalay Roads
PO Box 332
AIRLIE BEACH QLD 4802
ph (07) 4946 7022
fax (07) 4946 7023
9am–5pm weekdays

Campsite bookings: 13 13 04 or www.qld.gov.au/camping

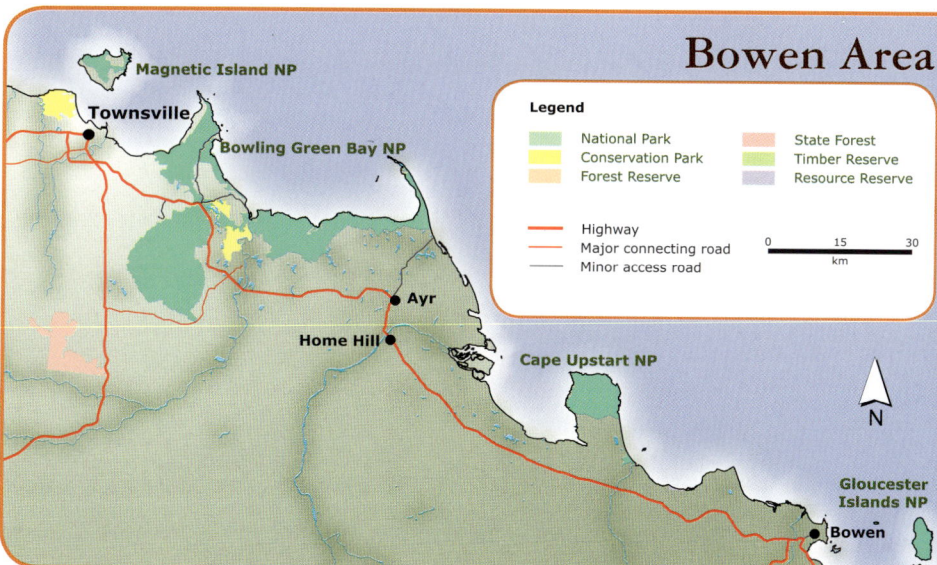

Bowen Area

Magnetic Island NP

Townsville

Bowling Green Bay NP

Ayr

Home Hill

Cape Upstart NP

Gloucester
Islands NP

Bowen

Legend

National Park	State Forest
Conservation Park	Timber Reserve
Forest Reserve	Resource Reserve

Highway
Major connecting road
Minor access road

0   15   30
km

N

Map 9

Central Outback

Map 10

Legend

- National Park
- Conservation Park
- Forest Reserve
- State Forest
- Timber Reserve
- Resource Reserve
- Highway
- Major connecting road
- Minor access road

0 35 70
km

N

NORTHERN TERRITORY

Kynuna
Combo CP

Winton

Muttaburra

Bladensburg NP

Lark Quarry CP

Longreach

Boulia

Barcaldine

Diamantina NP

Lochern NP

Blackall

Welford NP

Idalia NP

Simpson
Desert NP

Windorah

Birdsville

Adavale

SOUTH AUSTRALIA

Mariala NP

Sand ridges and spinifex, Simpson Desert National Park

Robert Ashdown

Bladensburg National Park

What's special?

Flat-topped mesas, plateaus and residual sandstone ranges are a scenic backdrop to Bladensburg National Park's vast grassland plains and river flats. This large, remote park protects examples of the Mitchell Grass Downs and Channel Country in outback Queensland.

Mitchell and Flinders grasses grow on the plains while river red gum and coolibahs fringe Surprise Creek. Open woodlands of western bloodwood and mulga grow on mesas and plateaus, lancewood and spinifex grass cover steep slopes and escarpments and Normanton box grows in the broad valleys.

The park is home to a wonderful variety of wildlife, from kangaroos and wallaroos to dunnarts, native marsupial mice and birds such as emus, spotted bowerbirds and brolgas. Many birds are at the extreme boundary of their range here.

Skull Hole is believed to be the site of an Aboriginal massacre in the late 1800s. Other sites in the park are reminders of the park's early pastoral history.

Exploring Bladensburg

Picnic or bush camp beside Bough Shed Hole or at Scrammy Gorge. Visitors must be self-sufficient. Take water.

Go stargazing at night. Away from city lights, the starlit skies are entrancing. Go birdwatching around the creek. Look for painted firetails and rufous-throated honeyeaters, two typical birds of central and northern Australia.

Go for a scenic drive in dry weather. The Scrammy Tourist Drive is 40km return from the park office. See the restored homestead which is now a visitor centre. The cooler months from March to September are the best times to visit.

Walking

Only experienced and well-equipped walkers should go bushwalking. There are no tracks.

Getting there

Bladensburg is 17km south-west of Winton. Take the "Route of the River Gums" starting about 8km south of Winton on the Jundah-Opalton road. Drive 6km to the park and a further 8km to the camping area. Check road conditions before visiting.

Bruce Cowell, Queensland Museum

Bladensburg National Park

Further information

Bladensburg NP
via WINTON QLD 4735
ph (07) 4657 1192
fax (07) 4657 0214
UHF channel 18

QPWS
Landsborough Highway
PO Box 202
LONGREACH QLD 4730
Ph (07) 4652 7333
fax (07) 4658 1778

Idalia National Park

Bats-wing coral tree flower
Damian Mc Greevy

Bridled nailtail wallaby
Adam Creed

What's special?

In central western Queensland, Idalia National Park protects extensive mulga woodlands, the headwaters of the Bulloo River, and tributaries of the Barcoo River system. The broad, sandy, river red gum-fringed watercourses are usually dry, except following rain.

Mulga covers most of the park. Mountain yapunyah, Dawson gum and lancewood occasionally grow in the low bendee woodlands on the escarpments and steep slopes. Open woodlands of poplar box and silver-leaved ironbark grow on sandy flats beside the Bulloo River. Brigalow, boree and gidgee also grow in the park. Fifteen native fuschia species occur in the park.

Yellow-footed rock-wallabies live in Idalia's high rocky escarpments. This rock-wallaby is threatened with extinction. A colony of bridled nailtail wallabies was re-introduced to the park as part of the recovery program for this endangered wallaby.

Exploring Idalia

There is plenty to do and see in this remote park. Go birdwatching. You might see mulga parrots, eastern yellow robins or common bronzewing pigeons. Look for wallaroos, red kangaroos, grey kangaroos or the occasional koala. See the rock-wallabies at Emmet Pocket lookout or along Bullock Gorge walking track.

Go spotlighting at night around the visitor centre and you might see the endangered bridled nailtail wallaby.

Explore Old Idalia, the site of an old musterer's hut and stockyards. Walk to a nearby wave-shaped cliff overhang for views over the park and stunning sunsets.

Explore the park and learn about the vegetation along a signposted self-guided drive from the information centre to the campground.

Drive 4·3km from Monk's Tank to Rainbow Gorge, colourful sandstone rock formations in the headwaters of a creek. Visit Murphy's Rockhole, a 8·9km drive north of Monk's Tank. This shady gorge is a watering point for wildlife.

Enjoy panoramic views over the northern end of the park from Emmet Pocket lookout, 12km from Monk's Tank.

Idalia National Park

Idalia Creek

Camp at Monk's Tank, 14km from the park office. Visitors must be self-sufficient. Take water and a fuel stove and extra supplies of food, fuel and water. (One fireplace is available.) Visit during the cooler months, April to September.

Walking

As the country here is fairly flat, walking is easy. Take drinking water and wear a hat and sunscreen. Check with the ranger about a 5km hike down the creek.

Accessibility

The toilets at Monk's Tank camping area are wheelchair-accessible.

Getting there

Idalia is south-west of Blackall via the Yaraka Road. Turn south at the Benlidi siding, 70km from Blackall. Follow the Idalia-Benlidi Road for about 70km to the park boundary. The office is a further 12·5km. When you arrive, call at the park office. Four-wheel-drive is not essential but high clearance vehicle access is recommended. Off-road caravans can be towed to the camping area with care.

Tracks

Emmet Pocket lookout track
4·4km return, 1·5 hours

Bullock Gorge circuit
1·2km, 30 minutes

Old Idalia ruins to Wave Rock track
1·6km return, 45 minutes

Further information

Idalia NP
via BLACKALL QLD 4472
ph/fax (07) 4657 5033

QPWS
Landsborough Highway
PO Box 202
LONGREACH QLD 4730
ph (07) 4652 7333
fax (07) 4658 1778

Mulga woodland, Idalia National Park

Adam Bruzzese

Welford National Park

Barcoo River, Welford National Park

Gary Cranitch, Queensland Museum

What's special?

Striking red sand dunes contrast with green spinifex grass and white ghost gums in this large diverse park in arid south-western Queensland.

Welford National Park protects examples of three of the State's natural arid regions, Mulga Lands, Channel Country and Mitchell Grass Downs. Some of Australia's most easterly wind-blown sand dunes occur in the park, which is also the extreme western range for many plants, including mountain yapunyah, poplar box, bendo and lancewood. The giant grey spinifex *Triodia longiceps* which grows on the lower slopes of the park's ranges is uncommon in the surrounding region.

Large permanent waterholes on the Barcoo River are a refuge for wildlife, especially birds. Yellow-footed rock-wallabies shelter in rocky outcrops in the park's rugged northern and eastern sections.

Evidence of Aboriginal occupation is scattered throughout the park. Remnants include wells and stone arrangements. The rammed earth homestead built on the former grazing property in 1882–3 is on the Queensland Heritage Register. This is a rare and fairly intact example of this type of construction.

Exploring Welford

Bush camp at Little Boomerang Waterhole on the Barcoo River. Take drinking water and a fuel stove. Go fishing.

Go scenic driving along two tourist drives. Allow two hours for each drive from the campground. The mulga drive leads to a picturesque waterhole on Sawyers Creek. See the sand dunes on the desert drive.

Go wildlife watching. See pelicans, brolgas, black swans and whistling kites around the waterholes. Look for brushtail possums at night. See emus on the grassy plains and pink cockatoos, mallee ringnecks, red-winged parrots and mulga parrots in the mulga woodlands.

Visit in the cooler, drier months, April to September. Nights can be frosty.

Welford National Park

Bruce Cowell

Getting there

Welford is 50km south-east of Jundah. Travel south-west
from Blackall on the Yaraka Retreat Road or north-west
from Quilpie on the Diamantina Developmental Road to the
Jundah-Quilpie Road.

Turn off the Jundah-Quilpie Road at the park entrance,
40km from Jundah and drive a further 10km to the park
office. Four-wheel-drive is recommended on the mainly
unsealed roads which are impassable in wet weather.

Further information

Welford NP
via JUNDAH QLD 4736
ph (07) 4658 5994
fax(07) 4658 5952
UHF channel 4 duplex

QPWS
Landsborough Highway
PO Box 202
LONGREACH QLD 4730
ph (07) 4652 7333
fax (07) 4658 1778

Sand dunes, Welford National Park

Gary Cranitch, Queensland Museum

Lochern National Park

Waterhole, Lochern National Park

Bruce Cowell, Queensland Museum

Red-kneed dotterel

Robert Ashdown

What's special?

Lochern is in the heart of boom and bust country where flooding rains and devastating drought are part of daily life. The park protects habitats in Queensland's Channel Country, Mitchell Grass Downs and Mulga Lands including mulga, hakea, western bloodwood and coolibah and gidgee woodlands.

All four species of Mitchell grass (bull, curly, barley and hoop) grow on the park. Whitewood and gidgee woodlands grow on stony ridges while sandplains support leopardwood and gidgee woodlands or mulga and eastern dead finish shrublands.

Lochern National Park has a 20km frontage to the Thomson River. The park's many lagoons and waterholes are a refuge for birds and other wildlife. Forrest's mouse, restricted to the arid inland, is at the eastern boundary of its range at Lochern. The threatened Major Mitchell (pink) cockatoo also lives in the park.

Exploring Lochern

Like the jolly swagman, you can camp beside a billabong at Broadwater Hole. Rediscover the park's pastoral past by staying in the old shearers' quarters. Visitors must be self-sufficient. Take fuel, food, water, first aid kit and vehicle spare parts.

Lochern is a great place for watching wildlife. See kangaroos, wallaroos, emus, brolgas and Australian bustards.

Go birdwatching early morning around the waterholes or in the sweetly-scented eastern dead finish and native fuchsia shrublands. See red-tailed black-cockatoos in spring and summer. Go fishing. Size and bag limits apply.

Explore the park along the 16km Bluebush Lagoon circuit drive which starts near the office. See Mitchell grass plains, gidgee woodlands and coolibah-fringed creeks.

See the shepherd's yards and old shearers' quarters. April to September are the best times to visit though nights can be cold. Summers are very hot.

Lochern National Park

Lin Martin

Walking

The park has no walking tracks but you can wander around the river and waterholes.

Getting there

Lochern is 140km south-west of Longreach or 40km north of Stonehenge. The best access is from Longreach or Stonehenge along the Longreach-Jundah Road. Turn off 100km south of Longreach then follow the unsealed road about 40km to the park boundary. Drive a further 10km to the park office. Allow 4–5 hours for the journey from Winton. This access route is rough and dusty. Always check road conditions before you visit. Rain makes the roads impassable.

Further information

Lochern NP
via LONGREACH QLD 4730
ph (07) 4658 5959
UHF channel 2 or 7 (duplex)

QPWS
Landsborough Highway
PO Box 202
LONGREACH QLD 4730
ph (07) 4652 7333
fax (07) 4658 1778

Thomson River, Lochern National Park

Bruce Cowell, Queensland Museum

Lark Quarry Conservation Park

Dinosaur footprints at Lark Quarry

What's special?

The land before time is near Winton in outback Queensland where the world's only known site of a dinosaur stampede is preserved in Lark Quarry Conservation Park.

The stampede happened 95 million years ago when a theropod, a large meat-eating dinosaur, startled and chased a horde of much smaller dinosaurs (coelurosaurs and ornithopods) on the muddy shores of a lake. The footprints made in the mud have been fossilised and can be seen today in a shelter at Lark Quarry Conservation Park, a major dinosaur tourism destination.

Formed over millions of years, the ancient rocks known as the Winton Formation have been eroded into a striking landscape known as "jump up" country with its flat-topped hills (mesas), gullies, and steep, broken escarpments.

Stunted mallee eucalypts, wattles and spinifex grass in the park provide a home for more than 90 species of birds (including black kites, rufous-crowned emu-wrens and spinifex pigeons), as well as lizards, echidnas and wallaroos.

The park's infrastructure, built using ecologically sustainable design principles, features solar energy, rainwater collection and minimal impact construction methods.

Lark Quarry is jointly managed by the Queensland Parks and Wildlife Service and Winton Shire Council. The Queensland Museum provides these agencies with scientific advice on ways to protect the trackways.

Exploring Lark Quarry

Step back in time to a primeval world where dinosaurs roamed lush, damp rainforests. Discover the fascinating dinosaur story and gaze in wonder at the evidence preserved forever here. Entry to the trackways is by guided tour only. Tickets can be purchased from the Waltzing Matilda Centre in Winton (07) 4657 1466 or on-site, www.matildacentre.com.au.

Have a picnic or go bushwalking. Entry to the park is free but a fee applies if you want to view the trackways. Signs and displays explain the dinosaur story.

Lark Quarry Conservation Park

Walking

Explore the "jump up" country along a short half-hour walking track from the entry building to a lookout over the surrounding countryside. Carry water and wear a hat, sunscreen and sturdy walking shoes.

Accessibility

The trackways building is wheelchair-accessible.

Getting there

Lark Quarry is 110km or 90 minutes south-west of Winton along the Jundah Road. The park is three hours from Longreach. The gravel access road may be impassable following rain.

Further information

Waltzing Matilda Centre
50 Elderslie Street
WINTON QLD 4735
ph (07) 4657 1466
e-mail: matilda@thehub.com.au

Dinosaur Trackway building, Lark Quarry Conservation Park

Diamantina National Park

Greater bilby
Darren Jew

What's special?

Vast open plains stretching towards the horizon are broken only by the coolibah-lined channels of meandering rivers and creeks in Diamantina National Park. This large, remote park in Queensland's Channel Country features sand dunes, claypans, ragged red-capped ranges, and the broad floodplains and braided channels of the Diamantina River, one of the state's longest rivers.

Beyond the river flats are vast gibber plains and Mitchell grasslands. Trees at the western limit of their range include mountain yapunyah, Normanton box and red mallee. Myall *Eremophila tetraptera*, a native fuschia which grows in the park, is considered vulnerable to extinction.

Diamantina is home to many rare and threatened species such as the greater bilby, kowari, dusky hopping-mouse, kultarr, plains wanderer, peregrine falcon and two rare skinks.

The Kirrenderri people who lived here for thousands of years call Diamantina "Kurrawoolkani" and regard this place as their heartland. The park has a rich Aboriginal history and is also the traditional land of the Maiawali people. Once a working cattle property, Diamantina contains old station buildings, remains of the Mayne Hotel, stone hut ruins near Warracoota Waterhole and cemeteries.

Exploring Diamantina

Rich colours delight photographers who visit this diverse park. Camp or fish, or go canoeing, scenic driving or birdwatching. Obtain a copy of the park guide and self-guided circuit drive brochure to help you explore the park.

You can bush camp at Hunter's Gorge or Gum Waterhole. Take drinking water and a fuel stove.

See the park along the 157km Warracoota self-guided circuit drive, which takes visitors past sand dunes, floodplains, claypans, gibber plains and grasslands. Stop at Warracoota Waterhole and visit the old cattle yards, a large constructed dam and an old stock camp.

Go birdwatching around seasonal lakes and waterholes. See spoonbills, darters, galahs and budgerigars. Fish for yellowbelly and Welsh's grunter in Mundewerra Waterhole at Hunters Gorge.

Diamantina National Park

See the "Diamantina Gates" from Janet Leap Lookout. Here, the river is funnelled between the Guyder and Hamilton Ranges.

Enjoy spectacular wildflower displays after rain. Visit in the cooler months, April to September. Summers are very hot.

Getting there

Head south from Winton or Boulia or north from Windorah and Bedourie. Access is suitable for four-wheel-drive vehicles only and roads may become impassable or flooded after rain. Always check road conditions before travelling to the park. Access is through working pastoral properties. Leave gates as you find them. Take extra fuel. The closest supplies are at Boulia (183km), Winton (306km) or Windorah (350km).

Hunters Gorge is 14km from the park headquarters or 4km from the Boulia-Springvale Road. Gum Waterhole is 11km past the Hunters Gorge turnoff.

Further information

Diamantina NP
via WINTON QLD 4735
ph (07) 4657 3024
fax (07) 4657 3977
UHF channel 29

QPWS
Landsborough Highway
PO Box 202
LONGREACH QLD 4730
ph (07) 4652 7333
fax (07) 4658 1778

Sunrise over the Diamantina River

Simpson Desert National Park

Triumfetta winneckeana,
Simpson Desert National Park

What's special?

In the dry heart of Australia, Simpson Desert National Park contains part of the world's largest and youngest parallel sand dune desert. This is Queensland's largest national park.

The parallel, wind-blown sand dunes up to 90m high are about 1km apart, extend up to 200km and run north-west to south-south-east. Between the dunes are gibber-ironstone flats, claypans, saltpans and sand plains.

Simpson Desert is home to the small carnivorous mulgara, which is vulnerable to extinction, and more than 180 bird species including the Eyrean grasswren which lives among the canegrass.

Exploring Simpson Desert

Enjoy the rich colours of this big sky country with its red sand dunes and ironstone pebbles, grey-green spinifex grass and clear blue skies. Camp under the stars. You can bush camp within 500m of the QAA line.

Robert Ashdown

Thorny devil

Robert Ashdown

Simpson Desert National Park

Robert Ashdown

Robert Ashdown

Ghost gums, Simpson Desert National Park

Find out the park's special stories on a self-guiding drive. Ten sites are signposted along the track between the eastern park boundary and Poeppel's Corner.

Discover the plants and animals which have adapted to this harsh place. Smell the pungent Georgina gidgee, a wattle growing in the dune swales. Look for tracks of desert animals in the sand. Look for white-winged fairy-wrens in clumps of sandhill canegrass.

Only experienced, self-sufficient visitors should explore Simpson Desert. Visitors must be well-equipped to cope with the harsh environment in the driest place in Australia. Leave a copy of your travel plans with your family or someone responsible. Travel in two-vehicle parties and stay on the track. Take a two-way radio and plenty of food, water, fuel and spare parts for your vehicle. Be prepared for temperature extremes with hot days and freezing nights. Visit only between April and October.

Walking

There are no tracks in the park and walking any distance is not recommended. Stay with your vehicle. Always wear a hat and sunscreen and drink plenty of water.

Getting there

Head west from Birdsville. For 74km, you pass through private property. The first 35km is a formed road but the remaining 130km is four-wheel-drive only and can take 5–6 hours to cross. Visitors must stay on the QAA line inside the park. The roads become impassable when wet. You need a Desert Pass to visit the South Australian part of the desert. The closest food and fuel are at Birdsville.

Further information

QPWS
cnr Billabong Boulevard and Jardine Streets
BIRDSVILLE QLD 4482
ph (07) 4656 3249
ph (07) 4656 3272
fax (07) 4656 3273

QPWS
Landsborough Highway
PO Box 202
LONGREACH QLD 4730
ph (07) 4652 7333
fax (07) 4658 1778

South Australian National Parks and Wildlife Service
PO Box 78
PORT AUGUSTA SA 5700
ph (08) 8648 5300 or
freecall 1800 816 078
fax (08) 8648 5301

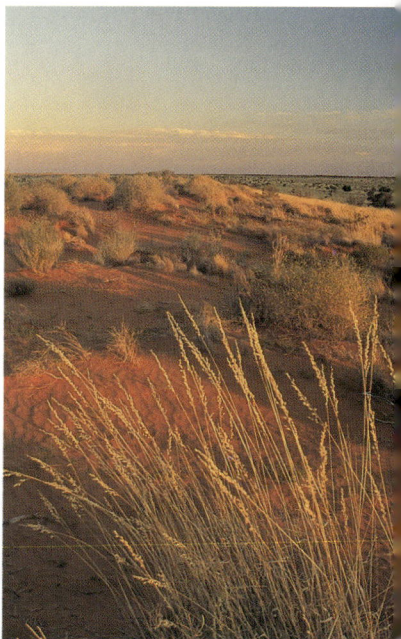

Robert Ashdown

Spinifex, Simpson Desert National Park

Combo Conservation Park

Hobby falcon
Robert Ashdown

What's special?

Did the jolly swagman camp by Combo Waterhole? We will probably never know for sure, but waterholes in this park reputedly inspired Banjo Paterson to write Australia's most popular folk song, Waltzing Matilda, while visiting nearby Dagworth Station in 1895.

Combo Conservation Park contains a string of semi-permanent coolibah-lined lagoons in outback Queensland. Combo Waterhole is on one of Queensland's longest rivers, the Diamantina. The park is a wildlife refuge, especially in dry times.

Exploring Combo

Have a bush picnic on the banks of this famous waterhole. Camping is not allowed.

Discover the park's fascinating past as you wander along the channels of the Diamantina River. See the historic stone-pitched overshot weirs (causeways) built by skilled Chinese labourers from 1883.

Walking

A 40 minute return walk to the waterholes starts in the carpark. Wear a hat and sunscreen.

Getting there

Combo is just near Kynuna, 145km north-west of Winton. Turn south off the Landsborough Highway 13km south of Kynuna or 132km north-west of Winton. A short drive leads to the park. Wet weather may restrict access to the park.

Further information

QPWS
Landsborough Highway
PO Box 202
LONGREACH QLD 4730
ph (07) 4652 7333
fax (07) 4658 1778

Combo Waterhole
Jeff Wright, Queensland Museum

Townsville Area

Map 11

Legend

National Park	State Forest	— Highway	
Conservation Park	Timber Reserve	— Major connecting road	
Forest Reserve	Resource Reserve	— Minor access road	

0   15   30
km

N

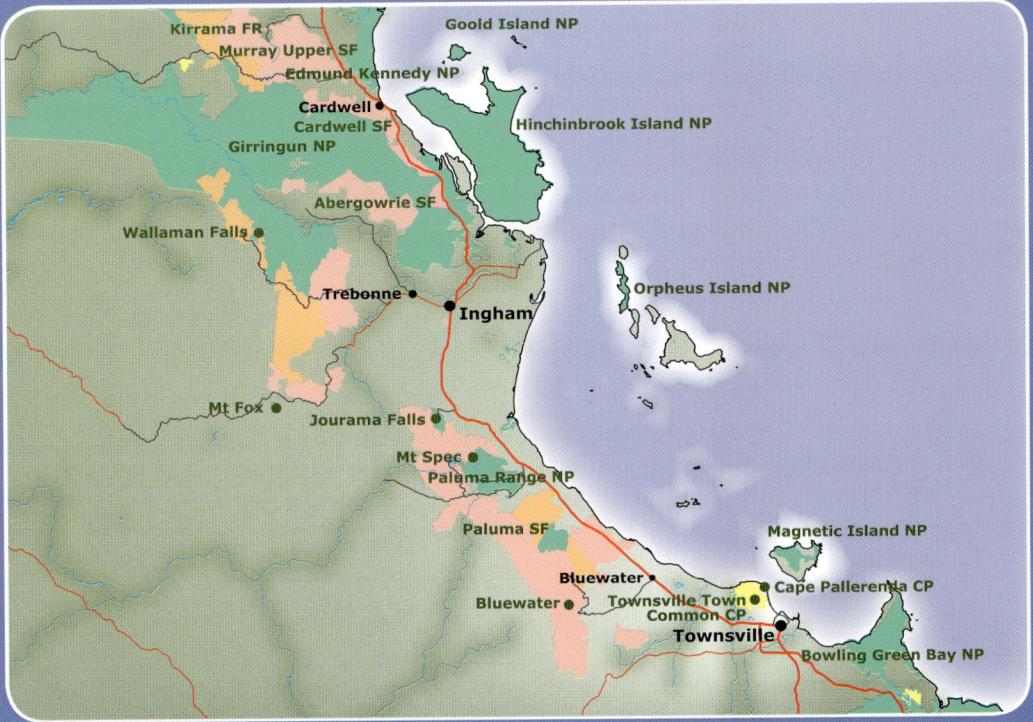

Kirrama FR
Murray Upper SF
Edmund Kennedy NP
Goold Island NP
Cardwell
Cardwell SF
Girringun NP
Hinchinbrook Island NP
Abergowrie SF
Wallaman Falls
Trebonne
Ingham
Orpheus Island NP
Mt Fox
Jourama Falls
Mt Spec
Paluma Range NP
Paluma SF
Magnetic Island NP
Bluewater
Townsville Town
Common CP
Cape Pallerenda CP
Bluewater
Townsville
Bowling Green Bay NP

Paul Candlin

Jourama Falls Section, Paluma Range National Park

Bowling Green Bay National Park

What's special?

Rugged granite mountains rise abruptly above the coastal plain in Bowling Green Bay National Park, the largest park between Bowen and Townsville. Coastal wetlands, saltpans and mangroves cover much of this coastal park. Alligator Creek flows through the park in a series of cascades, deep pools and waterfalls.

Tropical rainforest grows towards the summit of Mt Elliot, the highest peak in the park. Open forests and woodlands, riverine vegetation, mangroves and coastal vegetation also grow in the park.

Aboriginal people of the Wulgurukaba language group once lived in this area and have left behind rock paintings. Explorer Philip Parker King landed at Cape Cleveland in 1819 and the first white settlers lived here from 1846.

Exploring Bowling Green Bay

Have a picnic or camp at Alligator Creek. Picnic tables, a shelter shed, gas barbecues and toilets are provided. The camping area has hot showers and wood barbecues and is suitable for caravans and motorhomes. Remove your rubbish.

Go spotlighting at night. Look for brushtail possums, sugar gliders and northern brown bandicoots. See agile wallabies, allied rock-wallabies and rufous bettongs feeding early morning and late afternoon.

Visit the information centre to find out more about the park.

Walking

Walk along Alligator Creek to the falls. Wear a hat and sunscreen. Take drinking water. Beware of slippery rocks.

Accessibility

The camping and picnic area toilets, and a 100m boardwalk along Alligator Creek near the picnic area, are wheelchair-accessible.

Paul Candlin

Alligator Creek

Bowling Green Bay National Park

Bowling Green Bay

Getting there

Turn off the Bruce Highway 28km south of Townsville or 59km north of Ayr. Drive 6km to the park. Watch for wildlife between dusk and dawn. The park is closed at night (6.30pm–6.30am).

Rufous bettong

Tracks

Alligator Creek track
17km return, 5 hours

Cockatoo Creek track
3km return, 1 hour

Further information

QPWS
Reef and National Parks
Information Centre
Old Quarantine Station
Cape Pallarenda Rd
PO Box 5391
TOWNSVILLE QLD 4810
ph (07) 4722 5224
e-mail:
tsv.infocentre@epa.qld.gov.au

Campsite bookings: 13 13 04 or
www.qld.gov.au/camping

Townsville Town Common Conservation Park

What's special?

Mangrove-lined tidal estuaries, swamps, vine thickets, grasslands and woodlands on the northern side of Townsville are collectively known as "The Common". Townsville Town Common Conservation Park protects remnants of the once extensive Bohle River Basin.

The Town Common is ever-changing as wetlands fill and dry up with seasonal changes. When the waterholes are full, from December to June, thousands of magpie geese, brolgas and other birds flock here to feed as inland waterways gradually dry up.

This is a popular park for Townsville residents and visitors.

Town Common

Keith McDonald

Townsville Town Common Conservation Park

Paul Candlin

Exploring Town Common

Stop at the information shelter at the park entrance to find out about the park.

The Common is a great place for birdwatching. Six bird observation points are provided. The Jacana and Freshwater Lagoon bird hides overlook a seasonal wetland at the end of the Freshwater Lagoon Road. Signs help you identify the birds you are most likely to see. The Bald Rock bird hide is located at the end of the Causeway Road.

Look for wildlife all-year-round. Dingoes roam around and agile wallabies feed on grassy verges.

Enjoy spectacular views over the Common and along the coast from tracks through the Many Peaks Range. Discover how the local Wulgurukaba Aboriginal people used plants for food and medicine along the Plant trail starting behind the QPWS office.

Camping is not allowed in the park.

Walking

Three longer walks go over the Many Peaks Range. A forest walk and self-guiding Aboriginal plant trail are also provided. Wear sensible walking shoes, a hat and sunscreen and carry water.

Accessibility

The Freshwater Lagoon bird hide and the 50m track to the observation tower are wheelchair-accessible.

Getting there

Townsville Town Common is on the Cape Pallarenda Road at Townsville. The park entrance is near the golf club. Park gates are closed at night and open 6.30am to 6.30pm daily. Vehicles are allowed only on the 6km Freshwater Lagoon Road and the Causeway. Access to the Bald Rock bird hide may be restricted in wet weather. The Aboriginal plant trail and Teegoora Rock Lookout track are accessible from the carpark at Pallarenda near the QPWS office.

Paul Candlin

Dancing brolga, Town Common

Tracks

Forest walk
1·9km, 45 minutes

Aboriginal plant trail
800m circuit, 45 minutes

Teegoora Rock Lookout
1·6km return, 1 hour

**Bald Rock carpark to
Cape Pallarenda Road**
4·5km one-way, 4 hours return

**Bald Rock carpark to
Shelly Beach**
8km return, 4–5 hours

Further information

**QPWS
Reef and National Parks
Information Centre**
Old Quarantine Station
Cape Pallarenda Rd
PO Box 5391
TOWNSVILLE QLD 4810
ph (07) 4722 5224
e-mail:
tsv.infocentre@epa.qld.gov.au

Cape Pallarenda Conservation Park

What's special?

This scenic coastal park is the site of a former quarantine station for the port of Townsville. The original quarantine station was relocated here from Magnetic Island in 1915 and operated until 1973. The buildings are typical timber Queenslanders with high ceilings and wide verandas. Most are now used as offices for the Queensland Parks and Wildlife Service.

Cape Pallarenda Conservation Park contains the remains of gun emplacements and search light towers built on the headland as defences during World War II.

Open woodland and vine thickets in the park are home to a variety of wildlife including the yellow-bellied sunbird.

Exploring Cape Pallarenda

Have a picnic or barbecue on the foreshore overlooking Magnetic Island. Gas barbecues, toilets and parking are provided. See brush-turkeys scratching the leaf litter, sand goannas scurrying around, and agile wallabies feeding late afternoon.

Go birdwatching. See brahminy kites and white-bellied sea-eagles soaring high over the Many Peaks Range.

Walk over the headland to Shelly Beach. See the defence ruins and the heritage-listed homestead. Enjoy views over Townsville and Magnetic Island from the walking tracks. On a clear day, you can see the Palm Group and Hinchinbrook Island. Along the Graves circuit, see the weir built to supply water to the Quarantine Station and the graves of the Vietnamese deck passengers who died here in 1920.

Line fishing is allowed from the beach but restrictions apply to activities in the adjacent marine park waters. Beware of marine stingers October to May.

Camping is not allowed in the park.

Visit the information Centre and find out about other parks in the Townsville area.

Darren Jew

Agile wallaby

Cape Pallarenda Conservation Park

Darran Leal

Australian brush-turkey

Paul Candlin

Tracks

Graves circuit
2·5km, 1·5 hours

Forts track
2km return, 1 hour

Further information

QPWS
Reef and National Parks
Information Centre
Old Quarantine Station
Cape Pallarenda Rd
PO Box 5391
TOWNSVILLE QLD 4810
ph (07) 4722 5224
e-mail:
tsv.infocentre@epa.qld.gov.au

Walking

Short tracks lead to picnic spots and the beach. A short track past the museum (now closed) leads to the remains of the old jetty destroyed by a cyclone in 1971. Other tracks lead over the headland to the gun emplacements.

Accessibility

The picnic area and toilets are wheelchair-accessible.

Getting there

Cape Pallarenda is at the end of Cape Pallarenda Road, 10km from the Townsville GPO on the city's north-eastern outskirts. The gates are open 6.30am–6.30pm daily.

Magnetic Island National Park

Magnetic's hoop pine-dotted coastline

Paul Candlin

What's special?

Rocky granite headlands dotted with towering hoop pines and sandy bays contribute to the picturesque scenery of beautiful Magnetic Island off Townsville. Just over half this large continental island is protected in Magnetic Island National Park. The island was named by Cook during his 1770 voyage when he believed the island's landmass was affecting his compass.

Open eucalypt woodland of bloodwoods, stringybarks and grey ironbarks cover most of the island. Hoop pine rainforest dots the headlands and small pockets of rainforest grow in sheltered valleys. The littoral rainforest at Nelly Bay is the most accessible rainforest on the island. Mangroves grow on the sheltered side of the island between West Point and Cockle Bay.

The Wulgurukaba people, the "canoe people", lived on the island and nearby mainland for thousands of years. Shell middens, stone tools and art sites are physical reminders of their strong connection with the island.

The island's interesting past has included hoop pine logging, a quarantine station for the port of Townsville, early tourism in the 19th century and coastal defences during World War II. The island's forts are listed on the Queensland Heritage Register.

Magnetic Island is surrounded by marine park waters and fringing reefs.

Exploring Magnetic Island

Walk to a secluded sandy bay for a swim or snorkel. Take a picnic lunch. Observe fishing and collecting restrictions in the surrounding marine park waters. Beware of marine stingers between October and May.

Go wildlife watching. Look for allied rock-wallabies on steep slopes early morning or late afternoon. See koalas along the walk to the forts. Look for peaceful doves and yellow-bellied sunbirds in the forest and woodlands and swamphens, Pacific black ducks and Australian grebes around the wetlands. Listen to the mournful cry of the bush stone-curlew late afternoon.

Magnetic Island National Park

Paul Candlin

Enjoy spectacular views from the gun emplacements and observation and command posts built as part of the coastal defences during World War II. Explore the mangroves at Cockle Bay along the Picnic Bay to West Point track.

Camping is not allowed but there is plenty of private accommodation on the island.

Walking

A network of walking tracks provides easy access to the most picturesque spots around the island. Wear a hat and sunscreen. Take drinking water. Be careful exploring around cliff edges and the defence ruins.

Getting there

Magnetic Island lies 8km north-east of Townsville and can be reached by fast ferry services and vehicle barge from Townsville. The passenger ferry takes about half an hour. Bicycles, motor bikes and mini vehicles can be hired on the island.

Steve Parish

Yellow-bellied sunbird

Tracks

Hawkings Point track
1·2km return, 1 hour

Picnic Bay to West Point
16km return, 5 hours

Nelly Bay to Arcadia
5km one-way, 2·5 hours

The Forts walk
4km return, 1.5 hours

Horseshoe Bay Beach to Horseshoe Bay Lagoon
200m return, 15 minutes

Horseshoe Bay Road to Balding Bay
1·5km one-way, 30 minutes

Horseshoe Bay Road to Radical Bay
1·7km one-way, 30 minutes

From Forts carpark, Horseshoe Bay Road:

Arthur Bay walk
700m one-way, 15 minutes

Florence Bay walk
1·8km one-way, 30 minutes

Radical Bay
3km one-way, 1 hour

Further information

Magnetic Island National Park
22 Hurst Street
Picnic Bay
MAGNETIC ISLAND QLD 4819
ph (07) 4778 5378
fax (07) 4778 5518

QPWS
Reef and National Parks Information Centre
Old Quarantine Station
Cape Pallarenda Rd
PO Box 5391
TOWNSVILLE QLD 4810
ph (07) 4722 5224
e-mail:
tsv.infocentre@epa.qld.gov.au

Bluewater Paluma State Forest

Northern bettong
Adam Creed

What's special?

At the southern end of the Wet Tropics World Heritage Area, the Bluewater Section of Paluma State Forest has the closest rainforest to Townsville and great views over the coast and offshore islands.

Exploring Bluewater

This is a popular retreat in summer but few facilities are provided, so visitors must be self-sufficient. Camping is not allowed in the forest. Take drinking water.

Have a bush picnic on the site of the old Forestry camp.

Enjoy views over the northern beaches of Townsville and the islands from along the road.

Walking

See the rainforest along old Forestry roads.

Accessibility

The shelter shed and old gravel forestry roads are wheelchair-accessible.

Getting there

Bluewater is 30 minutes' drive north-west of Townsville. Turn off the Bruce Highway at Bluewater and drive 18km west along Forestry Road to the forest. The road is closed during the wet season but accessible by conventional vehicle in dry weather. Take care on the gravel road up the range.

Further information

QPWS
Halifax Bemerside Road
PO Box 1293
INGHAM QLD 4850
ph (07) 4777 2822
fax (07) 4777 2863
8am–5pm weekdays

Paluma State Forest

What's special?

Valuable remnants of upland rainforest along the Paluma and Seaview Ranges are protected in Paluma State Forest. The forest is in the Wet Tropics World Heritage Area.

Exploring Paluma

Head to this cool mountain retreat for a pleasant change from the coastal heat.

Explore the rainforest on three short tracks. The Paluma Rainforest walk starts opposite the Town Hall. The H track starts from the small ring road near the Police Station. The falls walk off the Paluma Dam Road heads through the rainforest to picturesque cascades on Birthday Creek.

Camping is not allowed in the forest but you can camp nearby at Lake Paluma, www.nqwater.com.au.

Getting there

Paluma is one hour's drive north-west of Townsville. Turn off the Bruce Highway about 50km north of Townsville and take the Mt Spec Road 20km to the forest. Birthday Creek Falls is 6km along the Paluma Dam Road.

Tracks

Birthday Creek Falls walk
1·2km return, 1 hour

Paluma Rainforest walk
600m return, 30 minutes

H track
1·3km return, 1 hour

Further information

QPWS
Halifax Bemerside Road
PO Box 1293
INGHAM QLD 4850
ph (07) 4777 2822
fax (07) 4777 2863
8am–5pm weekdays

Eastern water skink

Paul Candlin

Mt Spec Paluma Range National Park

What's special?

Straddling the summit and escarpment of the Paluma Range lies the Mt Spec Section of the Paluma Range National Park. Rising 1000 metres above the Big Crystal Creek floodplain, Mt Spec is the most southerly park in the Wet Tropics World Heritage Area.

Tropical rainforest grows on the cooler mountain tops and valleys while open eucalypt woodland covers the foothills. Casuarinas and paperbarks fringe the creeks in the lower, drier parts of the park. Bloodwoods, ironbarks, poplar gums and cocky apple trees grow here. The park is home to many animals found only in the Wet Tropics.

Exploring Mt Spec

Have a picnic at Little Crystal Creek halfway up the mountain. Toilets, gas barbecues and picnic tables are provided.

When you reach the top, enjoy the view from McClelland's Lookout. Have a picnic or walk through the rainforest. Toilets, a shelter shed, picnic tables, barbecues and tap water are provided.

Go birdwatching. Look for logrunners, Macleay's honeyeaters, brush turkeys and Lewin's honeyeaters. You might be lucky enough to see a golden bowerbird. These birds live in the wet tropical rainforest and decorate their bowers with green and yellow leaves and flowers. Look for green ringtail possums and giant white-tailed rats at night.

Camp or picnic at Big Crystal Creek at the bottom of the range. Tent and van sites, gas barbecues, picnic tables, a shelter shed, toilets and cold showers are provided.

Walks

Walk from McClelland's Lookout to Witt's Lookout and Cloudy Creek.

Accessibility

The toilets and shelter sheds at McClelland's Lookout and Big Crystal Creek and toilets at Little Crystal Creek are wheelchair-accessible.

Darran Leal

Riflebird

Tracks

Witt's Lookout
1·5km, 1 hour return

Cloudy Creek
2km, 1·5 hours return

Mt Spec, Paluma Range National Park

Getting there

Mt Spec is one hour's drive north of Townsville. Turn off the Bruce Highway onto the old highway 61km north of Townsville or 40km south of Ingham. The narrow, winding, 18km Paluma Range Road leads to Little Crystal Creek and McClelland's Lookout.

The turnoff to Big Crystal Creek is 2km north of the Paluma Range Road on the old highway. The gravel access road has several low level crossings that may be impassable during wet weather.

Little Crystal Creek

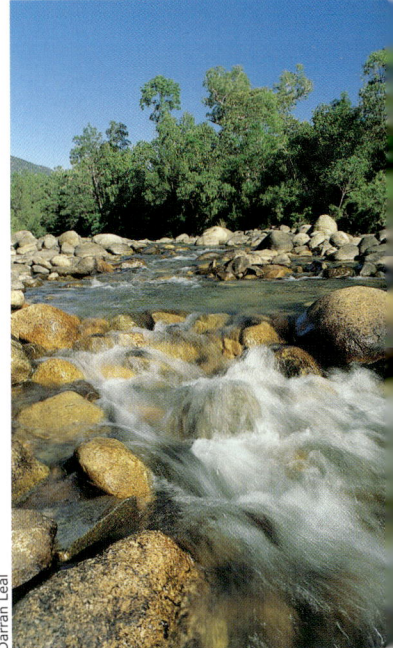

Little Crystal Creek

Further information

Mt Spec
Paluma Range NP
PO Box 1293
INGHAM QLD 4850
ph (07) 4777 3112
fax (07) 4777 3278
7.30am–4pm weekdays

QPWS
Halifax Bemerside Road
PO Box 1293
INGHAM QLD 4850
ph (07) 4777 2822
fax (07) 4777 2863
9am–5pm weekdays;
9.30am–12.30pm

QPWS
Reef and National Parks
Information Centre
Old Quarantine Station
Cape Pallarenda Rd
PO Box 5391
TOWNSVILLE QLD 4810
ph (07) 4722 5224
e-mail:
tsv.infocentre@epa.qld.gov.au

Jourama Falls Paluma Range National Park

Tracks

Jourama Falls track
3km return, 1 hour

Further information

Jourama Falls
Paluma Range NP
PO Box 1293
INGHAM QLD 4850
(07) 4777 3112
fax (07) 4777 3278
7.30am–4pm weekdays

QPWS
Halifax Bemerside Road
PO Box 1293
INGHAM QLD 4850
ph (07) 4777 2822
fax (07) 4777 2863
8am–5pm weekdays

QPWS
Reef and National Parks
Information Centre
Old Quarantine Station
Cape Pallarenda Rd
PO Box 5391
TOWNSVILLE QLD 4810
ph (07) 4722 5224
e-mail:
tsv.infocentre@epa.qld.gov.au

What's special?

A picturesque waterfall on Waterview Creek, rainforest, dry vine forest and dry open forest are protected in this section of Paluma Range National Park in the foothills of the Seaview Range.

Rainforest grows high on the slopes and fringes the creek. Poplar gum, bloodwood, Moreton Bay ash and cocky apple trees are common in the open forest.

Exploring Jourama Falls

Jourama Falls is a delightful stopover for travellers and well worth a longer stay. Have a picnic or camp in the park. Picnic tables, toilets, cold showers, gas barbecues and water are provided. Take a fuel stove for cooking. Campsite bookings are recommended for large groups.

Go birdwatching. Look for azure kingfishers, satin flycatchers, northern fantails and emerald doves around the creek and peaceful doves, kookaburras and honeyeaters in the forest.

At night, spotlight for sugar gliders and the endangered mahogany glider. Listen to the call of the southern boobook owl or large-tailed nightjar. See freshwater tortoises and goannas around the creek during the day.

Enjoy the view over the falls and forest from two lookouts along the walking track.

Walking

Walk 1·5km through open woodland to the Jourama Falls Lookout. The track starts 700m past the camping area. Be careful crossing the creek.

Accessibility

The toilets and shelter sheds are wheelchair-accessible.

Getting there

Jourama Falls is south of Ingham. Turn off the Bruce Highway 86km north of Townsville or 24km south of Ingham and drive 6km to the park. The park is accessible for conventional vehicles and caravans, except when the creek crossing is flooded.

Mt Fox Lumholtz National Park

What's special?

Mt Fox is a dormant volcano which erupted violently 100,000 years ago, spewing thick molten magma over the surrounding landscape. Today, rocks known as fusiform bombs can be seen in this section of Lumholtz National Park. These bombs, some more than 1m across, are smooth on the side exposed to the air while being ejected and have deep grooves on the other side.

The volcanic crater is covered in stunted trees and sparse grasses. Vine thicket grows in a steep gully on the southern slopes. Open eucalypt woodland of bloodwoods is the most common vegetation type.

The tussock grasses shelter many animals including rufous bettongs, skinks and ground-dwelling birds like the little button-quail.

Exploring Mt Fox

Go for a scenic drive to Mt Fox while camping at nearby Wallaman Falls or Broadwater in Abergowrie State Forest. Have a bush picnic.

Self-sufficient visitors can bush camp at Mt Fox. Take fresh water and a fuel stove for cooking. Remove your rubbish. Visit in the cooler months, April to September.

Walking

Only fit, experienced walkers should attempt the climb up Mt Fox. There are no formed tracks. The 2km return trail from the carpark to the top of the crater takes about 40 minutes each way.

Getting there

Mt Fox is 75km south-west of Ingham. Take the Trebonne Road from Ingham to the Wallaman Falls/Mt Fox turnoff at Trebonne. Follow this road for 14km to the Stone River/ Mt Fox turnoff. The turnoff to Mt Fox Road is a further 7km. Follow the Mt Fox Road up the range. The turnoff to Mt Fox crater is about 1 km past the Mt Fox School. The park is 2km from the turnoff and the crater's base is a further 2km along a bush track. The access road is unsuitable for caravans. Four-wheel-drive is recommended in the wet season.

Darren Jew

Wedge-tailed eagle

Further information

QPWS
Halifax Bemerside Road
PO Box 1293
INGHAM QLD 4850
ph (07) 4777 2822
fax (07) 4777 2863
8am–5pm weekdays

QPWS
Reef and National Parks Information Centre
Old Quarantine Station
Cape Pallarenda Rd
PO Box 5391
TOWNSVILLE QLD 4810
ph (07) 4722 5224
e-mail:
tsv.infocentre@epa.qld.gov.au

Orpheus Island National Park

Brahminy kite

Paul Candlin

Further information

**Rainforest and Reef
Information Centre**
142 Victoria Street
PO Box 74
CARDWELL QLD 4849
ph (07) 4066 8601
fax (07) 4066 8116
e-mail: hinchinbrook.camp@
epa.qld.gov.au

Campsite bookings: 13 13 04 or
www.qld.gov.au/camping

What's special?

Sheltered bays and spectacular fringing reefs make Orpheus Island National Park a popular boating destination. Orpheus Island is one of the hilly continental islands in the Palm Group off the Queensland coast, east of Ingham.

Caves and crevices around the headland and shores provide evidence of the island's geological past. Here, molten rock has intruded into the granite to form ring dykes which have since been eroded.

Dry woodlands of Moreton Bay ash and wattles, grasslands and rainforest grow on the island.

Orpheus Island is surrounded by marine park waters and has beautiful fringing reefs.

Exploring Orpheus Island

Visitors must be self-sufficient. You can bush camp at Yank's Jetty, South Beach or Little Pioneer Bay. Yank's Jetty has toilets, picnic tables, and a gas barbecue. South Beach has picnic tables and Pioneer Bay toilets and picnic tables. Take fresh water and a fuel stove for both sites. Campfires are not allowed. Remove all rubbish from the island.

Look for wildlife in the rainforest and along the shore. You might see echidnas, snakes, geckoes, ospreys or brahminy kites.

Go snorkelling or diving. Large coral bommies can be seen at Little Pioneer Bay, Cattle Bay and around Yank's Jetty. Anchor carefully to avoid coral damage. Fishing and collecting are not permitted in most of the surrounding waters. Beware of marine stingers between October and May.

A resort overlooks Hazard Bay. Only guests are welcome there. Tours of the James Cook University Orpheus Island Research Station can be arranged (07) 4777 7336.

Walking

A 100m track leads from Little Pioneer Bay to the Old Shepherds Hut.

Getting there

Orpheus Island lies off the north Queensland coast 23km south-east of Dungeness (Lucinda). Access is by charter or private boat.

Abergowrie State Forest

What's special?

In the scenic Herbert River Valley, Abergowrie State Forest contains tropical rainforest, open eucalypt forest and exotic pine plantations in the Wet Tropics World Heritage Area.

Exploring Abergowrie

Escape the summer heat in this forest retreat. Have a picnic on the banks of Broadwater Creek. A shelter shed, gas and wood barbecues, picnic tables and toilets are provided. Read about local attractions in the information shelter. Be careful swimming in the creek.

Go birdwatching. If you are lucky, you might even see a cassowary. Find out about the local wildlife along the Rainforest circuit. Signs along the Creek walk provide information about the local vegetation.

You can camp in a grassy open forest setting near the creek. The camping area has secluded tent sites, caravan and motorhome sites, toilets, shelter sheds, picnic tables, fireplaces, firewood, drinking water and cold showers. A separate group camping area with large barbecues, tables, a group fire ring and bus parking is available by prior arrangement.

Walking

See the rainforest on two short walks. Wear a hat, sunscreen and insect repellent.

Accessibility

See the massively buttressed white-haired fig tree on the wheelchair-accessible Rainforest circuit and boardwalk. The toilets, showers and shelter shed are also wheelchair-accessible.

Getting there

Abergowrie is 40km west of Ingham via Trebonne. Turn off the Bruce Highway at Ingham. The last 16km is gravel road which can be impassable in wet weather when a low-level causeway floods for short periods.

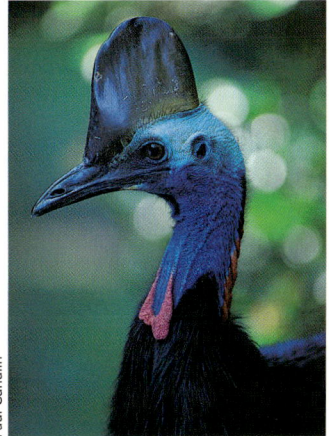

Paul Candlin
Southern cassowary

Tracks

Rainforest circuit
1·3km, 1 hour

Creek walk
3km return, 1·5 hours

Further information

QPWS
Halifax Bemerside Road
PO Box 1293
INGHAM QLD 4850
(07) 4777 2822
fax (07) 4777 2863
8am–5pm weekdays

QPWS
Gregory Street
PO Box 312
CARDWELL QLD 4849
ph (07) 4066 8779
fax (07) 4066 2041

Wallaman Falls Lumholtz National Park

Lewin's honeyeater

Darran Leal

What's special?

In the scenic Herbert River Valley, Lumholtz National Park protects waterfalls, gorge scenery, tropical rainforest, wetlands, and open eucalypt forest and woodland in the Wet Tropics World Heritage Area.

Wallaman Falls is the most accessible waterfall in this part of the coastal hinterland. Stony Creek tumbles 70m off the Seaview Range before dropping 268m in a clear fall, making this the highest, permanent single-drop waterfall in Australia.

Exploring Wallaman Falls

Escape the summer heat in this popular section of the park. Camp or have a bush picnic or barbecue at Wallaman Falls. Gas barbecues, picnic tables, a shelter shed, water, toilets and a public phone are provided.

Look for wildlife around the creek. See platypus, water dragons, saw-shelled turtles, lace monitors and southern cassowaries. Go birdwatching. Lewin's honeyeater, little shrike-thrush, golden whistler, crimson rosella and northern logrunner are some of the birds you might see. At night, look for pademelons, amethystine pythons, possums and bandicoots.

Enjoy the view over the Herbert River gorge from a lookout 300m along the Falls Lookout track.

You can also bush camp in the Yamanie section of the park. No facilities are provided but bookings are necessary. Seasonal canoeing is possible. Beware of estuarine crocodiles.

Tracks

Falls Lookout to Wallaman Falls
4km return, 1·5 hours

Picnic area to rockpool
1km return, 20 minutes

Walking

A short walk along the creek from the camping area leads to a rockpool. From a lookout over the falls, 2km by road from the camping area, a track leads to the base of the falls. If you plan to hike from the falls to the Herbert River, you must first contact the QPWS Ingham office. Only very fit, experienced walkers should attempt this walk.

Accessibility

The toilets and shelter shed in the camping area and the lookout and toilets at the falls are wheelchair accessible.

Wallaman Falls, Lumholtz National Park

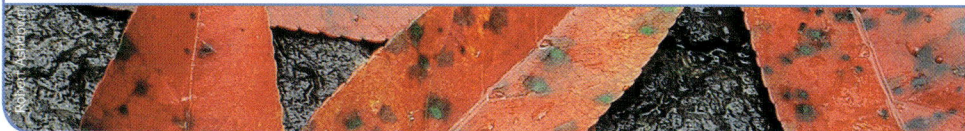

Getting there

Wallaman Falls is 50km west of Ingham. Conventional access is possible but the road is unsuitable for large caravans, and four-wheel-drive is recommended in the wet season. Four-wheel-drive is recommended to Yamanie, 54km west of Ingham.

Further information

QPWS
Halifax Bemerside Road
PO Box 1293
INGHAM QLD 4850
ph (07) 4777 2822
fax (07) 4777 2863
8am–5pm weekdays

Wallaman Falls

Cardwell State Forest

What's special?

Rugged mountain scenery, lush tropical rainforest, dry open forest, pine plantations, creeks and waterfalls are protected in Cardwell State Forest in the Wet Tropics World Heritage Area.

The Dalrymple Gap track which passes through the forest was the supply route linking cattle stations to the port of Cardwell in the 19th Century. Stone and wooden bridges, cuttings and stone paving remain.

Exploring Cardwell

Stop at Five Mile Waterhole for a picnic. Picnic tables and wood barbecues are provided on the banks of Five Mile Creek. For your safety, do not dive off the platform into the creek.

Take the 26km Cardwell Forest Drive starting at Cardwell. Allow two hours for the drive through open forest, rainforest and pine plantations. Have a picnic. Picnic tables and barbecues are provided at Attie Creek, Dead Horse Creek and the Spa Pool on Scrubby Creek. Attie Creek Falls is mostly dry.

Camping is not allowed in the forest.

Walking

The two short walks off the forest drive have steep sections. The historic Dalrymple Gap track starts 15km south of Cardwell and passes through the forest and Lumholtz National Park. Arrange to be dropped off at Cardwell end and collected at Broadwater near Ingham. Starting at Cardwell, walk to the top of the Gap to see the Gap and the 1865 Dalrymple Gap stone bridge (2 hours return).

Accessibility

The toilets and picnic tables at Five Mile Waterhole and Cardwell Lookout are wheelchair-accessible.

Getting there

Turn off the Bruce Highway 8km south of Cardwell then travel 1km to the Five Mile Waterhole picnic area. The Cardwell Forest Drive starts at Braesnose Street, Cardwell.

Spangled drongo
Darran Leal

Tracks

Cardwell Lookout
1·6km return, 40 minutes

Attie Creek walk
1·2km return, 30 minutes

Dalrymple Gap track
10km one-way, 3 hours

Further information

Rainforest and Reef Information Centre
142 Victoria Street
PO Box 74
CARDWELL QLD 4849
ph (07) 4066 8601
fax (07) 4066 8116
e-mail: hinchinbrook.camp@
epa.qld.gov.au

Edmund Kennedy National Park

What's special?

This section of coastline has changed little since explorer Edmund Kennedy passed this way during his ill-fated expedition to Cape York in 1848.

Edmund Kennedy National Park has a wonderful variety of vegetation including lowland rainforest, open eucalypt forest, paperbark woodland, sedge swamps and extensive mangrove forests. Most of the mangrove species found in Australia grow in this diverse wetland park in the Wet Tropics World Heritage Area.

The park provides valuable habitat for the endangered mahogany glider and the rare arenga palm.

Exploring Edmund Kennedy

Have a picnic on the foreshore at Rockingham Bay. Picnic tables and toilets are provided. Take drinking water and remove your rubbish. Enjoy the superb view over 13 offshore islands from the beach. Wear insect repellent and protective clothing, especially in summer.

Go birdwatching. Look for orioles, sunbirds, honeyeaters and nesting orange-footed scrubfowl.

Never cross any tidal creeks at high tide or swim in the creeks. Estuarine crocodiles, which live in the sea and estuaries here, pose a serious threat to humans. Be croc-wise.

The adjacent waters are protected in marine parks but most activities are allowed. Check zoning restrictions. Beware of marine stingers between October and May.

Camping is not allowed but you can stay at the caravan park opposite the park entrance or in nearby Cardwell.

Walking

Walk through the park along a series of boardwalks and tracks leading to the beach near Wreck Creek. Return along the beach at low tide only.

Accessibility

The toilets and picnic area are wheelchair-accessible.

Getting there

Turn off the Bruce Highway 4km north of Cardwell and drive 1km to the park entrance and a further 1km to the ranger station. The road beyond this point is unsuitable for caravans.

Paul Candlin

Wetland in Edmund Kennedy National Park

Tracks

Edmund Kennedy circuit
5km return, 1·5–2 hours

Further information

Rainforest and Reef Information Centre
142 Victoria Street
PO Box 74
CARDWELL QLD 4849
(07) 4066 8601
fax (07) 4066 8116
e-mail: hinchinbrook.camp@
epa.qld.gov.au

Kirrama Forest Reserve

Kirrama rainforest canopy

Bruce Cowell

What's special?

Rugged mountain scenery, lush tropical rainforest, open eucalypt forest and the spectacular Blencoe Falls are protected in Kirrama Forest Reserve in the Wet Tropics World Heritage Area. The Kirrama Range Road was built between 1937 and 1941 to provide access to the forest's rich resources.

Exploring Kirrama

Take the scenic 30·5km drive through Kirrama Forest Reserve along the Kirrama Range Road to Society Flat. Allow one to two hours for the drive which climbs to 850m above sea level.

Stop at Tuckers Lookout for views over the Kennedy Valley and Hinchinbrook and Goold Islands offshore. A monument commemorates G. W. Tucker who surveyed the road in the late 1930s. An example of the original stone pitching can be seen in an embankment 200m past the lookout.

Continue climbing through rainforest to the Murray Valley Lookout over Murray Upper State Forest. The drive continues past Brice Henry Lookout and the only remaining original bridge.

At the highest point along the range, there is an historic monument dedicated to Percey Pease, the Minister for Lands in the 1930s. The forest changes from dense rainforest to open forest and levels out to a large area known as Society Flat, once the centre of a thriving logging industry. The road continues past Blencoe Falls to Mt Garnet.

Bush camp at Blencoe Falls. No permit is required. Remove your rubbish. Have a bush picnic beside Blencoe Creek. No facilities are provided.

Horse riding, motorbike riding and four-wheel-driving are allowed by permit along Culpa Road.

Walking

See massive kauri pines and rose gums in the rainforest and eucalypt forest along the walking tracks.

Tracks

Society Flat circuit
800m, 20 minutes

Blencoe Falls track
2km return, 40 minutes

Kirrama Forest Reserve

Bruce Cowell

Accessibility

Wheelchair-assisted access is possible along the Society Flat boardwalk.

Getting there

To reach Kirrama Forest Reserve, turn off the Bruce Highway at Kennedy, 10km north of Cardwell. The forest is accessible by conventional vehicle and high clearance vehicles can travel along the road to see Blencoe Falls. Four-wheel-drive is recommended in wet weather. The road past Society Flat to Mt Garnet and Culpa Road may be impassable in wet weather. Check road conditions with the Kennedy Store (07) 4066 0135.

Further information

Rainforest and Reef Information Centre
142 Victoria Street
PO Box 74
CARDWELL QLD 4849
ph (07) 4066 8601
fax (07) 4066 8116
e-mail: hinchinbrook.camp@epa.qld.gov.au

Rainforest Creek, Kirrama Forest Reserve

Bruce Cowell

Murray Upper State Forest

Murray Falls

Photo credit: Darran Leal

Tracks

River boardwalk
300m return, 10 minutes

Rainforest walk and lookout
1·8km return, 45 minutes–1 hour

Further information

**Rainforest and Reef
Information Centre**
142 Victoria Street
PO Box 74
CARDWELL QLD 4849
ph (07) 4066 8601
fax (07) 4066 8116
e-mail: hinchinbrook.camp@
epa.qld.gov.au

What's special?

In the scenic foothills of the Kirrama Range lies Murray Upper State Forest, a magical place where rainforested mountains and tropical lowlands meet. Murray Falls is picturesque with tropical rainforest, open forest, water-sculpted boulders, cascades and clear mountain rockpools. Murray Upper State Forest is in the Wet Tropics World Heritage Area.

Exploring Murray Upper

Camp or picnic at Murray Falls. Toilets, picnic tables, cold showers, bins, wood barbecues and limited firewood are provided. Take your own firewood or a fuel stove. The camping area's grassy sites in an open forest setting are suitable for tents, caravans and motorhomes.

Walk through the open forest and rainforest to the lookout for a view over the falls. Learn about the special culture of the Girramay people from signs along the walk. You can photograph the falls from the river boardwalk. For your safety, stay on the tracks and avoid slippery rocks. Serious injuries and deaths have occurred here.

Walking

See the falls and the forest along two short walks.

Accessibility

The camping area toilets and the first 75m of the river boardwalk starting at the top end of the camping area are wheelchair-accessible.

Getting there

Murray Falls is just off the Bruce Highway 42km north-west of Cardwell or 38km south of Tully. Turn off the highway at Bilyana or Murrigal and drive 22km to the forest along partly sealed roads. The forest is signposted and accessible by conventional vehicle.

Goold Island National Park

What's special?

Granite outcrops and sandy beaches are features of Goold Island National Park, a hilly continental island off Cardwell. Eucalypt woodland covers most of the island but patches of lush rainforest grow in sheltered gullies. Noisy flocks of sulphur-crested cockatoos live in the island's forests.

Dugong and turtles feed on seagrass beds in the shallow waters surrounding the island, part of the Great Barrier Reef Marine Park.

Exploring Goold Island

Bush camp or picnic on the western beach. Toilets, picnic tables, a shelter shed, tank water and gas barbecues are provided. The tank water supply and creek flow are seasonal and unreliable. Take fresh water, insect repellent and a fuel stove for cooking. Do not rely on the barbecue for cooking. Campfires and generators are not allowed. Remove your rubbish. Visit in the cooler months.

Enjoy superb views of nearby Hinchinbrook Island.

Beware of marine stingers between October and May. Observe restrictions on collecting and fishing in the surrounding marine park waters.

Walking

Walk 1km through the woodlands and return along the western beach. Wear a hat and sunscreen.

Getting there

Goold Island is 17km north-east of Cardwell or 4·5km north-west of Cape Richards, Hinchinbrook Island. Access is by private boat or ferry from Cardwell.

Paul Candlin

Torresian imperial-pigeon

Further information

Rainforest and Reef Information Centre
142 Victoria Street
PO Box 74
CARDWELL QLD 4849
ph (07) 4066 8601
fax (07) 4066 8116
e-mail: hinchinbrook.camp@ epa.qld.gov.au

Campsite bookings: 13 13 04 or www.qld.gov.au/camping

Hinchinbrook Island National Park

Mulligan Falls

Terry Harper

What's special?

With its lush rainforests, rugged, misty and heath-covered mountains, sweeping sandy beaches, rocky headlands, paperbark and palm wetlands, mangrove-fringed shores and extensive open forests and woodlands, Hinchinbrook Island National Park is one of the world's most outstanding island parks.

The island's mangrove forests are some of the richest and most varied in Australia and an important breeding ground for many marine animals.

For thousands of years, the Bandyin Aboriginal people lived on Hinchinbrook Island. Middens and fish traps are reminders of their special culture.

The island's world-famous Thorsborne Trail was named after local naturalists Margaret and Arthur Thorsborne.

Hinchinbrook Island is surrounded by marine park waters where fringing reefs and seagrass beds are home to a variety of marine life including dugong and green turtles.

The Thorsborne Trail follows the east coast of Hinchinbrook Island

Darran Leal

Hinchinbrook Island National Park

Exploring Hinchinbrook Island

Experienced and fit bushwalkers can discover the special beauty of Hinchinbrook Island on a 32km trail along the island's east coast. Limits apply to the number of walkers allowed on the trail so you must book at least 12 months in advance for holidays. Take a topographic map and compass.

Fresh water is available along the trail. Take water containers, insect repellent and a fuel stove for cooking. Campfires are not allowed. Campsites and toilets are provided. Walkers are encouraged to minimise their impact. Where no toilets are provided, bury human waste. Use no soap or toothpaste in creeks. Leave no rubbish behind. For your safety, complete the log books at the Nina Bay, Little Ramsay Bay, Zoe Bay and Mulligan Falls campgrounds. Leave your itinerary with a reliable friend or relative and advise your safe return.

The cooler months, April to September are best for walking. Heavy rain can fall between December and April. Allow at least three days to complete the trail.

You can also camp at Macushla or The Haven camping areas. Toilets, picnic tables and barbecues are provided. Take water and a fuel stove. A resort is located on the northern end of the island.

Beach fishing is allowed. Be careful. Marine stingers are present in the sea and estuaries between October and May. Estuarine crocodiles live in the surrounding channel and estuarine waters. Be croc-wise.

Walking

Wear insect repellent and a hat and sunscreen. Carry drinking water. Walking in the mountains is by special permit only. The Thorsborne Trail is not graded or hardened and provides a wilderness experience for self-sufficient hikers. Allow at least three nights to walk between Ramsay Bay to George Point in either direction. Shorter return walks are possible.

Getting there

Hinchinbrook Island lies off the north Queensland coast just 8km east of Cardwell. Commercial water taxis from Cardwell and Dungeness (Lucinda) transfer campers and walkers to the island.

Tracks

Short tracks:
The Haven track
1km circuit, 15–30 minutes

Macushla track, Cape Richards
5–8km, 1·5–2·5 hours

Thorsborne Trail:
Ramsay Bay to Nina Bay
4km, 2·5 hours

Nina Bay to Little Ramsay Bay
2·5km, 2 hours

Little Ramsay Bay to Zoe Bay
10·5km, 6 hours

Zoe Bay to Diamantina Creek
6·5km, 4 hours

Diamantina Creek to Mulligan Falls camp
1km, 30 minutes

Mulligan Falls camp to George Point
7·5km, 2·5 hours

Further information

Rainforest and Reef Information Centre
142 Victoria Street
PO Box 74
CARDWELL QLD 4849
ph (07) 4066 8601
fax (07) 4066 8116
e-mail: hinchinbrook.camp@epa.qld.gov.au

Campsite bookings: 13 13 04 or www.qld.gov.au/camping

Northern Outback

Map 12

Legend

▮ National Park	▮ State Forest	▬ Highway
▮ Conservation Park	▮ Timber Reserve	▬ Major connecting road
▮ Forest Reserve	▮ Resource Reserve	▬ Minor access road

0   50   100
km

N

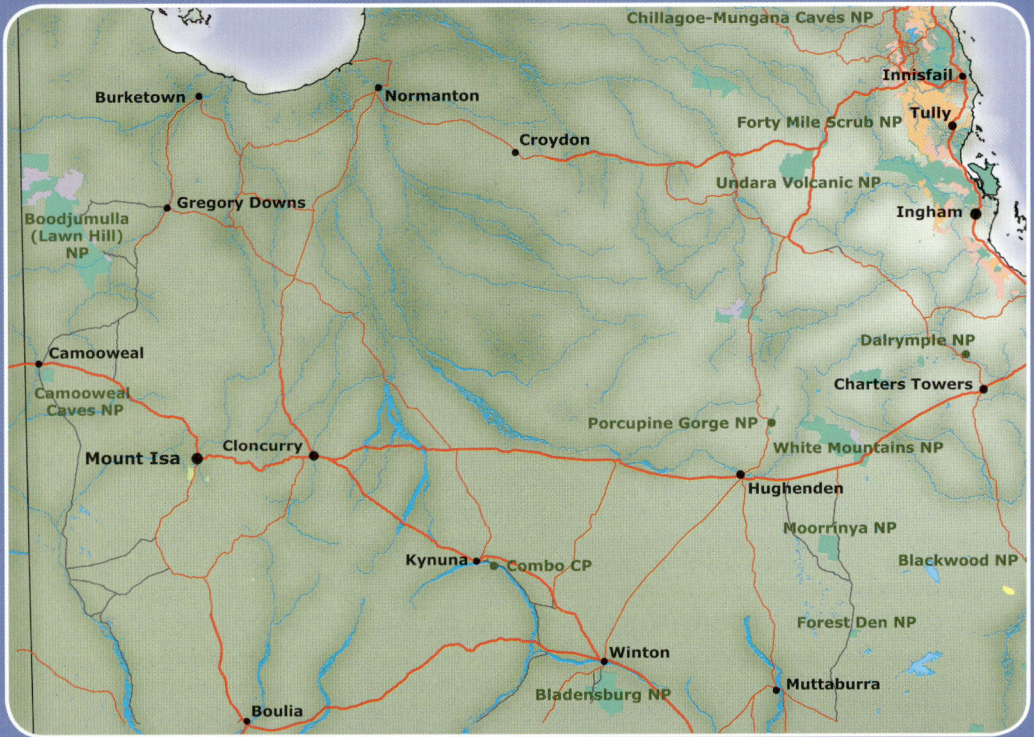

Chillagoe-Mungana Caves NP

Burketown •   • Normanton   Innisfail •

      • Croydon   Forty Mile Scrub NP   Tully •

    Undara Volcanic NP

Gregory Downs •

Boodjamulla (Lawn Hill) NP   Ingham •

Camooweal •   Dalrymple NP •

Camooweal Caves NP   Charters Towers •

    Porcupine Gorge NP •

Mount Isa •   Cloncurry •   White Mountains NP

             Hughenden •

         Moorrinya NP

Kynuna •   Combo CP   Blackwood NP

         Forest Den NP

   Winton •   Muttaburra •

Bladensburg NP

Boulia •

Lawn Hill Gorge, Boodjamulla (Lawn Hill) National Park

Paul Candlin

Blackwood National Park

What's special?

In Queensland's Brigalow Belt natural region, Blackwood National Park has a landscape of undulating hills, stony ridges and alluvial flats. Acacia woodlands of blackwood and lancewood trees, spinifex grass and pockets of dry rainforest grow on the stony ridges while box eucalypts and coolibah trees grow along the alluvial flats. The park conserves several plant communities which have been mostly cleared.

Blackwood National Park was named after the wattle known as Belyando blackwood, *Acacia argyrodendron*, a beautiful tree which grows up to 10m.

Exploring Blackwood

Self-reliant visitors can relax and enjoy the peace and quiet in this remote, undeveloped park. No facilities are provided.

Go birdwatching. See squatter pigeons and speckled warblers. Look for black-necked storks around watercourses.

A private campground at Belyando Crossing (07) 4983 5269 has tent and caravan sites, picnic tables, a shelter shed, toilets, water, showers and a public phone. Food and general supplies are available here. The Plain Creek farmstay is located just north of the park at Plain Creek.

Walking

Fire trails around the park boundary help you explore the park and look for wildlife. Please stay on the trails to protect the park. Walk from the camping area to Wallaroo Gully (10km return). Wear a hat and sunscreen and take drinking water. Hikers planning to go beyond the fire trails must contact the QPWS office at Charters Towers and complete a remote bushwalking form.

Getting there

Blackwood is off the Gregory Development Road (Great Inland Way) and is 180km south of Charters Towers or 15km north of Belyando Crossing. The road inside the park is gravel but conventional access is possible. Access is restricted in the wet season.

Black-necked stork

Adam Creed

Further information

QPWS
109 Hodgkinson Street
PO Box 1017
CHARTERS TOWERS QLD 4820
ph (07) 4787 3388
fax (07) 4787 3800

Dalrymple National Park

Paul Candlin

Sugar glider

Further information

QPWS
109 Hodgkinson Street
PO Box 1017
CHARTERS TOWERS QLD 4820
ph (07) 4787 3388
fax (07) 4787 3800

QPWS
Reef and National Parks
Information Centre
Old Quarantine Station
Cape Pallarenda Rd
PO Box 5391
TOWNSVILLE QLD 4810
ph (07) 4722 5224
e-mail:
tsv.infocentre@epa.qld.gov.au

What's special?

Part of the site of the former township of Dalrymple is in historic Dalrymple National Park. Built in 1864 on the western bank of the Burdekin, Queensland's largest river, Dalrymple was the first inland settlement surveyed in northern Australia. During the gold rush days in 1869, Dalrymple was a thriving town. Following destruction by floods, the settlement was reduced to ruins by 1901.

The park has a fascinating geological history with basalt flows and fossilised limestone. Mt Keelbottom rises 130m above the surrounding plain.

Open woodland with Moreton Bay ash and blue gum covers most of the park, providing a refuge for wildlife.

Dalrymple National Park is part of the traditional lands of the Kudjala people.

Exploring Dalrymple

Dalrymple is a quiet retreat for self-sufficient visitors. Bush camp under the river red gums on the banks of the Burdekin River. River flow is seasonal. Take fresh water and a fuel stove for cooking. Remove your rubbish.

Explore or go birdwatching around Fletcher Creek. Fishing is not allowed. Look for rock-wallabies at dawn and dusk and greater gliders and sugar gliders at night.

You can also camp in the local authority campground 2·5km away at Fletcher Creek where tent and caravan sites, picnic tables, a shelter shed, toilets, cold showers and wood barbecues are provided. Take fresh water and a fuel stove.

Walking

Rough trails follow the Burdekin River and Fletcher Creek. Experienced walkers can hike to Mt Keelbottom. Contact the ranger at Charters Towers first and complete a remote bushwalking form beforehand. Wear a hat and sunscreen and carry drinking water.

Getting there

Dalrymple is half an hour's drive or 46km north of Charters Towers. From the south, take Gregory Development Road (Lynd Highway) then turn right into an unsealed road at Fletcher Creek Crossing and drive 2·5km to the park entrance.

Moorrinya National Park

What's special?

In the heart of the Desert Uplands, Moorrinya National Park protects 18 land types in the Lake Eyre Basin, one of Australia's most important catchments.

Dry, flat plains are criss-crossed by watercourses in this remote park covered in open eucalypt, paperbark and acacia woodlands and grasslands. Moorrinya is a wildlife refuge protecting Australian icons like kangaroos, koalas, emus and dingoes as well as rare and threatened species such as the square-tailed kite, squatter pigeon and Julia Creek dunnart.

The former "Shirley Station", a sheep grazing property, operated here. In the late 1970s, cattle replaced sheep and grazing continued until the park was established in 1992. Much of the sheep station infrastructure, dating back to the late 1940s, remains as a reminder of the spirit and hard work of the people who made a living in this remote part of Queensland.

Exploring Moorrrinya

This low-key park is suitable for experienced bushwalkers and nature lovers. Go birdwatching or bushwalking, take photographs or paint, brush up on our grazing past, or simply enjoy the remoteness of Australia's outback.

Camp near the old shearer's quarters. Get your permit beforehand from the on-site ranger station or from the Charters Towers office. Toilets are provided. Take fresh water and a fuel stove for cooking. Remove your rubbish from the park.

Getting there

Moorrinya is about 90km south of Torrens Creek or 180km north of Aramac, on the Torrens Creek/Aramac Road. A "Ranger Station" sign marks the park turnoff. The unsealed Torrens Creek/Aramac access road to Moorrinya is easily accessible by four-wheel-drive vehicles, except during wet weather. Conventional vehicles are not recommended. Check road conditions before travelling to the park.

Darren Jew

Emu

Further information

Moorrinya National Park
TORRENS CREEK QLD 4816
ph/fax/answering machine
(07) 4741 7374

QPWS
109 Hodgkinson Street
PO Box 1017
CHARTERS TOWERS QLD 4820
ph (07) 4787 3388
fax (07) 4787 3800

Porcupine Gorge National Park

Red-winged parrot

Darren Jew

What's special?

Towering cliffs of vibrantly-coloured sandstone and lush green vine forest fringing Porcupine Creek provide a striking contrast with the surrounding sparsely wooded, dry flat plains in Porcupine Gorge National Park.

Over millions of years, Porcupine Creek has carved a gorge through the basalt-capped sandstone and conglomerate rocks laid down by ancient rivers.

Three Aboriginal groups have traditional links with this area. Artefact scatters located around the gorge are protected from floodwaters.

Deep permanent waterholes along the creek are lined with casuarinas and paperbarks while eucalypt trees and wattles grow along the cliffs. Most of the park is covered in open eucalypt forest with a heath understorey.

Exploring Porcupine Gorge

Stop for a view of the gorge and a picnic at the Gorge Lookout just off the Kennedy Developmental Road.

Bush camp at the Pyramid Lookout camping area. The Pyramid, a sandstone rock outcrop shaped like its namesake, is located in the wider section of the gorge. Obtain your camping permit from the Charters Towers office or on-site. Be prepared for cool winter nights. Tent and caravan sites, a shelter shed and toilet are provided. Take fresh water and a fuel stove for cooking. Boil the creek water for five minutes before drinking. Remove your rubbish.

Porcupine Gorge

Paul Candlin

Porcupine Gorge National Park

Robert Ashdown

Paul Candlin

The Pyramid

Further information

QPWS
Reef and National Parks
Information Centre
Old Quarantine Station
Cape Pallarenda Rd
PO Box 5391
TOWNSVILLE QLD 4810
ph (07) 4722 5224
e-mail:
tsv.infocentre@epa.qld.gov.au

QPWS
PO Box 67
HUGHENDEN QLD 4821
ph (07) 4741 1113
fax (07) 4741 1046

QPWS
PO Box 1017
CHARTERS TOWERS QLD 4820
ph (07) 4787 3388
fax (07) 4787 3800

Enjoy birdwatching, nature study and photography. See red-winged parrots, honeyeaters and black ducks around the creek. Look for wallaroos and rock-wallabies. Enjoy the wildflowers in spring and summer.

Visit in the cooler months. Summers are hot.

Walking

Walk 1·2km down into the gorge (about 30 minutes). The climb back up is quite strenuous. Allow one hour. Take drinking water and a first aid kit. Wear sturdy footwear, a hat and sunscreen. Anyone planning an extended bushwalk must contact the ranger at Hughenden and complete a remote bushwalking form.

Getting there

Porcupine Gorge is 61km north of Hughenden via the Kennedy Developmental Road or 190km if travelling from The Lynd. The camping area is a further 11km along an unsealed road. Conventional and caravan access is possible with care. Four-wheel-drive is recommended in wet weather.

White Mountains National Park

What's special?

Spectacular white sandstone bluffs and gorges make this rugged wilderness park well worth a visit. White Mountains National Park is an important catchment for wet season streams flowing north to the Gulf of Carpentaria, east to the coast and south towards Lake Eyre.

This is one of inland Queensland's most varied parks. Lancewood forests, laterite pastures, spinifex grasslands, open woodlands and heathlands are found around the white sandstone outcrops. Sand dunes and sandy flats occur in the Cann's Camp Creek area.

White Mountains is a wildlife haven. The spectacled hare-wallaby *Lagorchestes conspicillatus* and eastern pebble-mound mouse *Pseudomys patrius* are two of the more unusual animals which live in the park.

Exploring White Mountains

Stop on the Flinders Highway at Burra Range Lookout for a view over the park's steep gorges and peaks. This is a relatively undeveloped park but camping is allowed at Cann's Camp Creek. The campground is unsuitable for caravans or motorhomes and campsites are limited. A composting toilet is provided. Take fresh water and a fuel stove for cooking. Campsites must be pre-booked at Charters Towers.

Enjoy the wildflower display during late winter and spring. Go birdwatching or wildlife watching. See ducks, honeyeaters, friarbirds, bearded dragons and spiny-tailed geckoes.

Visit in the cooler months. Summers are hot.

Spiny-tailed gecko

Damian McGreevy

White Mountains National Park

Walking

No tracks are provided. Only experienced and well-equipped walkers should go buishwalking. For safety, walkers must register with the QPWS office in Hughenden or Charters Towers and complete a remote bushwalking form beforehand.

Getting there

White Mountains lies on the Flinders Highway between Hughenden and Charters Towers. The park is 80km northwest of Hughenden, 140km southwest of Charters Towers, 23km east of Torrens Creek or 27km west of Pentland. Conventional access is possible to Burra Range Lookout. Four-wheel-drive is recommended to reach the campground. The road to the campground is closed during wet weather.

Further information

QPWS
Reef and National Parks Information Centre
Old Quarantine Station
Cape Pallarenda Rd
PO Box 5391
TOWNSVILLE QLD 4810
ph (07) 4722 5224
e-mail:
tsv.infocentre@epa.qld.gov.au

QPWS
PO Box 67
HUGHENDEN QLD 4821
ph (07) 4741 1113
fax (07) 4741 1046

QPWS
PO Box 1017
CHARTERS TOWERS QLD 4820
ph (07) 4787 3388
fax (07) 4787 3800

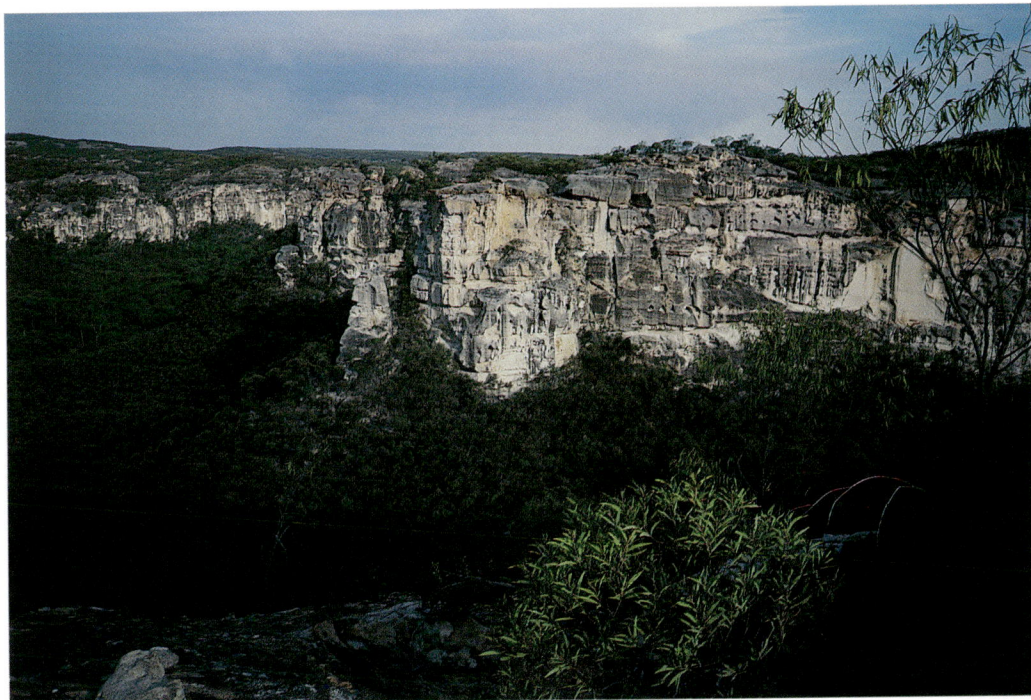

White Mountains National Park

Forest Den National Park

What's special?

Mitchell grass plains and black gidgee *Acacia argyrodendron* woodlands are protected in this remote park in the Torrens Creek catchment in central-western Queensland. Forest Den National Park is an important wildlife corridor and semi-permanent waterholes along Torrens and Paradise Creeks provide a refuge for wildlife.

River red gums, coolibahs and paperbarks fringe the creek and waterholes.

The park is named after one of five grazing paddocks which covered the property over the past century.

Exploring Forest Den

Stop at Forest Den when travelling between Townsville and western Queensland. Visitors must be self-sufficient in food, water, fuel and spare parts.

Picnic on the banks of Torrens Creek. No facilities are provided.

Take your binoculars and camera and go birdwatching. Dusk and dawn are the best times. See whistling kites, brown falcons, white ibis, egrets and rufous-throated honeyeaters. Try to spot squatter pigeons hiding in the grass.

Look for sugar gliders and brushtail possums in the trees or Beccari's freetail bats skimming over the water surface.

Camp beside Four Mile Waterhole. Take drinking water and a fuel stove. Bury human wastes away from the waterhole and remove your rubbish. Use no soap or detergent in the waterholes.

Visit in the cooler months, March to September. Summers are hot and can be wet.

Walking

Wear a hat and sunscreen. No tracks are provided but the flat ground makes walking easy.

Getting there

Forest Den is on the Torrens Creek Road 110km north of Aramac. Take the Corinda turnoff from Aramac. Turn left after 5km and head north 4·5km to Four Mile Waterhole. Four-wheel-drive is recommended and you may be stranded in wet weather.

Brown falcon

Steve Parish

Further information

QPWS
Landsborough Highway
PO Box 202
LONGREACH QLD 4730
ph (07) 4652 7333
fax (07) 4658 1778

Camooweal Caves National Park

What's special?

On the Barkly Tableland, dry open eucalypt woodland, turpentine wattle shrubland and extensive Mitchell grass plains cover Camooweal Caves National Park. The special beauty of this place lies underground. Here, water has percolated through 500 million years-old layers of soluble dolomite creating an extensive cave system unique in Queensland. Typical limestone cave formations are uncommon here due to the extreme temperatures and sudden flooding during the wet season.

Ghost bats, other insect-eating bats and owls roost in the caves. The ridge-tailed monitor which lives among the park's rocky outcrops is associated with a dreaming legend of the local Injilujji and Thethanu people.

Exploring Camooweal Caves

Picnic or bush camp at Caves Waterhole camping area. Toilets, a shelter shed, fireplaces and water are provided. Take fresh water and a fuel stove for cooking. Book campsites in holidays and long weekends.

Only experienced and well-equipped cavers should go caving. Always take a spare light source and go in groups for safety. Notify the local police and the QPWS Mt Isa office before caving. Great Nowranie is the best cave to explore but climbing gear is needed to negotiate the entrance.

Visit in the cooler, drier months in the middle of the year. Be prepared for cool nights. Summers are very hot and the caves may flood during the wet season.

Accessibility

The track to the caves is wheelchair-accessible.

Getting there

Camooweal Caves is 24km south of Camooweal. Take the Urandangi Road 8km south of Camooweal and turn left on the park boundary road. The camping area is 14km from the park entrance. Conventional access is possible with care in dry weather. Four-wheel-drive is recommended, especially in wet weather. The road becomes boggy for several days after rain. Check road conditions before travelling.

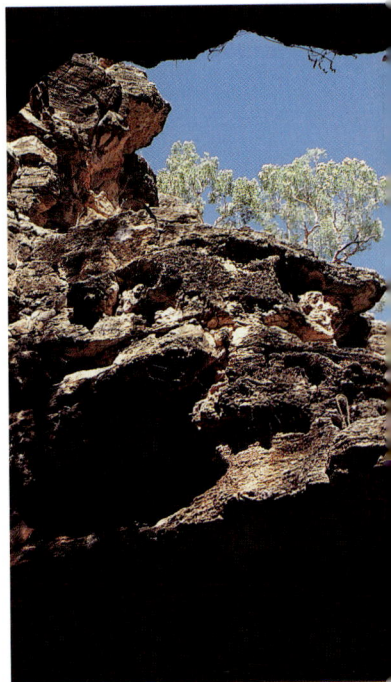

Cave entrance, Camooweal Caves National Park

Further information

QPWS
PMB 12
MT ISA QLD 4825
ph (07) 4748 5572
fax (07) 4748 5549
2–4pm

Camooweal Caves NP
ph/fax (07) 4748 5595

Boodjamulla (Lawn Hill) National Park

Darran Leal

Crimson finch

What's special?

Nestled in the parched plains of remote north-western Queensland is Boodjamulla (Lawn Hill) National Park with its permanent creeks and waterholes. Spectacular gorges, sandstone ranges and palm-fringed creeks make this one of Queensland's most scenic parks. Carved by Lawn Hill Creek, Lawn Hill Gorge is a rich oasis with cabbage palms and lush tropical vegetation.

Lawn Hill's ancient sandstones and limestones have been gradually stripped away over millions of years leaving behind rugged escarpments, gorges and rock outcrops.

The Waanyi people who have lived in the gorge area for at least 17,000 years know this place as Boodjamulla, or Rainbow Serpent country. Lawn Hill Gorge is sacred to the Waanyi people. Midden heaps, grinding stones and rock art are evidence of the importance of this place. Visitors are asked to respect this special culture. Today, the traditional owners help manage the park.

The park has a rich pastoral history and Lawn Hill Station was once one of the state's largest cattle properties.

The Riversleigh Section of the park is part of the Australian Fossil Mammal Sites World Heritage Area and contains the fossil remains of many of today's native animal ancestors. Animal bones dating back 25 million years are preserved in lime-rich sediments here. This living museum is an important record of the evolution of Australian mammals.

Paul Candlin

View towards Lawn Hill Gorge

Boodjamulla (Lawn Hill) National Park

Exploring Boodjamulla

Picnic in the gorge. Hire a canoe in the camping area and paddle around the gorge. Go birdwatching along the Indirri Falls loop track.

Enjoy the view from Island Stack, a steep climb best attempted early morning. See Aboriginal rock art at Wild Dog Dreaming and Rainbow Dreaming.

Go wildlife watching. See kangaroos, wallabies, echidnas, lizards, red-winged parrots and purple-crowned fairy-wrens. Look for spitting archer fish, turtles and freshwater crocodiles in the creek.

Camp near Lawn Hill Creek. Bookings are essential. Toilets, cold showers, shared fireplaces and water are provided. Take a fuel stove for cooking. Be self-sufficient in fuel, food, camping equipment and vehicle spare parts. You may be stranded in wet weather. Camping is not allowed at Riversleigh but you can camp outside the park at Adels Grove.

Access to the World Heritage Area is restricted to Riversleigh's D Site. Read about the fossils in the information shelter at Riversleigh then explore along a self-guided interpretive trail. Only toilets are provided. Commercial tours operate from Adels Grove.

Avoid visiting in the heat or wet season, October to March. Be prepared. Daytime temperatures can be very hot and nights can be freezing.

Walking

Wear sturdy shoes, a hat and sunscreen and carry drinking water when walking. Observe safety signs.

Getting there

The park base is 340km north-west of Mt Isa, 220km south-west of Burketown, or 425km north-west of Cloncurry. The Burketown route and the last 280km of the Mt Isa access route are unsealed and become impassable after rain. Four-wheel-drive is recommended. The Cloncurry route is best for towing vans and conventional access.

A light airstrip is located at Adels Grove, PMB2 Mt Isa (07) 4748 5502. Transport to the park can be arranged. Riversleigh is 51km from the gorge or 250km north-west of Mt Isa via Camooweal Road then a dirt road past Riversleigh Station. Fuel and some supplies are available at Adels Grove.

Tracks

Island Stack track
4km return, 2 hours

Cascades track
2km return, 1 hour

Wild Dog Dreaming track
4·5km return, 1·5 hours

Rainbow Dreaming track
100m return, 10 minutes. Access by canoe.

Constance Range track
4km return, 3 hours

Indarri Falls track
3·8km circuit, 1·5 hours

Upper Gorge track
7km return, 3·5 hours

Further information

Boodjamulla (Lawn Hill) NP
PMB 12 MT ISA QLD 4825
ph (07) 4748 5572
fax (07) 4748 5549
2–4pm

QPWS
Mt Isa House
Camooweal and Mary Streets
MT ISA QLD 4825
ph (07) 4744 7888
fax (07) 4744 7800

Darran Leal

Double-barred finches

Map 13

Cairns and Atherton Tableland

Legend

National Park	State Forest	Highway
Conservation Park	Timber Reserve	Major connecting road
Forest Reserve	Resource Reserve	Minor access road

0   10   20
km

N

Barron Gorge NP
Mt Whitfield CP
Cairns
Dinden FR
Fitzroy Island NP
Davies Ck NP
Mareeba
Dinden SF
Emerald Ck
Danbulla SF
Gordonvale
Frankland Group NP
Russell Heads
Hallorans Hill CP
Yungaburra
Goldsborough Valley SF
Atherton Curtain Crater
Fig FR Lakes NP
Russell River NP
Hasties Swamp NP
Wongabel SF
Gadgarra
Herberton Range SF
Malanda
Babinda
Herberton
Wooroonooran NP
Malanda Falls CP
Bramston Beach
Mirwinni
Eubenangee
Josephine Falls
Swamp NP
Mt Hypipamee NP
Millaa Millaa
Innisfail
Palmerston
Mourilyan
Millstream Falls NP

Dinner Falls, Mt Hypipamee National Park

Darren Jew

Palmerston Wooroonooran National Park

What's special?

Beautiful lowland rainforest, wild rivers, the North Johnstone River gorge and waterfalls make the Palmerston Section of Wooroonooran National Park one of the most scenic places in the Wet Tropics World Heritage Area. Both lowland and upland rainforests can be seen in the Palmerston Section.

Rainforest reaches its greatest diversity here in this high rainfall area. More than 500 rainforest trees occur here, including blackbean, milky pine, water gum and red tulip oak. Many wildlife live in this part of the park, including the tiny musky rat-kangaroo, double-eyed fig-parrot and chowchilla.

The Wari and Dulgubara people who lived in and near the Palmerston area have a special connection to this place. In 1882, explorer and bushman Christie Palmerston walked from Innisfail to Herberton with Aboriginal guides in 12 days, an incredible feat in those days. The highway follows the route he took and the park section and highway are named in his memory.

Exploring Palmerston

Have a picnic at Goolagan's picnic area or other spots along the highway. Look for platypus and freshwater turtles in Henrietta Creek.

Go birdwatching during the day or spotlight for possums at night. See many waterfalls along the walking tracks. Enjoy the view over the gorge from Crawford's Lookout.

Go white water rafting on the North Johnstone River. Permits apply.

Camp in the rainforest at Henrietta Creek. Tent and caravan sites, toilets, a shelter shed and picnic tables are provided. Boil the creek water for five minutes before drinking. Take a fuel stove. Remove your rubbish.

Walking

Wear a hat, sunscreen and insect repellent to protect you from leeches. Take drinking water. Many tracks are one way. Arrange a vehicle drop-off or pick-up if possible. Walking along the highway is not recommended.

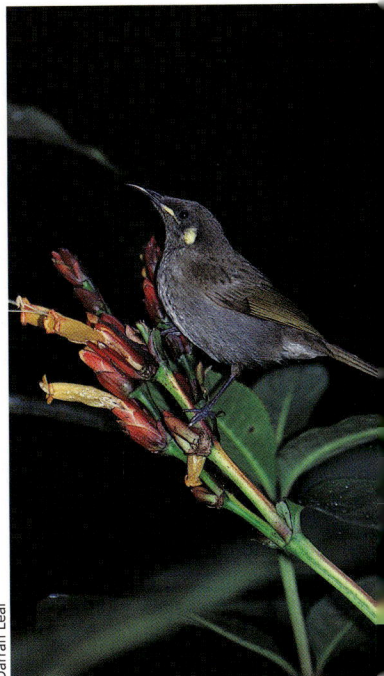

Darran Leal

Yellow-spotted honeyeater

Tracks

Tchupala Falls walk
1·1km return, 30 minutes

Crawford's Lookout to highway
5km return, 2–3 hours

Tchupala Falls entrance to Goolagan's picnic area
3km one-way, 1–2 hours

Goolagan's picnic area to Henrietta Creek camping area
800m one-way, 30 minutes

Nandroya Falls circuit
7·2km, 3–4 hours

Palmerston, Wooroonooran National Park

Bruce Cowell

Darran Leal

See many beautiful waterfalls along the walking tracks in Palmerston.

Further information

QPWS
Flying Fish Point Road
PO Box 44
INNISFAIL QLD 4860
ph (07) 4061 5900
fax (07) 4061 5999

QPWS
5B Sheridan Street
PO Box 2066
CAIRNS QLD 4870
ph (07) 4046 6600
fax (07) 4046 6751
e-mail: cic@epa.qld.gov.au

Accessibility

The toilets in the camping area are wheelchair-accessible.

Getting there

Palmerston is on the Palmerston Highway, 33km west of Innisfail or 25km east of Millaa Millaa.

Eubenangee Swamp National Park

What's special?

One of the wettest areas in Queensland is the coastal lowlands east of the Bellenden Ker Range. Eubenangee Swamp National Park protects seasonal coastal wetlands here around the Alice River, an important habitat for waterbirds.

Eubenangee Swamp is one of the most important wetlands between Ingham and Cairns. Lowland rainforest fringes Canal Creek's levee banks. This is the last remnant of this type of rainforest. Melaleucas and sedges grow around the edges of the swamp and rare plants grow in the park.

Exploring Eubenangee Swamp

Go birdwatching. You might see jabiru, herons, egrets, spoonbills and ducks feeding in the swamp. Finches flock around the sedgelands and honeyeaters feed on melaleuca blossoms at the swamp edges. Rainforest birds can also be seen.

Beware of estuarine crocodiles in the waterways. Never swim or wade through the water and stay on the boardwalks. Camping is not allowed.

Walking

Walk through the rainforest along the Alice River to the swamp. See Mt Bellenden Ker from the end of the track. Wear a hat, sunscreen and insect repellent, especially in summer.

Accessibility

The walking track is suitable for wheelchairs with assistance.

Getting there

Take the Bruce Highway south from Cairns to Miriwinni. Drive east along the Bramston Beach Road then turn south onto Cartwright Road and follow this road to the park entrance.

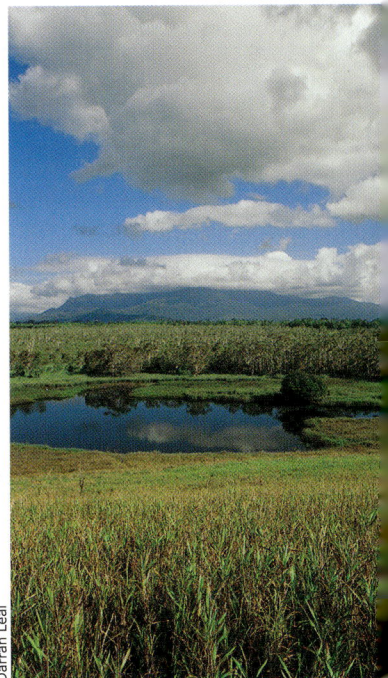

Darran Leal

Eubenangee Swamp

Tracks

Eubenangee Swamp walk
1·5km return, 45 minutes

Further information

**Josephine Falls Section
Wooroonooran NP**
PO Box 93
MIRIWINNI QLD 4871
ph (07) 4067 6304
fax (07) 4067 6443

Russell River National Park

Estuarine crocodiles live in the park.

Adam Creed

What's special?

This small coastal park in the Wet Tropics World Heritage Area protects lowland rainforest, paperbark swamps and mangroves near the estuary of the Russell and Mulgrave Rivers.

Exploring Russell River

Bush camp 6km north of Bramston Beach. Take drinking water, insect repellent and a fuel stove. No facilities are provided. Pay your camping fees on-site.

Go birdwatching or relax on the sandy beach. Beware of estuarine crocodiles in the waterways and marine stingers between October and May.

Getting there

Take the Bruce Highway south from Cairns to Miriwinni then drive 12km east to Bramston Beach. Access to the park is along a 6km rough track through private property. Four-wheel-drive is recommended.

Further information

QPWS
Josephine Falls
PO Box 93
MIRIWINNI QLD 4871
ph (07) 4067 6304
fax (07) 4067 6443

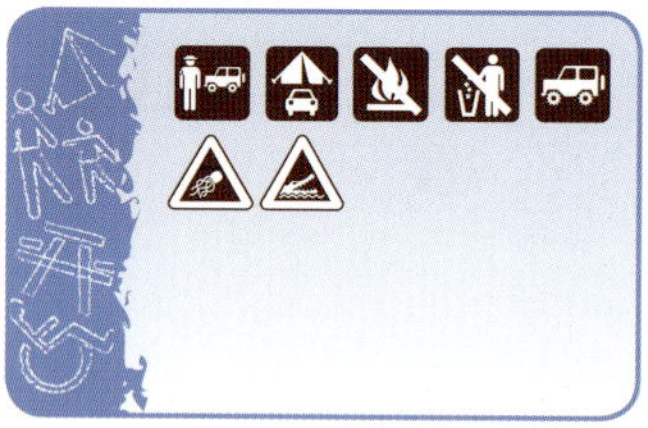

Frankland Group National Park

What's special?

Halfway between Cairns and Innisfail is the Frankland Islands, a group of five continental islands — High, Normanby, Mabel, Round and Russell Islands. Russell Island is a lighthouse reserve and the others are protected in Frankland Group National Park.

Rocky outcrops, dense rainforest, mangroves, coastal vegetation and surrounding fringing reefs make the Franklands a haven for wildlife.

The Franklands have special significance for Aboriginal people who fished, hunted and gathered foods on these islands and the adjacent sea country. Cook named the islands in 1770. The Franklands became a park in 1936 and the surrounding waters were protected in the Great Barrier Reef Marine Park in 1983.

Exploring the Frankland Group

Bush camp on Russell or High Islands. Visitors must be self-sufficient. Russell has toilets. Both sites have a bench seat, picnic tables and tarp posts. Take drinking water and a fuel stove.

Go birdwatching. See reef herons, ospreys, white-bellied sea-eagles, terns, ruddy turnstones and Mongolian sand plovers around the shores. See roosting pied imperial-pigeons in summer. Look for fruit-doves, varied honeyeaters and white-breasted woodswallows in the forest.

Observe fishing restrictions. Snorkel on the northern and south-western sides of Normanby Reef or the northern and western edges of Russell Island. Wear protective clothing if swimming in the marine stinger season, October to May.

Visit in the cooler months. Summers can be hot, wet and windy.

Walking

Take the nature trail around Normanby Island.

Getting there

The Franklands are 10km east of Russell Heads between Cairns and Innisfail. Travel by private boat at mid-high tide from Mulgrave and Russell Rivers. Daily cruises from Deeral Landing on the Mulgrave River take day visitors to Normanby and campers to Russell Island.

Paul Candlin

Ruddy turnstone

Tracks

Normanby Island trail
1·2km return, 30 minutes

Further information

QPWS
5B Sheridan Street
PO Box 2066
CAIRNS QLD 4870
ph (07) 4046 6600
fax (07) 4046 6751
e-mail: cic@epa.qld.gov.au

Campsite bookings: 13 13 04 or www.qld.gov.au/camping

Josephine Falls Wooroonooran National Park

What's special?

Rugged mountains, wild rivers and lush tropical rainforest make Wooroonooran National Park in the Bellenden Ker Range one of the state's most scenic parks. Queensland's highest mountains, Mt Bartle Frere (1622m) and Mt Bellenden Ker (1592m), are in this park in the Wet Tropics World Heritage Area.

Tropical rainforest grows from the foothills to the summit of the mountains. Many species of plants and animals are found here and nowhere else, including *Leptospermum wooroonooran* and the Bartle Frere skink.

This is the traditional land of the Ngadjonjii Aboriginal people who have maintained a close spiritual connection to the Mt Bartle Frere area for thousands of years. Explorer Christie Palmerston was the first European to climb Mt Bartle Frere in 1886. Today's Mt Bartle Frere trail follows the route taken by miners and adventurers since the 1890s.

Exploring Josephine Falls

Have a picnic at Josephine Falls. Picnic tables, a shelter shed, a coin-operated gas barbecue and toilets are provided in the picnic area near the carpark. Camping is not allowed.

Go for a short walk through the rainforest to the falls. For your safety, do not enter the restricted access area around the top of the falls. Serious injuries and deaths have occurred here.

Go birdwatching or wildlife watching. Lists of common birds and other animals are available from the Ranger.

Wooroonooran is a bushwalking haven for keen, experienced, fit walkers. Boil creek water for five minutes before drinking.

The historic 18km Goldfield Track from Goldsborough Valley to The Boulders Scenic Reserve near Babinda passes through the park. Bush camping is allowed on the banks of the East Mulgrave River.

The Mt Bartle Frere trail leads to the summit from Josephine Falls or the Atherton Tableland. Both routes are 7·5km, steep and very challenging. Allow two days.

Josephine Falls

Adam Creed

Josephine Falls, Wooroonooran National Park

Bush camping is allowed along the route. No facilities are provided. Obtain your permit from the self-registration station at the start of the trail.

The dry season from May to October is the best time for bushwalking. Be prepared for cold nights and strong winds. Rain can be heavy and prolonged in the Wet.

Walking

Wear a hat and sunscreen. Check track and weather conditions before hiking in the park. Leave your walking plans with a responsible friend or relative and advise your safe return.

Accessibility

The toilets, picnic shelter and picnic table are wheelchair-accessible. Wheelchair access along the Falls track is possible with assistance.

Getting there

Josephine Falls is 75km south of Cairns. Turn off the Bruce Highway 2km south of Miriwinni and drive 8km to Josephine Falls. The western approach is from Gourka Road, about 15km south-east of Malanda via Topaz Road.

Rockpool at Josephine Falls

Tracks

Josephine Falls track
1·2km return, 40 minutes

Josephine Falls to Broken Nose
10km return, 8 hours

Goldfield Trail
18km, 7–9 hours

Mt Bartle Frere trail:
Bartle Frere summit
15km return, 12 hours–2 days

Josephine Falls to The Junction Camp
15km one-way, 12 hours–2 days

Further information

Josephine Falls Section Wooroonooran NP
PO Box 93
MIRIWINNI QLD 4871
ph (07) 4067 6304
fax (07) 4067 6443

QPWS
5B Sheridan Street
PO Box 2066
CAIRNS QLD 4870
ph (07) 4046 6600
fax (07) 4046 6751
e-mail: cic@epa.qld.gov.au

Goldsborough State Forest
ph (07) 4056 2597

Campsite bookings
Goldfield Track: 13 13 04 or www.qld.gov.au/camping

Goldsborough Valley State Forest

Common jezebel

Darran Leal

What's special?

Nestled below the rugged Bellenden Ker Range, Goldsborough Valley State Forest protects beautiful lowland rainforest along the Mulgrave River in the scenic Goldsborough Valley.

This is the traditional home of several groups of Aboriginal people with a living rainforest culture. The discovery of gold in the Mulgrave River in the 1870s transformed the valley. Settlers, timber-getters, pastoralists and horse breeders followed the prospectors. Today, the forest is protected in the Wet Tropics World Heritage Area.

Exploring Goldsborough Valley

Picnic or camp on the grassy banks of the picturesque Mulgrave River. Two camping areas have a rainforest setting. Individual campsites, toilets, picnic tables, wood barbecues, firewood, drinking water and a shelter shed are provided. Pay your camping fees at the self-registration station.

Learn about Aboriginal culture and the rainforest along a short track to the base of Kearneys Falls. For your safety, do not attempt to climb the falls.

Follow in the footsteps of the prospectors on the historic 18km Goldfield Track through Wooroonooran National Park east to The Boulders Scenic Reserve near Babinda.

Canoeing is best between March and May, when the water levels are higher. Be very careful if canoeing in the wet season. Hidden obstacles are a hazard.

WARNING: Never dive or jump into the river — many pools are shallow. Bullrouts (freshwater stonefish) live in the river. Wear shoes when wading or swimming. If stung, apply hot (not scalding) water to the affected area. Seek medical attention.

Dogs are not allowed in the forest.

Tracks

Kearneys Falls track
1·6km return, 1 hour

Goldfield Track
8km, 7–9 hours

Walking

Wear a hat and sunscreen and carry drinking water when bushwalking. Check track conditions on the Goldfield Trail with the rangers at Wooroonooran (07) 4067 6304 or Goldsborough (07) 4056 2597.

Goldsborough Valley State Forest

Mulgrave River

Accessibility

The toilets are wheelchair-accessible.

Getting there

Goldsborough Valley is 25km south-west of Gordonvale or an hour's drive south of Cairns via the Gillies Highway. Access is along a narrow, winding gravel road unsuitable for buses and caravans.

Further information

QPWS
5B Sheridan Street
PO Box 2066
CAIRNS QLD 4870
ph (07) 4046 6600
fax (07) 4046 6751
e-mail: cic@epa.qld.gov.au

Goldsborough State Forest
ph (07) 4056 2597

Wooroonooran National Park
ph (07) 4067 6304

Campsite bookings
Goldfield Track: 13 13 04 or www.qld.gov.au/camping

Barron Gorge National Park

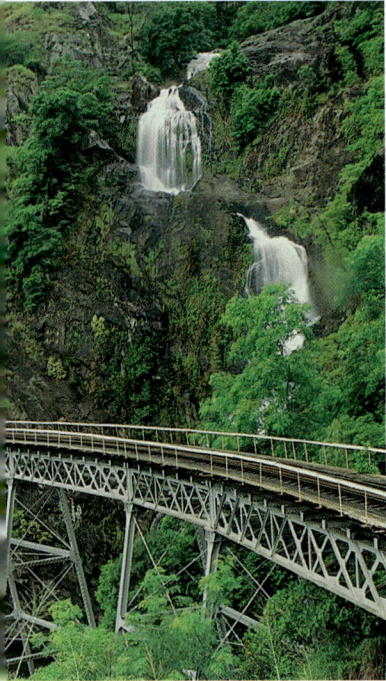

Stoney Creek Falls

Terry Harper

What's special?

Rugged mountain scenery, steep ravines, tumbling waterfalls, rich wildlife and tropical rainforest make Barron Gorge one of Queensland's most popular and picturesque parks. The park has the most accessible rainforest close to Cairns. Open woodland, grassland and heath also grow in the park.

Barron Gorge is the traditional home of the Djabaguy people who have many special connections to this place. The Douglas and Smiths tracks, traditional pathways for the Djabaguy for thousands of years, became the first pack routes linking the hinterland goldfields to the coast in 1876.

The 34km Kuranda Scenic Railway is considered a remarkable engineering feat. Built between 1882 and 1891, the railway has 15 hand-made tunnels and around 40 bridges. The park became part of the Wet Tropics World Heritage area in 1988.

The once-powerful Barron Falls have been harnessed to supply hydro-electric power and only flow after heavy rain.

Exploring Barron Gorge

Experience tropical rainforest in a variety of unusual ways, from bushwalking to the cableway or scenic railway.

Take the Skyrail cableway for a bird's-eye view of the forest. Stop and enjoy displays in the rainforest interpretation centre or go for a guided walk. Follow the traditional pathways of the Djabaguy people or the routes taken by the early pioneers.

Have a picnic on the shores of Lake Placid. Canoe around the lake or join a white-water rafting tour along the Barron River.

Enjoy the view over the gorge and falls from Wright's Lookout or the elevated boardwalk through the forest at Barron Falls lookouts.

Go birdwatching or wildlife watching. Join a free tour of Australia's first hydro-electric power station.

Camp at Speewah. Group and individual campsites, camper trailer sites, toilets, gas barbecues, cold showers and picnic platforms are provided. Take drinking water. The Djina-Wu track links the camping area to the historic Douglas and Smiths tracks.

Barron Gorge National Park

Walking

See the park's special features along the walking trails. Beware of cassowaries and stinging tree leaves. For your safety, do not walk along or below the railway line.

Accessibility

Near Kuranda at the Barron Falls Lookout, a wheelchair-accessible, elevated boardwalk lets visitors explore the rainforest. Two viewing platforms provide spectacular views over the falls and gorge. The Speewah camping area toilets and Skyrail facilities are wheelchair-accessible.

Getting there

Barron Falls is near Kuranda, just 15 minutes or 18km north of Cairns, or 50 minutes south of Port Douglas. Access is by conventional vehicle to Kuranda, railway from Kuranda, Redlynch or Cairns or cableway from Kuranda or Redlynch. Kuranda is 27km north-west of Cairns or 31km east of Mareeba. From Kuranda, take the 3km Barron Falls Road south to Barron Falls Lookout and other walking tracks. Speewah camping area is 15km west of Kuranda on the Speewah Road off the Kennedy Highway. The access road is unsuitable for towing caravans but camper trailers can be towed with care.

Barron Falls

Tracks

Barron Falls Lookout track
1·1km, 20 minutes

Wrights Lookout to Kuranda track
4·7km one-way, 1–2 hours

Douglas track Speewah to Kamerunga
6·8km one-way, 4–6 hours

Smiths track Speewah to Kamerunga
8·6km one-way, 6–7 hours

Djina-Wu track
765m one-way, 30 minutes

McDonalds track Wrights Lookout to Red Bluff
4·8km one-way, 1·5–2 hours

Gundal Wundal track
1·5km one-way, 45 minutes

Further information

QPWS
Moffatt Street
PO Box 2066
CAIRNS QLD 4870
ph (07) 4053 4533
fax (07) 4053 3100

QPWS
5B Sheridan Street
PO Box 2066
CAIRNS QLD 4870
ph (07) 4046 6600
fax (07) 4046 6751
e-mail: cic@epa.qld.gov.au

Mt Whitfield Conservation Park

Gilled fungus, Mt Whitfield

Darren Jew

What's special?

Right on Cairns' doorstep, Mt Whitfield Conservation Park protects the closest rainforest to Cairns. Mt Whitfield rises to 365m and is covered mainly in rainforest with patches of open forest and grassland. The park is home to the endangered southern cassowary.

Exploring Mt Whitfield

Have a picnic in the adjacent Botanic Gardens or go for a walk and take your picnic with you. Shelter sheds are provided along the tracks and on Lumley Hill.

Take your binoculars and go birdwatching. See brush-turkeys scratching in the leaf litter, cassowaries searching for berries to eat, and the intriguing scrub hen, one of the few birds born ready to fly. Look for agile wallabies feeding in the open grasslands early morning and late afternoon.

Enjoy spectacular views over Cairns and Trinity Inlet from lookouts along the tracks.

Camping is not allowed in the park.

Walking

Wear a hat and sunscreen and carry drinking water. Both walks are quite strenuous. Only very fit walkers should tackle the Blue Arrow circuit. If you see a cassowary, be very careful. Do not approach the bird and back away slowly if threatened.

Getting there

Mt Whitfield is next to the Flecker Botanic Gardens and just 4·3km north of the Cairns Post Office. Head north along Sheridan Street (Captain Cook Highway) and turn left into Collins Street. The park is signposted.

Tracks

Red Arrow circuit
1·3km, 1 hour

Blue Arrow circuit
5·4km, 4–5 hours

Further information

QPWS
5B Sheridan Street
PO Box 2066
CAIRNS QLD 4870
ph (07) 4046 6600
fax (07) 4046 6751
e-mail: cic@epa.qld.gov.au

Davies Creek National Park

What's special?

On the eastern edge of the Atherton Tableland, granite outcrops, boulder-strewn Davies Creek and open forest make Davies Creek National Park a picturesque alternative to the rainforest parks around Cairns.

Davies Creek rises in the Lamb Range and flows into the Barron River. A magnificent waterfall cascades over the huge granite boulders in the park. Vine forest grows along the creek but most of the park is covered in open forest and woodland studded with grasstrees and termite mounds. The park is home to the endangered northern bettong.

Exploring Davies Creek

Have a picnic or camp beside the creek. Toilets are provided. Take drinking water or boil the creek water for five minutes before drinking. Remove your rubbish. Bins are not provided.

Follow the circuit track to a lookout over the 75m Davies Creek Falls.

See the wildflowers in spring. Enjoy the local wildlife. Honeyeaters, lace monitors and tommy roundhead dragons are common. Visit nearby Dinden Forest Reserve where additional campsites are provided.

Walking

An unmarked 2km trail leads along the creek upstream to the base of Davies Creek Falls. The Falls circuit track starts from a carpark 2km up the road from the camping area. Wear a hat and sunscreen and carry drinking water.

Getting there

Turn off the Kennedy Highway 21km south-west of Kuranda or 15km east of Mareeba and drive 7km along an all-weather gravel road to the park. This road is corrugated and unsuitable for caravans.

Darren Jew

Davies Creek

Tracks

Davies Creek Falls circuit
1·1km, 20 minutes

Davies Creek Falls unmarked trail
4km return, 1–1·5 hours

Further information

QPWS
5B Sheridan Street
PO Box 2066
CAIRNS QLD 4870
ph (07) 4046 6600
fax (07) 4046 6751
e-mail: cic@epa.qld.gov.au

Campsite bookings: 13 13 04 or www.qld.gov.au/camping

Dinden Forest Reserve

What's special?

High in the Lamb Range on the Atherton Tableland, Dinden Forest Reserve contains tropical rainforest, tall eucalypt forest with flooded gum and turpentine, dry open forest and casuarina forest remnants. Many large rainforest trees remain, including kauri pine, red cedar and Queensland maple.

Bare Hill (Bunda Dalbanji), a granite outcrop surrounded by dry open forest, lies in the traditional land of the Djabaguy Bulwandji clan. Historic pack routes, used to transport supplies between the coast and the Tableland, pass through the forest.

Exploring Dinden

Enjoy spectacular views over Davies Creek from Kahlpahlim Rock, the highest point on the Lamb Range.

Bush camp beside crystal clear Davies Creek. Individual campsites, mostly in a tall open forest setting, and fire rings are provided. Take firewood or a fuel stove. You must obtain a permit to traverse to reach the camping area or drive on the road to Kahlpahlim Rock. Take drinking water or boil the creek water. Remove your rubbish.

Learn about the rainforest on the Clohesy fig-tree walk.

See Aboriginal rock art paintings along the Bare Hill track. To get permission to visit this cultural site, contact the Kuranda Mantaka Kowrowa Mona Mona Aboriginal Corporation (07) 4093 9296. Stay on the boardwalk and do not touch the paintings.

Visit in the dry season, May to November. Be prepared for cool weather in winter and at the top of Kahlpahlim Rock.

Walking

Only experienced walkers should tackle the trail to Kahlpahlim Rock. It is very steep and slippery when wet. The alternative return route along the Ridge trail is less steep and less diverse. Take drinking water. Wear a hat and sunscreen.

Accessibility

The Clohesy fig-tree walk is wheelchair-accessible.

Striped possum
Steve Parish

Tracks

Kahlpahlim Rock trail
12km return, 6–7 hours

Bare Hill track
2·8km return, 1 hour

Clohesy fig-tree walk
600m return, 15 minutes

Dinden Forest Reserve

Getting there

Dinden, 26km east of Mareeba, is next to Davies Creek National Park. Turn off the Kennedy Highway 14km east of Mareeba then drive 12km along Davies Creek Road to the camping area or 14·5km to the start of the Kahlpahlim Rock trail. Visit only in the dry. Four-wheel-drive is recommended.

The Clohesy fig-tree walk is on Clohesy River Road, 31km south-west of Mareeba. Access is only possible by four-wheel-drive and the creek crossings may be impassable after rain.

Further information

QPWS
PO Box 975
ATHERTON QLD 4883
ph (07) 4091 1844
fax (07) 4091 3281
8am–5pm weekdays

Pale-headed rosella

Fitzroy Island National Park

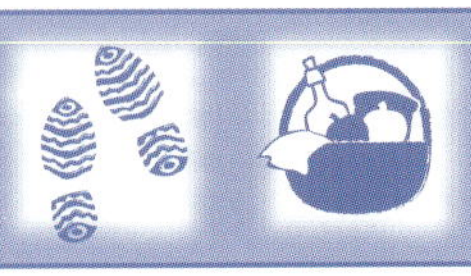

What's special?

Close to the north Queensland mainland, Fitzroy Island National Park is rugged and diverse with granite outcrops, open woodlands, rainforest, mangroves and coral beaches. The beaches and fringing reefs are protected in the Cairns Marine Park. This high continental island was connected to the mainland before sea levels rose.

For thousands of years, the Gungandji people hunted, gathered foods and held special ceremonies on the island they call "Gabar" or "Gabarra". Cook gave the island its current name in 1770. The island became a quarantine station for Chinese heading to the Palmer River goldfields in 1876 and later part of an Aboriginal mission growing fruit and vegetables.

Several lighthouses have been established over the past 80 years, from a carbide gas light on Little Fitzroy Island in 1923 to a wartime light built on the ridge above the old lightkeeper's residence in 1943. The lighthouse which is currently used as a visitor centre was built in 1970. This was the last staffed lighthouse purpose-built in Australia and probably the world. Today's automated lighthouse is again located on Little Fitzroy Island.

Fitzroy Island foreshore

Paul Candlin

Fitzroy Island National Park

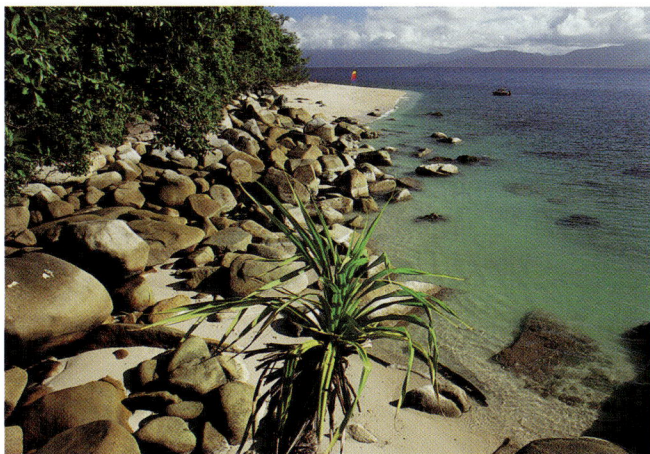

Fitzroy Island

Exploring Fitzroy Island

Spectacular vistas from almost any vantage point are a highlight of a visit to Fitzroy Island.

Go wildlife watching. See brilliantly-coloured Ulysses butterflies, emerald doves, sulphur-crested cockatoos, orange-footed scrubfowl, ospreys and migrating birds such as buff-breasted paradise kingfishers and pied imperial-pigeons.

Explore the island by walking. Signs on the Secret Garden track help you appreciate the rainforest. See the remains of the wartime lighthouse along the Summit trail.

The island is popular for boating. Protect the coral when anchoring, observe fishing and collecting restrictions, and dump no rubbish on the reef. Snorkel at Welcome Bay, Nudey Beach, the Playground or Sharkfin Bay. Beware of marine stingers between October and May.

Camping is allowed in the resort camping area or you can stay at the resort at Welcome Bay.

Walking

Wear a hat and sunscreen and take drinking water when walking. Walk in the cooler months. Be careful on the slippery and uneven track surfaces, especially when wet.

Getting there

Fitzroy Island is 29km south-east of Cairns. Access is by private boat or daily ferry services.

Tracks

Lighthouse Road
3·6km return, 2 hours

Summit trail
3·6km return, 2·5 hours

Lighthouse and Summit circuit
2·5 hours

Secret Garden
1km return, 45 minutes

Nudey Beach track
1·2km return, 45 minutes

Further information

QPWS
5B Sheridan Street Cairns
PO Box 2066
CAIRNS QLD 4870
ph (07) 4046 6600
fax (07) 4046 6751

Danbulla State Forest and Forest Reserve

Mobo Creek Crater

Paul Candlin

What's special?

Stretching from Tinaroo Range to Lamb Range on the Atherton Tableland, Danbulla State Forest and Forest Reserve surrounds picturesque Lake Tinaroo on the Barron River. This beautiful forest contains tropical rainforest and open forest remnants, softwood plantation forests, a crater lake and historic sites.

The forest is home to a wonderful variety of animals including the northern bettong, green-eyed treefrog, Lumholtz tree-kangaroo, Herbert River ringtail possum, red goshawk, and many rare plants.

Danbulla contains the magnificent Cathedral Fig, a strangler fig reputed to be the best place for a dawn bird chorus on the tableland. Danbulla State Forest is part of the Wet Tropics World Heritage Area. The forest is managed for a variety of sustainable uses for the benefit of the community.

Exploring Danbulla

You will need more than a day to discover Danbulla's special attractions. One of the best ways to explore the forest is the 28km unsealed forest drive. Allow at least an hour. Start your drive at the Tinaroo Dam spillway. Picnic tables, barbecues and toilets are provided below the dam wall. (You can also do the drive in reverse from the Gillies Highway.)

Drive along the shores of Lake Tinaroo, stopping at Platypus Rocks Lookout for a view over the lake and tableland. Have a picnic at Kauri Creek. Walk through the rainforest to a viewing platform over Lake Euramoo, a crater lake. Have a picnic at The Chimneys, the remains of an early 20th Century settlement. A shelter shed, gas barbecues and toilets are provided. Continue along the forest drive to the mysterious Mobo Creek Crater and the magnificent Cathedral Fig.

Go canoeing at Kauri Creek inlet or School Point. Take your binoculars and go birwatching.

Choose from five camping areas around the lake. Platypus camping and picnic area has a hoop pine plantation setting and is 5km from the dam wall. Tent sites, toilets, fire rings, wood barbecues, picnic tables and tap water are provided.

Danbulla State Forest and Forest Reserve

Camp in the rainforest at Downfall Creek, 7km from the dam wall. Toilets, tap water and fire rings are provided. Kauri Creek, a small camping area 10km from the dam wall, has cold showers, tap water, fire rings and toilets. School Point, the site of the former Euramoo school, is 18km from the dam wall and 1km off the forest drive. Toilets, seats, tap water and fire rings are provided for campers and picnickers. Fong-On-Bay, 18km from the dam wall and 4·7km off the forest drive, has toilets and fire rings and is popular for water sports, when the lake is full. Boil the water for five minutes before drinking.

The School House is available for group camping by prior arrangement. All camping areas are suitable for caravans, camper trailers and motorhomes.

Dogs are not allowed in any of the camping areas.

At 800m above sea level, Danbulla enjoys milder conditions than the coast, so is a popular summer escape. Be prepared for cool winter nights.

Walking

Wear a hat, sunscreen and insect repellent. Take drinking water. On the Kauri Creek walk, you have to be prepared to wade through the creek.

Accessibility

The toilets in all camping areas except Kauri Creek, Cathedral Fig boardwalk and Euramoo viewing platform are wheelchair-accessible.

Getting there

Danbulla is about 90 minutes' drive from Cairns on the north-eastern shores of Lake Tinaroo and accessible by conventional vehicle. The dam wall is 18km east of Atherton. Danbulla Forest Drive can be reached from the Gillies Highway or through Kuranda, Mareeba, Tolga, Kairi and Tinaroo. The Red Cedar Tree walk is off Gadgarra Road, 11km east of Yungaburra via the Gillies Highway.

Tracks

Lake Euramoo circuit
600m, 30 minutes

Mobo Creek Crater circuit
600m, 30 minutes

Cathedral Fig boardwalk
150m 10 minutes

From Downfall Creek or Kauri Creek camping areas:
"Regeneration walk"
2·6km one-way, 2–3 hours return

From Kauri Creek picnic area:
Kauri Creek circuit
5km, 2–2·5 hours return

Gadgarra
Red Cedar Tree walk
600m, 20 minutes return

Further information

QPWS
PO Box 975
ATHERTON QLD 4883
ph (07) 4091 1844
fax (07) 4091 3281

QPWS
PO Box 74
KAIRI QLD 4872
ph (07) 4095 8459
fax (07) 4095 8417

Campsite bookings: 13 13 04 or www.qld.gov.au/camping
School Point only

Crater Lakes National Park

Keith McDonald

Water whistle duck at Lake Barrine

What's special?

Forest remnants in Crater Lakes National Park reflect climate changes and volcanic activity over millions of years. With changing climate periods, the rainforests contracted and expanded. These changes have been recorded in sediments on the floor of the rainforest-fringed crater lakes or maars formed by volcanic activity, Lakes Eacham and Barrine. Crater Lakes National Park is in the Wet Tropics World Heritage Area.

The rainforest around both lakes contains large kauri pines, descendants of species which dominated the tableland forests for thousands of years. Lake Eacham's rainforests show how soil type affects the vegetation. On less fertile soils, the rainforests are simpler with more uniform trees and few buttresses. On the deeper, more fertile soils around the crater, the rainforest is more complex. The canopy is uneven and trees vary in size, have large buttresses and are covered in epiphytes like orchids and ferns.

Exploring Crater Lakes

Spend a perfect day touring the tableland and stop for a picnic and bushwalk at Lake Eacham or Lake Barrine. Both picnic areas have toilets, shelter sheds, picnic tables and tap water. Lake Eacham has gas and wood barbecues and Lake Barrine has a kiosk. A lake cruise operates at Lake Barrine.

Look for saw-shelled turtles and eastern water dragons around the lakes. See musky rat-kangaroos sheltering in the rainforest. Look for the colourful Boyd's forest dragon. Go birdwatching. More than 180 bird species have been recorded in the park.

Camping is not allowed in the park but there is plenty of accommodation nearby.

Visit the information centre at Lake Eacham to find out more about the park. A self-guiding trail from the ranger station to the picnic area helps visitors explore the forest.

Crater Lakes National Park

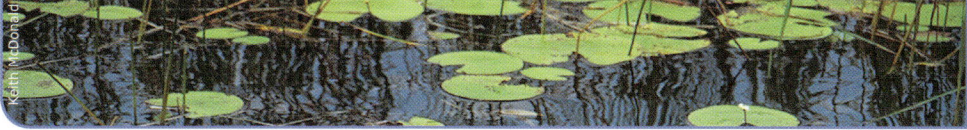

Walking

Take the self-guiding trail through the rainforest from the information centre or go for a walk around a lake.

Accessibility

The toilets at Lake Eacham and Lake Barrine are wheelchair-accessible. Wheelchair-assisted access is possible along the lake circuit tracks.

The rainforest safety and self-guiding trail brochures are in German and English.

Getting there

By road, Lake Eacham is 8km east of Yungaburra and Lake Barrine is 12km east of Yungaburra off the Gillies Highway.

Tracks

Self-guiding trail, Lake Eacham
1·5km return, 40 minutes

Lake Eacham circuit
3km, 1 hour

Lake Barrine circuit
5km, 1·5–2 hours

Further information

QPWS
Lake Eacham
PO Box 21
YUNGABURRA QLD 4872
ph (07) 4095 3768
fax (07) 4095 3403

Lake Eacham

Curtain Fig Forest Reserve

Curtain Fig

Bruce Cowell

What's special?

Beautiful tropical rainforest on the Atherton Tableland is protected in the Curtain Fig Forest Reserve in the Wet Tropics World Heritage Area. The huge fig tree in this reserve is a popular tourist destination.

Starting from a seed dropped by a bird in leaf litter high in the canopy, the strangler fig sends down roots which gradually thicken and interweave. The roots eventually strangle the host tree to death. The whole process can take hundreds of years. The Curtain Fig is unusual because one tree has fallen against another, forming a curtain of roots which give the tree its name.

Exploring Curtain Fig

At the Curtain Fig, an extensive "curtain" of aerial roots drops about 15m to the forest floor. A boardwalk has been built around the tree to provide access and protect the tree.

Dogs are not allowed in the forest.

Accessibility

The elevated boardwalk and viewing platform are wheelchair-accessible.

Getting there

The Curtain Fig is on the Atherton-Yungaburra Road, on the outskirts of Yungaburra.

Tracks

Curtain Fig boardwalk
10 minutes

Further information

QPWS
Lake Eacham
PO Box 21
YUNGABURRA QLD 4872
ph (07) 4095 3768
fax (07) 4095 3403

Emerald Creek Dinden State Forest

What's special?

On the Lamb Range west of Cairns, Emerald Creek in Dinden State Forest contains open forests and picturesque Emerald Creek Falls. The waterfall contrasts starkly with the surrounding dry, rocky landscape.

Exploring Emerald Creek

Have a picnic beside the creek in the shade of tall eucalypt trees.

Relax by the boulder-strewn creek or have a refreshing paddle. Enjoy the view towards Mareeba from a lookout over the falls and valley below.

Dogs and camping are not allowed in the forest.

Walking

Wear a hat, sunscreen and insect repellent.
Take drinking water.

Getting there

Emerald Creek is 15km south-west of Mareeba via the Tinaroo Creek Road and Cobra Road. The road to the falls can be very rough and is unsuitable for caravans or trailers.

Keith McDonald

Tapping green-eyed treefrog

Tracks

Falls walk
700m, 50 minutes return

Further information

QPWS
PO Box 975
ATHERTON QLD 4883
ph (07) 4091 1844
fax (07) 4091 3281
8am–5pm weekdays

Hasties Swamp National Park

Magpie goose
Darren Jew

What's special?

On the Atherton Tableland, Hasties Swamp National Park protects a wetland which is a valuable refuge for waterbirds. Local and migratory birds visit this swamp.

Only a few patches of the original open eucalypt woodland remain, a striking contrast to the lush rainforests found elsewhere on the tableland. The eucalypt forest remnant occurs on the change from basaltic to granitic soils.

Exploring Hasties Swamp

Go birdwatching from a large bird hide at the edge of the swamp. See plumed whistling ducks, brolgas and magpie geese.

Have a bush picnic. Camping is not allowed but you can stay nearby at Atherton or camp at Danbulla State Forest.

Accessibility

The toilets and bird hide are wheelchair-accessible.

Getting there

Hasties Swamp is just south of Atherton. Head along the Atherton-Herberton Road then turn left into Hasties Road and right into Kool Road.

Further information

QPWS
83 Main Street
PO Box 975
ATHERTON QLD 4883
ph (07) 4091 1844
fax (07) 4091 3281
8am–5pm weekdays

Hasties Swamp
Adam Creed

Hallorans Hill Conservation Park

What's special?

Rising above Atherton township, Hallorans Hill is an extinct volcanic cone on the Atherton Tableland. Hallorans Hill Conservation Park protects open eucalypt forest and rainforest remnants in sheltered places around the hill.

Exploring Hallorans Hill

Have a picnic on the top of the hill. Picnic tables, gas barbecues, water and toilets are provided by the local authority.

Enjoy the view or visit the information centre to find out more about the local area.

Camping is not allowed but you can stay in nearby Atherton.

Walking

Walk to the crater through the rainforest. Learn about Aboriginal culture along the way. The track has some steep sections.

Accessibility

The local government facilities are wheelchair-accessible.

Getting there

Hallorans Hill is just to the east of Atherton off the Kennedy Highway.

Darren Jew

Red-backed wren

Tracks

Aboriginal trail and crater walk
40 minutes return

Further information

QPWS
83 Main Street
PO Box 975
ATHERTON QLD 4883
ph (07) 4091 1844
fax (07) 4091 3281
8am–5pm weekdays

Wongabel State Forest

Lumholtz's tree-kangaroo

Darren Jew

Tracks

Wongabel Heritage trail
800m, 30 minutes return

Wongabel Forest walk
2·4km, 1·5 hours return

Further information

QPWS
PO Box 975
ATHERTON QLD 4883
ph (07) 4091 1844
fax (07) 4091 3281
8am–5pm weekdays

What's special?

Tropical rainforest on the Atherton Tableland is protected in Wongabel State Forest, an important wildlife refuge in the Wet Tropics World Heritage Area. The forest also contains hoop pine plantations, other plantations and early plantings of red cedar trees. The Barron River forms part of the eastern boundary of the forest.

Exploring Wongabel

Find out about the area's Aboriginal culture and history along the heritage trail. Learn about rainforest trees from signs along the Wongabel Forest walk.

Go spotlighting at night. You might see many different possums and even tree-kangaroos.

Dogs and camping are not allowed in the forest.

Walking

Wear a hat, sunscreen and insect repellent.

Accessibility

Wheelchair-assisted access is possible to the Heritage trail.

Getting there

Wongabel is on the Kennedy Highway, 8km south of Atherton.

Herberton Range State Forest and Forest Reserve

What's special?

Rainforest and open forest along the Herberton Range are protected in the Herberton Range State Forest and Forest Reserve in the Wet Tropics World Heritage Area.

The forest's upland rainforests are home to many unusual animals and plants including golden bowerbirds.

At 1107m, Mount Baldy provides panoramic views over Atherton and the tableland.

Exploring Herberton Range

Only experienced, fit walkers should attempt the walk to the summit of Mount Baldy. The walk is quite strenuous with steep sections and loose rock.

Walk or cycle through the forest along fire trails.

Dogs and camping are not allowed in the forest.

Walking

Walk or cycle along a 20km firebreak circuit or hike to the summit of Mt Baldy.

Wear sturdy walking shoes, a hat and sunscreen. Take drinking water.

Getting there

Herberton Range is just west of Atherton. From Atherton, go to the old Atherton Post Office on the road to Herberton, 1·6km from the centre of town. Head 600m along Rifle Range Road to the start of the walking track.

Steve Parish

Green ringtail possum

Tracks

Mount Baldy Summit walk
2km, 2 hours

Further information

QPWS
83 Main Street
PO Box 975
ATHERTON QLD 4883
ph (07) 4091 1844
fax (07) 4091 3281
8am–5pm weekdays

Mt Hypipamee National Park

Herbert River ringtail possum

Steve Parish

What's special?

High on the Evelyn Tableland in the Hugh Nelson Range, Mt Hypipamee National Park contains beautiful high altitude rainforests which are remarkably different from tropical rainforests found elsewhere on the tablelands. These upland forests contain species related to those in subtropical rainforests further south. Open forests also grow in the park, part of the Wet Tropics World Heritage Area.

Mt Hypipamee National Park is home to a wonderful variety of wildlife including possums found only in the wet tropical rainforests of north Queensland, such as the green ringtail, lemuroid ringtail and Herbert River ringtail possums.

The volcanic pipe or "diatreme" at Mt Hypipamee was formed when a volcanic vent exploded violently creating a sheer-sided crater. The explosion crater is 70m across with sheer granite sides and the lake is 58m below the rim and about 82m deep.

Exploring Mt Hypipamee

Have a picnic in the rainforest then go for a walk to a viewing deck over the diatreme. Picnic tables, wood barbecues, water and toilets are provided.

Look for golden bowerbirds, spotted catbirds and riflebirds in the forest and honeyeaters around the picnic area. Go spotlighting at night to see the possums or join a commercial tour.

Camping is not allowed in the park but you can stay nearby.

Walking

Walk 400m through upland rainforest to the crater or take the 1km return track to Dinner Falls, a series of cascades on the upper Barron River.

Accessibility

The track to the crater is wheelchair-accessible.

Getting there

Mt Hypipamee is 25km south of Atherton along the Kennedy Highway.

Tracks

Mt Hypipamee and Dinner Falls walk
1km return, 30 minutes

Further information

QPWS
Lake Eacham
PO Box 21
YUNGABURRA QLD 4872
ph (07) 4095 3768
fax (07) 4095 3403

Malanda Falls Conservation Park

What's special?

On the Atherton Tableland, Malanda Falls Conservation Park protects a small rainforest remnant. The falls on the North Johnstone River tumble over an ancient lava flow which originated from the Mt Hypipamee area, 15km away.

Exploring Malanda Falls

Have a picnic by the river. Toilets, a shelter shed, water, wood barbecues and picnic tables are provided.

See platypus in the river around dusk and look for brush-turkeys and orange-footed scrubfowl building mounds in the rainforest.

Visit the environmental centre next to the park to find out more about the history, geology, vegetation and wildlife.

Camping is not allowed in the park but you can stay nearby at Malanda.

Walking

The Tulip Oak walk features drier forests. The Rainforest circuit passes through undisturbed rainforest along the river.

Getting there

Malanda Falls is on the outskirts of the township of Malanda on the Atherton Road.

Tracks

Tulip Oak circuit
1km return, 20 minutes

Rainforest circuit
1km return, 20 minutes

Further information

QPWS
Lake Eacham
PO Box 21
YUNGABURRA QLD 4872
ph (07) 4095 3768
fax (07) 4095 3403

Grey-headed robin

Darran Leal

Millstream Falls National Park

What's special?

Millstream Falls is reputedly Australia's widest single-drop waterfall. The falls flow over the edge of a columnar basalt lava flow, a legacy of the Atherton Tableland's volcanic past. Millstream Falls National Park also protects a dry open woodland remnant on the tableland and is part of the Wet Tropics World Heritage Area.

Here, in the rain shadow of the eastern dividing ranges, the woodland is dominated by bloodwoods and stringybarks. Tall open forest of majestic rose gums is protected in nearby Millstream Conservation Park.

Tracks

Millstream Falls walk
1km return, 20 minutes

Further information

QPWS
Lake Eacham
PO Box 21
YUNGABURRA QLD 4872
ph (07) 4095 3768
fax (07) 4095 3403

Exploring Millstream Falls

Spend some time in the open woodland. Toilets, a shelter shed, picnic tables, wood barbecues and tank water are provided.

Camping is not allowed in the park.

Walking

See the falls and rockpools along the Millstream River.

Getting there

Millstream Falls is 3km south-west of the township of Ravenshoe.

Millstream Falls

Darran Leal

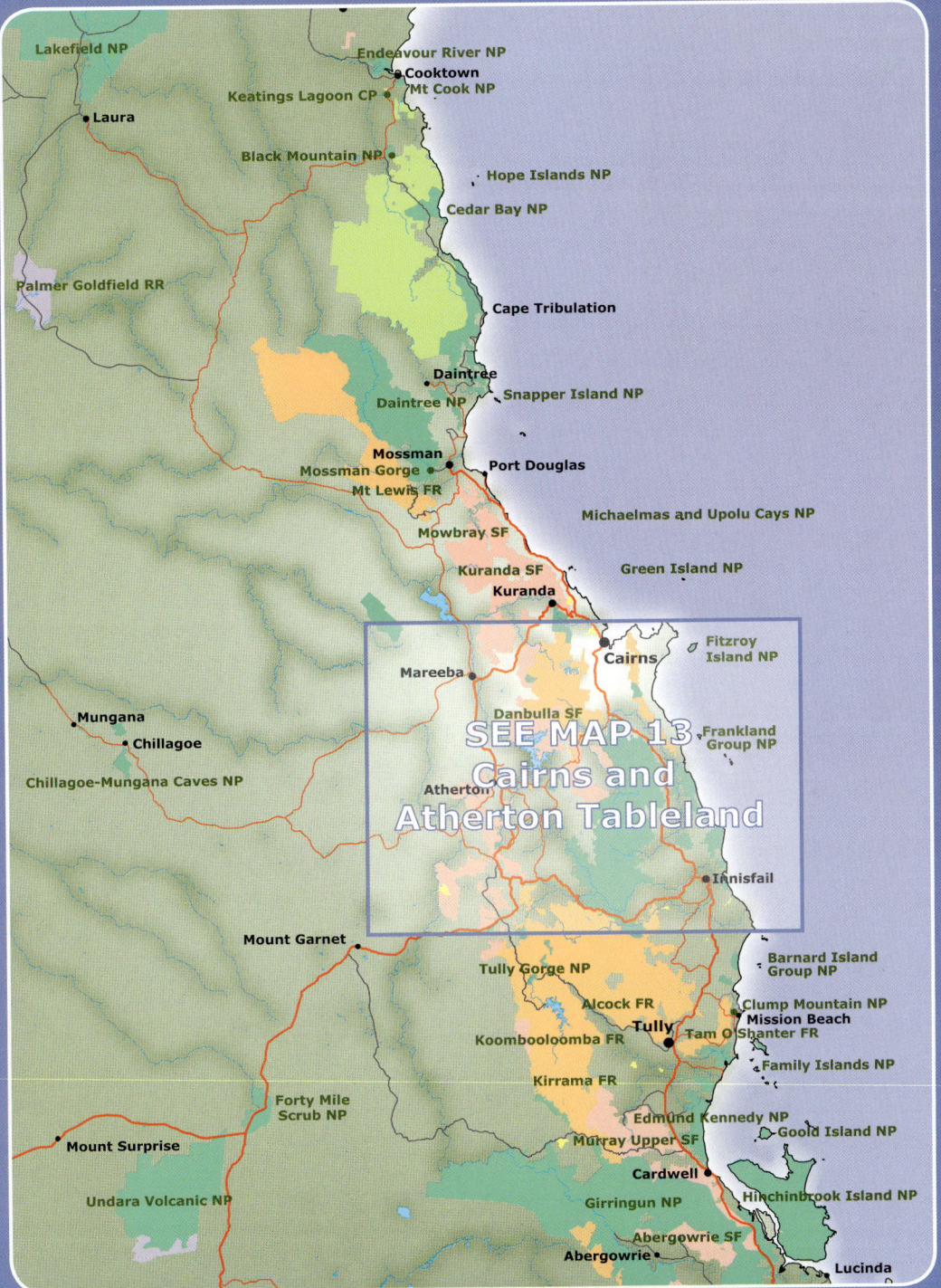

Cardwell to Cooktown

Map 14

Legend

National Park
Conservation Park
Forest Reserve
State Forest
Timber Reserve
Resource Reserve
Highway
Major connecting road
Minor access road

0   20   40
km

N

Lakefield NP
Endeavour River NP
Cooktown
Mt Cook NP
Keatings Lagoon CP
Laura
Black Mountain NP
Hope Islands NP
Cedar Bay NP
Palmer Goldfield RR
Cape Tribulation
Daintree
Daintree NP
Snapper Island NP
Mossman
Mossman Gorge
Mt Lewis FR
Port Douglas
Mowbray SF
Michaelmas and Upolu Cays NP
Kuranda SF
Kuranda
Green Island NP
Mareeba
Cairns
Fitzroy Island NP
Danbulla SF
Mungana
Chillagoe
Chillagoe-Mungana Caves NP
Frankland Group NP

**SEE MAP 13
Cairns and
Atherton Tableland**

Atherton
Innisfail
Mount Garnet
Barnard Island Group NP
Tully Gorge NP
Alcock FR
Clump Mountain NP
Mission Beach
Koombooloomba FR
Tully
Tam O'Shanter FR
Kirrama FR
Family Islands NP
Forty Mile Scrub NP
Edmund Kennedy NP
Goold Island NP
Murray Upper SF
Mount Surprise
Cardwell
Hinchinbrook Island NP
Undara Volcanic NP
Girringun NP
Abergowrie SF
Abergowrie
Lucinda

Family Islands National Park

Male Ulysses butterfly

Adam Creed

What's special?

A chain of scenic continental islands extends about 14km off the coast between Tully Heads and Mission Beach. Most of the Family Islands are in the national park. Dunk Island, the most northerly, is hilly and clothed in rainforest and open forest. Beachcomber E.J. Banfield, who lived on Dunk Island from 1897 until 1923, wrote four books about the island's natural history.

Wheeler, Coombe, Smith, Bowden and Hudson Islands are also in Family Islands National Park. Stunted woodlands of casuarinas, wattles and eucalypts grow between tumbled slabs of granite on the windswept south-eastern sides of the islands and lush rainforests grow on the sheltered northern sides.

Exploring the Family Islands

You can camp on Dunk, Wheeler and Coombe Islands.

Picnic or camp on Dunk Island. Facilities include picnic tables, toilets, a shelter shed, gas barbecues, hot and cold showers, water and a public phone. Campers and day visitors can access some of the resort facilities by purchasing a pass from Water Sports at the resort.

Wheeler Island has picnic tables and a toilet and Coombe Island has a picnic table. Visitors must be self-sufficient. Take fresh water, insect repellent and a fuel stove for cooking. Campfires are not allowed. Take your rubbish when you leave.

Go birdwatching on Dunk Island. More than 100 species of birds have been recorded.

Beware of marine stingers between October and May. Fishing restrictions apply in the surrounding marine park waters.

A private resort operates on Dunk Island. Day visitors are welcome. Visit in the cooler months.

Walking

Explore Dunk on 13km of walking tracks around the island. Wear a hat and sunscreen and take drinking water.

Tracks

Banfield's Grave track
1km return, 15 minutes

Mt. Kootaloo track
5·6km return, 3 hours

Muggy Muggy Beach track
2km return 30 minutes

Coconut Beach track
6km return, 2 hours

Island circuit
9·2km, 3 hours

Family Islands National Park

Dunk Island

Accessibility

The toilets and showers in the day facilities area are wheelchair-accessible.

Getting there

Water taxis from Mission Beach, boats from Clump Point and flights from Townsville or Cairns provide easy access to Dunk Island, 4·5km east of Mission Beach or 36km north of Cardwell. The other Family Islands are accessible by private boat from Mission Beach, Cardwell, Hull River or Tully River.

Further information

Rainforest and Reef Information Centre
142 Victoria Street
PO Box 74
CARDWELL QLD 4849
ph (07) 4066 8601
fax (07) 4066 8116
e-mail: hinchinbrook.camp@epa.qld.gov.au

Campsite bookings: 13 13 04 or www.qld.gov.au/camping

Dunk Island campsite bookings:
Water Sports building
Dunk Island Resort
ph (07) 4068 8199

Clump Mountain National Park

What's special?

One of the few remaining patches of undisturbed tropical lowland rainforest can be seen in Clump Mountain National Park. Rainforest once grew throughout these coastal lowlands but little remains. These remnants are important habitat for the southern cassowary, a large flightless bird found only in the tropical rainforests of Queensland and New Guinea.

Swamp mahogany and brush box dominate the rainforest canopy and Alexander palms, epiphytes and buttressed tress grow in the rainforest. The migratory buff-breasted paradise-kingfisher nests in termite mounds here in summer and the endangered southern cassowary lives and feeds in the forest. The arenga palm and palm cycad grow towards the summit of Bicton Hill.

This is the traditional land of the Dyiru Aboriginal people. Nearby Bingil Bay was a favourite camping spot and rainforest plants were used to make fish nets, shelters, tools, weapons and medicines.

Bicton Hill, overlooking the mainland and offshore islands, was a ship lookout for the first European settlers, the Cutten Brothers, who grew tropical fruits and other crops around Bingil Bay. They named their property "Bicton" after Bicton Hills in Devonshire, England.

Orchard butterfly

Darran Leal

Clump Mountain National Park

Bruce Cowell

Exploring Clump Mountain

See the tropical rainforest at Bicton Hill.

This is a great place for wildlife watching. See echidnas, rainforest skinks and lace monitors (lizards) along the track. Giant white-tailed rats feed on the red seeds of the palm cycad at night from May to June.

Go birdwatching. You might be lucky enough to see a buff-breasted paradise-kingfisher or a cassowary. Cassowaries can be aggressive towards people. Stay well back. Back away slowly holding your backpack in front of you if you feel threatened.

Go spotlighting at night to see the striped possum feeding on beetle larvae, flowers, fruit or the honey of native bees.

Camping is not allowed but there is plenty of accommodation in the Mission Beach area.

Walking

Walk uphill to lookouts over Mission Beach and the offshore islands. Wear a hat and sunscreen. Take drinking water.

Getting there

Clump Mountain is on the Bingil Bay Road north of Mission Beach.

Darran Leal

Southern cassowary

Tracks

Bicton Hill circuit
3·9km, 1·5 hours

Further information

QPWS
Garner Beach Road
PO Box 89
MISSION BEACH QLD 4854
ph (07) 4068 7183
fax (07) 4068 7878

Tam O'Shanter Forest Reserve

Cassowary chick

Adam Creed

What's special?

Tropical rainforest with graceful *Licuala ramsayi* fan palms and scenic creeks make Tam O'Shanter Forest Reserve well worth a visit. Tam O'Shanter protects a fan palm forest remnant and one of the largest tracts of coastal lowland rainforest left in north Queensland.

The forest is home to the southern cassowary, Australia's largest rainforest animal, which is threatened with extinction. The cassowary has disappeared from most of its former coastal rainforest range. Tam O'Shanter is one of the few places in Queensland where you are likely to see this unusual and colourful bird. Tam O'Shanter Forest Reserve is in the Wet Tropics World Heritage Area.

Exploring Tam O'Shanter

Lacey Creek is a cool rainforest retreat beside a creek for a bush picnic. Picnic tables and a gas barbecue are provided. Learn about cassowaries at the information shelter. Take the walking track to a viewing platform and look for tortoises, giant prawns and fish in the creek.

Go for a bushwalk at Licuala. See the fan palm forest once common in the wet coastal lowlands. Kids will love the children's walk complete with its own brochure, fun activities and cassowary footprints to follow. Keen walkers can tackle the longer walk linking Licuala to Lacey Creek which follows an old Forestry track, crosses creeks and passes through a variety of vegetation types.

Cassowaries are wild animals. If they attack, they can cause serious injury. Never feed them. If you see a cassowary, stay well back. Never run. Back away slowly holding your bag or backpack in front of you for protection.

Camping and dogs are not allowed in the forest.

Walking

Wear a hat, sunscreen and insect repellent.

Tracks

Lacey Creek walk
1·1km return, 45 minutes

Licuala walk
1·2km return, 45 minutes

Children's walk
350m, 20 minutes return

Licuala-Lacey Creek link trail
7km one-way, 4 hours return

Tam O'Shanter Forest Reserve

Accessibility

The toilets and the first part of the Lacey Creek walk from the carpark to the cassowary information shelter are wheelchair-accessible.

Getting there

Tam O'Shanter Forest Reserve is near Mission Beach south of Cairns. Travel to Mission Beach along the El Arish or Tully Roads off the Bruce Highway.

Further information

Rainforest and Reef Information Centre
142 Victoria Street
PO Box 74
CARDWELL QLD 4849
ph (07) 4066 8601
fax (07) 4066 8116
e-mail: hinchinbrook.camp@epa.qld.gov.au

Licuala palm forest, Tam O'Shanter Forest Reserve

Barnard Island Group National Park

Black-naped tern

Darren Jew

What's special?

Close inshore, the Barnard Island Group National Park includes Jessie, Kent, Lindquist, Bresnaham and Hutchison Islands in the North Barnard Group and Sisters and Stephens Islands in the southern group.

The Barnards have a fascinating geological history dating back 420 million years. The islands were isolated from the mainland 18,000 years ago when the ice caps melted and sea levels rose. Stephens Island has well-preserved volcanic tuff outcrops and steeply dipping basalt dykes exposed along the shoreline.

Dense rainforest cloaks the rocky slopes of the Barnards. Clambering vines form "vine towers" in the rainforest. Mangroves, pandanus and she-oaks fringe the shore.

The South Barnards are an important seabird rookery for six species of terns which breed there each year. This is the sea country of the Mamu people. Fish traps remain around the islands.

Some corals in the surrounding marine park waters have been badly affected by recent coral bleaching.

Exploring Barnard Islands

Go birdwatching. See 22 species of seabirds and 23 woodland species. Access is restricted to Sisters Island and most of Stephens Island during the seabird nesting season, September to April.

Bush camp on the western side of Stephens Island. Obtain your permit from Cairns. You can also camp on Kent Island. Take drinking water and a fuel stove. Be self-sufficient.

Do not swim in marine stinger season, October to May. Observe fishing and collecting restrictions in the surrounding marine park waters.

Getting there

The Barnards are 10–17km south-east of Mourilyan. Access is by private boat from Mourilyan Harbour or Kurrimine Beach. Sea kayak tours occasionally operate.

Further information

QPWS
5B Sheridan Street
PO Box 2066
CAIRNS QLD 4870
ph (07) 4046 6600
fax (07) 4046 6751
e-mail: cic@epa.qld.gov.au

Campsite bookings: 13 13 04 or
www.qld.gov.au/camping

Tully Gorge Alcock Forest Reserve

What's special?

The wettest place in Queensland contains Tully Gorge in the rugged Alcock Forest Reserve. The Tully River is renowned for white water rafting. The forest is the main exit point for commercial rafting tours. Alcock Forest Reserve is in the Wet Tropics World Heritage Area.

Exploring Alcock

As you enter the forest, stop at Frank Roberts Lookout for a view over the Tully Gorge. Continue to the picnic and camping area.

Have a picnic by the Tully River. A shelter shed, wood barbecues, picnic tables and toilets are provided. Find out about butterflies along the short Rainforest Butterfly walk. The best time to see the butterflies is between September and February.

You can camp near the river on grassy sites surrounded by rainforest. Tent sites, toilets, firewood, water and cold showers are provided. The camping area is suitable for caravans and motorhomes.

Tully River

Paul Candlin

Tully Gorge, Alcock State Forest

Be careful exploring around the creek. The Tully River is used to generate hydro-electricity, so the water level can change rapidly.

Beyond the picnic and camping area, the Flip Wilson Lookout provides a great view of a series of rapids on the river. Only experienced and skilled kayakers should attempt to negotiate the rapids. You must wear safety helmets and life jackets and carry throw-bags and first aid equipment. The best idea is to join a commercial rafting tour down the river.

Watch the rafters early afternoon from a boardwalk at Cardstone Weir at the end of the road. For your safety, stay on the boardwalk. The rocks can be slippery and water currents here are dangerous.

Dogs are not allowed in the forest. Avoid visiting in the wet season, January to April.

Walking

Wear a hat, sunscreen and insect repellent.

Accessibility

The toilets in the picnic and camping area and the Rainforest Butterfly walk are wheelchair-accessible.

Getting there

Alcock is 40km west of Tully along Jarra Creek and Cardstone Roads.

Paul Candlin

Tully River

Tracks

Rainforest Butterfly walk
375m return, 20 minutes

Further information

Rainforest and Reef Information Centre
142 Victoria Street
PO Box 74
CARDWELL QLD 4849
ph (07) 4066 8601
fax (07) 4066 8116
e-mail: hinchinbrook.camp@
epa.qld.gov.au

Koombooloomba Forest Reserve

What's special?

Surrounding Lake Koombooloomba, Koombooloomba Forest Reserve protects tropical rainforest, tall eucalypt forest and dry open forest remnants at the southern end of the Evelyn Tableland. The forest is part of the Wet Tropics World Heritage Area and located in one of the wettest areas in Queensland.

Several rare and threatened animals live in the forest including Lumholtz's tree-kangaroo, the Herbert River ringtail possum and the red goshawk.

Exploring Koombooloomba

Relax and enjoy nature in this undeveloped forest. Camping and picnicking facilities are provided at nearby Koombooloomba Dam.

Go for a scenic drive through the rainforest to Kirrama, Blencoe Falls and the Herbert River to the south. Four-wheel-drive access is possible in the dry season only. Permits are required.

Getting there

Koombooloomba is 34km south of Ravenshoe. Conventional vehicle access is possible along the Tully Falls Road.

Further information

QPWS
83 Main Street
PO Box 975
ATHERTON QLD 4883
ph (07) 4091 1844
fax (07) 4091 3281
8am–5pm weekdays

QPWS
Lake Eacham
PO Box 21
YUNGABURRA QLD 4871
ph (07) 4095 3768
fax (07) 4095 3403

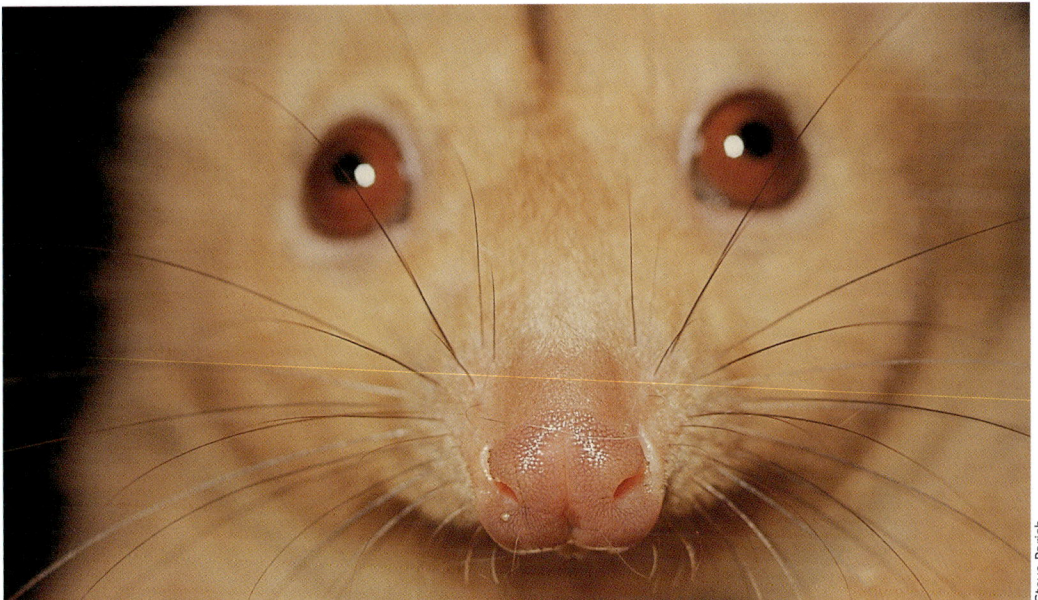

Young Herbert River ringtail possum

Tully Gorge National Park

Tracks

Tully River track
1·2km return, 30 minutes

Further information

QPWS
Lake Eacham
PO Box 21
YUNGABURRA QLD 4872
ph (07) 4095 3768
fax (07) 4095 3403

What's special?

The Tully River south of Ravenshoe is regarded as one of the State's most picturesque rivers. Tully Gorge National Park contains several sections partly surrounded by forest reserves. One park section is along the Tully River.

The park protects the western end of the gorge and beautiful upland rainforest in the Wet Tropics World Heritage Area. Water has been diverted to a hydro-electric power station, so Tully Falls is usually dry.

Exploring Tully Gorge

Most of the park is rugged and inaccessible with no visitor facilities.

Have a picnic in the upland rainforest in the Tully Falls Section of the park. Toilets, wood barbecues and picnic tables are provided. See the gorge along the Tully River from a lookout.

Camping is not allowed in the park.

Walking

Walk through the rainforest to the river.

Getting there

Tully Gorge is 24km south of Ravenshoe on the Lake Koombooloomba Road.

Rainforest creek along walk to Tully Falls

Bruce Cowell

Forty Mile Scrub National Park

What's special?

On the McBride Plateau, where ancient and recent volcanic flows occur side by side, a dry rainforest remnant, open grassy woodland, and the headwaters of Lynd, Barwon and Cleanskin Creeks are protected in Forty Mile Scrub National Park.

Bottle trees, white cedars, fig trees and forest red gums grow in the semi-evergreen vine thicket known as Forty Mile Scrub, one of the few inland dry rainforest remnants in north Queensland. This mountain rainforest vegetation was once quite extensive and is now considered nationally significant. Cypress pine, paperbarks, ironbarks, spotted gum and poplar gum grow in the park's open woodland.

At 900 metres above sea level, Forty Mile Scrub experiences chilly tropical evenings in winter. The heavy dew may be the reason so many native animals visit and live in the forests, feeding on the variety of foods in nature's garden.

Exploring Forty Mile Scrub

Stop for a walk or picnic. Toilets and sheltered picnic tables are provided in the day use area beside Kennedy Highway.

Information signs along the walking trail helps visitors understand the vegetation types and typical wildlife found in the vine scrub. The leaf litter is home to the giant cockroach which burrows into the moist soil looking for food. See black-striped wallabies sheltering in the vine thicket during the day.

Walking

Explore the unique stunted forest on a 10-minute, flat circuit walk. Signs guide you from the day-use area to the start of the track.

Accessibility

The picnic facilities, toilets and track are wheelchair-accessible.

Getting there

Forty Mile Scrub straddles part of the narrow Kennedy Highway 65km south-west of Mt Garnet and 108km south-west of Ravenshoe.

Paul Candlin

Forty Mile Scrub

Tracks

Forty Mile Scrub circuit
300m, 10 minutes

Further information

QPWS
5B Sheridan Street Cairns
PO Box 2066
CAIRNS QLD 4870
ph (07) 4046 6600
fax (07) 4046 6751
e-mail: cic@epa.qld.gov.au

Undara Volcanic National Park

What's special?

On the western slopes of the McBride Plateau, open woodlands give way to the vast open spaces of the Savannah. Here in Undara Volcanic National Park, rich volcanic basalt soils, covered in an endless sea of seasonal grass, conceal the Undara lava tube. This geological tunnel of global significance snakes westward under a ribbon of remnant deciduous rainforest.

"Undara" is an Aboriginal word meaning "long way". The park protects the longest lava tube cave system in the world. About 190,000 years ago, a large volcano erupted violently, spewing molten lava over the surrounding landscape. The lava flowed rapidly down a dry riverbed. The top outer layer cooled and formed a crust while the molten lava below drained outwards leaving behind a series of hollow tubes.

Surprisingly, semi-evergreen vine thicket grows in the moist, sheltered entrances to some of the lava caves. The roofs of some tubes collapsed creating ideal conditions for dry rainforest to grow and wildlife to shelter. Rock-wallabies, insectiverous bat colonies and owls roost here in the cool, birds shelter in the fruit-filled canopy and predators lurk in the tumbled basalt terrain to complete the food chain.

Exploring Undara Volcanic

Explore the "outback" on the Wet Tropics' doorstep at Undara. Visitors can climb a volcano, walk into the high country wilderness or see inside a lava tube on guided tours.

Go birdwatching. More than 120 species of birds, including the endangered red goshawk, can be seen in the park.

Picnic at Kalkani. Toilets, water and sheltered picnic tables are provided. Walk around the crater.

Camping is not allowed in the park but you can stay next door at Undara Lodge (1800 990 992).

Book a tour of the lava tubes through one of the park's commercial operators: Bedrock Village (07) 4062 3193, Cape Trib Connections (07) 4053 3833 or Undara Experience 1800 990 992.

Mareeba rock-wallaby

Adam Creed

Undara Volcanic National Park

Peter Lik

Walking

Follow the graded climb to the self-guiding trail around the eggcup-shaped Kalkani crater. Allow one hour to walk around the entire rim. Wear sturdy shoes, a hat and sunscreen. Take drinking water.

Accessibility

The Kalkani picnic area has wheelchair-accessible toilets and sheltered picnic tables.

The lodge also has wheelchair-accessible facilities.

Getting there

Undara Volcanic is 300km by road south-west of Cairns, 100km south-west of Mt Garnet and, 65km east of Mt Surprise. You can also travel by train and coach.

Tracks

Kalkani Crater circuit
2·5km, 1 hour

Further information

Undara Volcanic NP
c/- Post Office
MT SURPRISE QLD 4871
ph (07) 4097 1485
ph (07) 4097 1418
fax (07) 4097 1493
fax (07) 4097 1316

QPWS
5B Sheridan Street
PO Box 2066
CAIRNS QLD 4870
ph (07) 4046 6600
fax (07) 4046 6751
e-mail: cic@epa.qld.gov.au

Inside a lava tube

Peter Lik, Tourism Queensland

Chillagoe-Mungana Caves National Park

Decorated cave at Chillagoe

Paul Candlin

What's special?

Dry prickly vine scrub and jagged limestone outcrops at Chillagoe conceal the breathtaking beauty of the limestone caves underground. Many of these caves are protected in sections of Chillagoe-Mungana Caves National Park.

About 400 million years ago, limestone was deposited as calcareous mud and coral reefs surrounding underwater volcanoes. Subsequent tilting, folding and erosion exposed and weathered the limestone which today towers over the surrounding plains. Fluctuating groundwater levels slowly dissolved some of the limestone, creating caverns and passages, some of which have since been decorated by calcite stalagtites, stalagmites and flowstones, deposited by surface waters penetrating through the rock.

Few animals can survive inside the dark caves. The common bent-wing, little bent-wing, little brown, sheath-tailed, eastern horseshoe and diadem horseshoe bats roost and breed here. Chillagoe is one of five known nesting sites for the white-rumped swiftlet which, like bats, uses sound waves or echolocation to navigate around the dark caves. The caves are also home to the spotted python and a variety of insects and spiders. Fossilised bones of many animals including the extinct giant kangaroo have been found in the caves.

Aboriginal paintings are protected in the park. The Chillagoe Smelter site preserves relics of the state's mining and industrial heritage dating back to the 1890s.

Exploring Chillagoe

Spend some time in a country town and explore some limestone caves. Guided tours of Royal Arch, Donna and Trezkinn Caves operate three times daily except Christmas Day. The tours take about an hour and fees apply. Obtain your ticket beforehand from the Hub in Chillagoe. The Hub is open 8.30am–5pm daily and 8am–3.30pm weekends. Groups should make advance bookings.

You can explore The Archways, Pompeii and Bauhinia Caves on your own. Always take at least two torches when caving and never cave alone.

Chillagoe-Mungana Caves National Park

Paul Candlin

Explore above ground as well. See the brilliant red flowers of the bats-wing coral trees and kurrajong trees in winter. The ghost gum *Eucalyptus papuana* sheds its bark each year leaving behind white and yellow bark. See Aboriginal paintings at Balancing Rock and Mungana.

Discover the mining history of the area at the Smelter. Copper, lead, silver and gold were extracted here for a period of more than 40 years.

Go birdwatching. More than 75 bird species have been recorded around Chillagoe including pale-headed rosellas, apostle birds and blue-faced honeyeaters.

Camping is not allowed in the park but you can stay in the nearby township of Chillagoe. The winter months are a cooler time to visit, but the caves are a comfortable 22 degrees Celsius all year round.

Walking

Wear sturdy shoes and protective clothing when walking or caving. The limestone rock has sharp edges.
Take drinking water.

Accessibility

There are no disability facilities but you can drive around the short interpretive trail at the Chillagoe Smelters.

Getting there

Chillagoe Caves is 215km or three hours' drive west of Cairns via Mareeba and Dimbulah. The popular Royal Arch, Donna and Trezkinn Caves are just south of Chillagoe. The Archways is at Mungana, 15km north-west of Chillagoe. To reach the smelter site, take the Mungana Road and turn right at the signpost.

A bus service operates to Chillagoe from Cairns and Mareeba and charter flights operate from Cairns. Conventional vehicle access is possible in dry weather. Check road conditions in summer as roads may be impassable in the wet season.

Tracks

Donna Cave to Royal Arch Cave via Balancing Rock
4·5km one-way,
1 hour 15 minutes

Further information

Chillagoe-Mungana Caves NP
Queen Street
PO Box 38
CHILLAGOE QLD 4871
ph (07) 4094 7163
fax (07) 4094 7213

QPWS
5B Sheridan Street
PO Box 2066
CAIRNS QLD 4870
ph (07) 4046 6600
fax (07) 4046 6751
e-mail: cic@epa.qld.gov.au

Cave tour bookings:
The Hub
C/- Post Office
CHILLAGOE QLD 4871
ph (07) 4094 7111
fax (07) 4094 7122

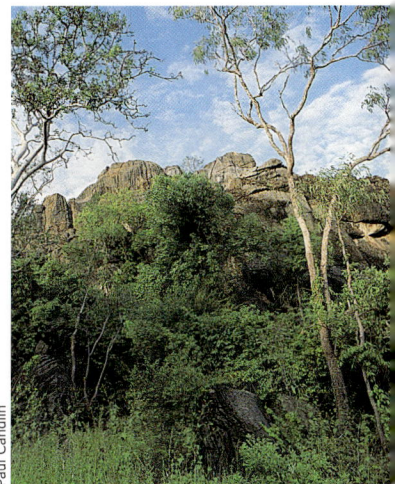

Paul Candlin

Karst outcrop at Chillagoe-Mungana Caves

Mowbray and Kuranda State Forests

What's special?

Tropical rainforest and open eucalypt forest are protected in Mowbray and Kuranda State Forests in the Wet Tropics World Heritage Area. Pyramid-shaped Black Mountain towers over the surrounding countryside.

Together, the forests form an important wildlife habitat between Lamb Range to the south and Carbine Tableland to the north. The tropical rainforest is home to the endangered southern cassowary and rare Lumholtz's tree-kangaroo.

The old Port Douglas-Thornborough Road, known as the Bump Track, was once a lifeline for isolated settlers, miners and townships. Blazed by renowned bushman, Christie Palmerston in April 1877, the Bump Track became the main route between the Hodgkinson goldfields near Mt Mulligan and Port Douglas.

Cycling through Kuranda State Forest

Adam Creed

Mowbray and Kuranda State Forests

Paul Candlin

Exploring Mowbray and Kuranda

Bushwalk or travel by mountain bike or horse along the historic 26·5km Bump Track. Obtain a permit for bike or horse riding. You need a permit to traverse if travelling beyond Julatten along the Black Mountain Road by four-wheel-drive vehicle.

Drive through spectacular rainforest along the 43km Black Mountain Road. The first 18km from the Kuranda end is conventional access. No permit is required to drive this section. Four-wheel-drive and a permit to traverse are needed beyond Flaggy Creek.

Walking

Allow a full day to walk the Bump Track and visit Big Mowbray Falls. Take drinking water. Wear a hat and sunscreen. Arrange to be collected from the top of the track near Julatten or the bottom of the track near Craiglee.

Getting there

Head south from Port Douglas along the Captain Cook Highway to Craiglee. Turn right into Mowbray River Road 1·5km south of Craiglea then travel along Connolly Road for 3·5km to the Bump Track. Black Mountain Road is a half-day trip for visitors from Cairns or Port Douglas.

To reach Black Mountain Road from Kuranda, take the Black Mountain Road turnoff, 300m on the eastern side of the Barron River Bridge at Kuranda, 27km from Cairns. From Julatten, take the Euluma Creek turnoff at the Julatten school.

Further information

QPWS
PO Box 2066
CAIRNS QLD 4870
ph (07) 4046 6600
fax (07) 4046 6751
e-mail:cic@epa.qld.gov.au

QPWS
1 Front Street
PO Box 251
MOSSMAN QLD 4873
ph (07) 4098 2188
fax (07) 4098 2279

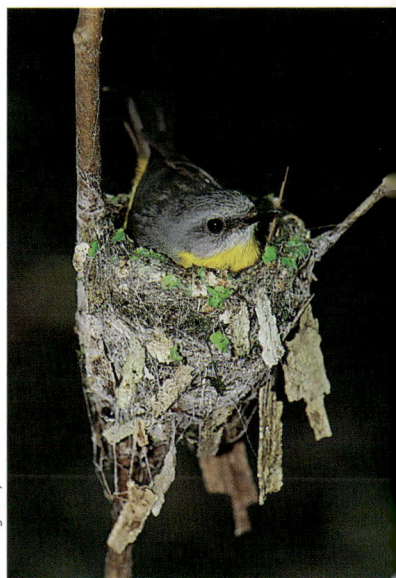

John Augusteyn

Eastern yellow robin

Green Island National Park

What's special?

The most popular destination on the Great Barrier Reef is Green Island. This 12ha island is a true coral cay formed over thousands of years by the build-up of sand and coral rubble deposited on the calm side of the reef. The eastern side of the island is covered in tropical vine forest. The surrounding coral reef is home to a variety of hard and soft corals, giant clams, fish and stingrays.

Even though beche-de-mer fishermen removed most of the vegetation in the 19th Century and recent crown of thorns outbreaks have affected the hard corals, this is still a very beautiful place. Pied imperial-pigeons roost on the island in summer and endangered green and hawksbill turtles are seen offshore.

This is part of the traditional sea country of the Gungandji people and the island is known as "Wunyami". The Gungandji people maintain a close connection with the island, a former initiation ground for young men.

Green Island has been a popular resort for close to a century. The island became a national park in 1937, marine park in 1974 and part of the Great Barrier Reef World Heritage Area in 1981. The island, reef and beaches are managed together as a recreation area.

Exploring Green Island

Spend a busy day exploring the island. Relax on the beach or wander through the forest. Snorkel over the lagoon.

Go birdwatching — Green Island is home to 35 species of seabirds and 28 species of woodland birds. Join a guided nature walk or explore the forest on your own.

Camping is not allowed but you can stay overnight in the resort, which has been operating on the island from the 1940s www.greenislandresort.com.au. Some resort facilities are available to daytrippers. Commercial attractions on the island include the world's first underwater observatory and Marineland Melanesia Crocodile Habitat.

Fishing restrictions apply in the surrounding marine park waters. Visitors are asked to help protect the island and reef by collecting nothing, and anchoring carefully to avoid damaging the coral. Beware of marine stingers between October and May.

Discover an underwater world at Green Island.

Green Island National Park

Walking

A 1km one-way track leads through the forest to the south-western beach. Return along the beach. Wear a hat and sunscreen. Allow about 50 minutes for the walk.

Accessibility

Boardwalks through the park are suitable for wheelchairs and strollers.

Getting there

Green Island is 27km east-north-east of Cairns. Daily ferry services operate to the island. The journey takes 50 minutes.

Further information

QPWS
5B Sheridan Street Cairns
PO Box 2066
CAIRNS QLD 4870
ph (07) 4046 6600
fax (07) 4046 6751
e-mail: cic@epa.qld.gov.au

Aerial view of Green Island

Michaelmas and Upolo Cays National Park

Michaelmas Cay

What's special?

One of the most important seabird breeding sites in the Great Barrier Reef is protected in Michaelmas and Upolo Cays National Park. Unlike nearby Green Island, Michaelmas is a small, low sand cay covered just by grasses and low-growing plants which provide an ideal habitat for thousands of ground-nesting seabirds.

At least 14 species of seabirds have been recorded on the island. Nesting peaks in summer when more than 30,000 birds have been observed. Sooty terns, common noddies and crested terns are the main nesting species.

The surrounding waters are marine park and part of the Great Barrier Reef World Heritage Area.

Exploring Michaelmas Cay

Visitors are asked to stay on the beach to avoid disturbing the nesting seabirds. When agitated, the adults fly off, leaving their chicks and eggs unprotected. Chicks are prey to scavenging silver gulls, and embryos can die from exposure.

Enjoy birdwatching, but never handle any birds or eggs. Look for black-naped terns, reef herons, roseate terns, ruddy turnstones and little terns.

Go snorkelling in the beautiful reefs around the island. Make sure your fins do not damage the corals.

Camping is not allowed on the island and visitors are not allowed on the cay between 3pm and 9am.

Beware of marine stingers between October and May. Help protect the island and reef — anchor in sand and snorkel carefully to protect the coral, and observe fishing, collecting and seabird nesting restrictions.

Walking

Wear a hat and sunscreen if walking around the island. No tracks are provided.

Getting there

Michaelmas Cay is 40km north-east of Cairns. Access is by charter or private boat.

Further information

QPWS
5B Sheridan Street
PO Box 2066
CAIRNS QLD 4870
ph (07) 4046 6600
fax (07) 4046 6751
e-mail: cic@epa.qld.gov.au

Mt Lewis Forest Reserve

What's special?

In the Daintree region, Mt Lewis Forest Reserve protects upland rainforests and a variety of rare and threatened wildlife, including the golden bowerbird, southern cassowary, Mt Lewis spiny cray, lemuroid ringtail possum and Daintree River ringtail possum. Mt Lewis Forest Reserve contains some of the most accessible and scenic upland rainforest in the area and is part of the Wet Tropics World Heritage Area.

Exploring Mt Lewis

Go birdwatching. See golden bowerbirds, blue-faced parrot finches, noisy pittas and chowchillas. The short walk to a small dam is popular for birdwatching.

Go for a scenic 28km drive through the forest. Have a bush picnic beside a boulder-strewn rainforest creek. No facilities are provided. Along the forest drive, enjoy views over the forest and mountains.

Dogs and camping are not allowed in the forest. You need a permit to traverse to travel further than 11km along the Mt Lewis Road.

Walking

A short track leads off the Mt Lewis Road to a small dam and communication tower. Wear sturdy walking shoes, a hat and sunscreen. Take drinking water. Allow about 45 minutes for the return walk.

Getting there

Mt Lewis is about 90 minutes' drive north-west of Cairns. Head north along the Captain Cook Highway. Turn onto the Rex Highway (Mossman-Mt Molloy Road) 4km south of Mossman and head towards Mt Molloy. Take the Mt Lewis Road 3km north of Julatten or 11km north of Mt Molloy. Drive 11km along this road to the walking track. Four-wheel-drive is recommended but conventional access is possible in dry weather.

Keith McDonald

Snail at Mt Lewis Forest Reserve

Further information

QPWS
1 Front Street
PO Box 251
MOSSMAN QLD 4873
ph (07) 4098 2188
fax (07) 4098 2279

Mossman Gorge Daintree National Park

Boyd's rainforest dragon

Keith McDonald

What's special?

Crystal-clear water cascading over smooth granite boulders in the Mossman River makes this picturesque section of Daintree National Park one of the most popular parks in the Wet Tropics World Heritage Area.

This section stretches from the coastal lowlands to rugged mountains, providing a home for a wonderful variety of rainforest animals including tree-kangaroos and the tiny musky rat-kangaroo. Tall dense rainforests clothe the lowlands and slopes while open forest and woodlands grow on the exposed slopes and mountaintops.

The Mossman Gorge Section is part of the traditional lands of the Kuku Yalanji people.

Exploring Mossman Gorge

Find a perfect picnic spot by the creek. Relax and enjoy this delightful place. Look for jungle perch, freshwater turtles and platypus in the creek. Swift currents, cold water and slippery rocks make swimming dangerous.

Go for a walk through beautiful lowland rainforest. Signs along the Rex Creek rainforest circuit help you explore the rainforest and explain why this place is so special to the local Kuku Yalanji people.

Mossman Gorge is a great place for wildlife watching. Birds from nearby upland areas and migratory birds visit the Gorge. See a colourful Boyd's rainforest dragon soaking up the sun. Watch a spectacular Cairns birdwing or vivid Ulysses butterfly flitting through the forest.

Most of this section of the park is rugged and inaccessible. For your safety, never leave the marked walking tracks.

Mossman Gorge is popular, so arrive early to avoid the crowds. Camping is not allowed but you can stay nearby at Mossman.

Mossman Gorge, Daintree National Park

Paul Candlin

Walking

A 400m track leads from the carpark along the river to a swinging bridge over Rex Creek at the start of a loop track through the rainforest. Wear a hat and sunscreen and insect repellent when walking. Only very experienced walkers should attempt hiking in this section of the park. Talk to a ranger first, complete a bushwalker registration form and let someone responsible know your plans.

Accessibility

The toilets are wheelchair-accessible.

Getting there

Mossman Gorge is 5km west of Mossman and 80km north of Cairns along the Cook Highway.

Tracks

Rex Creek circuit
2·7km, 1–1·5 hours

Further information

QPWS
1 Front Street
PO Box 251
MOSSMAN QLD 4873
ph (07) 4098 2188
fax (07) 4098 2279

**Mossman Gorge
Community Rangers**
ph (07) 4098 1305

Mossman Gorge

Paul Candlin

Snapper Island Daintree National Park

Bat fish

What's special?

At the mouth of the Daintree River, Snapper Island is part of Daintree National Park, one of north Queensland's most popular parks. The island is covered in rainforest and grassland and surrounded by coral rubble beaches.

The surrounding waters and reefs are protected in the Great Barrier Reef Marine Park and the World Heritage Area.

Exploring Snapper Island

Go snorkelling over the surrounding reef. Beware of marine stingers between October and May. Observe restrictions on fishing and collecting.

Camp at West Point. Toilets and picnic tables are provided. Take drinking water and a fuel stove.

Walking

A short (200m) track links the day-use are on the south-western beach and the beach on the north-western side of the island. Wear a hat and sunscreen when walking.

Getting there

Snapper Island is 2km east of Cape Kimberley and accessible only by private boat. The north-western side of the island is the best anchorage.

Further information

QPWS
5B Sheridan Street
PO Box 2066
CAIRNS QLD 4870
ph (07) 4046 6600
fax (07) 4046 6751
e-mail: cic@epa.qld.gov.au

QPWS
1 Front Street
PO Box 251
MOSSMAN QLD 4873
ph (07) 4098 2188
fax (07) 4098 2279

QPWS
Dixie Street
PORT DOUGLAS QLD 4871
ph (07) 4099 4709
fax (07) 4099 4849

Campsite bookings: 13 13 04 or www.qld.gov.au/camping

Snapper Island

Hope Islands National Park

What's special?

East and West Hope Islands are low-lying coral cays protected in Hope Islands National Park. The surrounding waters and reefs are protected in the Great Barrier Reef Marine Park and World Heritage Area.

Shingle cays like West Hope develop when piles of loose coral debris build up on the windward side of the reef during storms. Only hardy plants like mangroves grow on such cays. Mangroves grow on the northern and western sides of West Hope while shrubs grow on the eastern side.

East Hope is a typical sand cay, formed when fine reef sediments are deposited on the leeward side of a reef. The cay is vegetated by beach almond and red coondoo in its centre with sea trumpet, silverbush and nickernut around the edges.

Hope Islands are an important nesting site for pied imperial-pigeons.

The islands are part of the sea country of the Kuku Yalanji people who still hunt, fish and collect in the area. The islands were named by Cook in 1770 when he struck the nearby reef.

Exploring Hope Islands

Relax and enjoy the natural beauty of these islands.

East Hope Island has four campsites, toilets, picnic tables and fireplaces. Limits apply to camper numbers and the length of stay. West Hope has no facilities. All rubbish must be removed. Take drinking water and a fuel stove.

Go birdwatching. Twenty-five species of seabirds and many woodland birds can be seen on the islands. See terns, reef herons, pied oystercatchers, beach stone-curlews, ospreys, kingfishers, brahminy kites and bar-shouldered doves. Stay away from nesting seabirds. They are easily disturbed.

Go snorkelling but beware of strong currents and tides. Beware of marine stingers between October and May. Fishing is allowed but restrictions apply.

Paul Candlin

Bar-shouldered dove

Hope Islands National Park

Hope Islands

Further information

QPWS
5B Sheridan Street
PO Box 2066
CAIRNS QLD 4870
ph (07) 4046 6600
fax (07) 4046 6751
e-mail: cic@epa.qld.gov.au

QPWS
1 Front Street
PO Box 251
MOSSMAN QLD 4873
(07) 4098 2188
fax (07) 4098 2279

QPWS
Dixie Street
PORT DOUGLAS QLD 4871
ph (07) 4099 4709
fax (07) 4099 4849

Campsite bookings: 13 13 04 or
www.qld.gov.au/camping

Walking

Wear a hat and sunscreen if walking around the island. No tracks are provided.

Getting there

East and West Hope Islands are 37km south-east of Cooktown and north-east of Cedar Bay. Access is by charter or private boat.

Cape Tribulation Daintree National Park

What's special?

Lush tropical rainforests and coral reefs meet in this scenic and popular coastal section of Daintree National Park stretching between the Daintree and Bloomfield Rivers. Cape Tribulation is part of the Wet Tropics World Heritage Area. The beaches, reefs and offshore waters are protected in marine parks.

Away from the coast, the land rises steeply to cloud-swept Thornton Peak. The park is renowned for its rich diversity of plants and wildlife with lowland and upland rainforests, mangroves, swamps and heathlands. Rare and unusual species include primitive flowering plants, the giant white-tailed rat, southern cassowary and Bennett's tree-kangaroo.

The Kuku Yalanji people who have lived in this area for thousands of years call Cape Tribulation, "Kulki". The Cape was named by Captain Cook as the place his troubles began during the historic 1770 voyage of discovery.

Exploring Cape Tribulation

Break your journey with a picnic at Jindalba or Cape Tribulation. Go birdwatching. See beautiful rainforest birds such as the cassowary, wompoo pigeon or noisy pitta.

Camp at Noah Beach, 8km south of Cape Tribulation. Toilets, water and an outdoor shower stand are provided. Take a fuel stove. Campfires are not allowed. Remove your rubbish. Pay your camping fees at the on-site self-registration station. The camping area is closed in the wet season and after heavy rains. The maximum stay is seven nights. Supplies are available at Cow Bay and Cape Tribulation.

Find out about the rainforest and mangroves along the Maardja boardwalk at Oliver Creek or the Dubuji boardwalk at Cape Tribulation. Explore the rainforest along short tracks at Jindalba or walk along Kulki or Myall Beaches. Keen, very fit walkers can climb to a lookout over the Daintree coast along the Mt Sorrow ridge trail.

Go sea kayaking. Swimming is not recommended as estuarine crocodiles live in the park's creeks and nearby coastal waters. Beware of marine stingers from October to May. Fishing is not allowed in the park.

Paul Candlin

View from Cape Tribulation

Dainty green treefrog

Keith McDonald

Cape Tribulation, Daintree National Park

Bruce Cowell

Tracks

Jindalba rainforest walks and hiking trail
1·3km return, 30 minutes

Maardja boardwalk
2·2km return, 45 minutes

Kulki boardwalk
400m, 15 minutes

Kulki to Myall Beach track
1·6km return, 40 minutes

Dubuji boardwalk
2·4km return, 45 minutes

Mt Sorrow ridge trail
7km return, 6–7 hours

Further information

QPWS
1 Front Street
PO Box 251
MOSSMAN QLD 4873
ph (07) 4098 2188
fax (07) 4098 2279
e-mail:
cape.tribulation@epa.qld.gov.au

Cape Tribulation
PMB10
MS2041
MOSSMAN QLD 4873
ph (07) 4098 0052
ph (07) 4098 0127
fax (07) 4098 0074

You can also camp on Snapper Island just offshore. Toilet and barbecues are provided. You must pre-book your site through www.smartservice.qld.gov.au/AQ.

Visit one of the many tourist facilities in the area. Find out about Kuku Yalanji culture. Contact the Wujal Wujal Council on (07) 4060 8155 or the Mossman Gorge Community Rangers on (07) 4098 1305.

Walking

Wear a hat and sunscreen and insect repellent when walking. Carry water. Talk to the ranger and complete a bushwalker registration form if planning a longer walk. The tough, full-day Mt Sorrow ridge trail starts 150m north of the Kulki day-use area turnoff.

Accessibility

The toilets at Noah Beach are wheelchair-accessible.

Getting there

Travel 104km north of Cairns via the Cook Highway to the Daintree River crossing. The ferry operates 6am–midnight every day except Christmas Day and Good Friday. Take care on the narrow, winding roads. Conventional access is possible though high clearance is useful and towing caravans is not recommended. The road from Cape Tribulation to Bloomfield has many creek crossings and steep grades. Four-wheel-drive is strongly recommended. Wildlife is common along this road. Please drive carefully, especially at night. This road may be closed after heavy rain. Check current road conditions with RACQ (07) 4033 6433 or 1300 130 595.

Ant plant, Cape Tribulation

Adam Creed

Keatings Lagoon (Mulbabidgee) Conservation Park

What's special?

Freshwater wetlands in Keatings Lagoon (Mulbabidgee) Conservation Park are a refuge for thousands of waterbirds, especially in the dry season.

For thousands of years, this area was an important hunting and gathering place for the local Gungarde people who hunted and collected food and medicine at this special place they called "Mulbabidgee".

Exploring Keatings Lagoon

Learn about Aboriginal culture on the self-guiding trail through this small park. Obtain the brochure from the QPWS office in Cooktown or Cairns before you visit.

Go birdwatching. A bird hide is located on the lagoon foreshore. Camping is not allowed.

Walking

Walk along the edge of the lagoon to a bird hide and picnic area.

Accessibility

The walking track and bird hide are wheelchair-accessible, with care.

Getting there

Keatings Lagoon is 5km south of Cooktown off the Cooktown Developmental Road. Access is via a concrete causeway. Take care. The causeway may flood during the wet season.

Paul Candlin

Keatings Lagoon

Tracks

Keatings Lagoon track
1·5km return, 30 minutes

Further information

QPWS
5 Webber Esplanade
PO Box 611
COOKTOWN QLD 4871
ph (07) 4069 5777
fax (07) 4069 5574
e-mail: cooktown@epa.qld.gov.au

Cedar Bay (Mangkal-Mangkalba) National Park

What's special?

Dense tropical rainforest grows in Cedar Bay National Park, a remote coastal park south of Cooktown in the Wet Tropics World Heritage Area. Sandy beaches and fringing reefs are backed by rainforest. Tulip oaks, Daintree pendas, tall rainforest cycads, fan palms and milky pines grow in the rainforest. Much has never been logged or disturbed. Windswept vegetation covers exposed hillsides.

Cedar Bay is home to a wonderful variety of wildlife including the vulnerable southern cassowary and rare Bennett's tree-kangaroo. The adjacent waters are protected in marine parks.

This is the traditional land of the Kuku Yalanji people whose country extends along the coast to Mossman. Cedar Bay National Park was a major turtle hunting area and contains important story sites. The Kuku Yalanji people have kept their culture alive and ask visitors to respect this special place.

The Cedar Bay area was developed for tin mining from the 1870s. The remains of old tin workings can be seen between Black Snake Rocks and the park boundary.

Exploring Cedar Bay

Go birdwatching. See cassowaries, yellow-breasted sunbirds, double-eyed fig-parrots, mangrove kingfishers and beach stone-curlews. Pied imperial-pigeons feed on rainforest fruits during their annual summer migration from Papua New Guinea.

Look for the elusive Bennett's tree-kangaroo feeding on leaves and fruit at night in the rainforest. See rainbow skinks and lace monitors along the tracks.

Bush camp in the park. No facilities are provided. Take a fuel stove, insect repellent and a mosquito net. Campfires are not allowed. Remove your rubbish. Pay your camping fees on-site at the self-registration station at the southern end of the beach. Fresh water is available seasonally in creeks above tidal reaches. Boil the water for five minutes before drinking. Take drinking water in the dry season. Use no soap, detergent or toothpaste in the waterways.

Cedar Bay (Mangkal-Mangkalba) National Park

Adam Creed

Fishing and collecting are prohibited in the adjacent marine park waters. Boaties are asked to anchor only in sand, away from corals, and to watch for dugong and turtles. Beware of marine stingers October to May and estuarine crocodiles in the sea and estuaries. Never cross any tidal creeks at high tide or swim in the creeks. Be croc-wise.

Walking

The walking track into the park was a former donkey track used by tin miners. Only fit walkers should attempt this steep track. Wear a hat, sunscreen and insect repellent. Take drinking water and a first aid kit. Water is not available along the route. Avoid disturbing snakes. Some are venomous.

Getting there

Cedar Bay is 40km south of Cooktown. The park lies between Cape Tribulation and Cooktown and is accessible only by boat or walking. Boat access is not easy, especially during prevailing south-easterlies. Nearby Hope Isles provides a sheltered anchorage.

The walk begins at Home Rule Rainforest Lodge, private property 3km off the Cooktown-Bloomfield Road from Rossville. Overnight camping is allowed by prior arrangement at the lodge.

Tracks

Bush track
17km one-way, 6–8 hours

Further information

QPWS
Level 1 Centenary Building
1 Front Street
PO Box 251
MOSSMAN QLD 4873
ph (07) 4098 2188
fax (07) 4098 2279

QPWS
5 Webber Esplanade
PO Box 611
COOKTOWN QLD 4871
ph (07) 4069 5777
fax (07) 4069 5574
e-mail: cooktown@epa.qld.gov.au

Bruce Cowell

Cedar Bay

Black Mountain (Kalkajaka) National Park

What's special?

At the northern end of the Wet Tropics World Heritage Area, Black Mountain National Park contains an imposing mountain range of massive granite boulders. The wet tropics and drier savanna woodland natural regions meet in this park, making it a refuge for wildlife, many of which are either rare or threatened with extinction.

This park's vegetation is unique and only found in the park and Mount Simon area. Wildlife found only here and nearby Trevethan Range and Big Tableland include the scanty frog *Cophixalus exiguus*, a rainbow skink *Carlia scirtetis*, and the Black Mountain gecko *Nactus galgajuga*. Godman's rock-wallaby and the threatened ghost bat also live in this park.

Known as "Kalkajaka" (place of the spear), Black Mountain was an important meeting place for the Kuku Yalanji Aboriginal people and is the source of many dreaming stories.

Exploring Black Mountain

Read the signs in the carpark to discover the park's special history and wildlife.

Camping is not allowed in this rugged park.

Getting there

Black Mountain is 25km south of Cooktown and 4km north of Helenvale on the Cooktown Developmental Road.

Further information

QPWS
Level 1 Centenary Building
1 Front Street
PO Box 251
MOSSMAN QLD 4873
ph (07) 40982188
fax (07) 40982279

Black Mountain

Endeavour River National Park

Paul Candlin

What's special?

Just next to Cooktown, Endeavour River National Park contains coastal dunes, freshwater wetlands, and the estuary and parts of the catchment of the Endeavour River. Mangrove forests, heathlands and tropical woodlands grow in the park.

Cook named the Endeavour River after his ship when it struck a reef off Cooktown on 11 June 1770. Botanists Banks and Solander collected many plant specimens along the Endeavour River.

The Guugu Yimmithirr Aboriginal people have close spiritual ties with this place.

Exploring Endeavour River

Relax and enjoy nature in this undeveloped park. No facilities are provided so visitors must be self-sufficient. Camping is not allowed.

Beware of estuarine crocodiles in the Endeavour River. Never swim, dangle legs or arms in the water or prepare food near the water's edge. Be croc-wise.

Getting there

Endeavour River is just north of Cooktown. Most of the park is accessible only by boat. The southern side of the Endeavour River can be reached by vehicle along Starcke Street, Marton. The park is also accessible next to the Endeavour Valley Road 3km west of Cooktown. There are two boat ramps at the Cooktown waterfront.

Paul Candlin

Endeavour River

Further information

QPWS
5 Webber Esplanade
PO Box 611
COOKTOWN QLD 4871
ph (07) 4069 5777
fax (07) 4069 5574
e-mail: cooktown@epa.qld.gov.au

Mt Cook National Park

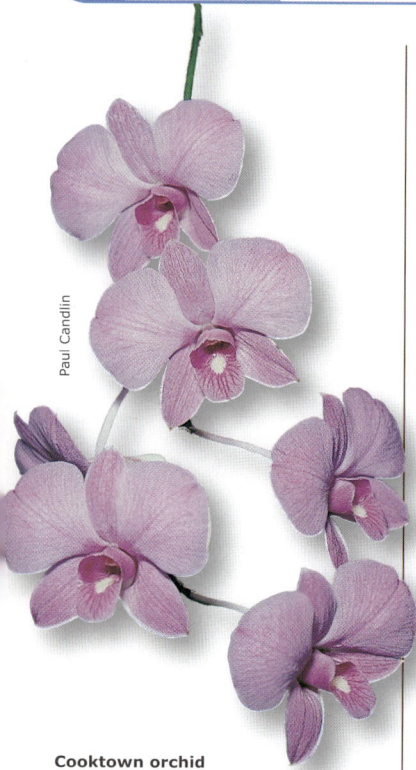

Paul Candlin

Cooktown orchid

What's special?

Rising to 431m, rugged Mt Cook provides a scenic backdrop to the township of Cooktown in Mt Cook National Park. Rainforest and tropical woodland with a heath understorey cover the mountain's upper slopes and sheltered gullies while grasslands grow on the southern slopes.

The park is home to the large amethystine python and northern quoll. Pied imperial-pigeons and buff-breasted paradise-kingfishers visit in the summer months.

Exploring Mt Cook

Spend a few hours exploring. Take your binoculars and go birdwatching.

Camping is not allowed.

Walking

A 3km circuit leads to a vantage point with views over the Great Barrier Reef to the east and the Endeavour Valley to the west. From here, an unmarked route leads to the summit. Take extreme care.

Getting there

You can see Mt Cook as you approach Cooktown by road or sea. Access to the walking track is from Ida Street and is signposted.

Further information

QPWS
5 Webber Esplanade
PO Box 611
COOKTOWN QLD 4871
ph (07) 4069 5777
fax (07) 4069 5574
e-mail: cooktown@epa.qld.gov.au

Mt Cook

Paul Candlin

Cape York Peninsula

Map 15

Legend

National Park	State Forest	—— Highway
Conservation Park	Timber Reserve	—— Major connecting road
Forest Reserve	Resource Reserve	—— Minor access road

0   40   80
km

N

Jardine River NP

Heathlands RR

Weipa

Iron Range NP
Lockhart River

Mungkan Kandju NP

Flinders Group NP

Cape Melville NP

Nymph Island
Lizard Island NP
Turtle Group NP

Three Island Group NP

Lakefield NP

Endeavour River NP
Keatings
Lagoon CP   Cooktown
Laura   Black Mt NP
Hope Islands NP
Cedar Bay NP

Cape Tribulation
Palmer Goldfield RR   Daintree NP
Daintree   Snapper Island
Mossman   Port Douglas

Mowbray SF

Cairns
Mareeba

Chillagoe
Chillagoe-Mungana   Atherton
Caves NP

Palmer Goldfield Resources Reserve

Palmer River

Paul Candlin

What's special?

Reminders of Queensland's rich gold mining history and biggest gold rush are protected in Palmer Goldfield Resources Reserve. Old mines, rusting machinery, Chinese alluvial workings and traces of the Maytown township remain from the once thriving settlements which sprang up around the Palmer goldfield in far north Queensland in the late 19th and early 20th Centuries.

The surrounding harsh, rugged countryside of many ridges dissected by creeks was formed over millions of years through deposition and subsequent uplifting, faulting and erosion. Ironbark woodland with paperbarks fringe the creeks.

William Hann named the Palmer River after the Colonial Secretary of Queensland during a government-sponsored mineral exploration expedition in 1872. James Mulligan made the first major gold discovery in June 1873, starting the gold rush. The old Maytown to Laura Coach Road was blazed in 1873 to carry supplies to the Palmerville diggings.

Exploring Palmer Goldfield

Spend a few days exploring the reserve and imagining what this place was like in its heyday when 9000 people flocked to this harsh landscape. Most were Chinese labourers. Be careful exploring. Watch for collapsed mine shafts and supervise children.

Metal detecting and treasure hunting are prohibited.

Bush camp beside a seasonal waterhole. Take water and a fuel stove. Remove your rubbish from the reserve. Prospecting, panning and the use of metal detectors are not allowed in the reserve.

Visitors must be totally self-sufficient. Take extra fuel, drinking water, food and spare parts for your vehicle. The closest supplies are at Mount Carbine, the Palmer River Roadhouse on the Cooktown Road, Laura or Chillagoe.

Visit in winter when days are more pleasant and nights are cool. Summer days can be very hot and humid.

Palmer Goldfield Resources Reserve

Getting there

Palmer Goldfield is 280km north-west of Cairns but the journey takes many hours. The best route is along the Peninsula Developmental Road, Whites Creek turnoff to Granite and Cannibal Creeks, then north to cross the Palmer River at Dog Leg Creek Junction above Maytown. You can also travel along the very rough old coach road from Laura. Allow six hours for this route. The reserve is about three hours' drive west of the Palmer River Roadhouse.

This is a remote reserve. Tracks are rough and suitable for four-wheel-drive vehicles only. Travel is slow. Roads become impassable in the wet season when flash flooding can occur.

Further information

Chillagoe-Mungana Caves NP
Queen Street
PO Box 38
CHILLAGOE QLD 4871
ph (07) 4094 7163
fax (07) 4094 7213
e-mail: cic@epa.qld.gov.au

QPWS
5B Sheridan Street
PO Box 2066
CAIRNS QLD 4870
ph (07) 4046 6600
fax (07) 4046 6751

A reminder of the once-thriving settlements around the Palmer goldfield

Lakefield National Park

What's special?

At 537,000ha, Lakefield National Park on Cape York Peninsula is Queensland's second largest park. The park is drained by large rivers and contains spectacular wetlands — home to waterbirds, barramundi and estuarine and freshwater crocodiles. Rivers become a series of waterholes in the dry season but the wet season transforms the park into a vast inaccessible wetland.

Lakefield has a rich and varied landscape with river estuaries, mangroves and mudflats to the north around Princess Charlotte Bay, extensive grasslands and eucalypt and paperbark woodlands on the river floodplains, and sandstone hills and escarpments to the south. Patches of the unusual *Corypha utan* palm grow in the grasslands on the marine plain. Gallery rainforest fringes parts of the Normanby and Kennedy Rivers. The park is a wildlife refuge and home to several rare or threatened animals including the golden-shouldered parrot, star finch, red goshawk, Lakeland Downs mouse and spectacled hare-wallaby.

Before European settlement in the 1870s, numerous Aboriginal clans speaking at least 11 different languages lived here and in the surrounding lands. Lakefield's traditional owners, the Lama Lama, Kuku Warra, Kuku Yamithi and Kuku Thaypan, are closely involved in managing the park.

Explorer William Hann crossed the North Kennedy River at the site now known as Hann Crossing, during his expedition to Cape York in 1872. Lakefield's grazing history dates back to the first lease for Laura cattle station granted in 1879.

Exploring Lakefield

Lakefield is a remote national park and offers a style of camping to match. It is also the most accessible park on the Cape and a great place to spend a few days relaxing and exploring. The best time to visit is April to October. Summers are hot and wet.

Bush camping is allowed at a number of sites near rivers and waterholes. Pay your camping fees on-site at self-registration shelters throughout the park.

Termite mound, Lakefield

Paul Candlin

Lakefield National Park

Few facilities are provided so visitors must be self-sufficient. Take drinking water, a fuel stove and mosquito nets. Generators are not allowed. Remove your rubbish. Bury human wastes well away from waterholes. Boil the water for five minutes before drinking. Do not use soap, shampoo or detergent in waterholes.

Campsites include Twelve Mile Waterhole on the Normanby River opposite New Laura Ranger Base, Old Faithful Waterhole, 23km north of New Laura, Mick Fienn and Dingo Waterholes, 33km north of New Laura, Kalpowar Crossing, 3km east of Lakefield Ranger Station, Seven Mile Waterhole, 13km north-west of Lakefield, or Hann Crossing, 6km south-west of Bizant Ranger Station. Kalpowar Crossing has grassy individual campsites, cold showers, tap water, picnic tables, fireplaces and toilets along an 8km stretch of a permanent fresh waterhole. Hann Crossing has individual campsites and pit toilets. Bookings are recommended for school holidays, long weekends and Kalpowar Crossing.

Waterhole, Lakefield

Gallery rainforest, Lakefield

Lakefield National Park

Steve Parish

Tracks

Kalpowar Crossing
Normanby River circuit
4·5km, 1–1·5 hours

Hann Crossing
North Kennedy River track
7km return, 90 minutes

Further information

Lakefield NP
Lakefield Ranger Station
PMB29
CAIRNS MAIL CENTRE QLD 4871
ph (07) 4060 3271

Lakefield NP
New Laura Ranger Station
PMB79
Cairns Mail Centre QLD 4871
ph (07) 4060 3260

QPWS
PO Box 611
COOKTOWN QLD 4871
ph (07) 4069 5777
fax (07) 4069 5574
e-mail: cooktown@epa.qld.gov.au

Aboriginal rock art

Go birdwatching early morning or late afternoon around the waterholes. See brolgas, sarus cranes, comb-crested jacanas, magpie geese and black-necked storks. Look for birds and enjoy the view towards Jane Table Hill from the treeless Nifold Plain, north of Hann Crossing.

Recreational fishing and boating are allowed in the park. Size and bag limits apply to barramundi. The Bizant boat ramp provides the best access to Princess Charlotte Bay. Canoeing is not recommended because this is crocodile country. Estuarine crocodiles live in the rivers and waterholes in this park. For your safety, never swim, canoe, clean fish or prepare food at the water's edge, or camp close to deep waterholes. Be croc-wise.

Visit the restored Old Laura Homestead on the former cattle grazing lease or the site of the former Breeza Homestead where horses were bred for the Palmer River goldfields. See spectacular displays of red lotus lilies and white lilies in the Red and White Lily Lagoons 8km north of Lakefield ranger station.

Walking

Tracks are provided at Kalpowar Crossing and Hann Crossing camping areas. Wear a hat and sunscreen and take drinking water.

Getting there

Lakefield is 7–8 hours north of Cairns along the Peninsula Developmental Road. Turn right to Lakefield 2km north of Laura. Four-wheel-drive is recommended. From Cooktown, travel via Battlecamp Road. This can be rough and takes about four hours. Access from Coen via the Musgrave Roadhouse is four-wheel-drive only. Allow three hours from Musgrave to Lakefield ranger station.

Roads are rough requiring higher than usual fuel consumption. The closest supplies and fuel are at Laura and Musgrave. The park is accessible only in the dry season, April to November, and closed to traffic in the wet season. Check current road conditions before travelling.

Cape Melville National Park

What's special?

Wild coastal scenery is protected in remote and rugged Cape Melville National Park on Cape York Peninsula. Tropical rainforest, mangroves, heathlands, woodlands and grasslands grow in this park.

Because the park is so remote and isolated, many plants and animals are found nowhere else, such as the rare and unusual foxtail palm, now a popular garden plant in northern Australia.

Traditional owners for Cape Melville belong to several clan groups including Daarba, Junjuu muli, Bagaarrmugu, Wurri, Manyamarr, Gambiilmugu and Yiirrku.

Skink, Cape Melville National Park

Keith McDonald

Exploring Cape Melville

Bush camp along the beach. Get your camping permit from the Cooktown QPWS office beforehand. No facilities are provided so visitors must be totally self-sufficient. Take plenty of drinking water and a fuel stove. Remove your rubbish.

Beware of estuarine crocodiles which live in the sea and estuaries here and pose a serious threat to humans. Never cross any tidal creeks at high tide or swim in the creeks. Be croc-wise.

Getting there

Cape Melville is on the eastern end of Bathurst Bay. The park's western boundary is 85km north-east of Lakefield Ranger Station. Access from the west is via Kalpowar Crossing in Lakefield National Park. The journey to Bathurst Bay takes five to six hours. The closest supplies are at Laura, seven to eight hours away.

The southern access road is north of Cooktown via Starcke Homestead, a difficult 225km journey which can take 12 hours. Visit the Cooktown office before travelling to Melville from the south for local advice and track conditions.

The park is accessible by four-wheel-drive vehicles only in dry weather. Plan your visit for later in the year. Access can be difficult before June or July. Check current road conditions with the Lakefield Ranger Station before travelling.

Further information

QPWS
5 Webber Esplanade
PO Box 611
COOKTOWN QLD 4871
ph (07) 4069 5777
fax (07) 4069 5574
e-mail: cooktown@epa.qld.gov.au

Iron Range National Park

Paul Candlin

Eclectus parrot

What's special?

Rugged, hilly country in the far north-east of Cape York Peninsula rises to 543m above sea level at Mt Tozer in Iron Range National Park, a place of spectacular natural beauty. The park protects Australia's largest lowland tropical rainforest remnant. Volcanic rocks overlie the older metamorphic rocks where the rainforest grows.

Iron Range is an important wildlife refuge and home to many unusual wildlife species such as the eclectus parrot, palm cockatoo, southern cassowary, fawn-breasted bowerbird, red-bellied pitta, green python and spotted cuscus. Most are found only here and in New Guinea.

Heath covers the Janet and Tozer Ranges, dense, tall lowland rainforest grows across the broad floodplains and open forest, woodland and paperbark forest grow closer to the coast. Sandy beaches and rocky headlands overlook the Coral Sea.

Aboriginal people of the Kuuku Ya'u language group occupied this area until they were forced into missions. Their descendants living at the Lockhart River Community retain close ties with their land and cultural heritage. Aboriginal lands border the park and the traditional owners help manage the park.

The first European contact was William Bligh's boat landing after the Bounty Mutiny. Explorer Edmund Kennedy left a party here during his ill-fated overland expedition in 1848. Relics of gold mining during the 1930s and 1940s can be seen near Gordon Creek. Iron Range was a staging post for thousands of American troops during World War II.

Exploring Iron Range

Relax and enjoy the unspoilt beauty of this special place.

Bush camp at Rainforests, Gordons Creek, Chili Beach or Cook's Hut camping areas. Few facilities are provided so visitors must be self-sufficient. Toilets are at Chili Beach. Take plenty of drinking water, a fuel stove and mosquito nets. Generators are not permitted in the camping areas. Remove your rubbish. Supplies and fuel can be purchased from the Lockhart River Community Store.

Iron Range National Park

Fishing is allowed at Chili Beach. Beware of estuarine crocodiles in the park's coastal beaches, rivers and waterholes. For your safety, never swim, canoe, clean fish or prepare food at the water's edge, or camp near deep waterholes. Be croc-wise.

Walking

The only track starts from Rainforests camping area. Wear a hat and sunscreen. Take drinking water.

Accessibility

The crocodile warning signs are in German and Japanese as well as English.

Getting there

Access to the park is along the Portland Roads Road which leaves the Peninsula Development Road 35 km north of the Archer River Roadhouse. From this turnoff, the drive to the ranger station takes about three to four hours.

From the north, take Frenchmans Road east from the Telegraph Road, 2km north of the Batavia Downs to Weipa Road. Drive about 50km or two hours to the intersection with Portland Roads Road and a further 30km to the ranger station. The ranger station is 3km south of the road junction, just past the new Claudie River bridge.

Four-wheel-drive is recommended. Visit only in the dry cooler months, April to September. Check road conditions before travelling on the Portland Roads Road or Frenchmans Road as both can become impassable following rain.

Tracks

Old Coen track
*4·7km one-way,
2–3 hours return*

Further information

Iron Range NP
"King Park"
CMB52
CAIRNS MAIL CENTRE QLD 4871
ph (07) 4060 7170
fax (07) 4060 7328

Waterhole, Iron Range National Park

Paul Candlin

Jardine River National Park

What's special?

Together with Heathlands and Shadwell Resources Reserves, Jardine River National Park at the remote northern tip of Cape York Peninsula forms almost 400,000ha of true wilderness. The park protects much of the catchment of the Jardine River, the largest perennial stream in Queensland.

Jardine River National Park lies between the old telegraph line and the coast and is bounded by the headwaters of the Jardine River to the south and the mangroves of Jacky Jacky Creek and the Escape River in the north.

Because the park had abundant fresh water in rivers, swamps and streams but little food for cattle and horses, early explorers such as Edmund Kennedy and the Jardine Brothers called this place a "wet desert". Heath, rainforest and open forest grow on low, broad sandy ridges with intervening swamps while shrublands and vine thickets cover the massive coastal dunes.

The park is home to several unusual species such as the spiny knob-tailed gecko and spotted cuscus.

The Attanbaya, Anggamurthi, Yadhaykenu, Gudang and Wathatni people lived here before Government Resident John Jardine was posted here in 1864. Explorer Edmund Kennedy was speared by Aborigines at the northern end of the park in 1848. The park's western boundary follows the historic telegraph line installed in 1887 to provide communications to the remote areas on the Cape. Jardine River National Park was established in 1977 and will be jointly managed by the traditional owners who maintain close spiritual ties to the park. The adjacent coastal and estuarine waters are protected in marine parks.

Spotted cuscus

Steve Parish

Jardine River

Damian McGreevy

Jardine River National Park

Exploring Jardine River

Relax and enjoy nature in this park. Go birdwatching. You might be lucky and see the yellow-billed kingfisher, the rare palm cockatoo or the fawn-breasted bowerbird.

Have a picnic at Fruit Bat Falls, where a boardwalk overlooking the falls and picnic tables have been provided.

You can camp beside the Jardine River or at Captain Billy Landing, Ussher Point or Eliot Falls. Only Eliot Falls has facilities (picnic tables, fireplaces and toilets) so visitors must be self-sufficient. Take drinking water, a fuel stove, a screened tent or nets for protection against insects at night.

Generators are not allowed. Remove your rubbish. Bury human wastes well away from waterholes. Boil the water for five minutes before drinking. Use no soap, shampoo or detergent in waterholes.

Be careful at Eliot Falls. People have been seriously injured here. Stay well back.

Beach fishing is allowed at Captain Billy Landing and Ussher Point. To protect the park, do not drive your vehicle on the beach between Captain Billy Landing and Ussher Point. Check the marine park zoning plan for restrictions on fishing and collecting at other places.

Estuarine crocodiles live in rivers and waterholes in this park, and along the entire coastline and offshore islands. For your safety, never swim, canoe, clean fish or prepare food at the water's edge, or camp close to deep waterholes. Be croc-wise.

Walking

Short walks lead along Eliot Creek and the Jardine River, and along the remote coastlines next to Captain Billy Landing and Ussher Point.

Accessibility

Eliot Falls has wheelchair-accessible toilets.

Getting there

Jardine River is near the tip of Cape York Peninsula. Follow the old telegraph line or the Peninsula Development Road to the park. Vehicle access is restricted to the road along the park's western boundary. Four-wheel-drive is necessary. Visit only in the dry season, May to October.

Further information

Jardine River NP
Heathlands
PMB76
CAIRNS MAIL CENTRE QLD 4871
ph (07) 4060 3241
fax (07) 4060 3314

Mungkan Kandju (Kaanju) National Park

Cape York tree gecko

Steve Parish

What's special?

Stretching from the foothills of the McIlwraith Range between the west-flowing Archer and Coen Rivers lies Mungkan Kandju National Park, a large wilderness park in central Cape York Peninsula.

Dry open eucalypt woodlands and wet melaleuca swamps cover most of the park. Dense rainforest cloaks the tops of the McIlwraith Range. The braided channels of the Coen River are fringed by deciduous vine thickets while gallery rainforest lines the Archer River. These riverine areas are important wildlife corridors. Both rivers flow all year round.

Aboriginal people of the Wik Mungkan, Kaanju and Ayapathu clans lived here before European settlement in the 1880s.

Exploring Mungkan Kandju

Bush camp at specific sites near rivers and waterholes. No facilities are provided. Be totally self-sufficient in fuel, food and vehicle spare parts. Take drinking water and a fuel stove. Generators are not allowed. Remove your rubbish. Bury human wastes well away from waterholes. Boil the water for five minutes before drinking. Use no soap, shampoo or detergent in waterholes.

Go birdwatching around lagoons and swamps. This is crocodile country, so visitors must take precautions. Never swim, canoe, clean fish or prepare food at the water's edge, or camp close to deep waterholes.

The park has no tracks but you can walk along the Archer River. See nesting mounds of the orange-footed scrubfowl.

Visitors must advise the ranger when leaving the park or travelling to the Archer Bend section of the park. Visit in the dry season. Summers are hot and wet.

Getting there

The ranger station is 95km north-west of Coen and about 10 to 12 hours from Cairns. Head north from Cairns along the Peninsula Development Road through Coen to the Rokeby turnoff to the west. Drive 66km to the ranger station. Access is only possible by four-wheel-drive in the dry season, May to November.

Be prepared. Driving on the rough roads in low gear uses more fuel than normal driving.

Further information

QPWS
Coleman Close
c/- Post Office
COEN QLD 4871
ph (07) 4060 1137
fax (07) 4060 1117
e-mail: cooktown@epa.qld.gov.au

QPWS
PO Box 611
COOKTOWN QLD 4871
ph (07) 4069 5777
fax (07) 4069 5574
e-mail: cooktown@epa.qld.gov.au

Three Islands Group National Park

What's special?

Two wooded islands south-west of Cape Flattery are protected in Three Islands Group National Park. The islands are important seabird nesting sites.

The surrounding waters and reefs are protected in the Great Barrier Reef Marine Park and World Heritage Area.

Exploring the Three Islands Group

Bush camp on the western side of the islands. No facilities are provided on these remote islands. Be totally self-sufficient. Take water and a fuel stove. Remove your rubbish to the mainland. Camping is closed from 1 September until 31 March during the seabird nesting season.

Check the marine park zoning plan for fishing and collecting restrictions in the surrounding marine park waters. Beware of crocodiles which live in the sea. Wear protective clothing or do not swim during the marine stinger season, October to May.

Getting there

The Three Islands Group is 13km south-east of Cape Flattery. Access is by private boat.

Further information

QPWS
5B Sheridan Street
PO Box 2066
CAIRNS QLD 4870
ph (07) 4046 6600
fax (07) 4046 6751
e-mail: cic@epa.qld.gov.au

Bridled tern

Darren Jew

Lizard Island National Park

Gould's sand goanna

Paul Candlin

What's special?

Lizard Island's stark beauty contrasts sharply with the surrounding sparkling blue Great Barrier Reef waters and colourful fringing coral reefs. The Lizard Island Group is the only continental island group close to the outer barrier. Six islands are protected in Lizard Island National Park.

Almost sixty percent of Lizard Island is covered in grasslands. Eucalypt and acacia woodlands and mangroves also grow on the island. More than 40 species of birds have been seen on Lizard, while nearby Osprey, Seabird, South and Palfrey Islands are important bird nesting sites.

The Dingiil Aboriginal people, the traditional custodians of Jiigurru (Lizard Island) lived here for tens of thousands of years. Jiigurru is a sacred place for the Dingiil people, a place where young boys were initiated and the site of tribal gatherings. In the creation story for the Lizard Island Group, Jiigurru is the body of the stingray and other islands form the tail.

Cook named Lizard Island in 1770 after the Gould's sand goannas he saw on the island. The island's past includes the tragic death of the wife and child of beche-de-mer fisherman Robert Watson following an encounter with Aborigines in 1881. The Australian Museum established a research station on the island in 1973 and the resort opened in 1975. Today, the island is popular for sailing and fishing. The waters and reefs surrounding the Lizard Island Group are protected in the Great Barrier Reef Marine Park and are part of the World Heritage Area.

View from Cook's Look

Paul Candlin

Lizard Island National Park

Steve Parish

Exploring Lizard Island

Lizard Island is a ruggedly beautiful and remote place to visit. Have a picnic overlooking Watsons Bay. Picnic tables, a barbecue and toilet are provided for day visitors. Walk to Cooks Look for a great view over the islands.

Go wildlife watching. Eleven species of lizards live on the island, and geckos, skinks, snakes and birds are commonly seen. Green and loggerhead turtles nest late spring and black flying-foxes often camp in the mangroves. Common birds include pheasant coucals, yellow-bellied sunbirds, white-bellied sea-eagles and terns.

Go snorkelling. See the giant clam gardens in Watsons Bay. Visit nearby Palfrey and South Islands. Beware of marine stingers between October and May. Observe fishing and collecting restrictions to protect the reef. Check the zoning plan for details.

Camp at Watsons Bay on Lizard Island. Campers must carry all their gear 1·2km from the airstrip and be self-sufficient in food, shelter and first aid. No supplies are available on the island but campers are welcome at Marlin Bar, a resort bar and restaurant for non-residents.

Toilets, a gas barbecue and picnic tables are provided. Open fires are prohibited. Water is available from a hand-pump. Take water containers and boil the water for five minutes or treat it before drinking. Please do not feed the wildlife, and secure all food and rubbish scraps.

You can also stay at the resort or go on a tour of the research station.

Walking

Explore Lizard Island in the cooler part of the day. Cooks Look is the most challenging. Wear a hat and sunscreen when walking.

Getting there

Regular flights operate to Lizard Island from Cairns. Charter flights operate from Cairns and Cooktown. Access is also possible by charter or private boat. Anchoring restrictions apply to protect the coral.

Tracks

Chinamans Ridge track
340m, 20 minutes one-way

Watsons Cottage and Pandanus track
685m, 30 minutes one-way

Watsons Walk
520m, 30 minutes one-way

Cook's Look
4·5km return, 2–3 hours

Airstrip to Research Road
2·2km, 30 minutes one-way

Airstrip to Blue Lagoon
900m return,
40 minutes one-way

Further information

QPWS
5B Sheridan Street
PO Box 2066
CAIRNS QLD 4870
ph (07) 4046 6600
fax (07) 4046 6751
e-mail: cic@epa.qld.gov.au

QPWS
5 Webber Esplanade
PO Box 611
COOKTOWN QLD 4871
ph (07) 4069 5777
fax (07) 4069 5574

Campsite bookings: 13 13 04
or www.qld.gov.au/camping

Turtle Group National Park

What's special?

Just west of Lizard Island, Turtle Group National Park protects four very small, vegetated islands. The surrounding waters and reefs are protected in the Great Barrier Reef Marine Park and World Heritage Area.

Exploring Turtle Group Islands

Bush camp on all three Turtle Islands or camp on the northern side of Nymph Island. No facilities are provided on these remote islands. Be totally self-sufficient. Take water and a fuel stove. Remove your rubbish.

Check the marine park zoning plan for fishing and collecting restrictions in the surrounding marine park waters. Estuarine crocodiles live in the adjacent waters and marine stingers are present between October and May.

Getting there

Turtle Islands are 30km west of Lizard Island. Nymph Island is 35km east of Murdoch Point. Access is by private boat.

Green turtle

Darren Jew

Further information

QPWS
5B Sheridan Street
PO Box 2066
CAIRNS QLD 4870
ph (07) 4046 6600
fax (07) 4046 6751
e-mail: cic@epa.qld.gov.au

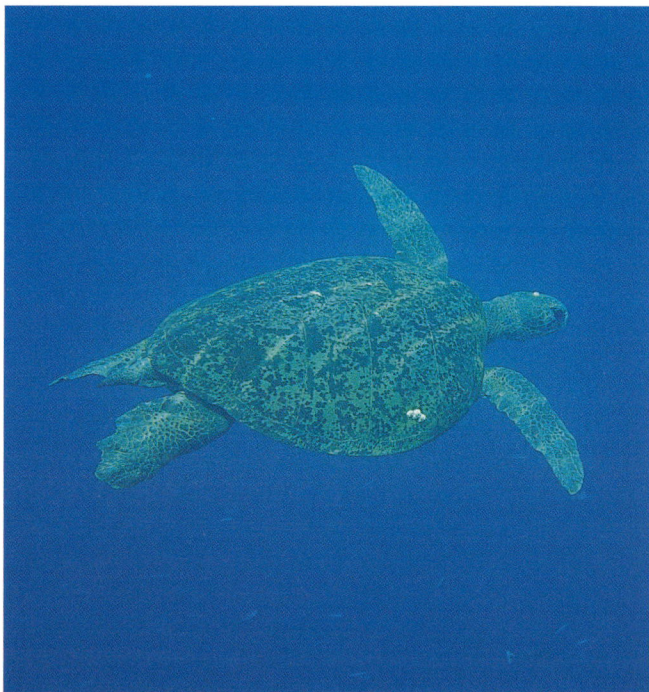

Flinders Group National Park

What's special?

Off the east coast of Cape York Peninsula in Princess Charlotte Bay lies Flinders Group National Park, a group of seven continental islands with rocky shores, rugged sandstone hills and escarpments, coastal mangroves and sand dunes.

The Flinders Group is part of the sea country of the Yiithuwarra Aboriginal people. Aboriginal rock art sites on the islands include art associated with early European contact.

The surrounding waters are protected in The Great Barrier Reef Marine Park.

Exploring the Flinders Group

Bush camp on Flinders Island. Obtain your camping permit first. Toilets, picnic tables and a shelter shed are provided. Take drinking water and a fuel stove. Open fires are not permitted and all rubbish must be removed.

Check the Great Barrier Reef Marine Park zoning plan for restrictions on activities in the waters around the islands. Beware of marine stingers October to May and crocodiles all year round.

Walking

A self-guiding bushfood trail and boardwalks to the rock art sites are along two tracks on Stanley Island. See the HMS Dart inscription site on a short walk from Apia Spit on Flinders Island. Both tracks have moderate grades. Wear a hat and sunscreen and take plenty of drinking water.

Getting there

The Flinders Group lies between Cape Melville and Princess Charlotte Bay. Access is by charter or private boat or seaplane.

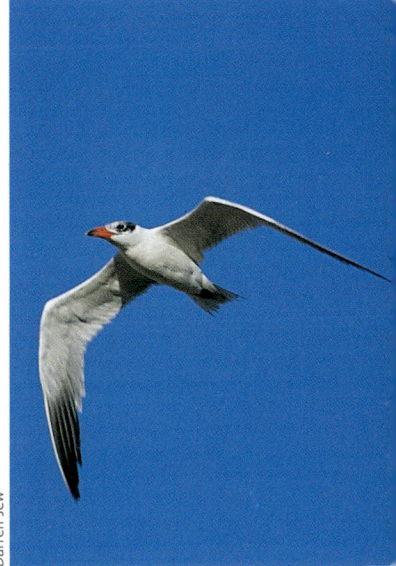

Darren Jew

Caspian tern

Tracks

Yindayin and Ship Shelter circuit walk
1·2km return, 1 hour

HMS Dart historic walk
1km return, 30 minutes

Further information

QPWS
5B Sheridan Street
PO Box 2066
CAIRNS QLD 4870
ph (07) 4046 6600
fax (07) 4046 6751
e-mail: cic@epa.qld.gov.au

Campsite bookings: 13 13 04 or www.qld.gov.au/camping

Alphabetical index

Alphabetical index

Lake McKenzie, Fraser Island, Great Sandy National Park

Paul Candlin

Notes

Emerald spotted treefrog

Robert Ashdown

Notes

Cairns birdwing

Adam Creed